The Redefinition of the EU Presence in Latin America and the Caribbean

Gian Luca Gardini

The Redefinition of the EU Presence in Latin America and the Caribbean

PETER LANG

Berlin - Bruxelles - Chennai - Lausanne - New York - Oxford

Library of Congress Cataloging-in-Publication Data
A CIP catalog record for this book has been applied for at the Library of Congress.

Bibliographic information published by the Deutsche Nationalbibliothek.
The German National Library lists this publication in the German National Bibliography; detailed bibliographic data is available on the Internet at http://dnb.d-nb.de.

This book is one of the deliverables of the project:
"The Reconfiguration of the EU presence in Latin America and the Caribbean" (EUinLAC) - 620093-EPP-1-2020-1-DE-EPPJMO-PROJECT

Cover image: An adaptation of the EUinLAC Logo

EUinLAC
Jean Monnet Project

ISBN 978-3-631-88977-0 (Print)
E-ISBN 978-3-631-90916-4 (E-PDF)
E-ISBN 978-3-631-90917-1 (EPUB)
DOI 10.3726/b21282

PETER LANG
Open

Published by: Peter Lang GmbH, Berlin, Germany

Acknowledgements

First and foremost, I would like to thank the European Union, and in particular, the Erasmus+ Programme for the generous support provided to the Jean Monnet Project "The Redefinition of the EU presence in Latin America and the Caribbean" (EUinLAC) – 620093-EPP-1-2020-1-DE-EPPJMO-PROJECT. This book is one of the key deliverables of that project.

I am very grateful to the colleagues who shared with me the co-organisation of the EUinLAC plenary events in Nuremberg (Germany), Concepción (Chile) and Venice (Italy). In particular, a big thank you to Sophia Ehrlinger and Helen Weiß, and to the entire team at my former Chair for International Business and Society Relations with focus on Latin America at Friedrich-Alexander University in Nuremberg. Many thanks to Paulina Astroza Suárez, Carolina Fuentealba, Javier Sepúlveda Estrada, Andrés Coo, and all the team members of the European Studies Programme, now the Centre of European Studies (congratulations!), for the successful event in Concepción. Last but not least, many thanks to Luis Fernando Beneduzi for the concluding event in Venice, the cherry on the pie of this three-year journey together.

I am indebted to Linda Borean, Director of the Department of Humanities (DIUM) at the University of Udine, for her participation in the Venice event and for her support for the two EUinLAC roundtables at the University of Udine. Great to be back home after 24 years and be able to count on such support.

Thank you to those colleagues who started the EUinLAC journey with us but who could not accompany us until the end due to prestigious appointments and other commitments. We have missed you, but we have made it.

Many thanks to the commissioning editor at Peter Lang, Hermann Ühlein, who believed in this project and offered help through difficult times. Unfortunately for us, he retired before seeing the book published. I am confident that we have honoured his trust. Of course, a big thank you to Adrian Stähli and the team at Peter Lang, who accompanied us in the final stage and successfully took the book through the publication process.

And of course, many thanks to all the contributors to this book for their hard work and intellectual efforts. Some of you have gone the extra mile to respond quickly and attend to all my editorial requests.

Gian Luca Gardini
Udine (Italy), February 2023

Contents

Notes on Contributors

Juan Carlos Aguirre is a Political Scientist with an M.A. in International Studies and a doctoral researcher at Friedrich-Alexander-Universität Erlangen-Nürnberg since October 2018. His research focuses on international politics in Latin America, foreign policy decision-making and regional integration processes. Juan Carlos Aguirre was an advisor for international affairs in different Ministries in Chile. He has also been a lecturer in international relations at various universities in Chile.

Paulina Astroza Suárez is a lawyer and a professor at the University of Concepción, Chile. She has a doctoral degree in Political and Social Sciences, a master's in Political Science and International Relations and a diploma in International Relations and Comparative Politics, all from the Université Catholique de Louvain, Belgium. She is the Director of the European Studies Program at the Universidad de Concepción. Her research areas are European political integration and EU-Latin America relations.

Luís Fernando Beneduzi is Full Professor of Latin American History. Since 2020, he has been the Chair of History and Institutions of the Americas at Ca' Foscari University of Venice. He has previously taught at The Johns Hopkins University, the University of Bologna, and the Lutheran University of Brazil. His main research interests cover international migration, the relations between Europe and Latin America, especially Italy and Brazil, and the nation-state building process in Latin America.

Sergio Caballero is a professor at the Department of International Relations in the University of Deusto, Bilbao (Spain), where he has been Vice Dean as well as the Principal Investigator of the research team "International Relations and Multidimensional Security". He holds a PhD in International Relations from the Universidad Autónoma de Madrid. His main research lines include Latin American regional integration and Brazil's foreign policy, as well as IR theories and EU-Latin American relations.

Belén Cabezas Araya has a degree in Political Science from the Faculty of Government of the University of Chile and is a master's student in Government and Public Management at the same university.

Carmen Fonseca is an assistant professor of International Relations at Nova University of Lisbon, Portugal, and a researcher at the Portuguese Institute of

International Relations (IPRI-NOVA). She was a Visiting Fellow at Getulio Vargas Foundation and at the Institute of Social and Political Studies of the State University of Rio de Janeiro, Brazil. She is the editor of the journal *Relações Internacionais*. Her research interests cover Brazilian foreign policy, Brazil-Portugal relations and emerging and regional powers.

María J. García is a senior lecturer and the Head in the Department of Politics, Languages and International Studies at the University of Bath (UK). Prior to that, she held a Marie Curie International Fellowship at the University of Canterbury in New Zealand. Her research focuses on EU trade policy, EU-Latin American trade agreements, labour and gender clauses in trade agreements, and, more recently, the trade implications of Brexit. She has published extensively on EU-Latin America relations.

Gian Luca Gardini is Chair of History of International Relations at the University of Udine, Italy, and Carlos Saavedra Lamas visiting professor in International Relations at Friedrich-Alexander University Erlangen-Nuremberg, Germany. He has previously taught at the University of Cambridge and at the University of Bath in the UK. His main research interests cover the international relations of Latin America, foreign policy analysis, and comparative regional integration.

Beatriz Larraín Martinez is a professor at the Faculty of Law and Social Sciences of the Universidad de Concepción in Chile. She holds a PhD in Law, Politics and Society from Northeastern University in Boston, Massachusetts. Her area of interest and research is the judicialisation of politics and judicial activism in Chile and the world. She has been a member of the European Studies Programme of the Universidad de Concepción since its inception in 2002.

Elena Lazarou is an associate fellow in the US and the Americas Programme at Chatham House, UK. She holds a PhD in International Studies from the University of Cambridge. Her research focuses on EU relations with Brazil and Latin America, multilateralism, regionalism, and foreign policy analysis. She was an assistant professor of international relations at the Getulio Vargas Foundation (FGV) in Brazil. She is currently working as the acting head of external policies at the European Parliament's Research Service.

Jaime León González is a lecturer at the Catholic University of Eichstaett-Ingolstadt, Germany. Formerly he was a researcher and teaching assistant at Friedrich-Alexander University in Erlangen-Nuremberg. His research focuses on Germany's foreign policy towards Latin America, the role of actors and decision-making processes. He has managed two projects on Latin America sponsored by the Bavarian Virtual High School (VHB). He has previously taught at the University of Bayreuth in Germany.

Paz Verónica Milet is an Associate Professor of the Institute of International Studies of the University of Chile. Her main lines of investigation are multilateralism, spaces for regional integration, Latin American foreign policy, Latin American relations with other regions and Chile's relations with its neighbours. She also coordinates the Chilean team of the Generation of Dialogue Chile-Perú/Perú-Chile Project and the Chile-Morocco Chair in the frame of the America Latina-Africa Foundation.

Diego Ponce is a research assistant and a student at the School of International Relations of the Getulio Vargas Foundation in São Paulo, Brazil, and a research trainee at ELIAMEP, the Hellenic Institute for European and Foreign Policy, Athens, Greece. Prior to joining ELIAMEP, he also took courses in political science at KU Leuven, Belgium, and at Universität Pompeu Fabra, in Barcelona, Spain.

Millán Requena is an Assistant Professor of Public International Law and International Relations at the University of Alicante, Spain. He is also a visiting professor at the University of Lisbon. He is the author of various publications in the field of International Investment Law; EU law and protection of national minorities in Europe. He was Academic Secretary of the Faculty of Law (2012–2016) and at present, he serves as the Head of the Department of Public International Law and Criminal Law.

Mauricio J. Rondanelli-Reyes is a Biologist, Master of Science, and Doctor of Biological Sciences. Associate Professor at the University of Concepción, Chile. Member of the European Studies Program at the University of Concepción. Researcher on environmental issues, plant ecology and biodiversity. Professor in the chairs of Research Methodology and Conservation Biology. Director of undergraduate and postgraduate theses and author of scientific publications in indexed journals of the discipline.

Javier Sepúlveda Estrada is a law graduate from the Universidad de Concepción, awarded the Rolando Peña López Prize for Best Bachelor Thesis in Public International Law. He was also part of the Chilean Delegation that negotiated at COP 27 in Sharm-El-Sheikh, Egypt. He is also a research assistant and member of the Centre for European Studies at the University of Concepción. His main research interests are integration processes, strategic autonomy, geopolitics and climate change.

Jeanne W. Simon holds a doctoral degree in International Studies from the University of Denver (USA). Her research interests are the democratization and territorialisation of social and economic policies, combining comparative analysis of (sub)national responses with the study of supranational governance, including the European Union and the United Nations. She has led several applied research grants on policy transfer, such as the adaptation of the Swedish EcoMunicipality model to the Chilean context.

Mario Torres Jarrín is Director of the Institute of European Studies and Human Rights at the Pontifical University of Salamanca in Spain. Previously, he was Director of International Relations at the Pontifical University of Salamanca, and Director of the European Institute of International Studies in Sweden. He holds a PhD in History from the University of Salamanca. His research interests include international relations and diplomacy, EU Foreign affairs and security, and EU-Latin America relations.

Alwine Woischnik is an independent consultant on Ecological and Social Transition. She holds a PhD in Economics and Social Sciences from Friedrich-Alexander University of Erlangen-Nuremberg, Germany. She was a member of the Environmental Advisory Council at the Ministry of Public Works, Transport and Environment in Spain and an Advisor on environment, employment and training at the Ministry of Labour in Chile. She was a lecturer at the Universidad Carlos III, Madrid and the Escuela Diplomática de Cuba.

Sandra Zapata is a post-doctoral researcher at the Friedrich-Alexander-Universität Erlangen-Nürnberg in Germany. She holds a PhD in Social Sciences from Salamanca University, Spain. She has a master's in International Relations from FLACSO-Ecuador and in Development Policies from Seoul National University in South Korea. Her research topics include US-China competition, South-South cooperation, regionalism and the international political economy of development.

Gian Luca Gardini

The Redefinition of the EU Presence in Latin America and the Caribbean: An Introductory Discussion

Changing circumstances and the need for a profound debate on EU-LAC relations

The project "The Redefinition of the EU Presence in Latin America and the Caribbean" (EUinLAC) was conceived and launched between 2019 and 2020. The European Union Jean Monnet programme generously financed it in 2020, and the project activities were carried out between 2020 and 2023. The project is the successor to another Jean Monnet programme entitled "Relations between Europe and Latin America: Future Scenarios in a Changing World" (Astroza and Larraín, 2022). This endeavour aimed at sketching some challenges and notable features of the bi-regional relationship in a fast-changing international context. Consequently, the timespan between 2019 and 2020 really seemed the appropriate moment to go further and reflect on a possible redefinition of the EU's role, activities and image in Latin America and the Caribbean (LAC).

Precisely at that moment, or better phrased, from that moment on, new unexpected challenges have been shaking the foundations of the international liberal order (which was already under strain), its underpinning values, and its most evident manifestation: globalisation and its associated governance. The Covid-19 pandemic, Russia's war in Ukraine, the need for a green transition altering modes of production and lifestyles have powerfully broken out and settled at the core of the international agenda between 2020 and 2023. This phase of transition and the changes that it brings with it call for an even deeper rethinking of the rationale underpinning the EU-LAC relationship (Sanahuja, 2022), and more specifically the EU's presence in the region and globally. This project, and this book along with it, is a response to this compelling call.

In the last few years, a number of events and initiatives have prompted a debate on the present and future of EU-LAC relations. Between 2019 and 2020, the scenario was not entirely favourable to a new European elan in LAC. There had been no EU-LAC political summit since 2015. On the one hand, the EU was still dealing with the consequences – more potential than actual in fairness (Gardini, 2019, 2020a) of Brexit for its outreach capacity. The image and reputation of the

EU in Latin America were overall positive but trailed way behind China's (in spite of growing fears of Chinese activism and assertiveness on the continent) and the Unites States' (in spite of Trump's unilateralism and his Latin American policies swinging between disinterest and imposition). In spite of a solid and satisfactory political, commercial, aid, and cultural bi-regional relationship, the support for the EU was quite lukewarm in Latin America (Latinobarometro, 2018).

On the other hand, between 2019 and 2020, Latin America itself was going through difficult times in the political, economic and social realms. Politically, LAC was divided on a range of topics spanning from the Venezuelan crisis to the development model and the position vis-à-vis China. In economic terms, three of the major economies in the continent (Brazil, Argentina and Venezuela) had experienced deep recessions in the previous years. Socially, protests and unrest shook some of the most stable and better-performing countries such as Chile, Colombia and Ecuador. Latin American regionalism reached a stalemate and was clearly under strain (Nolte & Weiffen, 2020). Overall, Latin America and the Caribbean as a region were consistently losing ground at the global level, continuing a trend of decline that has been lasting for the last century (Malamud & Schenoni, 2021). The situation on the LAC side also prompted a rethinking of the bi-regional links.

Against all odds, or perhaps in reaction to this negative perception, in 2019 several promising developments took place that made the need for a profound rethinking of the EU-LAC relationship even more evident. In April, after ten years of silence, the European Commission (2019) issued a new communication on the European Union, Latin America and the Caribbean aimed at designing the pillars of a new EU approach towards the region. In May, Germany identified Latin America as a key partner for its international strategy (Federal Foreign Office, 2019). The bi-regional partnership now enjoyed the full support of the EU's single most powerful political and economic player. In June of the same year, the European Union and Mercosur reached a political agreement on a trade deal. At the end of the year, a new Commission, on paper more favourable to Latin America, took office. All this created a basis to upgrade and strengthen the bi-regional relationship, which in turn prompted a need for a thorough reflection on where to take it and how to lead it. Therefore, there is a need for academic thinking on the topic.

That was back at the beginning of 2020. Then the Covid-19 pandemic came in early 2020 with its global political, economic, social, and lifestyle impact (Gardini, 2020b). Then Russia's war in Ukraine with its global implications broke out in 2022. In the meantime, the long-awaited 2019 Commission Joint Communication did not bear much fruit; Germany has not followed up on its enthusiasm towards Latin America and neither the German nor the Portuguese presidencies of the European Union have prioritised LAC in any way. The EU-Mercosur agreement is far from ratification and negotiations to finalise the agreement still have to address substantial issues such as the economic, social and environmental dimensions of sustainable development (Malamud, 2022; European Commission, 2023). The European Commission led by Ursula Von der Leyen has thus far not dedicated any special attention to Latin America and the Caribbean. This can all be justified and condoned by the urgencies, rescheduling and adjustments required by the pandemic and the war in Ukraine. Again, a new rethinking of the EU-LAC bi-regional interaction is required and both policy-makers and academia must contribute.

Furthermore, the pandemic, the war in Ukraine, and the green transition have highlighted a key challenge for the EU-LAC relation: the questioning of the common values underpinning the bi-regional relationship. This was perceived as largely based on shared values with a long historical and deep-seated cultural tradition (Borrell, 2020). One may wonder if this is still the case today. The Covid-19 pandemic has prompted a feeling in Latin America that Western powers had abandoned Latin America whereas China had come to the rescue. This is far from true: the EU committed nearly 1 billion Euros in the first few months of the pandemic to support Latin America's resilience (European Commission, 2020). Still, the pandemic has strengthened the role and image of China in Latin America (Heine, 2020). Solidarity and compassion between the two shores of the Atlantic seem to be questioned. If Europe moves towards "strategic autonomy" (Tocci, 2021), and Latin America towards "active non-alignment" (Fortin, Heine, Ominami, 2021), will the space for cooperation be curtailed?

Perhaps more importantly, Latin America was divided at the UN and the OAS when voting on resolutions regarding Russia's illegal and unprovoked invasion of Ukraine. The EU stayed united. This casts doubts on the fact that values such as democracy, rule of law, self-determination, non-interference are really shared by Europe and Latin America, to the point that one can wonder if a bi-regional community of values still exists (Nolte, 2022). Latin America's reaction before the US position vis-à-vis Cuba and Venezuela on the occasion of the 2022 Summit of the Americas confirms that the continent is going through a questioning of what democracy means and how it helps or hinders regional and global governance. If a redefinition of shared values occurs, then a redefinition of the relationship that was largely thought to be based on those common values may also be required.

Same as in 2020, also in 2023 there is not only bad news. In June 2023, the Commission's President Von der Leyen visited key partners in Latin America, such as Brazil, Argentina, Chile and Mexico, in search for rare-earth metals indispensable to the EU's green transition and support for the EU's position on the war in Ukraine. In July, a bi-regional summit at the highest level took place after eight years. While this was per se a significant development, it also showed the divergences that still exist between Europe and Latin America and the Caribbean. Furthermore, the EU's global presence and projection are kicking and alive; the EU Global Gateway is Brussels's response to the Chinese Belt and Road Initiative. The image of the EU in the perception of Latin American citizens in 2022 has improved in comparison to 2018 (Nueva Sociedad, 2022). Same as in the previous years, the context and the contingent interests associated to it largely dictated the agenda and positions of the bi-regional relationship

All these developments necessitate yet another deep and articulated discussion on the EU presence in LAC. The context, the actors and the tools moulding the EU-LAC relation all deserve attention. The structural circumstances affect the context where the bi-regional relation takes place. The foreign policies of single countries have the potential to drive EU-LAC interactions. Bold and innovative ideas are essential for an effective, practical, and result-oriented bi-regional agenda. This book is a timely effort to start a frank, open, informed and constructive discussion on all these matters and the redefinition of the EU presence in Latin America and the Caribbean.

The book ahead

The book is structured in two parts. Part I (Chapters 1–9) addresses the foreign policy and roles of some key European states towards LAC, and Brazil's policy towards the EU. Part I also analyses some systemic and contextual factors affecting the development of EU-LAC relations. Part II (Chapters 10–17) addresses some key topics on the EU-LAC agenda and proposes some new ideas and additional reflections on the nature and content of the bilateral agenda.

In Chapter 1, Sergio Caballero addresses the evolution and relevance of Spain's foreign policy towards Latin America. A historical overview is provided in order to highlight the main turning points in Spain's foreign policy towards the region since the transition to democracy. At the same time, the chapter emphasises Spain's role in bi-regional relations through Ibero-American Summits and other diplomatic efforts. The context plays an important role in making sense of both the main challenges and the potential synergies. Finally, a reflection on the current scenario highlights both Madrid's role as a bridge between Brussels and Latin America, and the impact of other extra-regional actors on EU-LAC relations.

In Chapter 2, Carmen Fonseca asks if the common wisdom that Portugal is a strategic player in and for Latin America stands a reality check. The chapter focuses on Portuguese foreign policy towards Latin America in the 21st century, exploring the connection between discourse, strategy and results. Despite the national narrative of Portugal as a bridge between the two continents, which is largely present at the EU level too, the author argues that the Portuguese presence and interest in Latin America can be illustrated through the yo-yo metaphor with swinging priorities and agendas. Hence, Lisbon's capacity to shape the EU-LAC dialogue remains unclear.

In Chapter 3, Jaime León González argues that Germany is a key player in the framework of a possible reconfiguration of EU-LAC relations. This is due to the fact that Berlin has developed a strong bilateral strategy with specific countries in the region, with an emphasis on the energy sector. However, while this is a crucial sector for the green transition and agenda, it may also cause tensions. German policy and regulations concerning the diversification of energy sources do not necessarily fit or converge with the Latin American reality. The chapter uses a normative and constructivist approach to account for the current developments and problems of German-Latin American and Caribbean relations.

In Chapter 4, Luis Fernando Beneduzi takes a historical and political approach to Italy's relations with LAC. Historically, the most important connection between Italy and LAC was the migration issues and the Italian communities abroad. The human relationship worked as a driving force of economic affairs and bilateral agreements. Only in the 21st century, with the economic and political growth of LAC, Rome developed a proper policy towards the continent. The chapter emphasises the connections between immigration, foreign policy and the international context and discusses the shortcomings of the Italian foreign policy toward Latin America.

In Chapter 5, María J. García addresses a sticky issue in European-Latin American relations: Brexit and the new LAC policies of the United Kingdom. Historically, the UK has been an important investor in Latin America and a key trade partner, although its political and economic significance declined with the rise of the US in the region. The chapter analyses UK policy documents since Brexit, as well as the trade and investment relationship to ascertain the significance of the region in London's post-Brexit foreign policy and identify any patterns of divergence with EU policies and with UK policies towards the region as a member of the EU. Post-Brexit policies very much resemble a continuation of past policies.

In Chapter 6, Elena Lazarou and Diego Ponce argue that the EU's relations with Brazil in the past decades have been viewed as a "two-level" strategy. On the one hand, the EU has pursued the strengthening of political relations with

Brazil to ensure an ally in the promotion of its values. On the other hand, Brazil has been viewed as a critical influencer in the future of EU relations with the wider LAC region, most notably through the EU-Mercosur Association Agreement. More recently, especially during the presidency of Jair Bolsonaro, stark divergences between Brasilia and Brussels on climate, indigenous rights and multilateralism, have led to a situation where Brazil-EU relations have reflected negatively on the relationship between the EU and the region.

In Chapter 7, Paulina Astroza Suárez and Javier Sepúlveda Estrada discuss the concept of autonomy, which has recently returned to the fore in IR academia and policy-making, both in Europe and LAC. In both regions, there is a long doctrinal tradition on the idea of autonomy, although the lines of action may differ, and the ways of exercising autonomy depend on how far processes of regional construction have developed. The EU and LAC have common interests in their different agendas, and bi-regional collaboration brings benefits to both parties. In that sense, the idea of autonomy could guide the way in which the different actors fit into the bi-regional relations and more broadly the complex international system.

In Chapter 8, Sandra Zapata suggests that the European Union is rethinking its international ties in the light of the growing US-China competition. Accordingly, Brussels has gone in search of allies, while Latin America is looking to its European partners in search for alternatives to the newly emerging bipolarism. The chapter argues that a stronger bi-regional relation can constitute a third pole. This would be useful to Europe to regain an edge globally, and to Latin America to counter its peripheral position geographically and politically. The implementation of appropriate autonomy strategies is key to reach these objectives on both sides of the Atlantic.

In Chapter 9, Paz Verónica Milet and Belén Cabezas Araya link the debates on regionalism and interregionalism. They identify three levels of crises: global, regional and national that affect Latin America and the Caribbean's ability to project the region internationally. The authors discuss Mercosur, Unasur, the Andean Community, CELAC and the Pacific Alliance to argue that, in the last two decades, Latin America has undergone a series of far-reaching processes that have conditioned the transitions and even the survival of its main multilateral initiatives. In this framework, a region-to-region approach with the European Union may be problematic.

The second part of the book is devoted to the discussion of the EU-LAC bi-regional agenda, its nature, purposes, content and possible innovations.

In Chapter 10, Gian Luca Gardini argues that a decoupling of the political and the functional agenda could help relaunch EU-LAC bi-regional cooperation. The chapter provides a number of policy proposals in three key areas: digitalisation, energy systems, and entrepreneurship and small and medium enterprises. Vocational education and training is a crucial transversal element for success in these three areas. Emphasis on the functional agenda does not exclude the political one, where three ideas are discussed: support for a summit of democracies, a joint EU-LAC agreement on China's investments, and a migration scheme prioritising Latin Americans who want to work in the EU.

In Chapter 11, Mario Torres explores two variables which until now have been under-considered in the study of inter-regionalism: cyberspace and big tech companies. Both need regulation and EU-CELAC inter-regionalism could serve as the basis for new global governance. Big tech companies are the new geopolitical actors and, as a consequence, new foreign policy instruments have to be created to deal with them. Techplomacy could be this new foreign policy instrument. EU-LAC joint efforts have been successful in the approval of the Paris Accords and the adoption of Agenda 2030. They can make a difference in designing the global tech governance too.

In Chapter 12, Jeanne W. Simon provides a bridge between innovation and regional policies. In the European Union, numerous regions have implemented the Smart Specialization Strategy (S3) to develop sub-national innovation systems based on public-private-academic networks. Since 2010, seeking to advance towards a more horizontal partnership with Latin America, the EU (through the DG REGIO program) has promoted S3 as a mutual learning process in several LAC countries. This chapter analyses the adaptation of the S3 approach to the socioeconomic and institutional contexts in Chile and Peru, focusing on the lessons learned with respect to governance and sustainability challenges.

In Chapter 13, Mauricio J. Rondanelli-Reyes tackles the challenge of the environment and climate change. The European Union and the Community of Latin American and Caribbean States (CELAC) are part of the 193 states that in 2015 approved the UN 2030 Agenda for the sustainable development of the planet. This chapter focuses on climate change and the life of terrestrial ecosystems (objectives 13 and 15 of the 2030 Agenda). Emphasis is placed on the climate-terrestrial ecosystem-biodiversity loss relationship. EU and LAC can advance not only with the proposals of mitigation and adaptation mechanisms but also by putting forward a strategic alliance for a global reconfiguration of the environmental issue.

In Chapter 14, Alwine Woischnik addresses the links between the ecological and the social transition. The chapter argues that it is difficult to compare the social and ecological transition in the European Union with similar processes in other continents. Ecological awareness is connected with relatively high levels of well-being. Consequently, historical, cultural, political, socio-economic, democratic development and citizen participation determine the evolution of perceptions and priorities in a society. An EU-LAC bi-regional dialogue and agenda aiming to achieve at least a shared understanding of the issue may facilitate both political and technical cooperation.

In Chapter 15, Millán Requena studies the processes and content of the Global Compact on Migration as well as its implementation focusing on the EU's role and engagement of Latin American and Caribbean countries. The analysis includes a comparative assessment of existing legal and political responses to protection needs and explores future options and their compatibility with the international human rights regime. Particular attention is paid to the regulatory issues pertaining to legal migration channels on the one hand, and migration trajectories and flows, voluntary and forced return policies, the role of diasporas and economic issues including remittances on the other.

In Chapter 16, Beatriz Larraín Martinez discusses an interesting and relatively new topic of the EU's presence in LAC: The influence exercised in different ways by Europe on the constitutional reform process in Chile. This shows a plethora of ways of interaction, spanning from academic publications and expert opinions, EU political cooperation through seminars, visits, and documents, to proposals presented to the Constitutional Convention. As China, Russia and other emerging powers are looking to expand their influence in Latin America, Europe continues to be a constitutional reference. Soft power, also in unexpected areas, seems to remain a major tool of the EU's international projection and presence in LAC.

In Chapter 17, Juan Carlos Aguirre addresses the traditional EU preference for a region-to-region approach by discussing the prospects for a closer EU-Pacific Alliance relationship. The collective identities of both organisations are similar, but their interests and objectives are different. How to take advantage of this similarity in collective identity to reconfigure EU-LAC relations? The chapter discusses two possible ways to do this. Firstly, by strengthening the common collective identity through regional initiatives. Secondly, by strengthening the Pacific Alliance's institutional design, whose extreme modesty and flexibility currently prevent progress in institutionalised relations with the EU.

In the concluding remarks, Gian Luca Gardini summarises some of the key findings of the book in the form of policy-oriented ideas for the reconfiguration of the EU presence in LAC. He also deals with more academic questions. At the empirical level, two dimensions emerge. On the one hand, the combination of change and continuity of the foreign policy of single EU member states towards LAC. On the other, new topics on the agenda have the potential to reshape the

EU-LAC relation. At the theoretical level, there emerge two tensions: the first between values and interests and the second between agency and structure. The book overall proposes a rebalance in these debates emphasising interests and structure.

Last but not least, the strongest asset of the EUinLAC project and this book is the quality and variety of the contributing team. All the authors have recognised expertise in their topic at their different career levels. They also reflect a variety of scholarly backgrounds, cultural and theoretical approaches, and geographical origin as well as a balanced gender composition and level of seniority. This diversity within a truly EU-LAC bi-regional team contributes to the richness in analysis, perspectives and plurality of the book. Overall, in times of alleged European decline (Webber, 2016) and mutually unfulfilled expectations (Maihold, Muscio Blanco and Zilla, 2023), this volume argues that the EU is still a very important actor in Latin America and the Caribbean and that there is considerable unexplored potential for a mutually beneficial redefinition of the EU presence in Latin America.

Bibliography

Astroza Suarez, P., & Larraín, B. (Eds.). (2022). *Relaciones entre la Unión Europea y América Latina: Escenarios futuros en un mundo de cambios*. Valencia: Tirant lo Blanch.

Borrell, J. (2020). Latin America-Europe: The "other" transatlantic relationship. *Blog post* 19 October 2020. Online: https://www.eeas.europa.eu/eeas/latin-america-europe-%E2%80%98other%E2%80%99-transatlantic-relationship_en (last accessed 4 January 2023).

European Commission. (2019). *Joint Communication to the European Parliament and the Council "European Union, Latin America and the Caribbean: joining forces for a common future"*, April, JOIN(2019) 6 final. Online: https://eur-lex.europa.eu/legal-content/EN/TXT/PDF/?uri=CELEX:52019JC0006&from=en (last accessed 4 January 2023).

European Commission. (2020),.*Coronavirus: EU global response to fight the pandemic* [press release 8 April 2020]. Online: https://ec.europa.eu/commission/presscorner/detail/en/ip_20_604 (last accessed 4 January 2023).

European Commission. (2023). *Meeting of the European Union-Mercosur chief negotiators*. Joint Communiqué of the European Union and Mercosur, 8 March 2023. Online: https://policy.trade.ec.europa.eu/news/meeting-european-union-mercosur-chief-negotiators-2023-03-08_en (last accessed 23 June 2023).

Federal Foreign Office. (2019). *Opening speech by Foreign Minister Heiko Maas at the Latin America-Caribbean Conference*, 28 May 2019. Online: https://www.auswaertiges-amt.de/en/newsroom/news/maas-latin-america-caribbean-conference/2222232 (last accessed 4 January 2023).

Fortin, C., Heine, J., & Ominami, C. (2021). *El No Alineamiento Activo y América Latina: una doctrina para el nuevo siglo*. Santiago de Chile: Catalonia.

Gardini, G. L. (2019). Brexit: seis consideraciones para la integración latinoamericana. *Pensamiento Propio*, *24*, 49–50, Noviembre 2019, pp. 395–405.

Gardini, G. L. (2020a). Europe and Germany on the relaunch of EU-LAC relations. In A. Mori (Ed.), *Latin America in the new multipolar world order* (pp. 31–50). Milan: The Italian Institute for International Political Studies (ISPI).

Gardini, G. L. (Ed.). (2020b). *The world before and after Covid-19*. Stockholm and Salamanca: European Institute of International Studies.

Heine, J. (2020). China and the prospects for Latin American recovery. *Global Times* 19.08.2020. Online: https://www.globaltimes.cn/page/202008/1198186.shtml (last accessed 4 January 2023).

Latinobarometro. (2018). *Informe 2018*. Online: www.latinobarometro.org (several entries, last accessed 4 January 2023).

Maihold, G., Muscio Blanco, T., & Zilla, C. (2022). *For a new conception of Germany's and the EU's relations with Latin America and the Caribbean*. SWP Comment Nr 1. Online: https://www.swp-berlin.org/publications/products/comments/2023C01_EU_LatinAmerica_Caribbean.pdf (last accesses 18 January 2023).

Malamud, A. (2022). *Assessing the political dialogue and cooperation pillar of the EU-Mercosur Association Agreement: Towards a bi-regional strategic partnership?*. In-depth Analysis for the European Parliament, Policy Department for External Relations, Directorate General for External Policies of the Union, Brussels, January. Online: https://www.europarl.europa.eu/RegData/etudes/IDAN/2022/653652/EXPO_IDA(2022)653652_EN.pdf (last accessed 4 January 2023).

Malamud, A., & Schenoni, L. (2021). *Sobre la creciente irrelevancia de América Latina*. Nueva Sociedad, N° 291, January–February. Online: https://nuso.org/articulo/sobre-la-creciente-irrelevancia-de-america-latina/ (last accessed 4 January 2023).

Nolte, D. (2022). *La guerra en Ucrania impacta las relaciones entre América Latina y la UE*, Latinoamérica21, 14 April2022. Online: https://latinoamerica21.com/es/la-guerra-en-ucrania-impacta-las-relaciones-entre-america-latina-y-la-ue/ (latest accessed 4 January 2023).

Nolte, D., & Weiffen, B. (2020). *Regionalism under stress. Europe and Latin America in comparative perspective*. London: Routledge.

Nueva Sociedad. (2022). *Cómo América Latina ve a Europa*. Online: https://nuso.org/articulo/como-AL-ve-a-europa/ (last accessed 4 January 2023).

Sanahuja, J. A. (2022). *La Unión Europea y América Latina en el interregno: autonomía estratégica, pacto verde y recuperación pospandemia*. High-level EU-LAC dialogue, Brussels 29–30.06.2022. Online: https://eurosocial.eu/wp-content/uploads/2022/05/UE-ALC-Sanahuja-Eurosocial-2022.pdf (last accessed 4 January 2023).

Tocci, N. (2021). *European strategic autonomy: What it is, why we need it, how to achieve it*. oma: Istituto Affari Internazionali. Online: https://www.iai.it/sites/default/files/9788893681780.pdf (last accessed 4 January 2023).

Webber, D. (2016). Declining power Europe: The evolution of the European Union's world power in the early 21st century. *European Review of International Studies*, *3*(1), 31–52.

Part I Foreign Policies and Contextual Factors Moulding EU-LAC Relations

Sergio Caballero

Spanish Foreign Policy Towards Latin America: Time for Redefinition?

Introduction[1]

A rigorous analysis of Spanish foreign policy reveals that Latin America has always been one of Spain's top priorities (Gobierno de España, 2019). Moreover, Spain's historical, cultural and socio-economic ties with Latin America have configured the region as the political space where Spanish diplomacy has had the most room for manoeuvre when seeking to incorporate "added value" in international forums or impact the global agenda. In light of this, Latin America has been the main focus of international policy at the *Palacio de Santa Cruz*, headquarters of the Ministry of Foreign Affairs, ever since Spain joined the European project in 1986 and subsequently internalised European policy, not only as foreign policy but also as a kind of *de facto* domestic policy. Latin America's centrality remained a cornerstone in Madrid's international agenda in spite of Spain's undeniable strategic interest in the Southern Neighbourhood (Mediterranean and Maghreb). This is an area of special interest that due to its geographical proximity and security and migration issues has often, and regrettably, overshadowed Latin America on Madrid's external agenda.

The discourse of both practitioners and scholars of foreign policy tends to simplify and homogenise Latin America, despite the high levels of diversity and heterogeneity in the region. Such approaches overlook the fact that there are "many Latin Americas" (Sanahuja, 2016: 241) which should also incorporate Brazil, a special case and something of an anomaly in the region (different colonial historical trajectory, different independence process, origins in a different political regime, etc.) (Ayllón, 2014). At the same time, Ibero-American[2]

---

1 Some ideas developed in this chapter are updated forms of an earlier version by Caballero (2021). "Oscilaciones en las relaciones Brasil-España: entre el pragmatismo económico y el desconocimiento mutuo," *Methaodos revista de ciencias sociales*, *9*(1), 124–134. https://doi.org/10.17502/mrcs.v9i1.436.

2 The concept of Ibero-America is mainly used by Spanish diplomacy to refer to the Latin American countries, Portugal and Spain. However, this label is not generally used either in multilateral forums or in the diplomatic language of Latin American countries due to its perceived colonial connotations.

relations assume mutual interests as a given, while simultaneously being formulated within a certain knowledge vacuum and based on stereotypes and biases, which are sometimes paternalistic and neo-colonial and can often hinder greater understanding.

This chapter adopts a historicist approach to foreign policy to examine political-diplomatic relations between Spain and Latin America. It works from a definition of foreign policy as "the sum of official external relations conducted by an independent actor (usually a state) in international relations" (Hill, 2016: 3). Nevertheless, the chapter goes a step further by understanding foreign policy as a public policy intended to ensure citizens' well-being by promoting higher levels of development. This process is shaped by two variables (Beneyto, 2011: 22–23): (i) national interest, defined in essentially pragmatic terms, which includes economic opportunities and analysis of the geopolitical context based on structural and conjunctural elements of the international system; and (ii) cultural values, which relate primarily to questions of identity, in the sense of how a society or a country perceives itself in the world (democratic, multilateral, peaceful, interventionist, etc.), thereby reinforcing its policies and actions in the international arena and, where appropriate, responding to the ideological shifts of its rulers that can redefine a country's role at either the regional or global level.

The chapter charts the milestones of these relations during recent decades via a historical overview of diplomacy and ties between Spain and Latin America. It examines the positions adopted by Spanish governments of differing political orientations, as well as specific policies implemented by Spanish diplomacy, such as the Ibero-American Summits. Then the analysis focuses on the current context, exploring both the main challenges as well as the potential opportunities and synergies, thereby allowing for some final conclusions that shed light on current redefinition processes. This approach casts Madrid's role as a bridge between Europe and Latin America, and shows how the emergence of other extra-regional actors (e.g. China) recalibrates mutual interests in Spain and Latin America, and with them the legitimate priorities and interests of each actor.

A brief history of Spanish foreign policy towards Latin America

Relations between Spain and Latin America have deep historical roots. They started with the colonial period and spanned through the independence processes (which took place in the period between 1810 and 1825 in most of the countries of the region) and the subsequent disquiet in the metropolis over the loss of the last overseas colonies in 1898. Later, the dictatorships of Primo de

Rivera and Francisco Franco instrumentalised the colonial legacy to construct the idea of *Hispanidad* with the aspiration of returning, at least symbolically, to the supposed "good old days" of the Spanish empire (Calduch, 1994).

The focus of this chapter will be on the democratic period, broadly the post-Franco years from the late 1970s in Spain and the re-democratisation phase in Latin America in the 1980s, in what Huntington called the third wave of democratisation (1994). Following Celestino del Arenal (2008), we can categorise various phases of Spanish foreign policy during the first years of the transition to democracy: (i) a sort of "tacit consensus" (1976–1980), during which foreign policy privileged Europe and Latin America; (ii) a "constituent phase in foreign policy" (1980–1986), during which Spain established relations with the US via NATO and completed its accession to the European project, and; (iii) a phase of "concretion" (1986–1988), during which Spain consolidated the main lines of its foreign policy and created the conditions for democratic and European foreign policy.

Beginning with what is known as "normalised foreign policy," that is, from 1988 onwards, we witnessed just over five years in which not only did a general consensus prevail among the various actors that defined and participated in designing and implementing foreign policy, but which could also be considered "the golden age of Spanish diplomacy," coinciding with the final years of the governments of Felipe González (1982–1996). This successful phase bore fruit both in terms of ambitions on the world stage and multilateralism, as well as in the capacity to "Europeanise" Spain's specific perspectives on the two it prioritises most highly: Latin America and the Southern Neighbourhood of the Mediterranean. Regarding Latin America, the establishment of the Ibero-American Summits in 1991, as will be explained later, has not only enabled closer relations with the region, but has also legitimised a role for Madrid to act as a privileged interlocutor – and set itself up as a kind of "bridge" – between Europe and Latin America, at least throughout the 1990s. This trend culminated in the Euro-Latin American Bi-Regional Strategic Partnership in 1999 (Ayuso & Caballero, 2018; Sanahuja, 2013). Regarding the Southern Neighbourhood, meanwhile, the launch of the Barcelona Process in 1995 regionalised and legitimised Spain's understanding of the Mediterranean basin, at least until the implementation of the European Neighbourhood Policy in 2004 and the subsequent Union for the Mediterranean, promoted by the French president Nicolas Sarkozy in 2007 (Neila, 2019).

These golden years came to an end during the government of José María Aznar, whose tenure was characterised by two significant events. The first of these occurred when Spain's ability to regionalise its Latin American policy at the European level crystallised with the "common position" in 1996, from which the EU imposed sanctions on Fidel Castro's Cuba (Diamint, 2009: 104). In addition to Spanish companies' increased presence in the region, an expansion due to their significant internationalisation during the 1990s, the appearance of a markedly ideological impetus within Spain's official policy consensus towards Latin America opened the door for future governments to adopt reductionist visions of foreign policy. To a certain extent, these reductionist perspectives diminished both the moral ascendancy that the Spanish transition had projected and Spain's status as the roadmap young Latin American democracies should follow. Moreover, this "common position" against Cuba would become a hindrance when José Luis Rodríguez Zapatero's government unsuccessfully tried to take it up (Sanahuja, 2016: 244), as the position provoked opposition from Eastern European governments with anti-communist sentiments. Ultimately, there would be no change at the European level until the normalisation of relations between Cuba and the US under the Obama administration.

The second notable characteristic of Spanish foreign policy under the Aznar government, meanwhile, was its decided renunciation of multilateralism and its alignment with the Bush administration (Arenal, 2003: 184–190). This trend was particularly pronounced during the Aznar administration's second term (2000–2004), when it enjoyed an absolute majority. This policy led Spanish diplomacy to strain its relations with Mexico and Chile, then non-permanent members of the UN Security Council, as Spain unsuccessfully attempted to pressure the two countries to vote in favour of a resolution legally endorsing the military intervention in Iraq in 2003. In short, Spanish foreign policy towards the region was subordinated to ideological concerns and a privileging of relations with Washington over traditional ties with Latin America.

Foreign policy during the two governments of José Luis Rodríguez Zapatero (2004–2011) centred around the idea of promoting a return to multilateralism, viewing closer relations with Latin America as crucial to this objective (Maihold, 2004: 172). This prioritisation inhered in the institutional design itself, which reorganised the Ministry of Foreign Affairs and Cooperation and divided the Secretariats of State between cooperation policies and the brand-new Secretariat of State for Ibero-America in 2006 (Europa Press, 2006). In this context and under Zapatero's leadership, two notable milestones in Spain-Latin America relations occurred. One of these milestones was the reopening of negotiations between the EU and Mercosur in May 2010. Taking advantage of Spain's occupation of the EU rotating presidency and the Argentine's government rotating presidency of Mercosur, both Zapatero and Cristina Kirchner relaunched these negotiations out of conviction, but also out of necessity, given that both were suffering economic crises and perceived the prospects for an ambitious political-commercial agreement as promising (Reuters, 2010; BBC, 2010). The second milestone that needs to be highlighted relates to the firm commitment to international cooperation.

> To comply with international Official Development Assistance (ODA) targets of 0.7% of GDP by 2015 and EU agreements to reach 0.50% by 2010, ODA increased from 0.24% in 2004 to a record high of 0.46% in 2009. That year, Spain, the only donor country in the Organisation for Economic Cooperation and Development that prioritises Latin America in its cooperation policy, ranked sixth in the world ranking of donors, and first in absolute terms for Latin America, ahead even of the United States (Sanahuja, 2016: 253).

However, the 2008 international financial crisis and its drastic effects on Spain from 2010 onwards led to a change of government and a consequent shift in foreign policy. The new government of Mariano Rajoy (2011–2018), in a context of economic crisis and a lack of confidence from international markets, opted to reinforce and absorb the economic austerity policies emanating from Europe, which would leave Latin America off the priority radar. Thus, according to Sanahuja (2016: 238):

> The duration of Mariano Rajoy's Partido Popular (PP) government has entailed a significant redefinition of Spanish foreign policy, partly by choice and partly by necessity. Informed by ideological considerations, the new PP government sought to move away from Zapatero's "cosmopolitan" and multilateralist vision, both symbolically and substantively. But the most important changes have been of necessity: the relationship with Brussels, centred on crisis management, has been the most obvious priority of the legislature. This is demonstrated by the appointment of high-ranking officials with experience and knowledge of the EU – and, on the other hand, less knowledge and concern for Latin America – such as José Manuel García Margallo as foreign minister, due to his extensive experience in European institutions, and Luis de Guindos as finance minister, to take on negotiations with the Eurogroup.

Consistent with the prevailing trend of austerity, Rajoy's foreign policy was subordinated to a pragmatic and reductionist vision which prioritised two markedly economistic objectives: boosting exports to stimulate the economy and encouraging the attraction of foreign direct investment. The so-called *Marca España* (Spain Brand) was designed according to these objectives, and was conceived as a commercial strategy for large Spanish companies facing challenges in widening diplomacy. *Marca España* was rebranded as *España Global* following the change of government in 2018 (El País, 2018). In this regard, the repeated dialectical clashes caused by the Spanish government's overreaction to the nationalisation of Spanish companies in Argentina and Bolivia are noteworthy. Far from finding solutions (as the companies themselves, with lower profiles and more open to dialogue, later succeeded in doing), Minister José Manuel García-Margallo's declaration that "Argentina had shot itself in the foot" (La Vanguardia, 2012) provoked heightened tensions that were counterproductive to national and business interests. In short, Spain's foreign policy towards Latin America was tinged with an ideological bias which artificially divided the region into friends and enemies, reliable partners (preferably the members of the Pacific Alliance) and unpredictable partners (the members of Mercosur), and designed foreign policy informed by a reading of the domestic political climate, rather than implementing a stable and lasting foreign policy. The case of Venezuela illustrates this tendency perfectly, insofar as the emergence of new political parties in Spain's traditional two-party scenario led Rajoy's government to attack Podemos while branding it as "Bolivarian and Chavist" (El País, 2017). In summary, we are witnessing the continued ideologisation of Spanish foreign policy, with the consequent loss of real interest in fostering predictable, lasting and sincere bilateral relations. On the other hand, Latin American policy was instrumentalised to serve domestic political objectives. During this period, Spanish diplomacy shifted, with Rajoy changing his stance from firm support for the Venezuelan opposition to Maduro (El País, 2016) to the delicate tightrope walking required regarding President Sánchez's declaration to recognise Juan Guaidó as the "acting president" in 2019 (RTVE, 2019). This shift was motivated by a desire not to dissociate himself from the European consensus, yet resulted in Minister González Laya recognising that the solution should not be to opt for either Guaidó or Maduro, but rather to move towards "free and democratic elections" (El Periódico, 2020).

This motivation was also evident in Spain's non-participation in the peace negotiations in Colombia (Spain felt participating in these negotiations would be risky due to any potential implications its participation would have for the Basque conflict) and also in the difficulties in resuming contact with Cuba after the aforementioned normalisation of relations with the US under Obama.

In parallel to this disinterest from Spain, China's economic slowdown led in turn to disinterest from Latin America, due to China's decreased demand for raw materials. This occurred despite the majority of Latin American countries' (especially South American) success in mitigating the harmful effects of the crisis in the early stages of the international financial crisis, thanks to their commodity exports to the Asia-Pacific area in general and to China in particular. This phenomenon was noticeable, for example, in countries such as Brazil, where the inertia and low international profile of Dilma Rousseff's administration led in turn to a limited, pragmatic and reductionist Brazilian foreign policy (Caballero, 2019).

Ibero-American Summits

At this point, greater attention must be given to one factor in particular, given its centrality in accounting for Spanish foreign policy towards Latin America: the idea of creating an Ibero-American Community of Nations with regular meetings and "family diplomacy" (Elcano, 2014: 15) through the Ibero-American Summits.

Madrid sought to establish the Ibero-American Community of Nations as an instrument for maximising historical and cultural ties with its former colonies (Diamint, 2009: 95–96). Although the Ibero-American Community of Nations was largely financed by Spain and responded to the former metropolis' strategic interests, it was developed in collaboration with Mexico (which hosted the first summit in Guadalajara in 1991) and achieved significant legitimacy in its early years. Almost from the outset, the three main countries, Spain, Mexico and Brazil internalised the dynamics of these summits (Cortés Lastra, 2013: 141), as evidenced by the venues chosen to host the following two summits (Madrid, 1992; Salvador de Bahía, 1993). Over time, not only have Latin American actors lost interest in these summits, viewing them as an instrument of Spanish penetration in the region, but the summits have also received criticism informed by a perceived need for "Latin Americanisation or de-Spanishisation of the summits" (Valle Gálvez, 2013: 31). In fact, this regrettable perception that the success of the summits should be measured in terms of the leaders in attendance rather than by the results actually achieved persists not only with academia but also within the Spanish Ministry of Foreign Affairs itself. Nevertheless, this simplistic perspective has gained even greater traction in recent years. Let us consider, for example, the ministry's note on the summit in Guatemala in 2018: "This was one of the most well-attended summits in the last decade, with 18 leaders in attendance, including heads of state and government, and with only 3 states absent" (Ministry for Foreign Affairs, European Union and Cooperation, 2018); now compare this to this reflection on the XXVII Summit held in Andorra in April 2021: "The media often tend to measure the success of a meeting at the highest political level by the number of participating leaders and, above all, by the attendance of those who supposedly have the greatest weight in decision-making in the international context. There is undoubtedly some logic to this [...] the absence of one or other member may be circumstantial, because the truth is that countries are always represented by some of their authorities while decisions are taken in the name of all of them. It goes without saying, by the way, that all this took place at the 27th Ibero-American Summit in Andorra, held on 21 April, under the extraordinary conditions in which it was held due to the COVID-19 pandemic" (Grynspan, 2021).

A useful exercise in these continuous re-evaluation processes was the report by former Brazilian president Fernando Henrique Cardoso at the Bávaro Summit (Dominican Republic, 2002), which claimed that the summit "represented an important political reflection on the values that distinguish us as a community and advocated deeper political dialogue, prioritising certain lines of cooperation and establishing a permanent Ibero-American Secretariat" (Casas, 2013: 131). Irrespective of the suitability of this "summit diplomacy" as an exercise in deliberative democracy, and despite its limitations arising from the summit fatigue informally known as "*summititis,*" this report clearly demonstrates Spain's desire for closer relations with Latin America. One episode is particularly instructive in this regard, namely the 22nd Ibero-American Summit in Cádiz (2012) to commemorate the bicentenary of the Constitution of Cádiz. The organisational effort of an event loaded with such symbolic significance necessitated the mobilisation of all diplomatic resources, to ensure a large representation of Latin American heads of state. This is particularly noteworthy given that Latin American leaders had less incentive to dialogue with their Iberian counterparts due to Spain and Portugal's weakened position in the wake of the financial crisis. In the specific case of Brazil, in addition to the excessive proliferation and overlapping of summits (whether regional summits such as UNASUR, Mercosur, CELAC, etc.; interregional summits, such as the EU-CELAC, which would take place in 2013 and 2015; or global summits, such as the G20, BRICS, etc.), Brazil had little incentive to participate, given that the Lula da Silva governments considered itself automatically invited to the global governance forums which decided on major global issues. President Cristina Fernández de Kirchner's absence, combined with certain tensions over the possible presence of the "suspended" Paraguayan president, Federico Franco, made ensuring President Dilma Rousseff's attendance even more imperative. Rousseff only agreed to attend after a direct invitation from the King of Spain, who was first forced to make an official visit to Brazil. In short, at a simplistic, cursory glance, this outcome may appear to be a success and proof of mutual interest; however, a more critical reflection leads to the conclusion that Brazil's doubts and lack of interest, despite its *de facto* presence at the summit as a matter of diplomatic courtesy, should be interpreted as evidence of both the intrinsic weaknesses of the Ibero-American summits themselves and the lack of concordance between Madrid and many Latin American capitals during years characterised by a narrow, reductionist, economistic and pragmatic vision of foreign policy.

Finally, and by way of conclusion, it is worth noting that the keenly contested election of the new secretary-general of the Ibero-American General Secretariat (SEGIB), the former Chilean foreign minister Andrés Allamand, represents both the ideological polarisation of the region and the renewed interest in placing political actors in top-level diplomatic posts (El País, 2021). This interpretation is evidenced by the inordinate effort required from the Chilean candidacy (Infobae, 2022) to obtain a post that used to be appointed with broad consensus, as in the case of his predecessors, Rebeca Grynspan (2014–2021) and Enrique Iglesias (2005–2014).

Current challenges and possibilities of Spanish foreign policy towards Latin America

More recently, President Pedro Sánchez's arrival at the Moncloa in June 2018 following a vote of no confidence in President Rajoy brought about substantial changes in Spain's approach to foreign policy. Spain's foreign policy (Carnero & Martín, 2011) exhibits the same presidentialist trait in its design, elaboration and execution that can be observed in Latin America (Danese, 2017). In addition to the major challenges of managing the Covid-19 pandemic and the Russian invasion of Ukraine, the most notable accomplishment over the course of Sánchez's two governments (2018–), was recalibrating the compass of Spanish foreign policy, aspiring to return to the multilateralism that was once a hallmark of the Zapatero government. With this in mind, the Foreign Action Strategy 2021–2024 (FAS), approved on 27 April 2021, sets out the four main lines of action:

> I. The promotion of human rights, democracy, security, feminism and diversity as a reference point for Spain's action in the world; II. The resolute promotion of a new global socio-economic model, based on the principles of integration, justice and equity; III. The firm defence of a more sustainable, habitable and green planet; IV. Activism in improving global governance through the promotion of greater regional integration and a renewed and strengthened multilateralism. (FAS, 27 April 2021)

In summary, the FAS proposes two possible responses (centrifugal and disuniting, or centripetal and inclusive), in addition to a holistic and comprehensive diagnosis of the current international scenario based on four fractures (socio-economic, ecological and environmental, technological, and political and governance). Seeking to put these principles into practice, the foreign minister herself, Arancha González Laya (2021), structured Spain's international projection priorities into four points: (i) defending multilateralism and international cooperation against unilateralism or nationalism; (ii) deepening European integration; (iii) promoting bilateral relations with specific regions of the world (the *Estrategia Foco África* [Africa Focus Strategy]), strengthening relations with Latin America and promoting the EU's Southern Neighbourhood with countries on the other side of the Mediterranean); and (iv) committing to modernising development cooperation. Links with Latin America regained a pre-eminent role in this scenario, not only in the economic-business sphere (which they did), but also in the political-cultural sphere.

Finally, in the case of Spain, in addition to the commitment to "reformed and strengthened multilateralism," another factor that contributed to the current aspiration to Europeanise Spanish relations with Latin America through Brussels was Josep Borrell's, former foreign minister in Sánchez's first cabinet, appointment as the new EU High Representative for Foreign Affairs and Security Policy in December 2019. His firm commitment to Latin America has amplified Spanish diplomacy's calls for Europe to redefine relations with Latin America, particularly in the context of the war on Europe's eastern flank and the need to unite partners for the "strategic autonomy" advocated by the EU in its recent document *A Strategic Compass for the EU* (2022).

Conclusions and room for redefinition

We now find ourselves in a *sui generis* scenario that demands a multi-faceted analysis. In light of this, the present article concludes by offering some reflections on the possibility of redefining relations between Spain – and therefore the EU – and Latin America via analysis of systemic, regional and conjunctural factors.

At the systemic level, both actors, Spain and Latin America, simultaneously face many of the structural challenges common in the international context: from the crisis of globalisation, with its consequent growing socio-political disaffection and the depletion of environmental resources (Sanahuja, 2018), to the health crisis and the acceleration of pre-existing trends, exacerbated by the Covid-19 pandemic (Haass, 2020; Rodrik, 2020). These systemic challenges are also framed by a perceived change of era (rather than an era of change), in which geopolitical tensions between China and the US are redefining not only relations between the two countries but also between other actors, while climate change, despite the continued postponement of drastic measures to tackle it, is becoming increasingly relevant to understanding the major transformations that are coming: digital, green and social (Verdes-Montenegro, 2022).

Secondly, at the regional level, recent years have witnessed a growing mutual disinterest. Structural problems have dominated the agenda in Latin America (inequalities, reprimarisation of exports, institutional weakness, taxation, etc.), in combination with the appearance of new opportunities and challenges: notably,

China's arrival in the region in the form of huge investments. Not only has China become the largest trading partner for the majority of Latin American countries, but it is now also a strategic political ally for many countries in the region, as demonstrated by the soft power exercised through "vaccine diplomacy" (Lee, 2021) and the diplomatic bid to side with China over Taiwan (BBC, 2021).

Reciprocally, from the Spanish side, and by extension, from the European side, we have witnessed several years of marked self-absorption in which Spain, far from projecting itself outwards as in the past, has prioritised domestic concerns in the face of three crises (Caballero, 2019b): the economic and euro crisis in wake of the international financial crisis of 2008, the refugee and values crisis following the war in Syria in 2015, and the political and institutional crisis caused by Brexit and the rise of the far right. In short, the increasing irrelevance of Latin America (Malamud & Schenoni, 2020) has contributed to a greater disconnection that is notably evidenced by the lack of high-level meetings since 2015, that is, after the first two EU-CELAC summits were held in Santiago de Chile in 2013 and in Brussels in 2015.

However, in terms of more conjunctural factors, certain events currently in progress suggest the existence of a kind of window of opportunity for redefining these relations. Spain, as a bridge between the EU and Latin America, led by a multilateralist government with a strong Latin Americanist focus, is seeking to promote and capitalise on Europe's turn towards Latin America. The fact that Spain will hold the European presidency in the second half of 2023, at the same time as the recently elected President Lula da Silva's Brazil will do the same in Mercosur, indicates a firm diplomatic commitment to redirect Euro-Latin American ties. Additionally, 2023 will be an election year in Spain and, although voters do not perceive foreign policy as a pressing issue, foreign policy could maximise political capital for a leader seeking international prestige and credibility as a presidential candidate in the run-up to a general election. In this scenario, Brussels will be the venue for a top-level summit between the EU and Latin America in July 2023, where Spain could, as in the past, regionalise its particular understanding of Latin America and instil this vision in its European partners. In fact, this would in itself constitute a kind of redefinition of the mutual disinterest that has characterised these relationships in the recent past.

Finally, and as if the factors mentioned above were not enough, the current conflict between Russia and Ukraine, with Spain's (and Europe's) resolute support for Ukrainian interests, has altered the geopolitical landscape. Although the 2016 EU Global Strategy (Sanahuja, 2021: 110) and the aforementioned Strategic Compass report reserved a marginal place for Latin America among the EU's priorities, it is more vital than ever for the EU to recruit partners and allies that respect international legality. On the one hand, this Spanish and European bid is intended to isolate Russia, to minimise the number of allies it can muster supporters for its expansionist activities; on the other hand, meanwhile, Spain and Europe's intention is to coordinate with Latin American countries with which it shares similar values and ideas, to allow it to have a voice in decision-making processes in multilateral forums that could become increasingly polarised by tensions between the US and China. Evidence of this was the signing of the EU-Mercosur agreement in June 2019 when the agreement was unexpectedly presented (although the final agreed text was never made public) in purely symbolic terms, projecting an image of a firm commitment to multilateralism and interregional dialogue when protectionist tensions between China and the US were rising and nationalist discourses were being promoted by Donald Trump and Xi Jinping, among others.

In summary, although in the short term, Spain's (and the EU's) strategic and economic interests do not correspond perfectly with those of Latin America, especially given Latin America's growing dependence on China, in the medium term there is no doubt about the potential for convergence between societies with shared values. Given this still-evolving outlook, Spanish diplomacy must certainly reorient its foreign policy towards Latin America, shedding its past paternalism and recognising that, in the current context, Latin America is more important to Spain than the other way around. This is true not only in terms of investment and economic relations but also because of the global importance of the Spanish language, with the 450 million Latin American speakers far outweighing the 47 million in Spain, but mainly because if Spain has anything to say on the global stage and in the highest echelons of international diplomacy, it owes this fact to its close ties with Latin America. This is where the potential, and the need, for Spain to redefine its current foreign policy towards Latin America resides.

Bibliography

Arenal, C. (2003). "Estados Unidos y la política latinoamericana de España", *Política Exterior*, vol. XVII, n. 93.

Arenal, C. (2008). "Consenso y disenso en la política exterior de España", *Documento de Trabajo Real Instituto Elcano*, n. 25, 2 junio de 2008.

Arenal, C. (2011). *Política Exterior de España y Relaciones con América Latina: Iberoamericanidad, Europeización y Atlantismo en la Política Exterior Española*, Siglo XXI Editores.

Arenal, C. (2013). “Brasil, las Cumbres Iberoamericanas y el papel de España en América Latina”, *Documentos CIDOB-América Latina*, n. 39, dic. 2013.

Ayllón, B. (2014). “De la asociación estratégica a la crisis: las relaciones hispano-brasileñas en un contexto de cambios estructurales”, *Revista de Estudios Brasileños*, ISSN-e 2386-4540, Vol. 1, n. 1, pp. 25–44.

Ayuso, A., & Caballero, S. (2018). *El interregionalismo de la Unión Europea (UE) con América Latina*, Bogotá, Ed. Universidad Cooperativa de Colombia. https://doi.org/10.16925/9789587601039.

BBC. (2010). “Cumbre de Madrid: comercio y reproches” 18 May 2010. https://www.bbc.com/mundo/economia/2010/05/100518_2059_cumbre_madrid_europa_latinoamerica_gm (last access 7 December 2022).

BBC. (2021). “Nicaragua receives China vaccines after cutting ties with Taiwan” 13 December 2021 https://www.bbc.com/news/world-asia-59633388 (last access 12 December 2022).

Beneyto, J. M. (2011). “La política exterior española en el nuevo escenario mundial”, en José María Beneyto & Juan Carlos Pereira (dirs.), *Política exterior española: un balance de futuro*, Ed. (pp. 19–60). Madrid: CEU.

Caballero, S. (2019a). “Política exterior brasileña tras Lula: inercia y caída”, en *Política brasileña en español. De la crisis al impeachment*. Editorial de la Universidad Nacional de Entre Ríos (EDUNER).

Caballero, S. (2019b). “Regionalismo latinoamericano, multilateralismo y transregionalismo: divergencias, retroalimentaciones y potencialidades”, en C. Ortiz Morales & E. Vieira Posada (Eds.), *Nuevas propuestas de integración regional: tendencias y retos de transformación* (pp. 23–44). Bogotá: Ediciones Universidad Cooperativa de Colombia. https://dx.doi.org/10.16925/9789587602036.

Caballero, S. (2021). “Oscilaciones en las relaciones Brasil-España: entre el pragmatismo económico y el desconocimiento mutuo”, *Methaodos revista de ciencias sociales, 9*(1), 124–134. https://doi.org/10.17502/mrcs.v9i1.436.

Calduch, R. (1994). “La política exterior española durante el franquismo”, en *La política exterior española en el siglo XX* (pp. 107–156). Madrid: Ediciones Ciencias Sociales.

Carnero Fernández, A., & Martín Frías, J. (2011). “¿Hacia una presidencialización de la Política Exterior? Algunas reflexiones sobre nuestra historia reciente (1973–2004)”, en José María Beneyto & Juan Carlos Pereira (dirs.), *Política exterior española: un balance de futuro*, Ed. (pp. 631–650). Madrid: CEU.

Cortés Lastra, R. (2013). “El futuro de las Cumbres Iberoamericanas”, en J. A. Valle Gálvez, I. González García, & M. A. Acosta Sánchez (coords.), *La cumbre de Cádiz y las relaciones de España con América Latina* (pp.141–146). Ministerio de Asuntos Exteriores.

Danese, S. (2017). *Diplomacia presidencial: história e crítica*. Brasília: FUNAG.

Diamint, R. (2009). "América Latina y España. Confluencias y disonancias", en Celestino del Arenal (coord.), *España y América Latina 200 años después de la Independencia: valoración y perspectivas* (pp. 87–122).

ELCANO. (2014). "Hacia una renovación estratégica de la política exterior española", *Informe del Real Instituto Elcano*, n. 15, Feb. 2014.

El País. (2016). "Rajoy apoya a la oposición venezolana ante las maniobras de Maduro", 11 January 2022 https://elpais.com/internacional/2016/01/10/actualidad/1452445903_732556.html (last access 7 December 2022).

El País. (2017). "Rajoy se aferra a Venezuela para hacer frente a las acusaciones de corrupción", 12 July 2017 https://elpais.com/politica/2017/07/12/actualidad/1499844141_967679.html (last access 7 December 2022).

El País. (2018). "España Global se centrará en defender la calidad de la democracia española" 20 November 2018. https://elpais.com/politica/2018/11/19/actualidad/1542657069_929908.html (last access 12 December 2022).

El País. (2021). "El canciller del chileno Piñera dirigirá la Secretaría General Iberoamericana", 26 November 2021. https://elpais.com/internacional/2021-11-26/el-canciller-del-chileno-pinera-nuevo-secretario-general-iberoamericano.html (last access 7 December 2022).

El Periódico. (2020). "Exteriores recuerda en plena polémica que España "lideró" el reconocimiento de Guaidó", 24 enero 2020 https://www.elperiodico.com/es/politica/20200124/gobierno-sanchez-guaido-venezuela-gonzalez-laya-abalos-7819604 (last access 7 December 2022).

Europa Press. (2006). "El Gobierno crea la Secretaría de Estado para Iberoamérica con Trinidad Jiménez al frente", 8 September 2006. https://www.europapress.es/nacional/noticia-consejo-gobierno-crea-secretaria-estado-iberoamerica-trinidad-jimenez-frente-20060908155450.html (last access 13 December 2022).

European External Action Service. (2022). "A Strategic Compass for the EU", 21 March 2022. https://www.eeas.europa.eu/eeas/strategic-compass-eu-0_en (last access 2 December 2022).

Foreign Action Strategy. (2021–2024). *Gobierno de España, 27 de abril de 2021*. https://www.lamoncloa.gob.es/consejodeministros/Paginas/enlaces/270421-enlace-exteriores.aspx (last access 2 December 2022).

García Casas, F. (2013). "Sobre el futuro de las cumbres iberoamericanas", en J. A. Valle Gálvez, I. González García, & M. A. Acosta Sánchez (coords.), *La cumbre de Cádiz y las relaciones de España con América Latina*, (pp. 129–140). Ministerio de Asuntos Exteriores.

Gobierno de España. (2019). "Los ejes de la política exterior española". Disponible en https://www.lamoncloa.gob.es/espana/eh18-19/pexterior/Paginas/ejespolext.aspx (last access 12 December 2022).

González Laya, A. (2021). "Intervención de Arancha González Laya", 27 abril 2021. Disponible en https://www.lamoncloa.gob.es/consejodeministros/Paginas/EnlacesTranscripciones_RPCMin_2021/270421-laya.aspx (last access 2 December 2022).

Grynspan, R. (2021). "La XXVII Cumbre Iberoamericana de Andorra: consenso, inclusión y cooperación", *Punto de vista Fundación Carolina*, 22 abril 2021. https://www.fundacioncarolina.es/la/ (last access 7 December 2022).

Haass, R. (2020). "The pandemic will accelerate history rather than reshape it", *Foreign Affairs*, July/August 2020.

Hill, C. (2016). *Foreign policy in the twenty-first century.* London & New York: Palgrave.

Huntington, S. (1994). *La Tercera ola. La democratización a finales de Siglo XX.* Ed. Paidós Ibérica.

Infobae. (2022). "Acusan al ex canciller de Chile de gastar miles de dólares en su campaña para su próximo puesto como secretario general Iberoamericano", 9 February 2022. https://www.infobae.com/america/america-latina/2022/02/09/acusan-al-ex-canciller-de-chile-de-gastar-miles-de-dolares-en-su-campana-para-su-proximo-puesto-como-secretario-general-iberoamericano/ (last access 7 December 2022).

La Vanguardia. (2012). "Margallo afirma que Argentina "se ha pegado un tiro en el pie", 17 April 2012 https://www.lavanguardia.com/politica/20120417/54284562862/margallo-argentina-pegado-tiro-pie-expropiacion-repsol-ypf.html (last access 7 December 2022).

Lee, S. T. (2021). "Vaccine diplomacy: Nation branding and China's COVID-19 soft power play". *Place Brand Public Dipl.* 2021 Jul 6, 1–15. https://doi.org/10.1057/s41254-021-00224-4.

Maihold, G. (2004). "Retorno a Europa, reencuentro con América Latina, ejes de la nueva política exterior de España en el Gobierno de José Luis Rodríguez Zapatero". *Iberoamericana, 4*(15), 168–173. https://doi.org/10.18441/ibam.4.2004.15.168-173.

Malamud, A., & Schenoni, L. (2020). "Sobre la creciente irrelevancia de América Latina", *Nueva Sociedad, NUSO* n. 291, Jan-Feb 2021.

Ministerio de Asuntos Exteriores y Cooperación. (2018) *XXVI Cumbre Iberoamericana de jefes de Estado y de Gobierno* http://www.exteriores.gob.es/

Portal/es/PoliticaExteriorCooperacion/Iberoamerica/Paginas/LasCumbres Iberoamericanas.aspx (last access 27 January 2021)

Neila, J. L. (2019). "El "giro mediterráneo" de España en un mundo en tránsito". *Pasado y Memoria. Revista de Historia Contemporánea, 19*, 51–77. https://doi.org/10.14198/PASADO2019.19.02.

Reuters (2010). "La UE y Mercosur relanzan sus negociaciones comerciales", 17 May 2020 https://www.reuters.com/article/oestp-zapatero-mercosur-idESMAE64G0XP20100517 (last access 12 December 2022).

Rodrik, D. "Will COVID 19 remake the world?", *Project Syndicate*, 6 April 2020.

RTVE. (2019). "España reconoce a Guaidó como 'presidente encargado' de Venezuela para que convoque elecciones cuanto antes", 4 February 2019 https://www.rtve.es/noticias/20190204/venezuela-espana-reconoce-guaido-como-presidente-encargado-venezuela/1878800.shtml (last access 7 December 2022).

Sanahuja, J. A. (2012). "Un Brasil suramericano y una España europeizada: relaciones en el marco iberoamericano". *Revista CIDOB d'afers internacionals, 97–98* (abril 2012), 245–261. ISSN 1133-6595 – E-ISSN 2013-035X.

Sanahuja, J. A. (2013). "Hacia un nuevo marco de relaciones entre la Unión Europea y América Latina y el Caribe", *Informe Fundación EU-LAC*, Hamburg.

Sanahuja, J. A. (2016). "España, América Latina y Cuba tras el periodo Rajoy. balance y perspectivas de la política exterior", en *¿Fin de ciclo y reconfiguración regional? América Latina y las relaciones entre Cuba y Estados Unidos*. Coordinadora Regional de Investigaciones Económicas y Sociales (CRIES).

Sanahuja, J. A. (2018). "Crisis de globalización, crisis de hegemonía: un escenario de cambio estructural para América Latina y el Caribe", en *América Latina y el Caribe frente a un Nuevo Orden Mundial: poder, globalización y respuestas regionales*. Icaria / CRIES.

Sanahuja, J. A. (2021). "América Latina y España: nueva mirada". *Política Exterior*, marzo-abril, 104–114.

Valle Gálvez, J. A., I. González García, & M. A. Acosta Sánchez (coords.) (2013). *La cumbre de Cádiz y las relaciones de España con América Latina*. Ministerio de Asuntos Exteriores.

Verdes-Montenegro, F. J. (2022). "La autonomía estratégica de la Unión Europea: ¿en qué lugar queda América Latina?", *Documentos de trabajo* nº 65 (2ª época). Madrid: Fundación Carolina. https://doi.org/10.33960/issn-e.1885-9119.DT65.

Carmen Fonseca

The Portuguese Foreign Policy Towards Latin America: A Yo-Yo Approach[1]

While it is common to assume that Portugal is a strategic player and a connecting element between Europe and Latin America, is that really the case? What is the weight and place of Latin America in Portuguese foreign policy? Does Portuguese foreign policy encompass a comprehensive and sustained strategy for the region? How does Portugal's relationship with Latin America fit in with the framework of its European orientation? Does Portugal maintain in Latin America a parallel or a complementary dialogue regarding the one pursued by the EU?

With these questions as its point of departure, this chapter sets out to analyse Portuguese foreign policy towards Latin America in the 21st century, exploring the connection between the discourse of the various governments and the strategy undertaken. This analysis will help understand and explain the place occupied by Latin America in Portuguese foreign policy, ascertaining whether Portuguese diplomacy has exerted pressure on the European agenda and managed to distance itself from Spain in the handling of Latin American affairs within Europe.

The foreign policy's axes of the democratic Portugal

Portuguese democratisation will be 50 years old in 2024. In the field of foreign policy, it has been 50 years since Portugal has seen any significant changes, after shifting its central axis to Europe and joining the European Economic Communities (EEC) in 1986, without, however, relinquishing its "Atlantic vocation".

At the same time, and progressively, there has been, on the one hand, an adjustment of some guidelines for external action, namely in relations with Africa, which began to unfold in a different framework, and with the Ibero-American axis, in which relations have adapted and expanded, in the face of the demands imposed by democratisation. On the other, some innovations also took place, notably economic diplomacy and cultural diplomacy (with a focus on the

1 This work was partially funded by the FCT (Refª UIDB/04627/2020, IPRI-NOVA).

Portuguese language), a trend which in Latin America was gaining ground later, mainly through Brazil. As Teixeira points out, by 1976 "Portugal then undertakes its full status as a Western country, at once European and Atlantic" and the two areas are perceived as complementary and no longer as contradictory (Teixeira, 2010: 54).

Portuguese democratisation in 1974 also marked a relaxation of the relationship with Brazil, which was normalised after the end of the African decolonisation processes and the stabilisation of the Portuguese political institutions. This normalisation was stressed with the visit of the President of the Republic, Ramalho Eanes, to Brazil in 1978.

Until 1985, Portugal's external interests were simultaneously focused on Africa and on Europe. In Africa, in view of the need to settle disputes which were pending due to the decolonisation process, and whose resolution was an essential requirement for the acceptance of the application to join the European Communities. In Europe, it was understood as the mechanism that could make democratic consolidation possible, contributing to the development of Portugal and enabling its international insertion.

In the Latin American context, given that Portugal was largely committed to the EEC adhesion process, Brazil's presence in Portuguese foreign policy was limited to the official rhetoric, on the one hand, and to the attempt to raise awareness in the European agenda for relations with Brazil, in particular (Carvalho, 2016: 347), and, with Latin America in general.

Likewise, Portugal was finding support in Spain, but also experiencing difficulty in differentiating itself from its neighbour, which was at the same stage as Portugal with regard to the definition of its international identity, the integration into the European Communities and the monetisation of the relationship with Latin America.

Under the leadership of Prime Minister Felipe González, Spain started to design its rapprochement with Latin America, which was also reflected at the European level. The Portuguese and Spanish membership to the EEC, which occurred at the same time, included a "Joint Declaration of intent on the development and intensification of relations with the countries of Latin America" demonstrating the importance awarded to Latin American countries. That adhesion was a turning point allowing that "Latin America had been declared a 'region of economic priority' for Europe" (Couffignal, 2013: 101).

Since democratisation and joining the European Communities, the evolution of Portugal's relationship with Spain was grounded in the notion that "we must be where Spain is, otherwise Madrid will 'represent' Lisbon and the differentiated image in the eyes of the world will fade", as the then Minister of Foreign

Affairs, Luis Amado, summed it up (2005: 214). This narrative rendered even more pressing the need for Portugal to define its element of differentiation vis-à-vis Spain and within the European Union.

In 1991, Portugal became the only European country to have high-level summits with Brazil, as well as concluding the General Agreement on Cooperation, which allowed the establishment of a new dynamic in the relationship. In that year, the Ibero-American Summits were launched, in which Portugal together with Spain shared a common forum with the entire region. In practical terms, the results attained were limited (Cruz, 2021).

Portugal has sought to differentiate itself in the EU, especially regarding Spain, through its links to Portuguese-speaking countries, in which only Brazil is included in the whole of Latin America. At the same time, in the European framework, the projection of the Portuguese-Brazilian relationship has gone beyond the Lusophone dimension, bearing in mind Brazil's international protagonism in the early 21st century.

Latin America in Portuguese foreign policy (2000–2021): Words and deeds

Guterres and the "Brazilian option"

Regarding Portugal's relationship with Latin America, the 20th century closed with the marks of economic diplomacy and the "Brazilian option", put into practice by the government of Prime Minister António Guterres. This strategy guided Portuguese trade and investments, preferably to Brazil, but reaching also other countries in the region. The magnitude of the figures made this the golden decade of Portuguese-Brazilian relations. In 1997, 1998 and 2000, Brazil stood out as the main target for Portuguese investment (AICEP, 2009). Comparatively, trade has always been less important, and although its weight has increased, it has not been possible to achieve high figures or outdo the main partners located in the European Union, with Spain in the lead.

Upon entering the new century, Guterres's second government intended to carry forward the programme underway (Portugal, 1999), which, however, was losing steam. Still, it was possible to breathe new life, politically speaking, into the relationship with Brazil through the joint organisation of the celebrations of the 500th anniversary of Portugal's arrival in Brazil, holding meetings and official visits by Brazilian and Portuguese authorities on each side of the Atlantic. To the traditional narrative of friendship and fraternal bonds, economic data were added (Sampaio, 2000). If the symbolic as well as the practical dimensions of official visits are considered, it is worth noting that during this period, the President of the Republic,[2] Jorge Sampaio, visited Brazil, Panama and Peru (all within the framework of the Ibero-American Summits), and the Minister of Foreign Affairs, Jaime Gama, only visited Brazil once to prepare the Portuguese-Brazilian Summit.

Barroso and Santana Lopes: Spain or Brazil?

Durão Barroso's election in 2002 changed Guterres's formula. It did not dispense the relationship with Brazil and Latin America, but it favoured Spain (Portugal, 2002), as illustrated by some international trips which still considered some Latin American countries.[3]

At the VI Portuguese-Brazilian Summit in 2002, held in Lisbon, the Portuguese Prime Minister, Barroso, stressed the need for Portugal to diversify its external investments and strengthen its relationship with Brazil in other areas. The Portuguese-Brazilian agenda then began to evolve. The political and economic issues were joined by the question of migration, in view of the exponential increase in Brazilian immigration in Portugal, as well as the cultural dimension.

Barroso's departure for the European Commission in 2004 placed Pedro Santana Lopes in the political leadership of Portugal. However, this was followed by the dissolution of Parliament by President Sampaio and the call for early elections. The brief time (from July 2004 to March 2005) in which Santana Lopes served as head of government nevertheless left a mark on the relationship with Brazil, when he chose it as the destination of his first official visit abroad.

Until that moment, Jose Maria Aznar was in charge of the Spanish government. Despite the emergence of the idea of the EU-LAC summits in the late 1990s in collaboration with France and Brazil and the creation of an Ibero-American

2 Portuguese Foreign Policy is a responsibility of the Prime Minister and the Minister of Foreign Affairs. Despite the constitutional prerogatives that attribute to the President of the Republic the power to appoint Portuguese Ambassadors and accept foreign diplomats, and to ratify international agreements, the President of the Republic *represents the State*, which gives him an important role in what concerns the projection of the country. In the foreign policy domain, the participation of the President of the Republic has a symbolic meaning but also stresses the weight and place of some Government priorities as State priorities as well.

3 President Jorge Sampaio visited Uruguay, and, with the Prime Minister Barroso, was in Bolivia for the Ibero-American summit. The Minister of Foreign Affairs, Teresa Gouveia, and Barroso also visited Brazil in 2004 for of the preparation and holding of the VII Portuguese-Brazilian Summit.

General Secretariat (SEGIB) in 2003, during the Aznar government, Spain lost prestige in Latin America (Ayuso, 2014). Perhaps the hesitation of Portuguese foreign policy towards Brazil and Latin America in that period could find an explanation in the relative absence of Spain.

Sócrates: From Spain to Latin America

The 2005 elections gave an absolute majority to José Sócrates' Socialist Party, which would be re-elected in 2009. His government programs reiterated the same objectives as those of Portuguese foreign policy, including the need for the internationalisation of the Portuguese economy. There is, however, no reference to a strategy of rapprochement with Latin America or Brazil, in particular (Portugal, 2002: 154). Moreover, not only was Spain the destination of his first official visit, but his words highlighted the rapprochement with the neighbouring country when he "summarized the priorities of his foreign policy at the beginning of his first term in three words: 'Spain, Spain, Spain'" (Gaspar, 2011: 150).

The global economic and financial crisis that followed, however, required some adjustments to be made. Spain, understood as the privileged partner, ended up moving down the list of priorities, not least because the effects of the economic crisis were taking a toll. The rapprochement that gradually developed with Latin America is part of this attempt to diversify partners prompted by the context of the crisis that was battering Europe and Portugal.

Jorge Sampaio's presidential diplomacy ended with a State visit to Chile and another one to Paraguay[4] in 2005. At that time, Brazil, Mexico and Chile were Portugal's main trading partners in Latin America. Socrates's Latin American tour, besides Brazil, included only Venezuela, with which economic and trade relations were strengthened. This economic agenda began to be outlined in 2008 when the President of Venezuela, Hugo Chávez, visited Lisbon three times, and the Portuguese Prime Minister, accompanied by a delegation of economic advisors, visited Venezuela on one occasion (El Pais, 2018). José Sócrates returned to Venezuela in 2010 when 19 cooperation agreements were signed to reinforce trade relations between the two countries (Expresso, 2010). The flagship of this partnership was the purchase, by Venezuela, of computers manufactured in Portugal for its primary schools.

4 A visit to Argentina was cancelled at the request of Néstor Kirchner due to the approaching elections.

Throughout the six years of socialist administration, two Portuguese-Brazilian Summits were held (in 2008 and 2010), along with seven official visits to Brazil by the President, the Prime Minister and the Minister of Foreign Affairs. During this period, the milestone of the EU policy towards Latin America occurred. Under the framework of the Portuguese Presidency of the EU Council in July 2007, the Strategic Partnership and the EU-Brazil Summits were institutionalised (which, until 2011, were held annually, as planned).

It is worth noting the statements of the Portuguese Minister of Foreign Affairs in the final stages of the second government in 2009, where he highlighted the strategic advantage of the relationship with Brazil and the notion that Portugal might play a central role in the Atlantic (Amado, 2009). In an interview given in 2010, the former Minister highlighted the economic dimension of Portuguese foreign policy, stating that "foreign policy action ought to contribute to strengthening the internationalisation of the country's economy (...) it ought to be the top priority of political and diplomatic action" (Amado, 2010).

Without compromising the relationship with the EU, Portugal diversified its partners, particularly in the search for Brazil and Latin America, later afflicted by the shockwaves of the crisis. The crisis even had an impact on Portugal's relations with Spain, which experienced its lowest point during this period – between 2009 and 2011 there were no Portuguese-Spanish Summits, a situation reversed with the visit of the Spanish Prime Minister, Mariano Rajoy, to Portugal in 2012 (even before his customary official visit to France).

It is important to register this turning point in the external strategy towards the end of Socrates's government: if, at the beginning of his first term, Brazil did not stand in the foreground, the same cannot be said five years later, with Portugal presenting a different economic conjuncture.

Passos Coelho and the management of the economic crisis

As mentioned above, the economic crisis entailed an adjustment in Portuguese foreign policy, but also in domestic policy. Portugal's bailout by the troika meant the resignation of José Sócrates' government and the holding of early elections in 2011, from which the right-wing coalition (PSD-CDS) led by Pedro Passos Coelho emerged victorious. It is therefore unsurprising that the Prime Minister's first official visit was to Germany and that of the Minister of Foreign Affairs, Paulo Portas, to China.

The program of the new Government specified European policy, relations with Portuguese-speaking countries and the "loyalty to the Atlantic alliance" as the goals of Portuguese foreign policy (Portugal, 2011: 104–105). In the second government of Passos Coelho, the novelty lay in the explicit reference to Latin America and Brazil in the programmatic text (Portugal, 2015a: 130). Passos Coelho's executive defined its approach to external affairs in very clear terms, which was understood as an instrument at the service of the interests and economic needs "for the international prestige" of the country (Portugal, 2015: 104). Economic diplomacy with Brazil and other Latin American countries was understood as a way to structure Portuguese external strategy. On his first visit to Brazil, the Minister of Foreign Affairs, Paulo Portas, said that he was "highly focused on economic diplomacy. The key is to build excellent economic diplomacy and improve Portugal's image abroad" (Portas, 2011). This view furthermore explains Paulo Portas's visits to Colombia and Venezuela shortly after taking up office.

With Passos Coelho, Guterres's "Brazilian option" appeared to be gradually replaced and extended to emerging markets, including the Lusophone ones. In the government's first eighteen months, five official visits to Brazil were made by the Prime Minister or the Minister of Foreign Affairs.[5] In addition to the (seven) official visits to Brazil, between 2011 and 2015 Portuguese foreign affairs authorities travelled to Colombia (three times), Venezuela, Peru, Paraguay, Panama and Mexico.[6] In 2013, the Venezuelan President, Nicolás Maduro, was received by Passos Coelho and several agreements were signed. At that moment, Venezuela was the main destination for Portuguese exports in the region. With Mexico, the Portugal-Mexico High-level Economic Dialogue was also established, which began in 2014 when the Vice-Prime Minister, Paulo Portas, visited the country. During the Ibero-American summit in Mexico, both Passos Coelho and the Portuguese President, Cavaco Silva, placed Latin America as a priority for Portuguese foreign policy (Observador, 2014).

If the economic crisis had occasioned an economic rapprochement with Latin America, it meant, on the other hand, a detachment from Spain since, during this period, "the Iberian alliance no longer existed" (Gaspar, 2011: 160). The Spanish-Portuguese Summits were also put on hold between 2009 and 2011, being resumed in 2012 after Rajoy visited Portugal. Once again, a strategic mismatch between Portugal and Spain was shown.

---

5 Minister of Foreign Affairs' first official visit during the second term was made to Brazil.

6 The visits to Paraguay, Panama and Mexico were made in the framework of the Ibero-American summits of 2011, 2013 and 2014, respectively.

Costa: What place for Latin America?

In 2015, in early elections, the Socialist Party returned to the government, led by Prime Minister, António Costa. The Government Program prioritised the rehabilitation of Portugal's image in the world, and, in addition to the European framework, the promotion of the Portuguese language and Lusophone citizenship would be the tools employed to achieve this goal (Portugal, 2015b: 246). The national identity was defined as "first and foremost, European, Lusophone, Ibero-American and Atlantic" (Portugal 2015b: 247).

However, despite this narrative advocating a global Portugal, the action of the Ministry of Foreign Affairs was aligned with European priorities. The Portuguese Minister Augusto Santos Silva rarely referred to Latin America without mentioning the importance of the region in the European context, as when he said, "we have a clear notion of the strategic importance of the relationship between Europe and Latin America – and of the decisive role of Iberian countries in this relationship. And that is why participation in CIB [Ibero-American Summits] is one of the lines of strength of our foreign policy" (Silva, 2018).

The second government of Costa, re-elected in 2019, presented a continuation of the main lines of the previous one. It highlights the benefits for the Portuguese economy of the EU-Mercosur agreement (Portugal, 2019: 38); however, until now, it still awaits ratification by some of the member states, including Portugal itself. Perhaps for that reason, the government re-elected in 2022 did not mention it (Portugal, 2022). Portugal continues to articulate foreign policy with cultural policy, given the emphasis on the promotion of the Portuguese language and culture. Oddly, however, the program of Costa's second government, which was dismissed in 2021 (but would be in office until 2023), did not include any reference whatsoever to the celebrations of the 200th anniversary of Brazil's independence.

Highlights of the official visits to Latin America during Costa's government are President Marcelo Rebelo de Sousa's visits to Brazil (four times), Cuba, Colombia, Argentina and Chile.[7] The Prime Minister, besides accompanying the President on these visits, was also engaged in a parallel work agenda on the two visits to Brazil in 2016, and the Minister of Foreign Affairs visited Brazil (twice), Venezuela and Argentina (for the inauguration of Alberto Fernandez in 2019).

7 The visits to Cuba and Colombia were made in the framework of the Ibero-American Summit.

Despite these official visits, a clear Portugal-Latin America strategy was not defined, and the results obtained are difficult to identify.

As presented, even before the crisis triggered by the pandemic, Latin America had already lost weight in the relationship with the EU as well as in Portuguese foreign policy, although the persistence of a narrative stated the opposite. It is worth noting that, given the Venezuelan crisis, the Minister of Foreign Affairs, and mainly the Secretary of State for the Portuguese Communities, José Luís Carneiro, went to Venezuela several times to follow the Portuguese community. Portugal was also part of the International Contact Group on Venezuela with other European (Germany, Spain, France, Italy, Portugal, United Kingdom and Sweden) and Latin American (Bolivia, Costa Rica, Ecuador, and Uruguay) countries. Despite this, and the strong European stance in repudiating Maduro's government, it has not been possible to find a way to exert influence on Venezuela's political situation.[8]

The Portuguese presidencies of the EU Council

It is important to look at Portugal's action upon taking over the Presidency of the EU Council in order to realise how Portugal articulates its foreign policy, namely its desired role as a privileged partner of the EU in Latin America – with EU interests. During the 21st century, the country has held three presidencies – in 2000, in 2007 and in 2021 – being its first-ever presidency in 1992.

At that time, the EEC was focused on completing the negotiating process that would lead to the Maastricht Treaty. Although some authors consider that Portugal did not pay due attention to Portuguese priorities in Africa and Latin America and that external relations were an imposition of the European agenda (Hermenegildo, 2014), the truth is that, during the first Portuguese presidency, the initiatives developed presented Portugal as a valid interlocutor with the Latin American region – it established the Framework Agreement for Cooperation between the EEC and Brazil, the I ministerial meeting EEC-Mercosur, and the ministerial meetings with the Rio Group and the Euro-Latin-American Forum. The existing network of agreements with the Andean Pact and Paraguay was also renewed, and a political statement was issued at the San José Group meeting regarding the political instability in Central America.[9]

8 In March 2021, the EU Ambassador to Venezuela, the Portuguese Isabel Brilhante Pedrosa, was considered *persona non grata* and expelled from the country.

9 Created in 1984, the San José Group is one of the main cooperation tools between the European Union and Latin America.

Portugal took over the Presidency again in 2000 in a quite different Portuguese and European context. It is a matter of consensus that national policies were adapted to the circumstances of the European project and reconciled it with its national interests (Magone, 2015; Ferreira-Pereira, 2008; Teixeira, 2014). At the time, Germany paid special attention to the Latin American region (Trueb, 2013: 83), and perhaps that is why Portugal chose to focus on Africa and India. Latin America was not fully off the agenda of the Portuguese presidency; ministerial meetings were held with the Rio Group, Mercosur, San José Group and the Andean Community.

Contrary to some European views (Kietz and Perthes, 2008) that perceived the European strategy should be oriented towards the conclusion of the Agreement with Mercosur instead of the bilateral rapprochement with Brazil, Portugal hosted the first bilateral summit between the EU and Brazil. The 2007 Presidency left a deeper, or at least symbolic, mark on the relationship with the region by establishing the EU-Brazil strategic partnership and launching the High-Level Summits with Brazil. Although the Portuguese agenda is deemed to have been "at some extent, dependent on the results of the German Presidency as well as the initiatives of the Commission" (Hermenegildo, 2014: 310), it was an active presidency in the external field, as well as, in institutional terms, it culminated with the signing of the Treaty of Lisbon.

Although during this period Brazil was not clearly defined as a priority of Portuguese foreign policy, as mentioned above, the Portuguese presidency seized the occasion to validate the importance of Portuguese-Brazilian relations. Portugal, perhaps against the expectations of a part of the Brazilian elites, managed to play a significant role within the EU, by and large advantageous to Brazil.

During the two previous decades, Brazil had favoured relations with major European powers such as Germany and approached Spain, but the holding of the first EU-Brazil Summit during the Portuguese Presidency of the EU Council was important to demonstrate Portugal's political credibility in the relationship between Brazil and the EU (as had been the case in 2000, with the EU-India Summit) (Fonseca, 2008).

The Portuguese Presidency of 2021 was radically different. In the face of a cascade of international events, from the outset of the Covid-19 pandemic to the US-China tension, external action was not the EU's top priority. Consequently, Latin America was also somewhat absent from this Presidency, even though the Portuguese official speech emphasised "historical, cultural and political proximity" with Latin America (Silva, 2021b) and on trade relations with Mexico or Mercosur (Silva, 2021a). The program of the three presidencies (Germany, Portugal and Slovenia) for the period 2020–2021, also pointed to the need to "strengthen EU's political partnership with Latin America and the Caribbean" (European Council, 2020: 27). Despite this, the Portuguese presidency was unable to relaunch the European agenda for Latin America (the agreement with Mercosur is still a quite long way from finalisation and the last EU-Brazil summit was held in 2014).

Indeed, while one may note the initiative by Federica Mogherini to deliver, in 2019, a communication to the Council and Parliament on "EU, Latin America: common future"; strong positions on sensitive issues, such as Cuba and Venezuela; the existence of a structured political dialogue; an intense attention from Germany to the region (Gardini, 2021) as well as some regularity on the EU-CELAC Summits, paradoxically, "the EU is losing appeal in the continent" (Gardini, 2021: 40), and the EU-Brazil strategic partnership is not working (Saraiva, 2019).

The interpretation of the political authorities was also in line with this view. Josep Borrell's statements shortly after taking over as High Representative of the EU for Foreign Affairs and Security Policy, titled "The other transatlantic relationship", acknowledged that "the attention awarded to the LAC region is not proportional to its importance" (Borrell, 2020, p. 3). The understanding of the Portuguese diplomacy was also similar. The Minister of Foreign Affairs stated that "the political dialogue between Europe and Latin America is loose, to not say that it is almost inexistent. Relationships (...) are stopped" (Silva, 2020: 197). The crises and challenges – social, migratory, economic and political, with the proliferation of extremisms – faced by the EU in recent times may partly account for the inability of the EU to become, as it succeeded in doing before, a model to follow in Latin America.

Portugal and Latin America: Diplomacy, economy and culture as needed

It is when economic diplomacy emerges on the Portuguese foreign policy agenda that Latin America jumps to the list of priorities. There is not, however, a Portuguese strategy for the region. Its role and place on the Portuguese agenda are neither straightforward nor constant, nor do they always have the same intensity.

Latin America has never been *the* priority of Portuguese foreign policy, even if at times that is the official narrative. And even when it is on the list of priorities (or fields of action) of Portugal's external action, it lacks a medium or long-term guiding strategy.

This place held by Latin America in Portuguese foreign policy derives (and oscillates) from its Atlantic dimension, which views Latin America as an extension of its foreign policy priorities and its European sensitive axis; and of its European (and continental) dimension, which drives the Portuguese agenda to adhere to the European agenda for external action. In recent years, this has been a persistent trend. Of course, these oscillations are not only due to ideological or partisan reasons but also to conjunctural reasons.

Between 1999 and 2002 Guterres sought to reconcile the opening of the Brazilian economy with economic growth and the expansion of the Portuguese business fabric, which benefited from European economic integration. Between 2011 and 2015, in the midst of the economic crisis, the government of Passos Coelho had the chief task of managing the troika rescue, and the Deputy Prime Minister revived economic diplomacy and defined Brazil and the core economies of Latin America as targets for Portugal's external action.

Barroso's government, between 2002 and 2004, as well as Sócrates's, from 2005 to 2011, did not attach the same importance to the relationship with Latin America or Brazil, and, instead, invested in the relationship with Spain. However, during Socrates's government, after the economic crisis broke out, there was a timid exercise in economic diplomacy. In this period, a greater deal of attention was paid to the relationship with Brazil and an articulation between foreign policy and cultural policy for the promotion of the Portuguese language began to be sketched. At the same time, the Portuguese mark in the institutionalisation of the EU-Brazil Partnership is possibly the best outcome for the maintenance of the Luso-Brazilian alliance. For António Costa's government (2015–2021), neither Latin America nor Brazil was a priority. Portuguese foreign policy has been an extension of European foreign action, added to the centrality of the promotion of the Portuguese language. The decline experienced by Latin American economies since 2015, the political and social crises in Latin America, topped by the emergence of far-right populist leaders, have pushed the region away from the radars of Portuguese foreign policy.

The cornerstone of Portuguese foreign policy in the last decade lies in the promotion of the Portuguese language – Portugal's differentiating element in the European Union.

The Portuguese presidencies are a reflection of the internal conjuncture in Portuguese foreign policy, which also coincides with its Europeanisation. The main extra-European theme that has been asserting itself throughout the 21st century is the Portuguese language and its potential benefits for Portugal's global image. In this context, Brazil stands out more due to its status as a Portuguese-speaking than as a Latin American country. Its position in that geographical space is in any case seen as an added value since it makes it possible for each continent to have a Portuguese-speaking country.

However, Portugal-Brazil relations themselves have been stagnant. Naturally, the historical foundations of the Portuguese-Brazilian relation dispense, to some extent, political action. However, this trend shrinks the possibilities to achieve concrete and long-term results. In the year marking the 200th anniversary of Brazil's independence, what stands out is a lack of political harmony between the two sides of the Atlantic.

Today, as in the past, Latin America has a marginal place in Portuguese foreign policy. Throughout the 21st century, the relationship has been characterised by moments of oscillation, in which Portugal reaches out and pulls away according to its interests, government perceptions and internal and European conjunctures.

Bibliography

AICEP – Portugal-Global. (2009). Mercados – informação global. Relações Económicas Portugal-Brasil.

Amado, L. (2010). Interview by Luís Amado to Teresa de Sousa. In Jornal Público, 3 January 2010. Available at: http://publico.pt/politica/noticia/luis-amado-portugal-sera-agora-na-europa-o-que-conseguir-ser-fora-dela-1416084

Amado, L. (2009). Luís Amado defende "recentramento" no Atlântico e sublinha papel de Portugal pelas relações com África e Brasil. In Jornal Público, 26 March 2009. Available at: http://publico.pt/politica/noticia/luis-amado-defende-recentramento-no-atlantico-e-sublinha-papel-de-portugal-pelas-relacoes-com-africa-e-brasil-1370993

Amado, L. (2005). Portugal e Espanha. In VVAA, Visões de Política Externa Portuguesa (pp. 211–215). Lisbon: Sociedade de Geografia de Lisboa and Instituto Diplomático MNE.

Ayuso, A. (2014). The recent history of Spain-Latin America relations. In D. G. Cantalpiedra & R. P. Pardo (Eds.), Contemporary Spanish foreign policy (pp. 106–130). London: Routledge.

Borrell, J. (2020). América Latina-Europa: la "outra" relación transatlântica, Análisis Carolina 51/2020. Fundación Carolina, https://doi.org/10.33960/AC_51.2020

Carvalho, T. (2016). Identidades de ânimos, diferenças de propósitos. As relações entre Portugal e o Brasil (1974–1985), PhD Thesis, Lisboa: ISCTE-IUL.

Carvalho, T. (2011). Portugal e as relações Brasil-União Europeia (1986–2007). Relações Internacionais, 29, 91–100.

Council of the European Union. (2020). Taking forward the Strategic Agenda. 18-month Programme of the Council (1 July 2020 – 31 December 2021, 8086/

1/20 REV 1, Brussels. Available at: https://www.2021portugal.eu/media/ldohjith/programa-do-trio-en.pdf

Couffignal, G. (2013). France: From uploads to disengagement. In L. Ruano (Ed.), The Europeanization of national foreign policies towards Latin America (pp. 89–111). New York: Routledge.

Cruz, A. M. (2021). Comunidade ibero-americana faz 30 anos. "Temos de atuar juntos". In Diário de Notícias, 16 November 2021. Available at: https://www.dn.pt/politica/comunidade-ibero-americana-faz-30-anos-temos-de-atuar-juntos-14320416.html

Efe. (2015). Passos Coelho afirma que México es una de las prioridades de Portugal en América Latina, April 24th. Available at: https://www.efe.com/efe/espana/portada/passos-coelho-afirma-que-mexico-es-una-de-las-prioridades-portugal-en-america-latina/10010-2595728

El Pais. (2018). Chávez y Sócrates cultivan su idilio, September 27th. Available at: https://elpais.com/internacional/2008/09/27/actualidad/1222466411_850215.html

Expresso. (2016). "Soy loco por ti América". In Expresso, August 9th. Available at: https://expresso.pt/dossies/diario/2016-08-09-Soy-loco-por-ti-America

Expresso. (2010). Sócrates visita Brasil e Venezuela para reforçar investimentos. In Expresso, 28 May 2010. Available at: https://expresso.pt/actualidade/socrates-visita-brasil-e-venezuela-para-reforcar-investimentos=f584965

Ferreira-Pereira, L. C. (2008). Portugal e a presidência da União Europeia (1992–2007). Relações Internacionais, 20, 131–143.

Fonseca, C. (2021). A Comunidade dos Países de Língua Portuguesa. In N. S. Teixeira & A. Cunha (Eds.), Dicionário Portugal Multilateral (pp. 201–217). Lisbon: Almedina.

Fonseca, C. (2020). O futuro do Acordo Comercial UE-Mercosul - uma visão europeia". In R. J. Themoteo (Ed.), O novo acordo Mercosul-União Europeia em perspectiva (pp. 109–124). Rio de Janeiro: Konrad-Adenauer-Stiftung.

Fonseca, C. (2017). Brasil e a União Europeia: a ilusão do excepcionalismo?. Iberoamericana, XVII(65), 223–224.

Fonseca, C. (2010). Intenções vs desempenho: o Brasil na política externa portuguesa, 1976–2007. Revista Brasileira de Política Internacional, 53(2), 49–69.

Gardini, G. L. (2021). The European Union in Latin America. A "neighbour" of values. In G. L. Gardini (Eds.), External powers in Latin America geopolitics between neo-extractivism and South-South Cooperation (pp. 29–43). London: Routledge.

Gaspar, C. (2011). Portugal, a Espanha e o futuro das relações bilaterais. In T. Rodrigues & R. Perez (Eds.), Portugal e Espanha. Crise e Convergência na União Europeia (pp. 145–162). Lisbon: Tribuna da História.

Giacalone, R. (2019). A cooperative scenario for Latin America regionalism and international insertion: How can the EU help?. The Jean Monnet/Robert Schuman Paper Series, 19(3). University of Miami.

Hermenegildo, R. S. (2014). As Presidências Portuguesas da União Europeia (1992, 2000 e 2007). PhD Thesis, NOVA University of Lisbon. Available at: http://hdl.handle.net/10362/14775

Joint Communication to the European Parliament and the Council: "European Union, Latin America and the Caribbean: joining forces for a common future", JOIN/2019/6 final, 16 April 2019. https://eur-lex.europa.eu/legal-content/EN/TXT/PDF/?uri=CELEX:52019JC0006&from=EN

Kietz, D., & Perthes, V. (Eds.) (2008). The potential of the council presidency. An analysis of Germany's chairmanship of the EU, 2007. Berlin: Stiftung Wissenschaft und Politik (SWP). Available at: http://www.swp-berlin.org/en/common/get_document.php?asset_id=4656

Lazarou, E., & Fonseca, C. (2013). Brasil e a União Europeia: a Parceria Estratégica em busca de significado. In A. C. Lessa & H. A. de Oliveira (Eds.), As Parcerias Estratégicas do Brasil: os significados e as experiências tradicionais (Vol. I, pp. 91–118). Belo Horizonte: Fino Traço.

Magone, J. M. (2015). The Portuguese presidency of the EU in 2000: An ambitious enterprise. International Journal of Iberian Studies, 28(2–3), 209–234.

Malamud, C. (2010). "As relações entre a União Europeia e a América Latina no século XXI: entre o voluntarismo e a realidade", Working Paper n. 10, Plataforma Democrática.

Observador. (2014). Exportações para a América Latina aumentaram 20% em cinco anos, 10 December 2014. Available at: https://observador.pt/2014/12/10/exportacoes-para-america-latina-aumentaram-20-em-cinco-anos/

Portas, P. (2011). Paulo Portas pede um "salto" nas relações económicas entre Brasil e Portugal. In Mundo Lusíada, 28 July 2011. Available at: http://www.mundolusiada.com.br/economia/paulo-portas-pede-um-salto-nas-relacoes-economicas-entre-brasil-e-portugal/

Portugal. (2022). Programa do XXIII Governo Constitucional 2022–2025. Available at: https://www.portugal.gov.pt/gc23/programa-do-governo-xviii/programa-do-governo-xviii-pdf.aspx?v=«mlkvi»=54f1146c-05ee-4f3a-be5c-b10f524d8cec

Portugal. (2019). Programa do XXII Governo Constitucional 2019–2023. Available at: https://www.portugal.gov.pt/pt/gc22/governo/programa-do-governo

Portugal. (2015b). Programa do XXI Governo Constitucional. Available at: https://www.portugal.gov.pt/ficheiros-geral/programa-do-governo-pdf.aspx

Portugal. (2015a). Programa do XX Governo Constitucional. Available at: https://www.historico.portugal.gov.pt/download.ashx?media=/media/18167052/20151106-programa-governo.pdf

Portugal. (2011). Programa do XIX Governo Constitucional. Available at: https://www.historico.portugal.gov.pt/download.ashx?media=/media/130538/programa_gc19.pdf

Portugal. (2009). Programa do XVIII Governo Constitucional. Available at: https://www.historico.portugal.gov.pt/download.ashx?media=/media/468569/gc18.pdf

Portugal. (2005). Programa do XVII Governo Constitucional. Available at: https://www.historico.portugal.gov.pt/download.ashx?media=/media/464060/GC17.pdf

Portugal. (2004). Programa do XVI Governo Constitucional. Available at: https://www.historico.portugal.gov.pt/download.ashx?media=/media/464054/GC16.pdf

Portugal. (2002). Programa do XV Governo Constitucional. Available at: https://www.historico.portugal.gov.pt/download.ashx?media=/media/464051/GC15.pdf

Portugal. (1999). Programa do XIV Governo Constitucional. Available at: https://www.historico.portugal.gov.pt/download.ashx?media=/media/464048/GC14.pdf

Sampaio, J. (2000). Discurso na Torre de Belém por ocasião da visita do Presidente da República Federativa do Brasil, Lisboa, 8 de Março de 2000. In J. Sampaio (2001) Portugueses (Vol. IV, pp. 555–559). Lisbon: Imprensa Nacional Casa da Moeda.

Sanahuja, J. A. (2013). Spain: Double-track Europeanization and the search for bilateralism. In L. Ruano (Ed.), The Europeanization of national foreign policies towards Latin America (pp. 36–61). New York: Routledge.

Saraiva, M. G. (2019). What next for Brazil-EU relations?, LSE Blog, September 4th. Available at: https://blogs.lse.ac.uk/europpblog/2019/09/04/what-next-for-brazil-eu-relations/

Silva, A. S. (2021b). As cinco tarefas da Europa global. In Folha de São Paulo, March, 29th. Available at: https://www1.folha.uol.com.br/opiniao/2021/03/as-cinco-tarefas-da-europa-global.shtml

Silva, A. S. (2021a). As dez primeiras semanas da Presidência do Conselho da União Europeia. In Expresso, March, 12th. Available at: https://www.portugal.

gov.pt/download-ficheiros/ficheiro.aspx?v=%3d%3dBQAAAB%2bLCAAAAAAABAAzNDQxNgMACkRHCgUAAAA%3d

Silva, A. S. (2020). Evoluir. Lisbon: Tinta-da-china.

Silva, A. S. (2018). Nós ibero-americanos. In Diário de Notícias, November, 20th. Available at: https://www.dn.pt/edicao-do-dia/20-nov-2018/nos-ibero-americanos-10202161.html

Teixeira, N. S. (2014). Portugal and European Integration (1974–2010). In L. Ferreira-Pereira (Ed.), Portugal in the European Union. Assessing twenty-five years of integration experience (pp. 30–42). London: Routledge.

Teixeira, N. S. (2010). Breve ensaio sobre a política externa portuguesa. Relações Internacionais, 28, 51–60.

Torreblanca, J. I. (2020). "Con los dedos de una mano". Felipe González y Helmut Kohl: una relación especial, Papeles nr. 5, Fundación Felipe González, November,

Trueb, B. (2013). Germany: From advocate to bystander – and back?. In L. Ruano (Ed.), The Europeanization of national foreign policies towards Latin America (pp. 62–88). New York: Routledge.

Jaime León González

Relations Between Germany and Latin America Through Energy Partnerships

Introduction

Although historically Germany and the European Union (EU) have described Latin America and the Caribbean (LAC) as "natural partners", there has been a growing estrangement in relations in recent years (Maihold, 2021: 1). The High Representative for Common Foreign and Security Policy, Josep Borrell, has himself pointed out the need to reconfigure EU-LAC relations on numerous occasions, even going as far as declaring that "The European Union must give more weight in its external relations to Latin America, as partners in the multilateral system and as a trade and investment destination. [...] We share values and institutions" (Borrell, 2021). This responds, on the one hand, to the political restructuring processes that many countries in the region are undergoing, and on the other hand, to the presence of China as a new actor in this part of the American continent. This has resulted in pressure on the relations between Germany-EU and LAC, especially because other regions of the world have become more attractive for German business and politics (Esch & Maihold, 2019; Maihold, 2021).

Therefore, if Latin America does not represent a priority for German foreign policy, how can Germany become a relevant actor in the reconfiguration of interregional relations?

Within this reconfiguration, Germany plays a central role due to its great economic weight within the EU, its international commitment to the promotion of renewable energies, and the fight against climate change. In the present times, in which the international order is under increasing pressure, international commitments to environmental protection call for global governance with a focus on energy transition. This is where Germany can play a much more important role in the European partnership with Latin America; nonetheless, it needs clear ideas about the role it intends to play in the region and in the partnership with it (Esch & Maihold, 2019: 117).

Germany is a large, industrialised country with high global recognition for "green energy". Despite this, its economy is highly dependent on fossil fuels. In terms of promoting renewable energy and energy efficiency through international cooperation, the country has a strong history as the world's second-largest supplier of this material (Röhrkasten et al., 2018). This has made it a key player in the area of foreign energy policy. To win imitators for this approach, Germany is pursuing a "soft power" strategy, where Energy Partnerships (EPs) are the central instrument of this foreign energy policy (Quitzow & Thielges, 2020). LAC has some of the most dynamic renewable energy markets and could become a relevant player on a global scale (Maihold, 2021). This has been identified by Germany, which has established bilateral EPs with Brazil, Mexico, and Chile.

This chapter analyses the development of German energy partnerships in LAC and addresses the question of how Germany can strengthen its bilateral relations with LAC countries through its foreign energy policy. This chapter argues that Germany can become a relevant actor in the reconfiguration of inter-regional relations through its role as a norm-setter in the international energy system. The chapter will also analyse why, despite Germany's positive image of the energy transition at the international level, which is used in high-level political dialogue in the framework of EPs, obstacles are being encountered in bilateral relations.

In theoretical terms, research is based on a norm-constructive perspective, arguing that states must be mindful of local circumstances. Accordingly, A. Acharya proposes a dynamic explanation of the discussion of the norm, whereby local actors reconstruct foreign norms intending to make them fit the identities and cognitive backgrounds of the actors. For this purpose, I will focus on norm takers, thus avoiding that universal norms prevail over local norms and vice versa (Acharya, 2004). To achieve this goal, I will conduct a study of bilateral relations between Germany and Brazil-Mexico-Chile, specifically in EPs, to emphasise the possible discordance generated in terms of climate change and renewable energy development in these three countries.

The chapter is structured as follows. First, I will conduct a theoretical review related to the norm diffusion approach in International Relations (IR) theory, with special emphasis on what Acharya defines as "norm subsidiarity" (Acharya, 2011), in order to have a conceptual framework that allows me to explain the case studies under a norm-beneficiary-entrepreneur approach. Secondly, I will develop the case studies of the Germany-Brazil, Germany-Mexico, and Germany-Chile Energy Partnerships with a focus on the localisation of the norm in a domestic context. Finally, in the concluding section, the possibilities for improving bilateral relations between Germany and LAC within the framework of the EP will be indicated.

Theoretical framework

The constructivist approach in International Relations theory argues that international reality is constructed through social interactions and intersubjectivities of repeated behaviors. The process of socialisation is a collective process and has been studied through the diffusion and internalisation of norms. Special emphasis is placed on the role of ideational factors such as social norms, ideals, and values in foreign policy making (Stevenson, 2013).

A state's interests are defined in the context of given norms and understanding of what is appropriate. Such a normative context influences rational behaviour. According to Cox (1981: 130), institutions can balance and perpetuate a particular world order by encouraging the adoption of ideas consistent with certain power relations. Norms influence the creation of identities, which play a fundamental role in society. Considering the relationship between norms and (state) identity, norms can influence what states want to do and what they actually do (Checkel, 1998).

We identify two relevant concepts of the socialisation process: individuals belonging to social groups and norms. On the one hand, identity refers to the belonging of individuals to social groups in a given territorial space that delimits what characterises it and what differentiates it from other groups. A country's foreign policy itself is constituted through these national ideas, so that collective ideas thus define the space of possible foreign policy actions (Risse, 2007). On the other hand, norms set standards for the appropriate behaviour of actors with a given identity (Katzenstein, 1996).

The process of norm diffusion from the international to the domestic sphere is not a linear process, but a dynamic and unpredictable one (Stevenson, 2013). The supposedly passive recipients (beneficiaries) of local norms may turn against external norms, as they fear that these new norms will undermine existing local practices, which the norm entrepreneurs consider desirable in local contexts (Acharya, 2004, 2011).

How a norm is adopted into local (normative) structures and how local actors reframe its original meaning in the process and how the elaboration of a counter-norm will come about if autonomy is endangered is what is referred to as norm subsidiarity (Acharya, 2011). The process of normative adjustment of localisation is identified as "the active construction, through discourse, framing, grafting, and cultural selection, of foreign ideas by local actors, resulting in the development of a meaningful congruence between international norms and local beliefs and practices" (Acharya, 2012: 201).

It is therefore important to consider how the process of localisation of a norm in the transnational context manifests itself:

1. *Local Resistance*: As no new instruments are created, the model remains (practically) unchanged;
2. *Norm Localisation*: The external norm reaches internal consensus and institutionalisation;
3. *Norm displacement*: This occurs when a foreign norm seeks to replace a local norm whose moral or functional adequacy claim has already been questioned from within.

This is why, "norm diffusion in world politics are not simply about whether and how ideas matter, but also which and whose ideas matter" (Acharya, 2004).

For the purpose of this research, the processes through which normative values and causal beliefs are institutionalised as a result of a process of norm localisation allow us to rethink bilateral relations between Germany and Brazil-Mexico-Chile within the framework of energy partnerships. Bearing in mind that, although one of the most enduring characteristics of the 'German identity is the promotion of international regulatory frameworks, its foreign policy is value-oriented, but guided by economic interests (Solera, 2012).

An opportunity for German foreign energy policy in the region

Latin America is home to some of the world's most dynamic renewable energy markets, with more than a quarter of its energy coming from renewable sources. Despite these very positive developments, aspects such as energy security, a solid democratic framework, and a stable rule of law are fundamental prerequisites for the expansion of renewable energies (IRENA, 2019; Hüber, 2016).

For Germany, an industrial and technological nation with the highest primary energy consumption in the EU, the struggle for a reliable and permanent energy supply is becoming increasingly important in terms of foreign policy and security. Therefore, two challenges stand out for the EU to address: (1) To cooperate regionally and globally in the future in order to ensure sustainable energy policy. (2) To actively promote the energy transition from fossil fuels to renewable energies (Auswärtiges Amt, 2022). In this area, Germany is internationally recognised for its "*Ernergiewende*", being among the first countries to implement the use of new renewable energies, as well as for energy efficiency and the fight against climate change through international cooperation.

This is where Germany has identified LAC as a strategic partner in the promotion of renewable energy and environmental protection. Until a decade ago, however, the security of energy supply in Germany had rested in the hands of private energy companies, whose business strategy is characterised by a profit-driven orientation. This had been in line with the energy strategy of the Federal Ministry of Economics and Energy (*Bundesministerium für Wirtschaft und Energie – BMWi*),[1] which maintained an apolitical approach, categorising energy resources exclusively as economic goods. However, Russia's multiple gas and oil supply problems in recent years have led the German government to consider the political framework conditions and the conditioning factors of producer and supplier countries in its policy (Umbach, 2011).

Germany is active in the region through various initiatives to promote renewable energies and combat climate change as part of its foreign energy policy. To this end, bilateral energy partnerships have been established with Brazil, Mexico, and Chile, as well as the multilateral energy dialogue within the G20 with Argentina, Brazil, and Mexico. The "Energy Partnerships" are the main instrument of German foreign energy policy and are aimed at promoting sustainable energy supply in Germany and partner countries in the long term. The German government describes the EPs as "...the federal government's most important instrument for the continuous exchange of ideas with partner countries around the world on energy policy and economic issues, as well as on progress in the energy transition" (BMWi, 2017: 4). Through the EPs, special attention is paid to the promotion of renewable energies, but the promotion of the private sector and investments in the energy sector are also formulated as objectives. This gives rise to a political dialogue that aims to support the activities of German companies on the ground and to create opportunities and channels of communication between companies and ministries "Business to Government" (B2G) (Quitzow, Thielges & Helgenberger, 2019).

Despite this global analysis, aspects such as the protection of human rights and the promotion of democratic values in German foreign policy are defined according to country and context, which in foreign energy policy means a prioritisation of German interests – Germany's foreign energy policy prioritises national interests over other integrative or democratic criteria (Solera, 2012). Germany's climate and energy diplomacy needs a new approach. The

1 This ministry will be renamed Federal Ministry of Economics and Climate Protection (*Bundesministerium für Wirtschaft und Klimaschutz – BMWK*) with the new government in 2021.

establishment of standards and norms as well as regulatory space should be guidelines for Germany's diplomatic toolbox (Dröge & Westphal, 2021). From this, the question arises whether Germany is considering the process of localising standards through the promotion of environmental regulation.

Germany and Brazil

In May 2008, former Chancellor Angela Merkel and former President Lula da Silva signed the "Action Plan for the German-Brazilian Strategic Partnership", in which both countries reaffirmed their interest in further intensifying their bilateral relations at all levels and in various areas. This agreement covers issues such as cooperation in multilateral organisations, human rights, trade relations, energy cooperation, and climate change, among others (Aktionsplan der deutsch-brasilianischen strategischen Partnerschaft, 2008, as cited in Birle, 2013).

Brazil has stood out as a pioneer in the field of the energy transition, currently having an electricity matrix of 83% from renewable sources, being one of the great exponents and players in this matter (García Howell, 2021). In terms of the production and use of renewable energies, both countries share synergies. This made Brazil the first Latin American country with which Germany formed an energy partnership. In 2008, the German-Brazilian EP was signed, with the promotion of renewable energies and energy efficiency as priority objectives. However, the political dialogue on renewable energies within this partnership has stalled mainly due to differences in the criteria and priorities pursued by the two sides regarding the expansion of renewable energies. Renewable energies, which are more important for Brazil, have been highly controversial in Germany (Röhrkasten et al., 2018).

Ethanol production has been a source of national pride and an opportunity for the South American giant to distinguish itself as an international pioneer. In this sense, the Brazilian executive stated the benefits of biofuel production for sustainable development, emphasising repeatedly the benefits of biofuel production for sustainable development, which would include both environmental protection and economic development (Kloss, 2012: 83–87). However, the other side of the EP has shown some mistrust. Both German state and non-state actors have raised concerns about food and environmental security, suggesting that biomass crops for fuel production cause famine. In a country like Brazil, with extensive arable land, this analysis is flawed, as it ignores the income poverty factor (Röhrkasten & Westphal, 2012; Röhrkasten, 2015). These concerns are not shared by the Brazilian side, as stated by the NGO Oxfam Brazil: "although Brazilian ethanol production is far from perfect and presents several problems of social and environmental sustainability, it is the most favourable biofuel in the world in terms of cost and greenhouse gas balance" (O Globo, 2008).

After a long period of paralysis between 2008 and 2015, in which the German government did not allocate any funding to the association, the EP was re-launched in 2017. An investment of €2.3 million was registered between 2016 and 2021 (BMWK, 2022). Nevertheless, with the Brazilian presidency of J. Bolsonaro, the European Partnership and thus the Strategic Partnership between Germany and Brazil has been further strained in terms of ecosystem protection. The Brazilian government's actions in environmental matters and disagreements over the administration of resources for forest and biodiversity protection projects have led the German Federal Ministry for Economic Cooperation and Development (*Bundesministerium für wirtschaftliche Zusammenarbeit und Entwicklung, BMZ*) to stop financial support in the amount of €35 million. Federal Environment Minister Svenja Schulze noted: "The Brazilian government's policy in the Amazon raises doubts as to whether a steady reduction in deforestation rates is still being pursued" (Ismer, 2019). Yet, the controversy is not only about protecting the biodiversity of the Amazon but also the indigenous populations that inhabit this area. It is estimated that in the period between 2019 and 2020, at least 163 indigenous people have been killed in the land conflict (Flemes & Schlöneich, 2020). Contradictorily, at the same time that Germany is suppressing funds for environmental protection in Brazil, German companies are working with controversial suppliers, which are linked to illegal logging companies in the country (Amazon Wacht, 2019).

Civil society plays a transcendental role in the normative context since its constructive participation in the creation of joint agendas makes the process of localising norms possible. The insertion of a bottom-up dimension is necessary for a possible negotiation of relations. It can be concluded that there is a "resistance" to the foreign norm, as the institutional model of the beneficiary remains the same. To overcome these challenges facing the bilateral energy relationship, a norm localisation approach would allow both parties to disclose the transformational rhetoric and insert new legitimacy into the relationship. Germany could help Brazil in the process of regulatory adjustment, according to local standards. At the same time, there is also a conflict of interest that interferes with regulatory localisation. While Brazil seeks to achieve the targets through ethanol exports, Germany limits biofuel imports in its markets through tariff and non-tariff trade barriers, even though production is insufficient to achieve the biofuel targets (Acosta & Zilla, 2011).

Germany and Mexico

For Germany, Mexico is a key partner for implementing environmentally friendly development strategies within the framework of the Paris Climate Agreement. This importance is manifested in several aspects. On the one hand, the Germany-Mexico EP was established in 2016, through which both countries aim to create learning opportunities in the liberalised electricity market, the integration of renewable energy sources, and fossil fuel transparency (Deutsche Gesellschaft für Internationale Zusammenarbeit, 2022). On the other hand, Mexico is one of the ten largest recipients of German climate finance, the only country in the region, along with Brazil, with an investment volume of 19 million euros in renewable energy (Deutscher Bundestag, 2020: 1). Mexico's own ambassador to Germany, Rogelio Granguillhome Morfín, stated that the most active sectors of cooperation between Germany and Mexico are energy and the environment. He described the EP between the two countries as perhaps the most ambitious cooperation project in the field of energy that Mexico has with any country in the world (Granguillhome Morfín & Jiménez Segovia, 2018).

The Mexican government has actively promoted the creation of wind farms in the Oaxaca region under the premise of converting "unproductive land" into energy (Terwindt & Schliemann, 2019: 51–56). Germany has taken advantage of this fact to create entry points for German companies in this growing sector. This has made Mexico the leading LAC destination for German companies in this field (Röhrkasten, 2018). However, despite the above, in 2015 a reform toward energy transition was implemented by the Mexican executive with legislative reform, energy production in the country is still concentrated on the exploitation of fossil resources such as oil. Data from the Mexican Ministry of Energy show that in 2020 only 29.67% of the energy produced came from renewable sources (Villavicencio & Millán, 2020; Secretaría de Energía del Gobierno de México, 2021).

While it is true that wind energy has been welcomed, especially because of its climate-friendly balance sheet, the way it is being implemented by the Mexican state, international partners, and the companies involved is problematic for several reasons. The vast majority of natural resource exploitation for energy purposes has contributed to changes in land use and thus to opposition from local communities. This, in turn, leads to a violation of the human rights of environmental and land rights defenders, and thus of Convention 169 of the International Labour Organisation (Terwindt & Schliemann, 2019: 51–56). The expectations raised by the establishment of wind farms have not been fulfilled. On the one hand, there has been a modification of the land, while no benefit has been observed in the local villages, which mostly live from agriculture and fishing. On the other, wind farms mainly follow the "self-supply" model of large companies (with the financial advantages of using "clean energy"), energy prices for ordinary consumers have increased (Terwindt & Schliemann, 2019: 51–56; Heydenreich & Paasch, 2017: 87–89). This was also expressed by Andrea Manzo, a defender of the territory of the indigenous Zapotec community Unión Hidalgo: "We already have a park in our territory, but the energy does not go to our territories, it goes to mining or cement companies. We denounce how they privatise the territory and do not want to recognise our territory, which is collective" (Moro, 2020). In the same vein, the Instituto Tecnológico Autónomo de México (ITAM), through its researcher Édgar Ocampo Téllez, indicated that: "The costs and implications of this type of project are not being taken into account; for example, only 2,000 hours of the 8,760 hours of the year are in operation" (Rodríguez, 2021).

The Paris Agreement explicitly states that the contracting parties must respect, promote and consider "human rights, the right to health, the rights of indigenous peoples, [...] and the right to development" (United Nations, 2015: 1–2). Paradoxically, European companies have been accused of failing to comply with human rights protections under the argument that they are promoting energy change. This fact was highlighted by Cristina Valdivia, a representative of the Ecumenical Peace and Justice Office in Munich, during the Siemens Annual General Meeting in 2019, where she said: "In Mexico, indigenous communities affected by Siemens Gamesa projects receive incomplete information, [...] communities are not adequately consulted before projects are approved; the projects and the energy generated in the region still do not directly benefit the inhabitants" (Valdivia, 2019).

In summary, it can be seen that there is a commitment on both sides to combat climate change through the implementation of renewable energies via the EP. This normative change is not only led by Germany but also by the beneficiaries of national standards, in this case, Mexico, who acted as active builders of foreign standards. However, this is only partially bottom-up, as it does not take into account all the local tensions arising from the implementation of wind farms and the human rights violations that this is entailing. We are, therefore, in an intermediate category between "local resistance" and "norm localisation", noting that the Mexican executive seeks to institutionalise the norm but that civil society is nonetheless rejecting the external norm in the terms in which it has been implemented.

Germany and Chile

Germany has identified Chile as an important partner in its foreign energy policy strategy, highlighting that the Andean country has an excellent geographical location for cooperation in the field of renewable energies (Deutsche Gesellschaft für Internationale Zusammenarbeit, 2022). For this reason, in April 2019, the German-Chilean EP was signed by BMWi and the Chilean Ministry of Energy, with the aim of promoting renewable energies and energy efficiency. It should be noted that Germany has been advising Chile on energy issues and assisting in the consolidation of its energy transition, enabling Chile to become the first country in the region with a national Green Hydrogen Strategy (Smink, 2022).

Within the framework of this Partnership, the objectives of improving bilateral dialogue and cooperation in the energy sector are pursued. To this end, the development and improvement of energy infrastructures and the promotion of modern energy efficiency are pursued. At the same time, the creation of an appropriate market environment for an increasing role of private sector activities is recognised, along with a strong public-private partnership framework (BMWi, 2019).

Within the EP, Germany's first green hydrogen project in Chile was presented in 2020 under the name "Haru Oni". With initial funding of about 48 million €, of which 8.23 million € came from the BMWi as part of the German National Hydrogen Strategy and the rest from corporate funding from the energy companies HIF, AME, and ENAP from Chile, ENEL from Italy, and Siemens Energy and Porsche from Germany, the latter with a planned investment of 20 million € (Heinrich-Böll-Stiftung, 2020). At the presentation of the project, the industry minister said: "German companies are world leaders in hydrogen technologies. The 'Haru Oni' project is a good example of this. [...]" (BMWi, 2020). The plant is located in Punta Arenas and will have a lifetime of 25 years and an estimated average production of more than 35 tonnes of green hydrogen in 2022. However, this project presents a paradox in that the fuel produced will be purchased by the Porsche company for use in Germany (Blanco, 2022a, 2022b). Chile is the country with the highest per capita energy consumption in the region, and at the same time a major importer of energy from external markets, with a high dependence on hydropower and external energy sources, mainly oil derivatives. Relying on a centralised and privatised energy system (Simsek et al., 2019; O'Ryan, Nasirov & Álvarez, 2020). In 2014, a series of energy policies and regulations were implemented which, according to former Chilean Energy Minister Máximo Pacheco, represented an energy revolution (Pacheco, 2018).

Despite this, the so-called Chilean energy transition has not led to a real decrease in the share of fossil fuels (Flores-Fernández, 2020).

Despite advancing towards an energy transition from an ecological perspective with the inclusion of clean energy in the energy matrix, this is not translating into a transition in social or political aspects of energy. Decision-making remains in the hands of private actors, who, with the blessing of the government, avoid citizen participation (Flores-Fernández, 2020). Luciano Cuenca, director of the Latin American Observatory of Environmental Conflicts (OLCA), remarked: "what worries me most is that history is repeating itself, it is an energy transition designed in the North without considering all its implications that we are once again paying for in the countries of the South" (Boddenberg & Birke, 2022). In May 2021, the debate reached the German Parliament, where the Green Party (Bündnis 90/Die Grünen) asked the coalition government (CDU/CSU & SPD) whether possible conflicts of social, ecological, and human rights interests in the production of green hydrogen in Chile had been examined. The executive's answer was: "Possible conflicts of social, ecological and human rights interests about the financed project were considered, with the result that, due to the sparsely populated area in the project area, which is mainly used for cattle breeding, no detriments are expected" (Deutscher Bundestag, 2021: 10).

In Chile, an energy transition is materialising, thanks to the incorporation of non-conventional renewable energies into the energy matrix, but social and political aspects related to energy are overlooked. According to Flores-Fernández (2020: 186): "In this way, energy decisions continue in the hands of private monopolistic and oligopolistic actors, who with the permission of the State define the location of projects without effective processes of citizen participation beyond the – often testimonial – instances of environmental qualification". In this strategic EP between the two countries, the localisation of regulations has not been taken into account. As mentioned above, local actors have not been involved in the negotiations or the ratification of projects. According to the theory addressed, an intermediate position between "local resistance" and "localisation of norms" is identified, with a disposition towards the latter dimension emerging. However, German interests are prevailing in the framework of this alliance.

Conclusions

Energy and environmental issues are currently high on the political agenda of governments. As a country committed to multilateralism, Germany is promoting the international energy transition, for which it has opted for closer relations with some Latin American countries.

In this context, the chapter has discussed how Germany can strengthen its bilateral relations with Latin American countries through its energy foreign policy. The model of the localisation of the norm in the local context has detected some mismatches in bilateral relations between countries through the EPs. These can be explained by a problem of diffusion of the environmental norm. In the case of Brazil, a rejection of the standard was detected, which resulted in a temporary stoppage of the EP due to a discrepancy regarding the green energies to be promoted. In the case of Mexico and Chile, there is an intermediate category between "local resistance" and "norm localisation", where the executive seeks to institutionalise the standard, but encounters the rejection of civil society in the terms in which it was proposed.

Germany may have neglected its relations with the Latin American region in trade matters at times. Yet, in energy matters, its presence has been gradually increasing. In this sense, the chapter argues in favour of energy partnerships that address the normative foundations, going beyond the logic of power and national and economic interests. The German government should keep this in mind for future energy partnerships.

Bibliography

Acharya, A. (2004). How ideas spread: Whose norms matter? Norm localization and institutional change in Asian regionalism. *International Organization, 58*(2), 239–275.

Acharya, A. (2011). Norm subsidiarity and regional orders: Sovereignty, regionalism, and rule-making in the third world. *International Studies Quarterly, 55*(1), 95–123.

Acharya, A. (2012). Ideas, norms, and regional orders en Paul, Thazha. In *International relations theory and regional transformation* (pp. 183–209). New York: Cambridge University Press.

Acosta, S., & Zilla, C. (2011). *Markets and minds. Trade and value conflicts over biofuels*, SWP Research Paper 07/2011, Stiftung Wissenschaft und Politik, Berlin.

Amazon Wacht. (2019). *Complicity in destruction II: How northern consumers and financiers enable Bolsonaro's assault on the Brazilian Amazon.*

Auswärtiges Amt. (2022). Energieaußenpolitik. https://www.auswaertiges-amt.de/de/aussenpolitik/themen/klima/energie (last access on 19 April 2022).

Birle, P. (2013). Die deutsch-brasilianischen Beziehungen. In P. Birle (Ed.), *Brasilien: Eine Einführung* (pp. 271–290). Frankfurt a. M., Madrid: Vervuert Verlagsgesellschaft.

Blanco, M. J. (25 January 2022a). Desde el sur del continente ya se construye la "nueva era del transporte" con hidrógeno. *Forbes Chile*. https://forbes.cl/sostenibilidad/2022-01-25/haru-oni-planta-de-hidrogeno-verde-chile/ (last access on 25 April 2022).

Blanco, M. J. (25 January 2022b). Desde el sur del continente ya se construye la "nueva era del transporte" con hidrógeno. *Forbes Peru*. https://forbes.pe/editors-pick/2022-01-25/chile-desde-el-sur-del-continente-ya-se-construye-la-nueva-era-del-transporte-con-hidrogeno/ (last access on 25 April 2022).

BMWi. (2017). *Jahresbericht Energiepartnerschaften 2017*. Berlin. https://www.bmwk.de/Redaktion/DE/Publikationen/Energie/jahresbericht-energiepartnerschaften.pdf?__blob=publicationFile&v=6(last access on 19 April 2022).

BMWi. (2019). *Joint declaration of intent between the Government of the Federal Republic of Germany and the Government of the Republic of Chile on the establishment of an energy partnership*. https://www.bmwk.de/Redaktion/DE/Downloads/J-L/joint-declaration-between-germany-and-chile.pdf?__blob=-publicationFile&v=3 (last access on 23 April 2022).

BMWi. (2020). *PtX-Projekt „Haru Oni": Altmaier übergibt ersten Förderbescheid für internationales Projekt für grünen Wasserstoff*. Bundesministerium für Wirtschaft und Klimaschutz. https://www.bmwk.de/Redaktion/DE/Pressemitteilungen/2020/12/20201202-ptx-projekt-haru-oni-altmaier-uebergibt-ersten-foerderbescheid-fuer-internationales-projekt-fuer-gruenen-wasserstoff.html (last access on 12 April 2022).

BMWK. (2022). *Schriftliche Frage an die Bundesregierung im Monat Februar 2022 – Frage Nr. 549*. Bundesministerium für Wirtschaft und Klimaschutz. https://www.bmwk.de/Redaktion/DE/Parlamentarische-Anfragen/2022/03/2-549.pdf?__blob=publicationFile&v=4(last access on 23 April 2022).

Boddenberg, S., & Birke, B. (2022. March 14). Öl aus Venezuela, Wasserstoff aus Chile: Hauptsache Energie. https://www.deutschlandfunkkultur.de/chile-102.html (last access on 24 April 2022).

Borrell, J. [@JosepBorrellF] (2021 November 01). *Empezando mi primera gira de Latinoamérica en la capital peruana. La UE debe darle más peso en sus relaciones exteriores a América Latina, como socios en el sistema multilateral y como destino comercial y de inversión. Compartimos valores e institucionalidad política* [Tweet]. Twitter. https://twitter.com/JosepBorrellF/status/1455204981406113794?ref_src=twsrc%5Etfw%7Ctwcamp%5Etweetembed%7Ctwterm (last access on 30 April 2022).

Checkel, J. T. (1998). The constructivist turn in international relations theory [Review of National Interests in International Society; The Culture of National Security: Norms and Identity in World Politics; Norms in International

Relations: The Struggle against Apartheid, by M. Finnemore, P. Katzenstein, & A. Klotz]. *World Politics, 50*(2), 324–348.

Cox, R. W. (1981). Social forces, states and world orders: Beyond international relations theory. *Millennium, 10*(2), 126–155.

Deutsche Gesellschaft für Internationale Zusammenarbeit. (2022a). *Deutsch-Chilenische Energiepartnerschaft*. https://www.giz.de/de/weltweit/82670.html (last access on 19 April 2022).

Deutsche Gesellschaft für Internationale Zusammenarbeit. (2022b). *Deutsch-Mexikanische Energiepartnerschaft*. https://www.giz.de/de/weltweit/40343.html (last access on 30 April 2022).

Deutscher Bundestag. (2020). *Deutsche Energiestrategie und Landkonflikte in Mexiko*. v. 05.05.2020, BT-Drs 19/18984 (S.1).

Deutscher Bundestag. (2021). *Wege in die Versorgung mit grünem Wasserstoff*. v. 04.03.2021, BT-Drs. 19/27338 (S.10).

Dröge, S., & Westphal, K. (2021). Klimaziele und Energiepolitikaußenpolitisch stärker gestalten. In G. Maihold, S. Mair, M. Müller,J. Vorrath, & C. Wagner(Eds.), *Deutsche Außenpolitik im Wandel: unstete Bedingungen, neue Impulse*. Berlin: Stiftung Wissenschaft und Politik.

Esch, F. L., & Maihold, G. (2019). Deutschlands Rolle und Interessen in Lateinamerika. *Handbuch für Wissenschaft und Studium, 117*.

Flemes, D., & Schöneich, S. (2020). *Indigene Völker unter Druck* (GIGA Focus Lateinamerika, 4). Hamburg: GIGA German Institute of Global and Area Studies - Leibniz-Institut für Globale und Regionale Studien, Institut für Lateinamerika-Studien.

Flores-Fernández, C. (2020). The Chilean energy "transition": Between successful policy and the assimilation of a post-political energy condition. *Innovation: The European Journal of Social Science Research, 33*(2), 173–193.

García Howell, D. (2021). ¿Estamos avanzando en la transición energética en América Latina?: Análisis y Consideraciones. *Boletín Política Comercial y Ambiental,* N° 13, enero 2021. Konrad-Adenauer-Stiftung e.V.

Granguillhome Morfín, R., & Jiménez Segovia, V. M. (2018). Las relaciones con Alemania y cómo fortalecer la presencia de México en el mundo de hoy. *Revista Mexicana De Política Exterior,* (112), 109–128.

H Villavicencio, D., & Millán, J. C. (2020). La transición energética en México: disyuntivas, tensiones y avances en la ejecución del proyecto nacional. Caravelle. *Cahiers du monde hispanique et luso-brésilien*, (115), 25–40.

Heinrich-Böll-Stiftung. (2022). *Haru Oni – highly innovative fuels project – geoengineering map*. https://map.geoengineeringmonitor.org/ (last access on 19 April 2022).

Heydenreich, C., & Paasch, A. (2017). Globale Energiewirtschaft und Menschenrechte: deutsche Unternehmen und Politik auf dem Prüfstand: Bericht 2017. *Germanwatch eV*. https://dserver.bundestag.de/btd/19/009/1900965.pdf

Hübner, C. (2016). *Trend zur Energiemarktöffnung in Lateinamerika*. Berlin: Konrad-Adenauer-Stiftung.

IRENA. (2019). *International Renewable Energy Agency. Plan de acción regional: Acelerando el despliegue de energía renovable en América Latina*.

Ismer, J. (2019 August 09). Bundesregierung legt Brasilien-Projekt auf Eis. *Tagesspiegel*. https://www.tagesspiegel.de/politik/regenwald-rodung-bundesregierung-legt-brasilien-projekt-auf-eis/24889568.htm (last access on 19 April 2022).

Katzenstein, P. (1996). Introduction: Alternative perspectives on national security. In Peter J. Katzenstein (Ed.), *The culture of national security: Norms and identity in world politics*. New York: Columbia University Press.

Kloss, E. C. (2012). *Transformação do etanol em commodity. Perspectivas para uma ação diplomática brasileira*. Brasília: Fundação Alexandre de Gusmão.

Maihold, G. (2021). *Vom Nebeneinander zu neuem Miteinander: die deutsche Lateinamerika-Politik braucht neue Ansatzpunkte*. SWP-Aktuell Nr. 58 09/2021. Berlin: Stiftung Wissenschaft und Politik.

Mella Polanco, M., & Berrios Silva, C. (2013). Gobernabilidad, democratización y conflictividad social en Chile: escenarios posibles para un nuevo equilibrio. *Polis. Revista Latinoamericana*, (35).

Moro, B. (2021. October 22). La comunidad zapoteca rechaza un parque eólico de una empresa francesa en Oaxaca. *France 24*. https://www.france24.com/es/programas/escala-en-par%C3%ADs/20211022-mexico-oaxaca-zapotecas-parque-eolico-medio-ambiente (last access on 23 April 2022).

O Globo. (25 Juni 2008). Etanol brasileiro é biocombustível mais favorável do mundo, diz Oxfam. *O Globo*. https://oglobo.globo.com/economia/etanol-brasileiro-biocombustivel-mais-favoravel-do-mundo-diz-oxfam-3612596 (last access on 28 April 2022).

O'Ryan, R., Nasirov, S., & Álvarez-Espinosa, A. (2020). Renewable energy expansion in the Chilean power market: A dynamic general equilibrium modeling approach to determine CO2 emission baselines. *Journal of Cleaner Production, 247*, 119645.

Pacheco, M. (2018). Revolución Energética en Chile, *Ediciones UDP, Santiago de Chile*.

Quitzow, R., & Thielges, S. (2020). The German energy transition as soft power. *Review of International Political Economy*, *29*(2), 1–26.

Quitzow, R., Thielges, S., & Helgenberger, S. (2019). Deutschlands Energiepartnerschaften in der internationalen Energiewendepolitik. *Bestandsaufnahme und Optionen für die Zukunft.*

Risse, T. (2007). Deutsche Identität und Außenpolitik. In S. Schmidt, G. Hellmann, & R. Wolf (Eds.), *Handbuch zur deutschen Außenpolitik.* VS Verlag für Sozialwissenschaften.

Rodríguez, Y. (2021. Januer. 16). Las energías limpias, reto para Yucatán. *El Universal.* https://www.eluniversal.com.mx/estados/las-energias-limpias-reto-para-yucatan (last access on 29 April 2022).

Röhrkasten, S. (2015 August 18). Debatte Energiedialog mit Brasilien:Unter Energiepionieren. *taz.* https://taz.de/Debatte-Energiedialog-mit-Brasilien/!5220355/ (last access on 23 April 2022).

Röhrkasten, S., & Westphal, K. (2012). Energy security and the transatlantic dimension: A view from Germany. *Journal of Transatlantic Studies, 10,* 328–342.

Röhrkasten, S., Thielges, S., Hübner, C., & Helgenberger, S. (2018). *Germany–Latin America: Fostering strategic alliances for a global energy transition.* Konrad-Adenauer-Stiftung e.V.

Secretaría de Energía del Gobierno de México. (2021). *Marco Jurídico del Reporte de Avance de Energías Limpias.* https://www.gob.mx/cms/uploads/attachment/file/610964/Cap10_-_Marco_Juri_dico_Reporte_Avance_de_Energi_as_Limpias_WEB.pdf (last access on 24 April 2022).

Simsek, Y., Lorca, Á., Urmee, T., Bahri, P. A., & Escobar, R. (2019). Review and assessment of energy policy developments in Chile. *Energy Policy, 127,* 87–101.

Smink, V. (2022, March 31). Hidrógeno verde: 6 países que lideran la producción de una de las "energías del futuro" (y cuál es el único latinoamericano). *BBC News Mundo.* https://www.bbc.com/mundo/noticias-56531777 (last access on 23 April 2022).

Solera, M. (2012). *La política exterior alemana de diversificación energética: principios y líneas de acción (1998–2012).* Documento de Trabajo 11/2012, Real Instituto Elcano.

Stevenson, H. (2013). *Institutionalizing unsustainability: The paradox of global climate governance.* Los Ángeles: University of California Press.

Terwindt, C., & Schliemann, C. (2019). Una situación complicada: el espacio de la sociedad civil en las luchas por los recursos naturales. *Heinrich-Böll-Stiftung e.V.,* 51–56.

Umbach, F. (2011). Deutsche Außenpolitik und Energiesicherheit. In T. Jäger, A. Höse, & K. Oppermann (Eds.), *Deutsche Außenpolitik.* Wiesbaden: VS Verlag für Sozialwissenschaften.

United Nations / Framework Convention on Climate Change (2015). *Adoption of the Paris agreement, 21st conference of the parties.* Paris: United Nations.

Valdivia, C. (2019). *Rede von Cristina Valdivia. Dachverband Kritische Aktionärinnen und Aktionäre.* https://www.kritischeaktionaere.de/siemens/rede-von-cristina-valdivia-3/ (last access on 23 April 2022).

Luis Fernando Beneduzi

Identity and International Relations: Italian Foreign Policy Towards Latin America

Scholars of History and International Relations have stressed, in Latin America and, in particular, in Brazil, the importance of the relationship between ethnic identity and foreign policy related to the Italian case (Cervo, 1991; Aledda, 2016; Bertonha, 1997; Di Santo, 2021; Bevilacqua, De Clementi, Franzina, 2001). Since the first years after the *Risorgimento*, in the second half of the 19th century, Italy had to manage an important migratory flow that was mainly directed towards Latin America. The highest concentration was achieved in Argentina, Brazil and Uruguay. Thus, the first agreements and relations sought to create an institutional framework for this movement of people.

In the early 20th century, Italian political discussion also spoke of "commercial colonisation", trying to exploit the immigrant community for national development and, at the same time, justify the national haemorrhaging of labour (Beneduzi, 2017). In the 1920s and 1930s this process reached a climax, when the Fascist project for Italian communities in Latin America produced an articulated set of actions in favour of the diffusion of Italian culture, but in association with political propaganda and Italian *grandeur*.

As Cervo (2011) claims, the Italian contribution to Brazilian national identity, through the long historical process based on immigration, is the common capital accumulated over time, which makes the bilateral relations between Brazil and Italy dynamic. The same argument could be applied to Uruguay or Argentina, whose "mark" of Italian presence can be found in their daily life and thinking of themselves as a nation (Devoto, 2008; Bresciano, 2003).

In fact, Amado Cervo – a renowned expert in International History and International Relations – emphasises the cultural characteristics brought by Italian immigrants, such as religiosity, the preoccupation with gastronomy, the culture of work and savings, the cult of family and entrepreneurship, as part of the construction of a Brazilian Italian spirit, in a connection that has produced different types of exchanges over time (Cervo, 2011).

Franco Cenni,[1] a renowned Italian Brazilian intellectual (1909–1973), recalling the visit to Brazil of the President of the Italian Republic, Giovanni Gronchi, in 1958, refers to this feeling of closeness of the population celebrating him in the streets and the Italian presence that is transversal to Brazilian society (Cenni, 2003). Among the ministers, governors, mayors, all sons of Italians who met Gronchi, Cenni stresses that the strong blood relations that had characterised the exchanges between Italy and Brazil, have turned into a new dialogue. In fact, he speaks of a new stage, which is not only based on the work of pioneers but also on investments in industry, from chemicals and pharmaceuticals to civil construction and automotive, in renewal and consolidation of common humanist values as well.

Starting from these premises, the aim of this chapter is to think, from a historical perspective, about the process of building cooperation between Italy and Latin America, considering the presence of Italian immigrants and their descendants in a double perspective. On the one hand, the presence of a community of Italian descendants in Brazil has facilitated bilateral relations; has created an idea of a communion of shared values; and, therefore, has brought some Latin American realities closer to the Italian one. On the other, this imagined proximity has identified the subcontinent with a strategic reserve, naturally intertwined with Western civilization, a resource to draw on in times of "need". By looking across the 20th century, a variety of intensities of Italian attention in relation to the Latin American world is marked by changes in international society and domestic politics, such as the fascist policies of the 1920s and 1930s, or by the subcontinent's economic boom, with the sharp rise in the value of commodities in the international market in the 21st century, and the birth of the Italy-Latin America Conference.

Before starting the analysis, a brief clarification on the concept of identity and its interactions with the dynamics of international politics in a global society is required. Both the contemporary identity processes and those of the 20th century are marked by interactions with different alterities that reinforce their characteristics of constant transformation, intersectionality and agency, whether on the part of individuals, communities or nation-states. Actually, belongings are plural, corresponding to different stages of personal experience, the historical past, and logics of power and oppression, within the interests played between

---

1 He worked at the Italian-Brazilian Cultural Institute. In 1960, he won the Italian Prize in San Paolo. In 1962, he received the silver medal from the Directorate General for Cultural Relations, which was a part of the Italian Ministry of Foreign Affairs.

ethnic communities and the states (Linhard; Parsons, 2018; Suárez-Orozco, 2004; Viola, 2015; Floriani, 2004).

Understanding identity as a dynamic process in time and space and, consequently, marked by social relations and transformation, is essential, in order to understand: (a) the relationship between Italian identity and the community of Italian origin in Brazil; (b) the Brazilian and Italian bilateral policies. Identity is not essential and fixed, but it must be associated with memberships reworked over time:

> Identity is, in fact, essentially comparative in nature and must be understood as originally connected to the dynamics of inclusion/exclusion. Identity is understood and best described as a relational and contextual process that refers to the way in which individuals and groups consider, construct and position themselves in relation to others according to social categories (La Barbera, 2015: 9).

Krause and Renwick (1996) associate this dynamic perception of identity with the specific studies of international relations. They seek to understand the concept from a global perspective, in an international reality in which the processes of identification are not reduced to the sphere of the nation-state as homogeneous and stable processes. The authors dwell on the disruptive perspective of the impact of globalization, which has challenged a linear reading that superimposed national identity and territoriality. Thus, it reinforces an idea of multiple loyalties and feelings of belonging, based on the different experiences of subjects, communities, national collectivities and even ethnic groups:

> In contemporary "national" societies, different models of loyalty and identity co-exist, and the globalization has disrupted the links between identity and the territorially based nations-state. [...] The identification with the nation can be strong or weak. At the same time, other identities, for example, gender, ethnicity, social class, race, sexual preference, which are not rooted in an attachment to a particular territory can be highly significant (Krause and Renwick, 1996:XI–XII).

This conceptual framework can be applied to the case of Italian immigrant communities in Latin America and to the difficulty of the effectiveness of a subcontinent perspective as a strategic reserve. On the one hand, the loyalty of Italo-Brazilians in relation to national belonging has changed over time, being more addressed to the country of birth or ancestors; or in the sense of the host country, depending on the different historical and contextual times: as Cervo (2011) claimed, the Brazilian Italian identity has been constructed. On the other hand, the proximity between Latin America, as an "extreme west" (Rouquié, 2007), and Europe cannot be understood as homogeneous and timeless, especially taking into account the contemporary challenges and the policies, such as the aggressive policies of China, in the commercial, cultural and political spheres, towards the subcontinent: if Europe is still a model today, this reality could change in the future.

Italy-Latin America relations from the 19th century to the fascist period

The Italian migratory phenomenon has been the central element of relations between Italy and Latin America since the second half of the 19th century. Annual and constant flows of Italian immigrants have strongly collaborated in the construction of the metropolitan cities such as Buenos Aires and São Paulo, where they represented an important part of the population in the first decades of the 20th century (Devoto, 2008; Fausto, 2000). Although other urban spaces such as Lima and Guayaquil, or Santiago de Chile, despite their much less representative numbers, cannot be overlooked. They also formed small rural communities in the southern states of Brazil, such as in Rio Grande do Sul or Santa Catarina (Beneduzi, 2008), or in the province of Santa Fe (Argentina), taking up cultural, architectural and social aspects of the country of origin.

At the turn of the 20th century, considerable attention was devoted to the place of the thematic debates in the newspapers on the connection between Italy and the immigrant communities in Latin America and also in the world of politics; and referring to the idea of a commercial colonization, in a distinction from the one that had just failed in the African context, with the Italian defeat in Adua, in 1896. For example, the newspaper "L'Italia coloniale" emphasised among its objectives the analysis of the advantages and opportunities of places of immigration for the development of Italian national production:

> To examine the repercussion they have and the repercussion they could have in the field of our industries, of our trade; to see how foreign competition can be overcome in the regions enlivened by our emigration (Aquarone, 1989: 268).

Even the Italian Member of Parliament, Vittorio Buccelli, defender of the idea of migration as a synonym for economic development, the creation of new markets, in his book-length account of a trip to the south of Brazil to the state of Rio Grande do Sul, makes an apology for migratory spaces as better than African ones for Italian business (Buccelli, 1906). His text is also an indictment of the Italian capitalists who fail to see the benefits of these Latin American realities: despite the emphasis he gives to the success of the migratory enterprise, he emphasises that it could be even greater if there were a managerial group – and he refers to the policy of the Kingdom of Italy – that provided adequate knowledge to immigrants. On the contrary, he lamented the fact that it was German traders who exploited the wealth produced by the Italian workforce.

In a forerunner to what was to become Fascist foreign policy, between the 1920s and 1930s, in the period following World War I, an Italian concern to expand relations with countries on both the South and North American continent can be observed. In this project, and we are talking about Brazil, Argentina, Chile and Uruguay, the bond to be welded between the two sides of the Atlantic, the bridge between Italy and Latin America, was constituted by immigrant communities:

> Firstly, the objective was to create the conditions to foster the revival of economic exchanges. Added to this was the Rome government's hope to revitalize the migratory movement; to re-establish links with the immigrant communities already present in the Americas, which [...] could prove to be effective vehicles for understanding between Italy and the American continent (Mugnaini, 2008: 35).

With the rise of Fascism, a strengthening of this policy in relation to Latin American migratory spaces can be noticed. As Bertonha (1997) points out, the first years of the Duce's policy were characterised by Italian expansion through the economy and culture, in the construction of a Latin world culturally bound to Italy. Indeed, there will be no lack of actions by the Italian government: Nave Italia, for example, in 1924 will circumnavigate South America in a propaganda project of the regime and Italian power. It would stop in major Latin American centres, opening up to the immigrant community and local citizens, so that they could see the country's technological greatness. This would be the first step in the improvement of relations between Italy and Latin American states. It would give rise to multinational mercantile treaties; encourage Italian migration and colonization; implement new agricultural, mining and operational concessions; develop new maritime communications with the region; create new agreements and redefine customs rates. The project was not only about increasing the export of Italian products or the establishment of new Italian companies in Latin America, but also to develop a large-scale and well-planned program of commercial expansion that would strengthen Italy's economic potential, creating important trade agreements with the region (Brandalise, 2020).

The presence of Italians in some Latin American states was considerable, which is why one of Mussolini's strategic goals involved conquering the Italian community and instrumentalising it for his own objectives (Scarzanella, 2005). Therefore, the fascist propaganda machine expanded its reach in the 1930s, reaching many countries. The radio, which was a very effective means of communication used by the regime and managed to reach the masses, including foreigners, made it possible to switch from a defensive cultural policy (which promoted Italian values) to another, more proactive approach, as an instrument of foreign and geopolitical policy.

According to Trento (2005), the strategy of Fascist Italy was based on the construction of a different expansion in relation to that of classical imperialism, which would have been impossible given the Italian reality. In this sense, there were many events organised by the regime that emphasised Italians living outside their national borders, indicating them as part of the same community and brotherhood. Benito Mussolini's speech in 1923 in Milan can be considered emblematic of this policy: "Wherever there is an Italian, there is the tricolor, there is the homeland, there is the defense of the government" (Trento, 2005: 3). Consequently, in 1926, the Duce's words were turned into action, corresponding to the transformation in the name of the Italian community abroad: from immigrants they became Italians abroad. This was not just a play on words, but a policy aimed at creating an ethnic-national bond, where Italians in the world and in Latin America, in particular, acted as instruments of state policy.

From the post-World War II years to the end of the 20th century

In the post-war period, Italy experienced a weakened situation during the reconstruction process and didn't resume the Latin American projects of the previous period. In contrast, it concentrated on the European dimension of its foreign policy, participating in the creation of the European Coal and Steel Community in 1951; and in 1955, took part in the Treaty of Rome, which established the European Economic Community. In relation to Latin America, as well as Brazil, Cervo (1991) points to a less dynamic moment in relations between governments, associating it with the negative adjective "laziness". Nevertheless, Italian entrepreneurship expanded in the subcontinent, also through the consolidation of big brands, such as Fiat and Pirelli; although it cannot be emphasised on cultural relations or university exchanges, which were much lower than in the fascist period, and different from the relations between other European states.

In 1989, it was clear that this phase, which began in the post-war period, was scarce in bilateral relations, compared to what it could have produced, between Italy and Latin America. However, during this time, the business community was able to build stable relations. In the same year, while Romano Prodi, then president of the Institute for Industrial Reconstruction, spoke at a conference in São Paulo, lamenting a much lower Italian presence in relation to the actual possibilities of cooperation; in Milan, at a meeting between Brazilian and Italian entrepreneurs, Piero Sierra, then president of the Pirelli Group in Brazil, emphasised the company's persistence and continuity of design since 1929 as fundamental aspects of its success in Latin America:

> The secret of this success was to be found in a long-term vision based on the country's potential, the ability to get things right and not to be stopped by red tape (Cervo, 1991: 258).

Towards the end of the 20th century, a wave of the neoliberal policies began to change the Latin American economic and social reality, with privatizations and market openings, but also with the birth of the Common Market of the South (Mercosur) in 1991 – an agreement between Argentina, Brazil, Paraguay and Uruguay. One can observe a resurgence of Italian interest in the subcontinent, especially through interactions conducted and supported by Italy at the European Union level. In the 1990s, the interest in the construction and interaction of common markets acted as a lever for the dynamics of bilateral policies; in the 21st century, it was the important international growth of commodity prices and the consequent surge in the GDP of Latin American states that created the conditions for a strong impulse in bilateral relations.

Italy and Latin America in the 21st century

Gian Luca Gardini and Peter Lambert (2011) emphasised, in a context of strong economic growth in Latin America accompanied by crisis and stagnation in most of the developed world and particularly in the EU after 2008, some relevant positive features of the region, such as the sophistication of its integration projects, the long absence of conflict since 1936, and the presence of important natural resources: "its economic and industrial growth, and the growth of its multinational corporations" (Gardini & Lambert, 2011: 5).

Since the beginning of the 21st century, Latin America has experienced a positive economic moment, with a robust GDP growth rate and substantial macroeconomic improvement:

> In the five-year period 2004–08, growth was high, inflation low, public accounts improved, public debt decreased and the balance of payments went into surplus. [...] In 2008, almost all large South American countries had high growth rates; Argentina 6.8%, Brazil 5.9%, Peru 9.4% and Venezuela 4.8% (Mori, 2009: 115).

With an average increase in regional GDP of 5.7% in 2007 and 4.6% in 2008, according to data from the Economic Commission for Latin America and the Caribbean (ECLAC) (Mori, 2009), a variety of primary resources were gaining importance in international society. Governments aimed at policies of income redistribution and infrastructural investments, as in the case of the PAC (Plan for Accelerating Growth) in Lula's Brazil. The subcontinent, once again, became a strategic reserve that the EU and Italy could draw upon. In this sense, the first fifteen years of the new millennium were marked by manifestations of interest by Italy in Latin American states, with bilateral projects indicating a renewed focus, at least rhetorically, on the region.

Therefore, Brazil and Mexico, two countries of strong economic relevance in Latin America, caught the attention of European institutions in 2007 and 2008, as Calandri (2009) states, with the construction of "strategic partnerships". While in the case of Mexico, we observe the deepening of already consolidated relations, with what had then become the tenth world economic power; in the Brazilian case, we have greater complexity, not only in the recognition of Brazil as a global political actor, given the economic weight gained during the Lula government (then the sixth economy), but also in action in foreign policy and inclusion in the BRICS, as well as a bridging role in relation to Lusophone Africa and Mercosur.

In the Italian sphere, the 21st century is marked by the creation of the Italy-Latin America and Caribbean Conference. Since 2003 in Milan, it was carried out every two years, promoting meetings between Italy and the governments of the region, at the level of foreign ministers, organised by the Ministry of Foreign Affairs and Cooperation (MAECI), in collaboration with the Italian-Latin American Institute[2] (IILA).

The first meetings – in 2003 and 2005 – with the important collaboration of the Lombardy Region Chamber of Commerce, had a more economic and entrepreneurial approach, in search of mutual understanding, in a space that was not yet strictly intergovernmental. It was in 2007, with the Prodi government and the strategic agenda directed at Latin America (economic growth, BRICS and the re-establishment of the subcontinent's priority in Italian foreign policy) that the event took on a more political and intergovernmental approach. In this event in Rome, the President of Chile, Michele Bachelet, attended, along with several representatives of Latin American governments. On the Italian side, it counted on the participation of the entire country system (institutional leaders from government, business, trade unions, academia and civil society).

2 The IILA is an intergovernmental organization established in 1966, consisting of Italy and 20 Latin American republics. It was formed with the aim of enhancing relations among its member states. Since 2007, it has collaborated on a permanent basis with the Italian Ministry of Foreign Affairs. It is an observer member of the United Nations Assembly and since 2018, of the EU-ECLAC ministerial meetings.

Since 2012, Latin American states began to participate in the organization of the Conference, which further strengthened its intergovernmental character and affirmed the relevance of the event. Its importance was demonstrated in two key points: in the final declaration of 2013, with the creation of the Italo-Latin American Forum of Parliamentarians (Rossi, 2015); and, in 2014, with Law 173/2014, which provided a formal character to the congregation.

The first parliamentary forum took place in 2015, and it was established as a tool that, on the one hand, proposes actions to governments, considering the issues considered priorities in relations between Italy and Latin America; and, on the other hand, monitors their development. As a first objective, also present in the discussions of all Italy-Latin America Conferences, it proposes a development agenda primarily focused on the promotion and support of Small and Medium Enterprises (SMEs). Other topics considered important in the forum are infrastructure and renewable energy, which should serve as a link for closer cooperation between governments, bilateral agreements aimed at protecting migrants, or the fight against organised crime, supported by the Italian government, with the provision of training projects in the field of security. A final point in the priorities of the forum directly concerned the IILA. This organisation was seen as a unique international body in the European context due to its characteristics and should be supported by the forum for the relaunch of relations between the European Union and Latin America. This initiative to strengthen IILA as a privileged interlocutor in relations between the two sides of the ocean was intended to guarantee Italy a leading role in opening up Italian foreign policy to the South Atlantic.

It is noteworthy the temporal concomitance between the EU's interest in Latin America and Italy's, as well as the construction of spaces for interregional and intergovernmental dialogue. In both cases, this coincided with the moment of growth of the subcontinent's relevance in the world economy and international politics.

In fact, in 2012, a study conducted by CeSPI (Centre for International Policy Studies), a think-tank that advises the Chamber of Deputies, the Senate and MAECI on issues concerning Italian foreign policy, recommends – in a framework of high economic growth rates of Latin American countries, in an international scenario of increasing interdependence – the deepening of dialogue with Latin America, which was considered a crucial actor in relation to new common challenges: economic, social, environmental and energy (CeSPI, 2012).

CeSPI's study goes further and indicates the need for Italy to place the region at an unprecedented centrality in its foreign policy, given the rich potential of Latin American domestic markets. In spite of the weakness of the data regarding trade exchanges in terms of interaction, which marked ninth place for Italy at the time in relation to the subcontinent, and an incidence of the latter of about 2% on Italian relations, the wealth lies in the significant percentage increase of national exports, in the turnover of Italian companies in Latin America[3] (of which ¾ in Brazil, Argentina and Mexico), second globally, and in the region's status as the first foreign market for Italian construction companies. These data on bilateral relations between Italy and Latin America provide an important picture of the relevance of the region in the process of internationalisation of the Country System (CeSPI, 2012: 7, 12).

In fact, a previous CeSPI study in 2010 showcased the role of Italian entrepreneurship – as a model and as a driving force – in a renewed attention from Italian government institutions in relation to the subcontinent:

> Once again, Italy has become interested in Latin America. This turnaround was inspired above all by the Italian business world, attracted by a series of factors: the positive economic cycle of the Latin American subcontinent, which was slowed down but not stopped by the global crisis; the continued openness of Latin American markets to foreign investments; the convergences with Spanish companies that allowed some large Italian groups – such as ENEL – to gain an important position in the Latin American market (CeSPI, 2010, p. 18).

In this way, the 2012 CeSPI report emphasises the Brazilian context, in which the presence of the Italian industry had strengthened during the analysed period: specifically, it emphasises the fact that construction companies obtained 1/3 of the contracts at the national level in Brazil (CeSPI, 2012). However, the rest of the Latin American reality is also impacted by the entrepreneurial interest of significant Italian companies, such as ENEL, for example, indicated as the leading private operator in the region, even though it points out a 2/3 concentration of exports in three relevant states, such as Brazil, Argentina and Mexico, two of which, Argentina and Brazil, were strongly affected by the migratory phenomenon coming from the peninsula (Rossi, 2015).

In November 2018, a new CeSPI report takes stock of the priorities that emerged in the different Italy-Latin America conferences that took place up to 2017. Although it is possible to observe some more concrete interests, such as energy cooperation agreements with Colombia and opportunities in the coal and oil mining sector, or in infrastructure, water, transport and telecommunications in Peru, most of the indications concern projects of intent. The document refers

3 The 34% of Pirelli's turnover is generated in Latin America and Fiat's 36% (CeSPI, 2012: 14).

to the promotion of sustainable development, gender equality, combating climate change, strengthening the rule of law, collaboration in peace processes and the promotion of human rights, and the development of energy networks and infrastructure. Nevertheless, the proposals made are not reflected into action. Even the affirmed interest in the Pacific Alliance remains in a vague "strengthening the participation of our economic system in a very large market" (CeSPI, 2018: 90).

Possibly, the discussion on Mercosur presented a more concrete and proactive approach, proposing a strong participation in the negotiations with the EU, with the aim of guaranteeing not only economic opportunities but also protecting Italy's food industry. Alongside Germany and Spain but unlike other European countries, Italy was one of the EU Member States most interested in reaching an agreement between the EU and Mercosur. One of its main goals was to gain access to public procurement contracts in the Mercosur bloc (CeSPI, 2018).

Finally, the March 2020 CeSPI report emphasised the importance and need for Italy to assert its leading role as an interlocutor between the EU and Latin America. Indeed, it spoke of the progress of Sanchez's Spain in the subcontinent, which required an urgent stance on the part of the country and the consequent counter-movement. It is worth noting the suggestions of how to achieve this main role, for example, to look at immigrant communities, which is associated with the exploitation of export opportunities and international remittances from small and medium-sized enterprises. In support of the relevance of the subcontinent, the document reports the turnover of Italian companies abroad, showing a volume of 54.2 billion in Latin America, compared to 38 billion in Asia or 20 billion in Eastern Europe (CeSPI, 2020: 15). It dwells again on the number of Italians in Latin American countries; in December 2018 there were 1,651,278,[4] of which 842,615 were in Argentina and 447,067 in Brazil, and on the links between this community and Italy: the many Italian-Latin American associations, the foreign constituencies since 1998, and the postal vote since 2001 (CeSPI, 2020: 4). Thus, the concrete links that connect Italian descendants and the national community residing in Italy are shown. In this sense, the report mentions the meeting of parliamentarians from Latin American states of Italian origin (350), of which 166 were in Argentina, Brazil and Uruguay. In summary, Italy would have all the cards in order to be the protagonist in the relations between the EU and Latin America – product attractiveness, human presence, and

---

4 Pointing out that this number corresponds to those who hold Italian citizenship, the numbers of Italian-descendants is much higher, and going well over 30 million.

cultural affinities. However, this potential is not expressed in a political and economic projection towards the subcontinent.

This report on the latest Italy-Latin America Conference also emphasises the importance of the subcontinent for the business of Italian SMEs (in Brazil alone, they exceed 300 units). Italian SMEs need greater support from national policymakers with the main aim of building partnerships, gaining a greater understanding of subcontinental trade legislation, and advancing technological development: they need a "system of accompaniment from institutions and the central state" (CeSPI, 2020: 17). Indeed, this highlights how a study on the internationalisation dynamics of Italian companies is much more significant than one on trade volumes in order to understand the potential offered by Latin American countries to the Italian economic system.

Conclusions

This chapter shows a wave-like relationship between Italy and Latin America, with certain moments when Italian interest turned towards the subcontinent. In fact, during both periods of increased attention to Latin American countries – during fascism and in the 21st century – the impetus was provided by Italian companies. On one hand, immigrant communities are understood as an important link between the two sides of the Atlantic and a resource. Nevertheless, the fluid and changing aspect of identity is not taken into consideration, which often produces romanticised readings of an unchanged Italian identity in migratory spaces, both today and in the 1930s. In addition, the contemporary Italian policy, in relation to Latin America, is characterised by low investment in qualified professionals and "brain circulation" of academics, as well as a lack of any research or mobility program linked to Latin American countries.

Indeed, this chapter supports CeSPI's argument that there is a lack of Italian institutional action in relation to the subcontinent (CeSPI, 2020). This chapter also echoes the words of the intellectual of dependency theory and former Brazilian president Fernando Henrique Cardoso, in a speech he delivered on European influence in Latin American society in 2000. On that occasion, he mentioned European countries like Spain, England, France and Portugal, but referred to Italians instead of Italy. This choice by Cardoso indicates how the country is perceived by the international community and several actors in Latin America: "a great and influential people that does not have behind it an equally strong system and an equally strong nation, with all the structures it implies: a people without a nation" (CeSPI, 2020: 23).

The director of Pirelli Brazil, in 1989, made a strong point for the company's success: the continuity of its relationship over time. In the case of Italian foreign policy, a lack of this persistence is observed and instead, there is strong intermittence. Moreover, the moments of revival of Italian interest are also characterised by little institutional action. Following the discussions of the Italy-Latin America Conferences, and the reports provided by experts for the International Policy Observatory,[5] a repetition of the same problems and potentialities can be noticed, with indications that are repeated on the role that the peninsula's foreign policy must play. All this suggests untapped opportunities, a lack of action by the institutions, and an absent organic economic policy aimed at Latin America.

A more pragmatic policy towards immigrant communities, one that actually sought to understand the terms of this Italian-Latin American identity, would also be of great relevance. The development of effective support networks not only for entrepreneurs, but also for the dissemination of Italian culture and the national university system, as done by other European states such as Germany, France, England or even Spain, would allow for a new foreign policy approach, where cultural and economic diplomacy would be associated with building new bonds with immigrant communities. Finally, breaking with the assumption of Latin America as the "Extreme West" (Rouquié, 2007), something distant, but close at the same time, would allow for a real understanding of the political and economic culture of the region, which is often falsely presumed to be understood.

Bibliography

Aledda, A. (2016). *Gli italiani nel mondo e le istituzioni pubbliche. La politica italiana nei confronti dell'emigrazione e delle sue forme di volontariato all'estero*. Milan: Franco Angeli.

Aquarone, A. (1989). *Dopo Adua: politica e amministrazione coloniale*. Città di Castello: Tibergraph editrice.

Beneduzi, L. F. (2008). *Imigração italiana e Catolicismo: entrecruzando olhares, discutindo mitos*. Porto Alegre: EDIPUCRS.

5 The International Policy Observatory is a cooperative project between the Italian Parliament and the International Affairs Institute, born in 2008. The objective of the project is to support members of parliament, the staff of the Ministry of Foreign Affairs, and members of the diplomatic-consular network with updated analysis of relevant international topics.

Beneduzi, L. F. (2017). Quando a imigração se transforma em colonização: algumas leituras sobre a presença italiana no sul do Brasil. *Revista Latino-americana de História, 6*, 35–58.

Bertonha, J. F. (1997). O Brasil, os imigrantes italianos e a política externa fascista, 1922–1943. *Revista Brasileira de Política Internacional, 40*(2), 106–130.

Bevilacqua, P., De Clementi, A., & Franzina, E. (2001). *Storia dell'emigrazione italiana. Partenze* (Vol. 1). Rome: Dondelli Editore.

Brandalise, C. (2020). *A Itália sob o fascismo e a latinidade das américas*. Jundiaí: Paco Editorial.

Bresciano, J. A. (2003). L'immigrazione italiana in Uruguay. In C. M. Rita (Eds.), *Un paese che cambia. Saggi antropologici sull'Uruguay tra memoria e attualità*. Rome: CISU.

Buccelli, V. (1906). *Un viaggio a Rio Grande del Sud*. Milan: L.F. Pallestrini & C.

Calandri, E. (2009). Eppur si muove! Unione Europea e America Latinadal vecchio a nuovo secolo. In G. Chiaramonti (Eds.), *Tra innovazione e continuità. L'America Latina nel Nuovo Millennio*. Padova: CLEUP.

Cenni, F. (2003). *Italianos no Brasil*. 3ed. São Paulo: Editora da USP.

Cervo, A. L. (1991). *Le relazioni diplomatiche fra Italia e Brasile dal 1861 ad oggi*. Turin: Edizioni della Fondazione Agnelli.

Cervo, A. L. (2011). *As relações entre o Brasil e a Itália: formação da italianidade brasileira*. 2ed. Brasília: Editora da UnB.

CeSPI. (2010). Il Brasile, motore dell'integrazione regionale dell'America del Sud. *Osservatorio di Politica Internazionale*, Approfondimenti (08).

CeSPI. (2012). L'Italia e l'America Latina. Insieme verso il futuro. *Osservatorio di Politica Internazionale*, Approfondimenti (46).

CeSPI. (2018). I processi d'integrazione in America latina e nei Caraibi. *Osservatorio di Politica Internazionale*, Approfondimenti (145).

CeSPI. (2020). America Latina: nuove tendenze in atto, vecchia e nuova emigrazione italiana. *Osservatorio di Politica Internazionale*, Approfondimenti (155).

Devoto, F. (2008). *Historia de los italianos en la Argentina*. Beunos Aires: Biblos.

Di Santo, D. (2021). *Italia e America Latina. Storia di una idea di politica estera*. Rome: Donzelli Editore.

Fausto, B. (Eds.). (2000). *Fazer a América, a imigração em massa para a América Latina*. São Paulo: Editora da USP.

Floriani, S. (2004). *Identità di Frontiera Migrazione, biografie, vita quotidiana*. Soveria Mannelli: Rubbettino Editore.

Gardini, G. L., & Lambert, P. (2011). Introduction: Ideology and pragmatism in Latin America foreign policy. In G. L. Gardini & P. Lambert (Eds.), *Latin America foreign policies: Between ideology and pragmatism*. New York: Palgrave MacMillan.

Krause, J., & Renwick, N. (1996). *Identities in international relations*. London: Palgrave MacMillan.

La Barbera, M. C. (2015). Identity and migration: An introduction. In M. C. La Barbera (Ed.), *Identity and migration in Europe: Multidisciplinary perspectives*. Berlin: Springer.

Linhard, T., & Parsons, T. (2018). *In mapping migration, identity, and space*. New York: Palgrave Macmillan.

Mori, A. (2009). L'economia in America Latina: Progressi e sfide. In G. Chiaramonti (Ed.), *Tra innovazione e continuità. L'America Latina nel Nuovo Millennio*. Padova: CLEUP.

Mugnaini, M. (2008). *L'America Latina e Mussolini. Brasile e Argentina nella politia estera dell'Italia (1919–1943)*. Milan: Franco Angeli.

Rossi, G. (2015). Italia-America Latina e il Forum Italo-Latinoamericano dei parlamenti. *Osservatorio di Politica Internazionale*, Approfondimenti, (108).

Rouquié, A. (2007). *L' America latina. Introduzione all'Estremo Occidente*. Milan: Bruno Mondadori.

Scarzanella, E. (2005). Il fascismo italiano in Argentina: al servizio degli affari. In E. Scarzanella (Ed.), *Fascisti in Sud America*. Florence: Le lettere.

Suárez-Orozco, C. (2004). Formulating identity in a globalized world. In M. Suárez-Orozco & D. B. Qin-Hilliard (Eds.), *Globalization: Culture and education in the new millennium* (pp. 173–202). Berkeley: University of California Press.

Trento, A. (2005). Dovunque è un italiano, là è il tricolore. La penetrazione del fascismo tra gli immigrati in Brasile. In E. Scarzanella (Ed.), *Fascisti in Sud America*. Florence: Le lettere.

Viola, F. (2015). Negotiation of identities and negotiation of values in multicultural societies. In M. C. La Barbera (Ed.), *Identity and migration in Europe: Multidisciplinary perspectives* (pp. 29–36). Berlino: Springer.

María J. García

Brexit, UK and Latin America

Introduction

Since independence, relations between Latin American republics and the UK have been characterised by private economic exchanges. The end of colonial monopolies afforded British traders an opportunity to trade and invest in a continent renowned for its mineral and agricultural wealth. The strong presence of British investment and commerce in the 19th century has led to descriptions of relations as part of an "informal empire" (Brown, 2008; Miller, 2014). Although the precise nature of such an informal empire has been contested (Thompson, 1992; Platt, 1968), the significance of the relationship, and the benefit that British investment brought to Latin American elites until the First World War is not disputed (Miller, 2014).

Latin America was a major destination for British industrial exports until the Second World War. As Victor Bulmer-Thomas (1999: 4) highlights, the complementarity between Britain's abundance of capital in The City and Latin America's mineral, resource and land wealth, laid the base for deepening economic ties. The irony, as he, and Platt (1968) point out, is that the economic relationship did not run deeper. Bulmer-Thomas (1999) argues this was due to a combination of mismanagement of mines and companies, leading to defaults on loans, and the impossibility for Latin American states to increase exports to the UK, given UK imperial preferences. The end of imperial preferences, and the UK's accession to the European Economic Community (EEC) in 1973, did not reverse this situation. Bulmer-Thomas's econometric analysis reveals the UK underperforming in trade with Latin America since the 1970s, and especially since the 1990s (1999: 18). An informal survey conducted by Chatham House in October 2021 revealed that insufficient local information, lack of contacts, UK focus on other regions, and misperceptions account for its underperformance. Together, the economies of Brazil, Mexico, Chile and Argentina accounted for just 0.9% of total UK service exports in 2020, with a value of £2.57 billion (Chatham House, 2021). Brexit provides an opportunity to reinvigorate the relationship, but as this chapter suggests, the urgent need to rearrange the relationship with the EU, focus on the US and Asia, and lack of a coherent Brexit foreign policy indicate that the relationship with Latin America will likely remain unchanged.

This chapter proceeds as follows. The second section comments on the UK's role within EU policies towards Latin America. The third section considers the UK's own policies towards Latin America prior to Brexit, with a focus on the Coalition Government's Canning House Agenda. The chapter proceeds to chart key aspects of the initial post-Brexit relationship, with a section explaining the trade challenges with Latin America presented by Brexit, and how these were mitigated. A final section locates Latin America within the context of the much-vaunted post-Brexit 'Global Britain' discourse. An analysis of documents and search for UK government documents on Latin America reveals that the profile of Latin America in UK foreign policy has not increased, and post-Brexit policies show little salience of the region. The chapter, thus, concludes that in the short to medium-term, significant changes in the UK's policies towards Latin America are unlikely.

UK within EU Latin American policies

Throughout the UK's membership of the EEC and EU (1973–2020), its policies towards Latin America were a combination of its own policies and those of the EU. In terms of political and cooperation relations at the EU level, the UK was a supporter and participant in the multiplicity of bi-regional institutionalised summits and dialogues that the EU established. The multiplicity of official channels for transatlantic relations have continued to flourish at the formal level, but their overall achievements have been modest due to the lack of monitoring and follow-up, and the heterogeneous interest of Latin American governments (Gratius, 2022). Leadership changes in Latin America, resulting in more left-leaning states and more internationally-oriented states, have complicated integration within Latin America stymieing the evolution of truly interregional relations (Gardini & Ayuso, 2015).

In combination with other geopolitical concerns like the growing importance of emerging countries, this has led to the simultaneous evolution of closer EU ties with specific states in Latin America (Santander, 2009), most notably the Strategic Partnerships with Brazil and Mexico. These partnerships are meant to foster greater economic cooperation and collaboration in political and security affairs. In Brazil's case, the key areas for cooperation are sustainability and energy security. However, the usefulness of these Strategic Partnerships has been criticised for lacking long-term strategy (Whitman & Rodt, 2012). Nonetheless, these do create additional bilateral summits and forums for discussions.

In terms of economic relations, it is the companies of individual EU states that trade and invest, and individual states engage in trade and investment promotion activities, including trade missions, ministerial visits, trade fairs, but the rules governing trade relations and policy are an EU prerogative. As an EU member, the UK supported an EU trade policy geared towards the promotion of greater liberalisation in trade and investment. EU trade policy towards Latin America is where the most obvious progress in the relationship has been made in the early decades of the 21st century, in line with that liberalising ethos.

Throughout these decades the EU has negotiated comprehensive preferential trade agreements (PTAs) with Mexico (2000), Chile (2003), Central American states (2012), Peru and Colombia (2013) and Ecuador (2017). It has also implemented an Economic Partnership Agreement with Caribbean states in CARIFORUM (2008) under the aegis of the EU's trade and development relationship with Africa, Caribbean and Pacific states as guided by the Cotonou Agreement of 2000. In July 2019, after 20 years of negotiations, the EU and MERCOSUR reached a political agreement on an Association Agreement. However, the agreement has not been ratified. Even though all EU member states represented in the Council of the EU agreed to the conclusion of the agreement, farmers' concerns over potential increases in imports from Brazil and Argentina, and environmental concerns regarding the Amazonian basin have led to delays on the EU side in the ratification process (Baltensperger & Dadusch, 2019).

These PTAs have been framed in the literature as defensive reactions to a USA shift towards the negotiation of bilateral trade agreements outside the WTO (Garcia, 2013; Meissner, 2018). The initial agreement with Mexico responded to the need to improve market access for EU firms after they lost 20% market share in Mexico following the entry into force of the North American Free Trade Agreement (NAFTA) (Barrau, 1999). Other partners in Latin America have also negotiated PTAs with the USA, helping to increase EU interest in negotiating with Central American and Andean states (Garcia, 2015). These agreements have, thus, been characterised by the pursuit of market access, but have also served to promote the economic agenda that the EU (and USA) were unable to pursue at the WTO due to developing states' opposition.

Successive UK governments have been proponents of such policies. It was under a British EU Commissioner for Trade, Peter Mandelson, that the European Commission launched its "Global Europe" trade strategy in 2006, emphasising the need to pursue bilateral trade agreements with growing markets, and with countries negotiating with key competitors (DG Trade 2016: 11). If anything, parts of the UK establishment felt frustrated by slow EU trade negotiations. Prime Minister David Cameron was a supporter of the controversial Transatlantic Trade and Investment Partnership negotiations between the EU and USA (2013–2016). Even as he renegotiated the terms of the UK's EU membership as the Brexit referendum neared in the Spring of 2016, he called for political courage to finalise TTIP, countering French President Hollande's objections to the deal (*The Guardian* 2016). During the Brexit referendum in 2016, the ability to conclude free trade agreements without the rest of the EU was heralded as a benefit of Brexit (Vote Leave, 2016), even though trade agreements with the rest of the world received very little attention during the campaigns. In this context, a foreign policy supportive of trade liberalisation could be expected to emerge post-Brexit.

UK Latin American policies pre-Brexit

At the national level, UK relations with Latin America focused on trade and investment, but have been complicated by geopolitics and security. Relations were particularly tense in 1982 during the Falklands-Malvinas war. The EEC, siding with the UK, imposed trade sanctions on Argentina, following UN Security Council Resolution 502 demanding a diplomatic resolution and the withdrawal of Argentine troops. Latin American states responded to Argentina's call for solidarity and condemnation of what it portrayed as a colonial struggle, even though many were no fans of the Argentine Junta government (Krepp, 2017: 352). Only Colombia and Chile took a more critical stance. In Chile's case, this included providing logistical support to UK forces, albeit covertly (Krepp, 2017: 353). Although the UK was victorious, the challenges posed by the status of the Islands continued (Beck, 2014). The presidencies of Néstor Kirchner and Cristina Fernández de Kirchner in Argentina in the 2000s and 2010s revived nationalist discourses regarding the Falklands-Malvinas, especially given the prospects of underwater oil resources. This reignited tensions with the UK, as Argentina sought to promote the notion that the islands should be under its sovereignty, encouraged its companies to boycott UK trade, and tried to discourage investment in the Islands (Dodds, 2012). This prompted a sovereignty referendum in the Falklands-Malvinas in March 2013, where 99.80% of the islanders voted to remain a UK overseas territory (Falklands Government, 2022). In spite of these tensions, the economic relationship between the UK and Latin American countries, including Argentina, has remained stable.

2010 was a key year in UK-Latin America relations. Attempting to reinvigorate the relationship and exploit economic opportunities, and aligning with EU negotiations of PTAs, the Conservative–Liberal Democrat coalition government (2010–2015) launched the Canning House Agenda, with a speech by the then Foreign Secretary, William Hague. This was part of efforts to strengthen relations with emerging powers (Diplomat, 2011), following the financial crisis of 2008 and reduced demand in Europe during the euro crisis.

In the speech, Hague (2010) acknowledged that the UK had tended to underestimate Latin America, and recognised they had been turning away from the region with the closure of four embassies in the late 1990s. He highlighted it was time "for Britain at last to think afresh about Latin America and the opportunities it presents for political cooperation and trade and investment". Although ecology, culture and activities in support of democracy were mentioned in passing, the speech extols the economic possibilities of the relationship. It highlights the desire for the UK to be the access point to Europe for Latin American companies as they commence to internationalise, and comments on the potential for economic growth in the region. Commentators at the time criticised the emphasis on economic exchanges and absence of strategy and partnership (Allen & Edwards, 2011). Hague's speech claimed the UK's decline in the region was over, and they would seek new opportunities for trade investment, lowering trade barriers, and for collaboration. At the time, any lowering of trade barriers would have to be achieved through the PTAs that the EU was negotiating with Latin American states. Increasing other opportunities through trade fairs, trade promotion, increased diplomatic activity could be achieved through unilateral UK actions.

The outcomes of the Canning House agenda have been modest. Diplomatic ties have strengthened, notably through increased ministerial visits. Politically, the UK has provided support to Colombia's government in the peace processes with the FARC. It has signed a Defence Cooperation Treaty with Brazil, initiated a defence dialogue, and has supported Brazil's bid for a permanent seat at the UN Security Council (Mills, 2018). The emphasis on Brazil, as a member of the BRICS and the largest economy in the region, is also evident in economic cooperation through the establishment of a UK-Brazil Financial Dialogue in 2015, mirroring the EU's trend of structured dialogues with Latin America. Nonetheless, the relevance of Latin America remained limited in terms of UK foreign policy. A search on the Government's website for policy papers and documents (2010–2015) relating to foreign policy strategies reveals that out of 143 documents, only five directly related to Latin America under the Coalition Government. One related to the Falkland Islanders' right to self-determination, three were broader documents on policies and funding for emerging countries in general (Emerging Powers Fund, 2012; Prosperity Fund, 2011, 2015 Government policy on UK prosperity and security in Asia, Latin America and Africa), and one related to the launch of the "Britain Open for Business" campaign in May 2011 by UK Trade and Invest.

In terms of trade, increased visibility and diplomatic support helped grow the economic relationship. Between 2010 and 2015 UK direct investment in Brazil more than doubled to £15 billion, and trade with Colombia grew to £1 billion by 2016 (Mills, 2018: 1395). Between 2010 and 2019 UK exports in goods and services to Latin America increased by 20% to a value of £18 billion (Canning House, 2020: 5). Exports of services improved by 42%, and increased trade was particularly noticeable with Brazil, Colombia and Peru (Canning House, 2020: 5). The former is the largest economy in the region, and where the UK placed the greatest focus, and the latter two experienced increased trade with all EU countries, as a consequence of the 2012 trade agreement.

However, as with the rest of the EU, despite an increase in the value of trade, the relative importance as a trade partner for Latin American states has waned. The UK's share of Latin American imports was low in 2010 at 1.1% and declined further to 0.7% by 2018, and the UK accounts for just 1% of Latin American exports (Canning House, 2020: 5). The UK lags behind other European countries like Germany and France who account for 4 and 1.6% of Latin America's imports, respectively (BFPG, 2018: 7). As can be seen in Table 5.1, the major export market for the UK is Europe, followed by North America and East Asia and the Pacific. In context, it is evident that the economic relationship with Latin America pales in significance with other parts of the world.

Table 5.1: Percentage share of UK export markets

	2010	**2012**	**2014**	**2016**
Latin America & Caribbean	2	3.3	1.9	1.9
Europe & Central Asia	60.5	56.9	58.5	56
North America	15.7	15	13.9	16.5
East Asia and the Pacific	10.8	13.2	14.3	14
Middle East & North Africa	5.5	5.4	6.1	6.6
Sub-Saharan Africa	2.7	3	2.2	1.8
South Asia	1.8	1.8	1.5	1.4

Adapted by the author from BFPG, 2018: 7

A key reason for the relative decline in significance, despite increased trade, is the growing presence of other states, especially China, as trade partners for Latin America. In terms of investment, the UK remains one of the top 10 investors in Latin America, representing 10% of total investment in 2015, although this is far less than the USA's 32% or EU's 40% (Mills, 2018: 1396). In an informal survey of business leaders and commercial attachés, Chatham House (2021) suggested that there remains much room for growth in the UK-Latin American trade relationship, especially as Brazil accounted for only 0.4% of UK services exports in 2020, and Mexico, Chile and Argentina accounted for just 0.3%, 0.1% and 0.1%, respectively. Their respondents pointed to lack of familiarity with the markets, regulations and contacts, misconceptions of the region, as well as the UK's traditional focus on other emerging markets, notably in Asia, as the key reasons behind the underperformance of the relationship.

The Canning House agenda was meant to address these hurdles. However, despite the new opportunities created by it and the PTAs, the relationship between the UK and Latin America has largely remained unchanged. Progress has been stymied by the challenges in the relationship throughout the 20th century, namely, "the decline in Britain's economic competitiveness; the challenges posed by the role of other external powers in the region; the significance granted to Latin America in Britain's global strategic priorities; and the difficulties encountered in responding to the political character and ambitions of Latin American governments" (Mills, 2018: 1393).

Trade continuation agreements: Brexit and the need to recast relations with Latin America

Although it has not been a panacea, the Canning House agenda has formally continued throughout the Brexit process. A search on the Government's website for policy documents mentioning Latin America between 2016 and 2022 reveals Latin America remains a lower priority in UK policy. Nonetheless, of the documents that stand out, two are general ones (Board of Trade report: Britain, local jobs March 2021 and Global Britain in a Competitive Age: Integrated Review of Security, Defence, Development in Foreign Policy July 2021), and a series of others relate to annual reviews of the programmes implemented in the Americas within the Conflict, Stability and Security Fund.[1] In contrast to the Coalition

1 A similar search of the Foreign, Commonwealth and Development Office (FCDO) database revealed 123 policy papers, including those related to Latin America, among

era, a series of documents specific to Latin America can be identified. These are on the Colombia-UK Partnership for Sustainable Growth (climate), Brazil-UK Financial Dialogue, and parliamentary reports on continuing the UK's trade relationship with various Latin American countries. Brexit meant that the UK also ceased to be a party to the various PTAs that the EU had negotiated with Latin American states. A newly created UK Department for International Trade, set to work on the urgent task of ensuring trade continuity with states linked to the EU through PTAs to limit uncertainty for businesses.

The complex and lengthy negotiation between the UK and EU on the terms of their future relationship, limited the scope for negotiations with other parties. Moreover, the resources required to negotiate also put pressure on UK resources. For these reasons, a pragmatic approach was taken for trade agreements with other countries, where the aim was to prevent a deterioration in the terms of trade, by ensuring that the existing agreement could continue to operate beyond Brexit day, at least for an initial period. Because the aim was to adapt existing agreements, these are commonly referred to as "rolled-over" agreements. Upon the realisation that this would be necessary, the UK commenced economic dialogues with various Latin American states, a key remit of which was to ensure trade continuation agreements.

PTAs with Latin American states were rolled over ahead of the 31 December 2020 deadline, when the EU agreements would cease to apply to the UK. These agreements changed references to the EU and EU agencies for references to the UK, clarified the territorial application, changed the list of geographic indicators (GIs) to a shorter list that only includes UK GIs. The biggest changes relate to tariff-rate-quotas (TRQs) for goods. TRQs had to be renegotiated, as the UK is a smaller market than the EU. Negotiations for rolled-over agreements started in 2017, and the UK had a self-imposed deadline of two years to complete these (to coincide with the initial estimated time of Brexit).

Chile was the first country to agree a rolled-over agreement in February 2019. In the negotiations, new UK TRQs of 16.66% of the EU quota were agreed, except for poultry where Chile managed to extract a TRQ of 55.6% of the EU quota (Gobierno de Chile, 2022). They also agreed to roll-over the agreement on organic products between the EU and Chile. The UK also signed rolled-over agreements with the countries of the Andean Community and Central American states. It signed individual bilateral agreements with these; nonetheless,

---

other regions. These covered themes such as social investment, corruption, education (including Newton Fund), healthcare systems, pensions and climate.

the negotiations were conducted simultaneously as these derived from a single text with the EU. These agreements maintained the rights and obligations and the timelines for tariff reduction established in the agreements with the EU and adapted TRQs in a proportional manner.

More complicated was the case of Mexico, which at the time of Brexit negotiations and "roll-over" agreement negotiations was negotiating a modernisation of the 1997 Global Trade Agreement with the EU. As the first Latin American country to negotiate a PTA with the EU, Mexico's agreement is less encompassing in scope. In August 2019, the UK and Mexico signed a UK-Mexico Alliance for Sustainable and Inclusive Growth, agreeing that their economic cooperation and negotiations should be guided by these principles. This agreement was rolled over *in extremis* in December 2020 to avoid a disruption in terms of trade and was accompanied by a compromise to begin negotiations for a new and modernised PTA as soon as possible in 2021. The aim is to finalise it no later than within three years, with an agreement that the new agreement would be at least as liberalising as the EU-Mexico modernised agreement (Gobierno de Mexico, 2020).[2] At the end of March 2022, it was expected that negotiations would commence soon (House of Commons Library, 2022).

An important element of the "rolled-over" agreements is that, while they aim to maintain the status quo as much as possible, there are small but significant changes. Under the Rules of Origin (RoO), cumulation of EU inputs into UK products allows for EU components not to count as non-originating content, provided the final transformation is carried out in the UK. This is beneficial to UK producers and exporters. However, as the EU has tighter conditions for products to count as originating in the UK in its RoO with the UK, UK manufacturers who previously could use content from countries with PTAs with the EU without affecting the origin will no longer be able to do so (Vines et al., 2019: 25). These changes will affect companies in different ways depending on their supply chains and availability of alternative suppliers and will become apparent over the longer term, as businesses adjust.

Trade negotiations and economic dialogues have become a critical part of the UK's policy towards Latin America post-Brexit. This is due to the immediate challenges presented by Brexit with regards to trade between the UK (and EU) and the rest of the world. Agreements based on existing texts with the EU will

2 In the continuity agreement, the parties agreed to only partial access to government procurement markets (for certain procurements in the case of Mexico), and the UK agreed to extend access only until the end of 2021.

require renegotiation in the future, at least of certain sections, if the UK deviates from the EU regulations and standards that it has inherited from its EU membership. Given this reality, trade negotiations and the economic relationship will remain a critically important aspect of the relationship. The prioritisation of economic matters continues the trajectory delineated in the Canning House Agenda, as well as the free-trading tropes promulgated by the Brexiteers, who eventually gained a parliamentary majority in the December 2019 election in the UK, and which have been incorporated in the initial post-Brexit foreign policies, as highlighted in the following section.

"The more things change": Global Britain and the future of UK-Latin America relations

The outcome of the UK's 2016 referendum on Brexit and Prime Minister Cameron's resignation led the way to Prime Minister Theresa May's government, hamstrung by a hung Parliament with an unclear mandate for Brexit following the 2017 national election. Prime Minister May set about trying to define Brexit and started to clarify a vision steered towards a full withdrawal from the EU's single market. May's Government coalesced around a diffuse idea of a "Global Britain" seeking business opportunities as a way of giving Brexit a meaning that would be acceptable to the variety of positions even within the ruling Conservative Party (Zapettini, 2019).

"Global Britain" was a response to the loss of influence through the EU. It was a signal that Britain "continue[d] to be open, inclusive and outward-facing; free trading; assertive in standing up for British interests and values; and resolute in boosting our international standing and influence. It is a Britain with a global presence, active in every region; global interests, working with our allies and partners to deliver the global security and prosperity that ensures our own; and global perspectives, engaging with the world in every area, influencing and being influenced" (FCO, 2018: 7). Although it referred to being active in every region, the memorandum outlining the policy placed emphasis on the EU (not least given the need to negotiate Brexit), the USA, and the Indo-Pacific, including China. It also outlined the importance of ties to the Commonwealth. The memorandum already showed signs that Latin America would remain at the bottom of UK foreign policy priorities.

Oppermann et al. (2020: 135) argue that the UK has tried since 2016 to avoid being cast as an isolationist in the international community by positioning itself as a global trading state, a great power, a loyal ally to the USA, a regional ally to the EU and a leader of the Commonwealth. Nonetheless, these differing roles and interpretations of what Brexit meant can create conflicting aims and run the risk of leading to unclear policies. Gaskarth and Langdon's (2021: 172) analysis of House of Commons debates since 2016 finds a "technocratic discussion legitimised with reference to the dominant tradition of pragmatism", which facilitated compromises but marginalised questions of ideology, identity and future policy, helping to crystallise a particular vision of post-Brexit foreign policy, centred around an open, free-trading Global Britain agenda, which diverges from the domestic character of the Brexit referendum.

The aims of "Global Britain" contrast with a reality in which the UK is forced to concentrate more on Europe while its global influence dwindles (Major & von Ondarza, 2018: 7). Moreover, as Wright (2017) highlights, Brexit entails risks to the UK's international reputation and credibility as a responsible member of the international community. The controversy and unilateral attempts to change the Northern Ireland Protocol in the Withdrawal Agreement with the EU have instigated concerns over the UK's credibility as an international partner. The strong rhetoric, inherited from the referendum campaign, around regaining sovereignty and independence of action also clash with the reality of new and "rolled-over" trade agreements, as all trade agreements constrain sovereignty. This is all the more the case in modern agreements, like the Comprehensive and Progressive Trans-Pacific Partnership (CPTPP) which the UK hopes to join, which include rules on intellectual property rights, investor-state dispute settlement mechanisms that can constrain domestic policy space (Dallingwater, 2021).

Brexit and the "Global Britain" agenda present opportunities for enhanced relations, as indeed Brazilian and Colombian Ambassadors to the UK enthusiastically highlighted (Mills, 2018: 1398). The need to secure "rolled-over" agreements and new trading opportunities has led to increased visits to Latin America, including Boris Johnson's as Foreign Secretary and PM May's trip to Argentina for the G20 summit in 2018. DIT, as part of its efforts to forge closer trade ties with other parts of the world, created nine positions of Trade Commissioners in early 2018 to work with Ambassadors and Government to coordinate and promote UK trade abroad. One of these was dedicated to Latin America. It is undeniable that in terms of trade, Latin America is firmly on the UK policy radar, as the various economic dialogues and negotiations confirm. DIT's establishment of a Latin American and Caribbean Investors Club, grouping 200 investors from the region with a view to providing a single channel for support for their investments in the UK, is further evidence of this (DIT, 2019).

However, the reality of resource constraints and the necessity to maintain close relations with Europe meant that, despite the rhetoric of "Global Britain" in 2017, diplomatic resources were reallocated from Latin America, Asia and Africa to increase UK's diplomatic presence in Europe (Mills, 2018: 1399). From a more fundamental and strategic perspective, Latin America barely gets a mention in the 2021 Integrated Review of Defence, Development, Security and Foreign Policy, which sets out the objectives of the next phase of UK post-Brexit foreign policy. The 110 pages of the Integrated Review mention Latin America on three occasions. One mention appears alongside Asia in reference to fighting poverty globally (UK Government, 2021: 27). There is a paragraph specifically on Latin America (which contains the other two references), and it reaffirms existing policies towards the region: namely, partnerships on issues like biodiversity, sustainable growth, and fostering ties with Brazil and Mexico on trade, innovation, climate change, security and development, as well as working with Argentina, Chile and Colombia (UK Government, 2021: 64). There is also a mention of defending the UK's interests in the Falklands and South Georgia (UK Government 2021: 64). By contrast, the Review clearly signals the Indo-Pacific as an area of increased activity, including through the UK's accession to CPTPP, as well as the alliance with the USA, collaboration with the EU and the Commonwealth.

In practice, once again, Latin America appears at the bottom of UK foreign policy priorities. A number of Latin American states are members of CPTPP (Mexico, Colombia, Chile), and if the UK accedes to CPTPP, trade between these could be enhanced, although the UK has PTAs with all three already. The UK will also need these states' support to join, so stronger diplomatic activity with these countries is likely. Notwithstanding this, it is evident that, for now, the UK has not crafted a long-term strategic policy towards Latin America. Instead, Latin America appears to be one geographic component of broader thematic policies (e.g. climate, development, trade opportunities). The UK's tradition of pragmatism in foreign policy and the necessity to be pragmatic given the challenges of Brexit are likely to prolong this approach.

Conclusion

Brexit created a rupture in UK foreign policy trajectories. It created an opportunity and need for the UK to recast itself as an international actor. However, the polarisation of views on foreign policy and on the relationship with the EU, challenging Parliamentary arithmetic following the 2017 national election, led to certain views being crystalised. Some emerged from the referendum (full separation from the EU, regaining sovereignty), others harked back to historical myths about the UK as a global advocate of free trade, leader of the Commonwealth and the Anglosphere (Kenny & Pearce, 2016). The election of a majority Conservative government led by Boris Johnson at the end of 2019, facilitated the passage of a Withdrawal Agreement from the EU that encapsulated the Brexit ideas of independence from the EU's single market. "Global Britain" as a foreign policy ambition to retain UK global influence presented a diffuse concept, and one challenging to operationalise in practice given resource constraints, and the immediate post-Brexit urgency to negotiate a future relationship with the EU.

Latin America has gained more visibility in post-Brexit UK policies, not least given the numerous economic dialogues established to try to capture opportunities, mitigate the losses incurred through Brexit, and the necessary negotiations to "roll over" various EU PTAs that ceased to apply to the UK upon Brexit. However, the region remains practically absent from high-level policies like the Integrated Review. This signals a continuation of UK policies towards Latin America from the 20th and early decades of the 21st century when even the concerted efforts of the Canning House agenda to enhance the profile of the region and economic ties led to modest outcomes. As the UK finds its way in a post-Brexit world, its emphasis on Latin America and policies may change. However, the early years of Brexit show a continuation with past policies rather than a rupture. The emergence of new pressing challenges in the international arena (e.g. trade disruptions due to Covid-19 and economic recessions, China's economic status, war in Ukraine and NATO-Russia tension) are likely to keep Latin America as an area of low priority in UK foreign policy, supporting the adage "the more things change, the more they stay the same".

Bibliography

Allen, L., & Edwards, G. (2011). UK-Latin America: Rearranging the deckchairs. *The World Today, 67*(3), 29–31.

Baltensperger, M., & Dadush, U. (2019). *The European Union-Mercosur free trade agreement: Prospects and risks*, Bruegel Policy Contribution, No. 2019/11, Bruegel, Brussels. https://www.econstor.eu/bitstream/10419/237634/1/1687136467.pdf (accessed 15 January 2022).

Barrau, A. (1999). *Union Européene et Mercosur: Marriage ou Union Libre? Rio, 28–29 Juin 1999*. Les documents d'information Assamblée Nationale Délègation pour L'Union européenne. Rapport d'information no. 1721. Paris.

Beck, P. J. (2014). *The Falkland Islands as an international problem (Routledge revivals)*. Abingdon: Routledge.

BFPG. (2018). *Revitalising UK-Latin American engagement post-Brexit*. November 2018, https://bfpg.co.uk/wp-content/uploads/2018/11/BFPG-LATIN-AMERICA-NOV-2018.pdf (accessed 20 November 2021).

Canning House. (2020). *The Canning House agenda-10 years on*. https://www.canninghouse.org/canning-insights/the-canning-agenda-10-years-on (accessed 20 November 2021).

Chatham House. (2021). *Room to grow*. https://www.chathamhouse.org/2021/10/uk-latin-america-trade-room-grow (accessed 30 March 2022).

Dallingwater, L. (2021). *Britain's post Brexit trade deals: Taking back control or a threat to sovereignty?*, Angles, 13/2021.

DG Trade. (2006). *Global Europe: Competing in the world*, COM(2006)567, https://eur-lex.europa.eu/LexUriServ/LexUriServ.do?uri=COM:2006:0567:FIN:en:PDF (accessed 25 September 2021).

DIT. (2018). *New HM trade commissioners announced news release*, 3 April 2018, https://www.gov.uk/government/news/new-hm-trade-commissioners-announced (accessed 12 April 2022).

DIT. (2019). *DIT launches LAC investors club news release* 2 April 2019, https://www.gov.uk/government/news/department-for-international-trade-supports-latin-american-and-caribbean-investors (accessed 15 January 2022).

Dodds, K. (2012). Stormy waters: Britain, the Falkland Islands and UK–Argentine relations. *International Affairs, 88*(4), 683–700.

Falklands Government. (2022). *Falklands government website-our history*, https://www.falklands.gov.fk/our-history (accessed 20 September 2021).

FCO. (2018). *Global Britain memorandum from the Foreign and Commonwealth Office*, https://publications.parliament.uk/pa/cm201719/cmselect/cmfaff/780/78008.htm#_idTextAnchor035 (accessed 10 March 2022).

Garcia, M. (2013). From idealism to realism? EU preferential trade agreement policy. *Journal of Contemporary European Research, 9*(4), 521–541.

García, M. (2015). The European Union and Latin America: "Transformative power Europe" versus the realities of economic interests. *Cambridge Review of International Affairs, 28*(4), 621–640.

Gardini, G. L., & Ayuso, A. (2015). EU-Latin America and Caribbean Inter-regional relations: Complexity and change. *Atlantic Future Working Paper, 24*, 1–24.

Gaskarth, J., & Langdon, N. (2021). The dilemma of Brexit: Hard choices in the narrow context of British foreign policy traditions. *British Politics, 16*(2), 170–186.

Gobierno de Chile. (2022). *Acuerdo de asociación entre Chile y Reino Unido*, https://www.subrei.gob.cl/acuerdos-comerciales/acuerdos-comerciales-vigentes/reino-unido/ (accessed 12 April 2022).

Gobierno de Mexico. (2020). *Comunicado Conjunto. México y Reino Unido firman el Acuerdo de Continuidad Comercial México-Reino Unido*, 15 December 2020. https://embamex.sre.gob.mx/reinounido/index.php/es/masavisos/1813-mexico-y-reino-unido-firman-el-acuerdo-de-continuidad-comercial-mexico-reino-unido (accessed 12 April 2022).

Gratius, S. (2022). EU–LAC: A relationship beyond trade: Political dialogues between unequal partners. In M. Garcia & A. Gomez-Arana (Eds.), *Latin America–European Union relations in the twenty-first century* (pp. 24–43). Manchester: Manchester University Press.

Hague, W. (2010). *Canning House Lecture*, 9 November 2010, https://www.gov.uk/government/speeches/britain-and-latin-america-historic-friends-future-partners (accessed 10 November 2021).

House of Commons Library. (2022). *Research briefing. Progress on UK free trade agreement negotiations*. https://commonslibrary.parliament.uk/research-briefings/cbp-9314/ (accessed 12 April 2022).

Kenny, M., & Pearce, N. (2016). After Brexit: The Eurosceptic dream of an Anglosphere. *Juncture, 22*(4), 304–307.

Krepp, S. (2017). A view from the South: The Falklands/Malvinas and Latin America. *Journal of Transatlantic Studies, 15*(4), 348–365.

Meissner, K. L. (2018). *Commercial realism and EU trade policy: Competing for economic power in Asia and the Americas*. Abingdon: Routledge.

Miller, R. (2014). *Britain and Latin America in the 19th and 20th centuries*. Abingdon: Routledge.

Mills, T. C. (2018). British foreign policy towards Latin America in the twenty-first century: Assessing the "Canning Agenda". *International Affairs, 94*(6), 1391–1408.

Oppermann, K., Beasley, R., & Kaarbo, J. (2020). British foreign policy after Brexit: Losing Europe and finding a role. *International Relations, 34*(2), 133–156.

Santander, S. (2009). EU-LAC relations: From interregionalism to selective bilateralism? In C. Franck, J. C. Defraigne, & V. de Monriamé (Eds.), *The European Union and the rise of regionalism: Source of inspiration and active promoter* (pp. 263–272). Brussels: Bruylant.

The Guardian. (2016). *David Cameron calls for political courage to seal TTIP deal*, 4 May 2016, https://www.theguardian.com/business/2016/may/04/david-cameron-political-courage-ttip-trade-deal (accessed 12 March 2022).

The Independent. (2018). *Boris Johnson first foreign secretary to visit Argentina in 25 years* (Peru, Chile, Argentina), 9 May 2018, https://www.independent.

co.uk/news/uk/politics/boris-johnson-argentina-visit-first-foreign-secretary-25-years-falklands-brexit-a8359376.html (accessed 18 January 2022).

UK Government. (2021). *The integrated review 2021*, https://www.gov.uk/government/collections/the-integrated-review-2021 (accessed 15 January 2022).

UK Government. (2022). *UK trade agreements*. https://www.gov.uk/guidance/uk-trade-agreements-with-non-eu-countries (accessed 12 April 2022).

Vines, D., Gretton, P., & Williamson, A. (2019). Developing trade. *National Institute Economic Rveiew*, N. 250, R2, https://www.rhysmichaelbidder-economist.com/_files/ugd/6143e8_b5b31a20dbae44ab9d08459385580eb5.pdf#page=23 (accessed 10 April 2022).

Vote Leave. (2016). *Why vote leave. Vote Leave*. http://www.voteleavetakecontrol.org/why_vote_leave.html (accessed 12 March 2022).

Whitman, R. G., & Rodt, A. P. (2012). EU-Brazil relations: A strategic partnership?. *European Foreign Affairs Review, 17*(1), 27–44.

Wright, N. (2017). *Brexit & the re-making of British foreign policy*. UCL European Institute, Working Paper. https://discovery.ucl.ac.uk/id/eprint/10082216/1/WP_Wright_ForeignPolicy.pdf (accessed 16 February 2022).

Zappettini, F. (2019). The official vision for "global Britain" Brexit as rupture and continuity between free trade, liberal internationalism and "values." In V. Koller, S. Kopf, & M. Milgbauer (Eds.), *Discourses of Brexit* (pp. 140–154). Abindon: Routledge.

Elena Lazarou and Diego Ponce

Brazil-EU Relations: Driver, Enabler or Negotiator for Interregionalism?

Introduction: EU-Brazil relations across history

Despite historically strong bilateral ties with individual EU member states, Brazil did not harbour strong ties with the EU's precursors, the European Communities. Since the 1960s, diplomatic relations have been maintained between the Communities and Brazil, with examples including the cooperation agreement between EURATOM and Brazil, a diplomatic mission to Brussels and commercial agreements throughout the 1970s. Yet, during this time, Brazil ranked as a low priority on the European agenda (Lazarou, 2011). For instance, the European Economic Community (EEC) and Brazil's 1974 economic and commercial cooperation agreement governed economic relations between the parties. As integration in the EEC deepened towards the single market, Euro-Brazilian relations were marked by "relative indifference" (Ferreira-Pereira, 2015). This gradually started to change following the Iberian enlargement in 1986, which saw relations with Latin America assume a more important place on the EEC's map of the world. As of the early 1990s, and as the EU began to construct its foreign policy and sought to position itself as a global actor, activity with Brazil intensified, first through interregional relations, and later through attempts to forge a tailored bilateral partnership.

The past two decades offer themselves for the study of the ebbs and flows of the EU-Brazil relationship. Among the questions to pose is the degree to which Brazil, representing over 50% of South America's GDP and population, has been an enabler of relations between the EU and the region as a whole. An overview of European expert perceptions of Brazil reveals that the assessment of Brazil's role in the interregional relation has varied across the years and correlated with changes in the Brazilian political setting, most importantly, the succession in the Brazilian presidency (Reisdorfer & Mattos, 2021). During the Lula era, for example, Brazil was viewed by Europeans as cooperative and moderately reformist. It was thus seen as a potential mediator in Latin America capable of stabilising the region, engaging with regional crises (for example Venezuela), and promoting regional integration (Reisdorfer & Mattos, 2021). Some German think-tanks referred to it as an "ordering power" (Ordnungsmacht) in the region

(Reisdorfer & Mattos, 2021: 25). As a partner, Brazil was thus increasingly seen as an asset in promoting European interests in Latin America.

By 2019, this view of Brazil had radically transformed to one of a "power of chaos" (regionale chaosmacht) – alluding to the chaotic foreign policy of President Jair Bolsonaro and the subsequent loss of trust from the EU side (Reisdorfer & Mattos, 2021: 32). Brazil's international standing has been weakened by Bolsonaro's efforts to use international relations as a distraction in domestic politics with commensurate effects on relations with the EU. The next sections look at the recent history of EU-Brazil relations, initially exploring the interregional and bilateral dimensions of engagement. They then proceed to assess the degree to which Brazil may have contributed to the promotion of the EU's relations with the wider (South American) region during three distinct phases coinciding with the Lula and Rousseff presidencies and the right-wing administrations of Temer and Bolsonaro. The chapter concludes with some final thoughts on Brazil's role in interregional cooperation.

From interregional to bilateral relations

Interregionalism, in the form of bilateral engagement between the EU and other regions, groupings of states or regional organisations, has been viewed as a vehicle for the EU to diffuse its own norms and values, such as the rule of law, democracy and human rights, as well as its own model of cooperation and integration (Torrent, 2002). It is also a way to engage other regions in the EU's stated aim to strengthen global governance based on multilateralism (Lazarou, 2011).

The institutionalization of interregional relations at the EU and Latin American level was marked by the first EU – Latin American and Caribbean (LAC) Summit in Rio de Janeiro in 1999. With the joint Declaration and Program of Action adopted by the Conference, the EU-LAC strategic partnership was founded on the basis of common history and common values. In the same year, the EU and Mercosur (the Common Market of the South, with Argentina, Brazil, Paraguay and Uruguay as members) began negotiating a comprehensive interregional partnership, including a free trade agreement. The launch of negotiations for an Association Agreement, with two components – political and trade agreement – followed the signature of the 1995 Interregional Framework Cooperation Agreement.

Meissner (2018) points to the fact that in its interregional engagement, the EU consciously chose Mercosur as a promising interlocutor, given Mercosur's relatively high level of institutional cohesion from 1997 to 2003, with regard to the settlement of disputes, establishment of institutions, and in the group's external dimension. During this time, trade between Mercosur and European countries had also increased (Meissner 2015: 5). However, in the face of gradually decreasing Mercosur institutional activity and cohesion, the EU pivoted to more bilateral engagement with Brazil as of 2004 (Meissner, 2018: 58). Notwithstanding setbacks in matters of regional integration during this period, Mercosur integration was increasingly seen in Brasília as a means to bolster Brazilian regional leadership. Brazil sought not only an economic relationship in a common market and customs union, but also to emulate EU institutions to a degree, including a Mercosur parliament (Lazarou, 2013). Consequently, the interregional engagement observed and the EU's "model power" projected through this engagement aligned with some of the foreign policy objectives of the Lula government. The strengthening of Mercosur and the deepening of its ties with the EU would thus satisfy both EU and Brazilian visions of the region.

In 2004, however, EU-Mercosur negotiations stalled, reaching a deadlock most notably on the trade front. They would be revived only after the global financial crisis that set on in 2008. Interestingly, it was during this time that the EU reached out to Brazil to establish a bilateral Strategic Partnership.

Conceptualised by the EU as an instrument of a bilateral nature but in support of effective multilateralism, strategic partnerships (SP) constituted a channel of EU engagement with major international actors in the aftermath of the 2003 European Security Strategy. In Brazil's case, in particular, the Commission's proposal to launch an SP went hand in hand with the perception of the country as a key interlocutor for the whole region. In the very first paragraph of its communication "Towards an EU-Brazil Strategic Partnership", which set the scene and the argument for such a step, the Commission referred to Brazil as having become "an increasingly significant global player and emerged as a key interlocutor for the EU" and a "natural leader in South America" due to its geographic, economic and diplomatic heft. It also explicitly stated that EU-Brazil dialogue had not been sufficiently exploited and had been carried out mainly through EU-Mercosur dialogue, confirming the interregional approach (European Commission, 2007: 1). The Commission concluded that "the time had come to look at Brazil as a strategic partner as well as a major Latin American economic actor and regional leader" confirming the shift in approach to bilateral engagement, but also the intrinsic link between its planned deepening of ties with Brazil as a part of an EU vision for the region (European Commission, 2007: 1). The communication recognised Brazil's regional leadership, calling on continued engagement with Brazil in the EU-LAC Forum on Social Cohesion and in international organizations. The EU also expressed the intention to exchange experiences of regional integration with Brazil and expected Brazil to aid in the completion of the ongoing EU-Mercosur agreement in addition to taking leadership in Mercosur's political and economic integration. It specifically encouraged Brazil to reduce tariff and non-tariff barriers and to promote economic reform, and saw the SP as an opportunity for dialogue on intellectual property, industrial policy and regulatory issues, including a regular macro-economic dialogue. On those latter issues, the communication explicitly posited that the EU-Brazil SP would complement and feed into the EU-Mercosur discussions.

Bilaterally, it highlighted the alignment of interests and core values with respect to human rights, rule of law, climate change, the pursuit of economic growth, and justice. Regarding the aims of the SP, the Commission began with setting a common agenda between Brazil and the EU to strengthen multilateralism. This would include checking in ahead of UN meetings to converge positions, cooperating in peacekeeping efforts (Haiti), developing the non-proliferation regime, and engaging in the WTO. Thereafter came provisions with respect to human rights, democracy, and governance, according to which Brazil and the EU would jointly advocate human rights initiatives at UN bodies. The environmental clauses called for increased dialogue on environmental policy, including international aid for renewable energy priorities, together with the EC-Brazil Energy Policy Dialogue, which began in 2007.

While the communication foreshadowed that the defining mechanism of the partnership would be the increase of bilateral dialogues on a variety of fronts (on social issues, regional policy, employment, environmental protection, energy, human rights, trade and economic relations, financial issues, information and communication technologies, maritime governance, and science and technology), the expected – or desired – effect of "regionalization" of cooperation is – at least discursively – quite discernible. Partnership with Brazil is framed as a road to engagement and alignment with South America and to a lesser extent Latin America. On the security front, a regional dimension is also envisioned: transnational threats (namely crime, corruption, drug trafficking, and migration) are the SP's main security-related threats. To meet them, the SP suggests the promotion of "regional multidisciplinary law enforcement cooperation" (European Commission, 2007: 13).

The two parties officially launched the SP on the first EU-Brazil Summit on 4 July 2007. Institutionally, it established annual summits between Brazil and the EU – which took place between 2007 and 2014. Two Joint Action Plans (2008–2011; 2012–2014) were elaborated but as of 2015 no summits or action plans materialised.

The agreement equally placed emphasis on the role of the bilateral relationship in the EU's engagement with the region and on the promotion of regional integration through Brazil's role in the region. According to the joint statement issued at the Summit, the EU and Brazil "attach high importance to strengthening EU-Mercosur relations and are committed to concluding the EU-Mercosur Association Agreement, which will further deepen region-to-region economic relations as well as enhance the political dialogue and cooperation initiatives" (European Council, 2007: 2). They stress the great economic and political importance that this agreement will have for both regions and its role in reinforcing their integration processes. Equally, the statement reaffirmed the commitment to strengthen the bi-regional EU-LAC process.

A series of reasons for the EU's choice of timing and content for an SP with Brazil have been enumerated. First, the international setting, in which the world was seen to be increasingly multipolar, with the main threats being transnational, as laid out in the 2003 European Security Strategy. The second is linked to Brazil being seen as an emerging power, especially considering Lula's activist foreign policy (Ferreira-Pereira, 2015; Lazarou, 2017; Ferreira-Pereira, 2021). The third attributed the decision to the stalled negotiations in the EU-Mercosur Accession Agreement and general divisions inside Mercosur. In that context, Brazil was seen as a reliable partner to use as an anchor in the region. In this sense, the move has either been labeled as a "resort to bilateralism" (Meissner, 2018) or as a pivot to "realist bilateralism" (Gratius, 2017). The fourth explanation has to do with stated "shared values", namely, multilateralism, democracy, and human rights. In practice, however, the literature shows that EU and Brazilian positions rarely converged on these matters (Pavese, 2014; Saraiva & Gomes, 2016). Fifth, the strategic partnership served to project Brazil and the EU as international actors (Ferreira-Pereira, 2015; Santander, 2016). Lastly, the agency is attributed to José Manuel Durão Barroso, at the time presiding the EU Commission (Saraiva, 2017; Ferreira-Pereira, 2021). Regardless of the explanation, the texts analysed above suggest that considerations of the role of Brazil as an enabler of EU relations with the region played an important role.

The foreign policy of Brazilian Presidents and its impact on the role of Brazil in the EU's relations with the region

The signature of the EU-Brazil strategic partnership coincided with a specific period in the history of Brazilian politics and, most importantly for the purposes of this chapter, of Brazilian foreign policy. Under President Lula, Brazil's international activism, designation as an emerging power and aspiration to exercise – discrete – leadership in the region became trademarks of Brazil's engagement with the world. It can be argued that the text of the EU-Brazil strategic partnership reflects a perception of Brazil that matches Lula's project. But the potential of the partnership to deliver would, among other factors, depend on the continuity of Brazilian foreign policy, including with regard to regional cooperation. This section explores the foreign policy of Brazilian presidents during the past two decades, in order to assess the degree to which the assumption that Brazil would leverage EU relations with South America and Latin America materialised.

Luis Inácio da Silva (Lula): 2003–2010

Brazil's increased international activism under Lula was a conduit for the strategic partnership. Ferreira-Pereira (2021: 156) describes the era as "an exceptionally non-conformist, counter-hegemonic, proactive and resourceful phase of presidential diplomacy, which saw the emergence of a Brazilian self-image marked by self-esteem and self-assurance, both regionally and on the international stage". Lula's foreign policy has also been characterised as "autonomy through diversification", by building bridges with a diverse set of countries, as Lula's foreign policy projection was marked by the defense of national sovereignty and seeking privileged alliances in the Global South (Vigevani & Cepaluni, 2007: 1).

Domestically, Brazil enjoyed an economic boom from increased commodity demand between 2003 and 2011. The country was praised for its poverty reduction programmes, and the 2008 financial crisis reached the Brazilian shores only marginally and belatedly. Internationally, the main achievements of the Lula era include the institutionalised coordination of global south countries such as in the WTO, BRICS and IBSA dialogues, the inauguration of a peacekeeping mission in Haiti, UNSC ambitions, and the mediator role in the Iran nuclear crisis. In addition to that signed with the EU, Lula concluded strategic partnerships with Japan, China, India, and South Africa. Brazil also increased humanitarian assistance to entities such as the UNDP, UNHCR, the WFP, the World Bank, and bilaterally, with Lusophone African countries, through Brazil's cooperation agency.

Regionally, Lula's presidential diplomacy was crucial in forging close ties with left-leaning South American presidents in Argentina, Uruguay, Venezuela and Bolivia (Carson & Power, 2009). The EU's choice to engage interregionally with Mercosur occurred in tandem with Brazil's investment in Mercosur during the Lula era. Indeed, during the first decade of the 21st century, Mercosur integration was increasingly seen in Brasília as a means to bolster Brazilian regional leadership. In a 2010 piece, Brazilian Foreign Minister at the time, Celso Amorim, recognised that working with regional partners made Brazil stronger and more influential globally and would contribute to growth and stability and increase overall South American bargaining power (Amorim, 2010: 227).

Indeed, the regionalism agenda flourished in the Lula years. In 2004, a free trade agreement between Mercosur and the Andean Community was established. In 2008, Lula oversaw the establishment of UNASUR. This became a dispute resolution forum, which helped reconcile the political situation in Bolivia, Colombia-Venezuela tensions, and Ecuadorian domestic politics. Late in his presidency, Lula also pushed for the establishment of CELAC, the Community of Latin American and Caribbean States. CELAC brought together the Rio Group, created in 1986 to enhance dialogue among Latin American states, with the Latin American and Caribbean Summit (CALC). Following CELAC's establishment, it subsequently became the EU's region-wide interlocutor in Latin America (Lazarou and Luciano, 2015). The first EU-CELAC Summit took place in 2013 with a focus on sustainable development.

Overall, under the Lula governments, Brussels perceived EU-Brazil relations as inextricably linked to the EU's relations with South America and as leverage for relations between the EU and the whole of Latin America. Amorim confirmed that from the Brazilian perspective and described the dialogue between the leaders of the EU and Brazil as a medium for coordination on region-wide issues such as energy and climate (Amorim, 2010).

Dilma Rousseff (2011–2016)

Lula's successor, Dilma Rousseff, oversaw an observed retraction of Brazilian foreign policy. Conceptually, there was definite continuity from Lula to Dilma. Rousseff's government retained the main figureheads, talking points and groups of diplomats responsible for drafting Lula's foreign policy. However, domestically, changes contributed to the rolling back of Brazil's foreign policy. Rousseff was relatively uninterested in foreign policy (Saraiva, 2016). She took nearly 50% fewer trips abroad than Lula did. During her presidency, the foreign ministry saw its budget slashed, Brazil paid out less international aid, and Lula's Africa policy was, to a large extent, abandoned.

Economic considerations forced Dilma to look inwards. Lower commodity prices battered the Brazilian economy. By 2013, nationwide protests began to reveal a crack in the political establishment when masses took to the streets to denounce cronyism, rising costs and lack of public-sector investments. During Rousseff's tenure, Lava Jato (an anti-corruption operation) became a major political force, cracking down on major members of the PT, eroding the party's legitimacy and compounding calls for impeachment. Having lost political support in the lower house of Congress, she would be impeached in August 2016.

Rousseff's engagement with Brazil's neighbours was based on the regional policy of past PT governments: that also included the vision of less US influence in the region. Despite this, regional leadership was not a priority of Rousseff's government (Saraiva & Zimmer, 2016). Under Rousseff, the economic crisis revealed Brazil's reluctance to pay the costs of regional leadership. A case in point, Brazil refrained from a leading role in the attempts to resolve the Venezuelan crisis.

On political issues, such as Venezuela and the regional stance on the impeachment of Paraguay's president Lugo, Brazil gave a clear preference to engagement through the South American format of UNASUR rather than to CELAC (Saraiva, 2014). This in turn led to observations that the EU-CELAC strategic partnership was less valued by Brazil at that time. Instead, the policy choice was to engage with the EU bilaterally, not interregionally (Saraiva, 2014). Gradually, Brazilian initiatives in the Council of South American Defence and UNASUR, previously political under Lula, became reoriented towards development projects and technical cooperation (Saraiva, 2020). Due to the economic situation, Brazil experienced a decline in its foreign direct investment in the region (Mariano, 2015). All this contributed to a weakening of Brazil's influence in the region (Saraiva & Zimmer, 2016).

The Rousseff government continued Lula's policy in Mercosur. During the negotiation of the EU-Mercosur trade agreement, economic actors and opposition politicians pressured the government to sign a bilateral EU-Brazil deal, but the government rejected the idea and remained committed to the regional integration format (Saraiva, 2014). Nevertheless, developments in Paraguay and Venezuela, among other issues, halted the process of Mercosur integration. In fact, Rousseff's government supported and aided Venezuela's accession into Mercosur – facilitated by the suspension of Paraguay from Parlasur in 2012.

At the multilateral level, Brazil's attempt to become a permanent member of the UNSC (for which it had always sought EU support) continued, although the country pursued this objective less fervently. Indeed, the BRICS did not form a joint position regarding Brazil's entry into the UNSC. In the WTO Doha round, Brazil found it hard both to unify the positions of emerging countries and to change the preferences of the status quo powers. After revelations of the US National Security Agency wiretapping, Brazil did manage to articulate a successful digital privacy resolution at the UN alongside Germany.

With respect to the Strategic Partnership, Brazil and the EU found little space for convergence. According to Santander and Saraiva (2016), during this time, it became clear to Brazilian diplomats that the stances of both partners rarely converged. Under Rousseff, the main advancement in the bilateral relationship was through academic exchanges, namely, the *ciência sem fronteiras* program (Saraiva, 2014; Saraiva & Zimmer, 2016). At the same time, due to the impact of the financial crisis in Europe, the EU's normative power as an economic model began to be questioned in Brazil and in the region.

Michel Temer (2016–2018)

Rousseff's moderate Vice-President, Michel Temer, took office after a dramatic impeachment trial. A centrist, Temer sought to reform Brazilian foreign policy, although the country's international footprint continued to shrink. Upon taking office, the president appointed José Serra to lead the foreign ministry, who promised a "new foreign policy" to put an end to the PT's deemed "ideological" foreign policy (Agência Brasil, 2016). The most pronounced change in Temer's foreign policy was a pivot to the West while still retaining principles emanating from Brazil's constitution, with respect to democracy, human rights, multilateralism and the environment.

Regionally, the Temer government pursued the return of *open regionalism*, associated with free markets, globalization, and the Washington consensus (Santos et al., 2021). It focused on trade policy, such as increasing ties between Mercosur and the Pacific Alliance, and bilateral trade deals. It introduced business-friendly policies through domestic reforms such as the enactment of a constitutional spending cap, a pro-business labour reform, and the impetus to pursue pension reform. Under Temer, Brazil applied for OCDE membership aiming, among other things, to bolster its image in the eyes of foreign investors. Nonetheless, by the time of Temer's presidency, Brazilian construction firms like Odebrecht were already embroiled in corruption scandals in neighbouring countries, weakening the country's foreign standing and regional image (Morini, 2015).

As part of its approach to the region, the Temer administration suspended Venezuela from Mercosur in 2016, while encouraging the EU-Mercosur Free Trade deal, which, however, did not advance owing to European limitations in agriculture and Brazilian industrial protectionism (Saraiva, 2020).

Other regional initiatives, made prominent under Lula, were reformed under Temer. The government oversaw Brazil leaving (and disbanding) UNASUR alongside right-leaning leaders in Chile, Paraguay and Colombia. Brazil began favouring OAS as the main conflict resolution organ in the Americas. (Rodriguez-Dominguez, 2017). In 2017, the administration condemned Venezuela's democratic backsliding in the OAS; the next year it vouched for the country's expulsion from the regional organization (Saraiva, 2020). In August of the same year, Brazil formed the Lima Group, aimed at restoring democracy in Venezuela. The general retrenchment regarding regional integration was in detriment to the EU's stated aim of engaging with Brazil to encourage regional cooperation. Multilaterally, a trend of reduced Brazilian engagement emerged. Brazil did not renew its participation in the UN peace operation in Haiti, in spite of the relevant UN request. Moreover, in the UN Human Rights Council, Temer's government became a target, mainly owing to agrarian, indigenous and environmental matters, as deforestation spiked (Saraiva, 2020).

A transitional president, Temer struggled with legitimacy, domestically and abroad. Internationally, he was perceived as a coup leader against the country's first female president, which harmed his appeal in the eyes of left-leaning South American governments (Pérez & Silva, 2019). Moreover, the first policy implemented by Foreign Minister Serra was to criticise countries that expressed consternation at Dilma's impeachment, namely, Venezuela, Cuba, Bolivia, Ecuador, Nicaragua and the Bolivarian Alliance – all in the South American and broader region (Casarões, 2016). Internally, corruption scandals were rife. Domestic backlash pitched up at the 2016 Olympic Games in Rio (Pérez & Silva, 2019). Various international leaders avoided official visits to Brazil, thus contributing to a sense of marginalization of the country (Fox, 2017).

In this context, Brazil's ability to act as an enabler of the EU policy's objectives in the region diminished significantly, as did its regional leadership potential. The peace agreement in Colombia was a case in point. Brazil did play a very limited role as a mediator or otherwise. The EU saw the peace agreement as a goal-shared issue in the region with significant potential for regional cooperation (Pérez & Silva, 2019).

Jair Messias Bolsonaro (2019–2022)

Jair Bolsonaro, a conservative illiberal populist who took office after campaigning against establishment politics, provoked a reorientation of Brazilian foreign policy by rejecting previous notions of Brazilian pragmatism and instead using foreign policy as a platform for domestic conservative and religious discourse. In contrast with several of the EU's foreign policy objectives, Bolsonaro's foreign policy is characterised by the rejection of multilateral institutions, an alliance with transnational right-wing populist groups and governments, anti-globalism, anti-communism, and emphasis on religious nationalism (Casarões, 2020; Pérez & Silva, 2019; Weiffen, 2022). According to Ferreira-Pereira (2021: 165), Bolsonaro's foreign policy agenda emphasised "very close relations with the Trump administration while de-emphasising and ultimately questioning the country's commitment to the protection and strengthening of multilateral arrangements (e.g. Paris Agreement on climate change), global public goods (e.g. Amazon rainforest) and even democratic values". Nonetheless, his foreign policy was often moderated by members of the military in the cabinet and by interest groups represented by legislators in Brazil's multiparty Congress.

Bolsonaro's regional policy further retracted Brazil from the regional scene. Upon taking office, Bolsonaro formalised Brazil's exit from UNASUR and joined the newly created Prosur (Forum for the Progress and Integration of South America), meant to replace it, along with other right-wing leaders (Weiffen, 2022). In 2020, Brazil's foreign minister, Ernesto Araújo, announced Brazil's decision to suspend its participation in CELAC, arguing that the organization did not bring satisfactory results in the defence of democracy and regional management, besides being a pulpit for non-democratic regimes such as Venezuela, Cuba and Nicaragua. To European eyes, Brazil's absence in the bloc rendered a bi-regional EU-CELAC dialogue impossible (Uol, 2021). In turn, an EU-LAC Leaders' Meeting, including Brazil, was carried out in December 2021.

Bolsonaro's government is noteworthy for its lack of regional initiatives. During the Venezuelan crisis of 2019, Brazil played only a marginal role in the Lima group. When a left-wing government was elected in Argentina, relations between the leaders of the two countries became difficult. The disengagement with regional initiatives was accompanied by alignment with the US and its policies in the region, exemplified by Brazil's support of the US candidate to the Inter-American Development Bank and support for the OAS.

At the same time, however, significant progress was made in EU-Mercosur relations with the signature of the trade and political components of the EU-Mercosur Association Agreement in 2019 and 2020, respectively, in spite of the limited progress of integration within Mercosur. The Brazilian government did not pursue any significant step to increase cooperation with the Pacific Alliance or other regional formats.

Despite advancements in interregional EU-Mercosur relations, the Bolsonaro government sought to weaken the Mercosur's symbolic recognition in favour of national sovereignty. For instance, one of Foreign Minister Ernesto Araújo's first orders of business was to do away with the Mercosur logo on the Brazilian passport. Before becoming President, Bolsonaro criticised Mercosur's "ideological moorings": he defended the idea that the bloc's preferential trade agreements are not only a result of former PT governments' ideological bias, but that these commitments restrict the Brazilian autonomy to form bilateral trade deals with other countries (Bolsonaro, 2017). During the presidential campaign, Bolsonaro's finance minister, Paulo Guedes, mentioned that the bloc would not be a priority (Agostine & Ramalho, 2018). Although his discourse with respect to the organization eventually moderated, Bolsonaro defended a narrower, commercial scope for the regional organization, whose multilateral commitments – such as the common external tariff – were considered constraints to Brazilian action.

Under Bolsonaro, Mercosur's commercial policy saw advances. Brazilian officials concluded the technical details of the Association Agreement. In 2022, Mercosur concluded its trade agreement with Singapore. Brazil also emerged as a supporter of Mercosur negotiations for free trade agreements with Indonesia and Vietnam (Leiroz, 2020).

The EU-Mercosur Association Agreement

In pursuing the completion of negotiations between the EU and Mercosur, Brazil has – at least in principle – enabled an agreement which would bring to fruition several of the EU's objectives in the region on trade, climate, labour standards and regional cooperation. If implemented, the trade pillar of the EU-Mercosur Association Agreement (AA) would eliminate tariff and non-tariff barriers for the large majority of the EU-Mercosur trade. The EU would gradually remove tariffs on 92% of Mercosur exports in ten years, whereas Mercosur would remove tariffs on 91% of EU exports in 15 years. The agreement serves the EU's long-standing objective of bi-regional and intra-regional integration. It is also an opportunity for Mercosur's economies to enter global value chains and signals in favour of rules-based multilateral trading systems. EU-Mercosur trade is worth 88 billion euros annually, of which 64 billion stems from Brazil. The agreement would also reduce non-tariff barriers (e.g. administrative delays, technical barriers, sanitary requirements, tax exemptions). Through the agreement, the EU aims to foster sustainable development and environmental standards, implement labour rights, and shape global trade rules in accordance with liberal and multilateral values (Grieger, 2019).

The AA also contemplates increased dialogue on climate. It includes commitments to implementing the Paris accord, and on issues such as biodiversity, circular economy, waste management and corporate social responsibility, alongside the encouragement of green public procurement practices, intellectual property and green technology transfers.

At the same time, it is also indisputable that a range of domestic policies implemented under the Bolsonaro government – many in policy areas with regional implications, such as the environment – were in absolute contrast to the EU's stated foreign policy goals. Under Bolsonaro's presidency, forest fires in the

Amazon experienced an uptick. In response to criticisms, Bolsonaro provoked the abandonment of environmental cooperation through Germany and Norway's Amazon Fund.

Bolsonaro's environmental policy – characterised by the hollowing-out of environmental institutions, dismissal of prominent scientists, non-enforcement of environmental crimes and protection of land-grabbers – made the ratification of the EU-Mercosur Trade Agreement impossible after its signature. During 2021, the resignation of Brazilian environment ministers, deforestation, masking of emissions at the Paris Agreement, corruption scandals related to vaccines and violence against indigenous people in the Amazon contributed to the stalling of ratification of the EU-Mercosur agreement on the EU side. In that sense, Brazil this time functioned as an obstacle to the EU's relations with the region.

In November 2021, as part of the European Green Deal, the EU Commission introduced a proposal to limit imports of products connected to the deterioration of climate change, potentially having a large impact on Brazilian produce. At the same time, the Bolsonaro government committed to ending illegal deforestation by 2028 and subscribed to the COP26 commitment of net-zero carbon emissions by 2050. The move was welcomed by the EU's High Representative, Josep Borrell, as crucial for concluding the EU-Mercosur deal. While the debate on Brazil's climate policy may appear to be a bilateral issue between Brussels and Brasília, this rhetoric, but also the reality of the agreement's progress, demonstrates Brazil's weight in enabling, stalling or blocking closer and deeper trade relations between the EU and the region. This time Brazil has functioned as an obstacle to the EU's relations with the region.

Conclusion

During the past two decades, the EU has pursued the strengthening of political relations with Brazil, recognising Brazil's potential as an ally in the promotion of its values, but also as a critical influencer in the future of EU relations with the wider LAC region, most notably with Mercosur, through – inter alia – its role in the EU-Mercosur Association Agreement. This assumption has presupposed that Brazil is interested in and capable of exercising regional leadership, but also that the values and interests of the EU and Brazil continue to align.

The deterioration of the Brazilian economy, which began in the first half of the past decade, and its subsequent social and political implications weakened these assumptions. Successive Brazilian presidents have diverged significantly in their approach to the region and to policy issues linked to EU interests. Most recently, stark divergences between Brasília and Brussels on climate policy, indigenous rights and multilateralism, have led to a situation where Brazil-EU relations have reflected negatively on the relationship between the EU and the region. These observations, analysed in this chapter, should serve to inform our understanding of Brazil's role as an enabler, but also as a potential veto point of the EU's policies for the region and should serve to explain potential recourse to a multi-level framework for the EU's relations in Latin America.

Bibliography

Agência Brasil. (2016). "Discurso do ministro José Serra por ocasião da cerimônia de transmissão do cargo de ministro de estado das Relações Exteriores – Brasília, 18 de maio de 2016". 18 May 2016, https://www.gov.br/mre/pt-br/canais_atendimento/imprensa/notas-a-imprensa/discurso-do-ministro-jose-serra-por-ocasiao-da-cerimonia-de-transmissao-do-cargo-de-ministro-de-estado-das-relacoes-exteriores-brasilia-18-de-maio-de-2016. Press Release.

Agostine, Cristine & Ramalho, André. (2018). "Paulo Guedes diz que Mercosul não é prioridade de Bolsonaro." Valor Econômico [São Paulo], 28 October 2018, https://valor.globo.com/politica/noticia/2018/10/28/paulo-guedes-diz-que-mercosul-nao-e-prioridade-de-bolsonaro.ghtml

Amorim, Celso. (2010). "Brazilian foreign policy under president Lula (2003–2010): An overview." *Revista Brasileira de Política Internacional,* vol. 53, pp. 214–240.

Blanco, Luis Fernando. (2016). "The functions of 'strategic partnership' in European Union foreign policy discourse."*Cambridge Review of International Affairs,* vol. 29, no. 3, pp. 35–54.

Bolsonaro, Jair. (2017). @jairbolsonaro "Temos que ter outras opções fora das amarras ideológicas do MercoSul! Partamos para o bilateralismo em prol do desenvolvimento real do país!" *Twitter,* 11 October 2017, https://twitter.com/jairbolsonaro/status/918112409520410626

Carson, Jeffrey & Power, Timothy. (2009). "Presidentialization, pluralization, and the rollback of the itamaraty: Explaining change in Brazilian foreign policy making in the Cardoso-Lula Era". *International Political Science Review,* vol. 30, no. 2, pp. 117–140.

Casarões, Guilherme. (2016). "A política Externa e riscos à integração regional." *Conjuntura Austral,* vol. 7, no. 37, pp. 81–93.

Casarões, Guilherme. (2020). "Religião e Poder: a Ascensão de um Projeto de "Nação Evangélica no Brasil?" *Interesse Nacional,* vol. 13, no. 49, pp. 9–16.

Council of the European Union. (2007). *EU-Brazil Summit Joint Statement*, 11531/07 (Presse 162). https://www.consilium.europa.eu/ueDocs/cms_Data/docs/pressData/en/er/95167.pdf

European Commission. (2007). *Communication to the council and the European Parliament: Towards an EU-Brazil strategic partnership*. https://www.eesc.europa.eu/en/documents/eu-brazil-strategic-partnership

Ferreira-Pereira, Laura C. (2015). "The European Union's partnership policy towards Brazil: More than meets the eye." *Cambridge Review of International Affairs*, vol. 29, no. 3, pp. 55–77.

Ferreira-Perreira, Laura C. (2021). "European Union-Brazil relations: A strategic partnership in suspended animation." In *The European Union's strategic partnerships: Global diplomacy in a contested world,* edited by Micheal Smith. London: Palgrave Macmillan, pp. 151–175.

Fox, Micheal. (2017). "Brazil rolls back on regional integration". *NACLA Report on the Americas*, vol. 3, no. 49, pp. 284–286.

Government of Brazil, Mercosur and Singapore conclude trade pact. Press Release, 25 July 2022. https://www.gov.br/en/government-of-brazil/latest-news/2022/mercosur-and-singapore-conclude-trade-pact

Gratius, Susanne. (2017). "Brazil and the EU: From liberal interregionalism to realist bilateralism." *Revista Brasileira de Política Internacional,* vol. 61, no. 1, pp. 1–21.

Grieger, Gisela. (2019). *The trade pillar of the EU-Mercosur Association Agreement.* European Parliamentary Research Service. https://www.europarl.europa.eu/RegData/etudes/BRIE/2019/640138/EPRS_BRI(2019)640138_EN.pdf

Lazarou, Elena. (2011). "Brazil and the European Union: Strategic partners in a changing world?" *Hellenic Foundation for European and Foreign Policy,* Working Paper nr. 24/2011.

Lazarou, Elena. (2012). "A model in crisis? The crisis of the Euro and its impact on the European 'model' for regional integration". In *Regions in crisis*, edited by Lorenzo Fioramonti. Abingon: Routledge.

Lazarou, Elena. (2013). "Brazil and regional integration in South America: Lessons from the EU's crisis." *Contexto Internacional,* vol. 35, no. 2, pp. 353–385.

Lazarou, Elena & Fonseca, Carmen. (2011). "The EU-Brazil strategic partnership and beyond". *Parcerias Estratégicas do Brasil: A construção do conceito e as experiências em curso,* edited by Antônio Carlos Lessa, Argumentum.

Lazarou, Elena & Luciano, Bruno Theodoro (2015). "Regionalism as an instrument: Assessing Brazil's relations with its neighbourhood." *Global Society*, vol. 29,no. 3, pp. 390–408.

Leiroz, Lucas. "Mercosur about to sign agreement with Vietnam and Indonesia". *Infobrics*, 17 December 2020. https://infobrics.org/post/32476/

Mariano, Marcelo et al. (2015). "A cooperação sul-sul na política externa brasileira dos governos Lula da Silva e Dilma Rousseff." https://alacip.org/cong15/int-mariano8cd.pdf (Accessed 22 May 2022).

Meissner, Katharina. (2018). "Resorting to bilateralism: The EU, MERCOSUR, and the strategic partnership with Brazil." *Journal of European Integration*, vol. 40, issue 1, pp. 51–61.

Morini, Thiago. *América Latina olha o Brasil com desconfiança*. El Pais, 28 August 2015. https://brasil.elpais.com/brasil/2015/08/20/economia/1440085710_908688.html

Pavese, Carolina. (2014). *Level-linkage in European Union – Brazil relations: An analysis of cooperation on climate change, trade and human rights*. London School of Economics and Political Science, PhD Thesis. http://etheses.lse.ac.uk/917/1/Pavese_Level-linkage-in-European-Union-Brazil-relations.pdf

Pérez, José & da Silva, André. (2019). "Lula, Dilma, and Temer: The rise and fall of Brazilian foreign policy". *Latin American Perspectives,* Issue 227, vol. 46, no. 4, pp. 169–185.

Preusser Mattos, Fernando & Rohr Reisdorfer, Bruna. (2021). "De Parceria Estratégica a Potência do Caos: o Brasil segundo os Think Tanks Europeus (2003–2021)." *O Brasil visto de fora: os think tanks e as representações sobre o Brasil num mundo em mudança*, Edited by Eduardo Munhoz Svartman and Luciana Wietchikoski. Konrad Adenauer Stiftung, pp. 11–46.

Rodriguez-Dominguez, Maria. (2017). "No longer Activa e Altiva: Brazil's Foreign Policy Stumbles under Temer". *Council on Hemispheric Affairs*. https://www.coha.org/no-longer-activa-e-altiva-brazils-foreign-policy-stumbles-under-temer/

Santander, Sebastian & Saraiva, Miriam. (2016). "Brazil-European Union Partnership: irc high expectations to limited results." *L'Europe en Formation*, vol. 3, no. 381, pp. 103–123.

Santos, Leandro et al. (2021). "Explaining the changes in Brazilian foreign policy towards South America under Michel Temer's administration (2016–2018): The return to the logic of open regionalism". *Contexto Internacional*, vol. 43, no. 3, pp. 490–513.

Saraiva, Miriam. (2014). "Balanço da Política Externa de Dilma Rousseff: Perspectivas Futuras?" *Relações Internacionais,* no. 44, pp. 25–35.

Saraiva, Miriam. (2020). "The democratic regime and the changes in Brazilian foreign policy towards South America." *Brazilian Political Science Review,* vol. 14, no. 3, pp. 1–39.

Saraiva, Miriam & Gomes, Zimmer. (2016). "Os limites da política Externa de Dilma Rousseff para a América do Sul". *Relaciones Internacionales,* vol. 50, pp. 81–97.

Torrent, Ramón. (2002). "Regional integration in Europe and the Americas and bilateral transatlantic relations." In *An integrated approach to the European Union-Mercosur Association,* edited by Paolo Giordano. Presses de la Fondation Nationale de Sciences Politiques, pp. 207–223.

Uol Notícias (2021). "União Europeia estuda como realizar cúpula após saída do Brasil na Celac", 2 October 2021, https://noticias.uol.com.br/ultimas-noticias/efe/2021/10/02/uniao-europeia-estuda-como-realizar-cupula-apos-saida-do-brasil-na-celac.htm (Accessed 22 May 2022).

Vigevani, Tullo & Cepaluni, Gabriel. (2007). "Lula's foreign policy and the quest for autonomy through diversification." *Third World Quarterly,* vol. 28, no. 7, pp. 1309–1326.

Paulina Astroza Suárez and Javier Sepúlveda Estrada

Autonomy as a Foreign Policy Objective: Perspectives from Europe and Latin America

Introduction

Today we are facing a period of liquidity, fragmentation, and multiple simultaneous changes. From general events such as climate change, economic crises and pandemics to concrete events such as armed conflicts, mass migrations, and social unrest, the international reality is in full reconfiguration, and therefore, the creation of a foreign policy – by a given actor – cannot but count on this scenario to make its interests effective. Pragmatism, therefore, becomes a necessary factor when exercising a specific international guideline, being aware of the dynamics of the system, and thus, creating a holistic approach.

However, what dynamics does the international system present today? Various authors (Sanahuja, 2008; Smith & Xie, 2009) have indicated that the international environment can be described mostly by a complex interdependence scenario, following Keohane and Nye's ideas, referring to situations characterised by reciprocal effects among countries or among actors in different countries (Keohane & Nye, 1989: 8). Similarly, Barbé (2020: 90) characterises the international system as the interpenetration of societies resulting from the flows of goods, services, capital, ideas, and people, associating societies with others in a multitude of dimensions, in the economic, the human, the scientific and the intellectual aspects. The author emphasises that these links are expected to have political consequences, to the extent that they modify the interests, preferences, and perceptions of more or less relevant parties in the different States, thus altering the incentives of decision-makers.

Therefore, interdependence in the external environment has marked a profound change in the way in which power is used: the typical means to exert influence in the international arena, such as armed power or *hard* elements, have given way to new *soft* ones, especially those related to the economic sector, the demonstration of values or international prestige. Consequently, what Fagaburu (2017: 11) points out as characteristics of this paradigm is important: the existence of multi-level relationships given the plurality of actors, the non-existence of a thematic hierarchy at the international level, the blurring of the line that divides internal issues from external ones, and the use of seductive means to obtain presence characterises the international realm.

Likewise, the multiple relationships between actors have also brought various problems to the public arena, whose scope is neither national nor regional, but global. In this way, pandemics, the climate emergency, economic crises, contemporary wars, and internal changes no longer have only an impact on their main actors, but also indirectly impact all the participants on the international scene, in multiple areas and in varied intensities. Consequently, uncertainty becomes the rule and liquidity in the general order.

What can be done, within the field of foreign policy, to respond to an increasingly difficult scenario? What deeper dynamics are taking place in a structure that is already interdependent? This chapter aims to answer these questions and to analyse the multiple proposals that have been made both in Latin America and Europe on a common concept: autonomy. What is it? What is it based on? What means would operationalise it? Is there any agreement regarding this concept? These are questions that will be studied in the following sections, through an analysis of various academic texts, first studying the systemic characteristics of contemporary international society, later examining the main concept in greater depth.

The current situation of the world under a paradigm of complex interdependence

In order to study the concept of autonomy, we must first analyse the contemporary scenario. After the various events that have occurred since 2001,[1] despite being diffuse and confusing, international relations ended up in 2008 in an open struggle for influence, ending the clear US hegemony that was present at that time. Thus, the beginning of the 2008 economic crisis meant the relative rise of emerging powers, especially for an already economically inserted China, which adopted increasingly assertive foreign agendas (Schulz, 2016). Consequently, the redistribution of power from the West to new actors (China, India, Brazil, Indonesia, among others) or resurgents (Russia) has encouraged the competition for power, a fact that was absent or concealed in previous phases.

---

1 September 11 attacks, the start of the war in Afghanistan and Iraq, the start of the War on Terror and the advancement of an openly warmongering US foreign policy that stressed the multilateral structures of that time.

The best case study to understand this new competition for influence is Sino-American relations of the last decade. The first approaches made by Washington towards China in this new scenario were made under the Obama administration, taking a hybrid strategy called the "Pivot to Asia" (Dueck, 2015: 72): on the one hand, presenting elements of anchoring and integration; and on the other, elements of containment and dissuasion. The idea of the Obama strategy was, through a selective approach, to achieve reciprocal cooperation with Beijing in important areas and to avoid the appearance of zero-sum thinking (Clinton, 2011). However, it did not yield the expected results, and Chinese diplomacy did not show signs of reciprocity in sensitive sectors for the United States: In the negotiations at COP15, it did not respond as expected to the proposal to reduce carbon emissions, nor did it show signs of collaboration in the situation of North Korea and nuclear disarmament, and even exerted more pressure on the claims over the South China Sea (deLisle, 2016: 146).

Yet, the tensions between the declining power and the rising one became more evident with the eruption of the Trump administration. The period between 2016 and 2020 was one marked by the withdrawal of the United States from various international instances, worsening its relative decline in comparison with other actors: denouncing the Paris Accord on Climate Change and the Non-Proliferation Treaty; launching commercial *wars* against partners and rivals such as the EU or China; or retreating from instances such as the WHO or the UNHRC; exemplifies the damage that the Trump Administration did to American presence in the world. Consequently, the *Wilsonian* ideal that the United States has promoted since the end of the Cold War was undermined by these events, souring the position of Washington with its allies, third countries and adversaries; something that the actual Biden Administration is trying to reverse (Astroza & Sepulveda, 2022).

On the other hand, China appears as a more assertive player in the international arena. Since the presentation of projects like the Belt and Road Initiative in 2013; the beginning of investments in infrastructure in African countries such as Nigeria, Angola and Sudan (Lechini, 2013); the displacement of important commercial partners in Latin America (Bonialian, 2021); and the rejection with Russia of a new expansion of NATO (El Pais, 2022), the *Middle Empire* has known how to take a stance as a relevant actor and undoubtedly as a global economic power.

Therefore, the increase in tension between the two powers is undeniable. From the consideration by the United States government that China has become a strategic rival (US Senate, 2021: 301) up to the failure of bilateral negotiations in Alaska (El Mundo, 2021), it has been clear that both states mutually recognise each other as competitors in the international arena.

However, it is not possible to describe this relationship as similar to a New Cold War. The level of economic exchange, the multiple political and cultural relations, and the existence of a systemic multipolarism show that the relationship between Beijing and Washington is diametrically different from the one it had with Moscow. In situations where the challenges are increasingly global and interdependent, the relations between the two powers should be rather approximated to a *cooperative rivalry* scenario (Nye, 2018) instead of an *adversarial rivalry* one (as during the Cold War). In this sense, there will be areas where there will be intense competition between both actors – new technologies, the space race and international trade – but at the same time, there will be other instances where cooperation will be required to face challenges that the actors alone cannot counteract, such as climate change or upcoming pandemics. Therefore, in some cases, power should be exercised jointly between China and the United States, in a type of positive-sum game where all the intervening subjects win, rather than the dominance of one actor over another.

So, in this new international dynamic, which guideline is the most appropriate? What kind of foreign projection and strategy may provide appropriate responses and mechanisms for an entropic world in transition? Several academics on both sides of the Atlantic, such as Sanahuja (2021) and Tokatlian (2022), have argued that autonomy should be the main factor to consider. But what is autonomy as a concept? What development has it had both in Europe and Latin America?

Autonomy as a concept: European understanding

Etymologically, autonomy comes from the Greek *autos* (*αυτος* – by itself), *nomos* (*νομος* – rule), and the suffix *ía* (quality), thereby expressing the quality of being under one's own rule or within one's government. But what exactly is autonomy? What does it point to? The concept is diffuse, but it is not due to an ambiguity in its content, but rather it is the consequence of great richness in terms of its development.

In the Old Continent, the idea is already a long-standing concept. The first approaches to an idea of *autonomy* occurred in post-war Europe, specifically within NATO circles and the European integration process. However, with the rejection of the European Defence Community during the 1950s and the consolidation of NATO as the guarantor of security in Europe, the concept was relegated to a secondary plane and with little theoretical relevance during the Cold

War (Le Gleut & Conway-Mouret, 2019: 15). Only after the fall of the Berlin Wall did the idea of European autonomy re-emerge.

One of the first references made to it in a formal declaration occurred in Saint-Malo in 1998 when the French and British governments indicated that the newly European Union "must have an autonomous capacity for action, supported by credible military forces" (Sénat, 1998). Consequently, the first constructions that arose around the concept were closely related to the field of defence and security, framed within the expression of *capacity for action*, having three important factors to consider (Arteaga, 2017; Kempin & Kunz, 2022):

1. *Political Capacity*, in terms of defining strategies and following them;
2. *Operational Capacity*, in terms of logistical and institutional power to execute the defined strategy;
3. *Industrial Capacity*, regarding the construction, development and maintenance of said faculties.

However, it was necessary to wait until 2013 for the term *strategic autonomy* to appear. It was the Foreign Affairs Council of the European Union that first created the concept and elevated it to the European Global Strategy in 2016 after the Brexit referendum (Tocci, 2021). Thus, only from 2017 was it possible to give a concrete definition of this idea: the ability to act and cooperate with international and regional partners whenever possible, while being able to operate autonomously when and where necessary (High Representative of the EU, 2016). Unlike what was mentioned before, here the term is broader and far from the conceptions of international security that had marked it for nearly twenty years, applying to new non-traditional areas: "Europe's strategic autonomy allows it to reduce dependence on others in relation to the most necessary things: critical materials and technologies, food, infrastructure, security and other strategic areas" (European Commission, 2020).

So, what motivated this change for Europe? Two precise facts were what caused a transformation of what has been understood by *Strategic Autonomy*: the arrival of Donald Trump to the Presidency of the United States in 2016 and the Covid-19 pandemic in 2020. On one hand, the arrival of the magnate caused a severe setback to transatlantic relations, especially in terms of compliance with Article V of the NATO Treaty (Kempin & Kunz, 2022: 6–7), meanwhile, the pandemic exposed Europe's dependence on foreign countries in strategic sectors, such as energy, medical supplies and pharmaceuticals (Ayuso, 2020). Therefore, Brussels is facing a situation that is delicate, which is part of other events that have already marked the European agenda, like the deterioration of the European neighbourhood from the Sahel to the Horn of Africa and Turkey, mass migration flows, terrorism, cyber threats, Brexit, among others (Molina & Benedicto, 2021: 10).

Thus, European Strategic Autonomy is trying to respond to new challenges that were not previously related to geopolitics, but that have become relevant due to the growing interdependence that exists between the multiple international actors. In this way, progress has been made in certain areas:

First, in the economic sector, by strengthening the euro as an international currency and as an element of economic sovereignty (European Council, 2021); the development of efforts to maintain global economic governance, especially within the WTO (Pellicer, 2022); the rethinking of trade policy as a tool of European foreign policy (European Commission, 2021).

Second, in the field of Industry, there is a strong look towards the technological, competitive and productive capacity of the EU. The Union itself has pointed out that it "gives European industry the opportunity to develop its own markets, products and services that boost competitiveness" (European Commission, 2021) as a manner to respond to external events. In this regard, Brussels has encouraged investment and innovation as the primary tools to rebuild Europe's industrial capacity and take it to the next stage of development, as seen with initiatives like *Next Generation EU* or *SURE*.

Third, in the realm of Security and Defence, the objective is to create a common defence culture as well as distinct European identity in response to new threats. Because of this, it was approved the European Global Strategy in 2016, creating the Permanent Structured Cooperation (PESCO) and the subsequent European Intervention Initiative (EI2), the endowment of a European Defense Fund in 2017, the encouragement of associativity between agents within the Common Foreign and Security Policy (CFSP) and the creation of the Military Planning and Conduct Capability (MPCC) (Molina & Benedicto, 2021: 10). In addition, in mid-February 2022, the Commission unveiled proposals for actions to contribute to community defence, drive innovation and address strategic dependencies (European Commission, 2022), as well as the unprecedented financing of the Ukrainian war effort against Russian aggression.

However, not all the Member States of the European Union agree on which direction Strategic Autonomy should point, both geographically and functionally.

France is the country that most strongly advocates for a notion based on European sovereignty and interests. Paris considers that the establishment of autonomy within the EU is crucial for France's own strategic autonomy (Direction Générale, 2017). Therefore, a development at the European level would imply a greater French presence on the international scene. On the other hand, Germany maintains that strategic autonomy should be developed as a pillar within the EU, not as a mutually exclusive project with NATO but rather a complementary one. Thus, Berlin considers that adopting the French proposal would imply matching European interests to French ones, which would mean putting their own interests and the geopolitical closeness with Washington at stake (Arteaga et al., 2022).

In addition to these positions, there are other proposals done by other European capitals. At the beginning of 2021, Spain and the Netherlands jointly proposed a point of synthesis between the French and German ideas, indicating that the European Union must become a global player with real capabilities based on tailor made solutions (Government of the Netherlands and Government of Spain, 2021). In contrast, states like Poland consider that the issue of strategic autonomy is really a discussion about how to update NATO in the face of new Russian pressure (Zielinski, 2020: 14), meanwhile, Sweden and Austria consider certain proposals as controversial to their historical neutralities, for which they have placed greater emphasis on operational or logistical autonomy rather than in defence (Franke & Varma, 2020). However, the start of the Kremlin's invasion of Ukraine has been a major shock, once again launching the discussion of community security within the EU.

Notwithstanding these different approaches and the dilemmas currently facing Europe, the concept of strategic autonomy is a reality that the EU is likely to implement in one way or another, and could receive an important boost under the French presidency and the so-called "Strategic Compass".

Autonomy in Latin America

The concept of autonomy has had continuous and successive development in Latin America as well, constituting a true current of thought of its own (Briceño & Simonoff, 2017). In this sense, it is a highly valuable aspect, since these are proposals that arise from a peripheral space within international dynamics, as is the case in Latin America, and not based on a rearrangement of doctrines brought from abroad.

A first approach to this concept was carried out by Juan Carlos Puig in Argentina and Helio Jaguaribe in Brazil at the beginning of the Cold War, through the so-called *heterodox autonomy* (Puig, 1980; Jaguaribe, 1979). The authors try to answer the various criticisms that ECLAC had made regarding the dependence of the Latin American States of that time, both economically and politically, on international dynamics, emphasising the role of local elites in this relationship. In this way, Jaguaribe (1979: 95–96) considers autonomous actors those that have a "margin of self-determination in domestic affairs and the capacity for independent international action", being conditioned by two essential factors: national viability (internal element) and international permissibility (external element).

Puig, on the other hand, delves further into the role that Latin American elites have in the dependency relationships that an actor has with a foreign entity, which can range from complete dependency to full autonomy. In consequence, and according to the interpretation done by Míguez (2022: 211), he considers the latter as "the maximum self-decision capacity that can be achieved, taking into account the objective constraints of the real world".

In reaction to what was pointed out by the previous authors, and after the disintegration of the Soviet Union, Escudé reformulated the concept of autonomy within his utilitarian vision of foreign relations: *peripheral realism* (Escudé, 1992). In it, he proposes an association of the concept with the idea of confrontation resulting from an overestimation of the room for manoeuvre of weak States, which did not distinguish between the autonomy that a State possesses (which is a consequence of its power) and the use of it. In that way, autonomy for Escudé is achieved through an in-depth analysis of the costs and benefits that a certain actor has in his decisions, trying to ensure the maintenance or increase of the material well-being of the population, without contradicting the guidelines established by the then hegemon – the United States – according to what is affirmed by Tokatlian and Russell (2002: 172).

Subsequently, and after the arrival of the new century, Tokatlian and Russell distanced themselves from the propositions of Escudé and they took up the autonomist current through their postulates on *relational autonomy*. In this sense, they indicate that in the face of the irruption of new factors (such as globalization, the end of the Cold War and the deepening of democratic and integration processes in the region), there has been a modification of the "context of action" in Latin America, being necessary a new definition of autonomy, no longer based on contrasts but on relationships with other actors.

Therefore, the authors considered that this new approach should be understood as "the capacity and willingness of a country to make decisions with others of its own free will and to jointly deal with situations and processes occurring within and outside its borders" (Tokatlian & Russell, 2002). Thus, the definition in terms of *conditioning* would be the aforementioned capacity and disposition, done in a competent, committed and responsible manner. Meanwhile, as a *national interest* (in order to increase the degrees of freedom) it is based on a new pattern of activity in the international orchestra, coming with new structures, identities and ideas, as well as gaining relevance within foreign relations the understanding that the other is no longer something opposite, but something integral to the international agent itself (Tokatlian & Russell, 2002: 179).

Similarly, in South America, especially in a Brazilian context, the so-called *autonomies with adjectives* appear, represented by the ideas of Tullo Vigevani and Gabriel Cepaluni (2007: 283). In that sense, they point out three different progressive degrees when talking about the concept in question:

1. *Autonomy in the distance* when the country confronts international norms and institutions and the great power, while tending towards isolation and self-sufficient development;
2. *Autonomy in participation* when external guidance is based on a commitment for global governance and multilateral institutions;
3. *Autonomy in diversification* when it is based mainly on relations with the global South.

As well, Miriam Gomes Saraiva (2010: 48) indicated the several currents that had happened in Brazilian diplomacy, especially an autonomic position that occurred during the presidency of Lula da Silva: the ability to manoeuvre on the international stage, universalism, and above all, strengthening Brazil's presence on the international stage.

Finally, it is also interesting to highlight the contributions made by Actis and Malacalza (2021), who propose their own notion: liquid autonomy. They point out that faced with an entropic scenario, and where there is a double tension between "Westphalia" and "Globalization" (the interactions between States on the one hand, and on the other, globalization and transnational relations), it is necessary to focus on the recognition of the fragility of the global and regional scenarios, the capacity for resilience in the face of adverse events by taking opportunities, and mitigating impacts.

Towards a new definition of autonomy for Latin America?

Given this long theoretical development, what can we consider as autonomy today in a Latin American context? In the first place, and starting with the European context, it is possible to define it as "the ability to set one's own priorities and make one's own decisions in matters of foreign policy and security, together with the institutional, political and material wherewithal to carry these through – in cooperation with third parties, or if need be alone" (Lippert, von Ondarza & Perthes, 2019: 5).

Despite this, adopting foreign definitions without adapting them to the local reality would result in an error. Latin America does not work under European logics, nor does Europe work under Latin American ones, despite having common interests. Thus, for establishing a *strategic autonomy for Latin America*, it is important to put on the table the notions of autonomy that already exist in the continent. In this way, the closest definition to the prevailing type of paradigm is the *relational autonomy* (Tokatlian & Russell, 2002). This constitutes an important basis since it has two important traits: first, the capacity and willingness of a country to make decisions with others of its own free will; and then, that said capacity to face, jointly with other actors, situations and processes that have occurred in the international scenario. However, it lacks further development in terms of areas of an operational or productive nature, explainable due to the period in which the theory was developed.

As well, new contributions in the area must also be brought to light, especially the proposal of *liquid autonomy* (Actis & Malacalza, 2021). The identification of the fragility of the global and regional scenarios, resilience in the face of adverse events by taking opportunities, and the mitigation of the various impacts that may occur in the future are necessary points to emphasise in a chaotic, highly changing international arena.

Thus, a Latin American-style strategic autonomy could be conceptualised as the ability and willingness to act, cooperate and relate to other international and regional actors voluntarily, whenever possible, with a view to expanding the spaces for action and the areas related to them by opportunity taking; or to maintain them through resilience or the mitigation of external shocks.

Consequently, autonomy should not be related to concepts such as autarchy or isolationism. In the first place, it is not comparable to autarchy, understood as a No State policy by which it tries to subsist with its own resources, since strategic autonomy is based on association with other actors, and therefore, it is a foreign policy open to the world. Neither is it isolationism, such as a policy of separation or non-intervention in international relations, on the contrary, the autonomy in question requires a willingness to act, to establish the necessary positions in the foreign arena, and even socialise it with other entities in order to expand the spaces for action or to maintain them.

It is also necessary to emphasise that the adoption of a policy of this type imposes certain challenges at the same time. Neither the creation of spaces nor the development of inherent aspects can be conceived spontaneously, but it is necessary adequate means that allow the realization of these objectives. Thus, the strategic management of the State will be decisive in the coming year, especially in terms of the domestic sphere, since the current economic opening must be reconciled with vulnerability to foreign events, in addition to the construction of agreements by internal politics that make it viable (Bywaters, Sepúlveda & Villar, 2021: 40).

In this way, what means are adequate to carry out an agenda based on strategic autonomy? In the first place, the same authors mentioned above indicate that there must be a deployment of an *entrepreneurial diplomacy*, within an approach that integrates policies at the domestic level in a holistic manner or a *whole-of-government* sense (Cooper, 2018: 596–608). They explain that given the lack of *hard power* capabilities that distinguishes the great powers, small and medium-sized countries – such as Latin American and some European countries – can exert influence on their external environment by concentrating their diplomatic activities on alternative courses of action that contribute to good international governance (Bywaters, Sepúlveda & Villar, 2021: 47). Consequently, the deployment of foreign action of this type implies a greater strategic role for the state in identifying and developing areas where there are interests of its own, especially those where there are comparative advantages over other players on the global scene (*niche diplomacy).*

On the other hand, and as mentioned above, an autonomous agenda also implies the association and diversification of ties with strategic partners. In this case, Euro-Latin American relations represent a potential axis, due to their cultural and political proximity. However, both regions have different challenges.

Regarding Latin America, the priority corresponds to retaking the various regional spaces that have been abandoned in the last decade. In this sense, it is a substantial requirement to overcome what Covarrubias calls a circumstantial regionalism, characterised by repetitive cycles of optimism and creation of institutions, followed by stagnation and negligence on the part of governments that prefer to act unilaterally (Covarrubias, 2019). Thus, it should be promoted the laying of foundations for a serious, pragmatic regionalism, that constitutes a source of governance in the region, especially through actions such as the search for minimum consensus.

Regarding the European Union, this constitutes a fundamental point. With Europe, the region shares more than democratic values, economic relations or political contacts; but also cultural, linguistic, historical ties and common challenges. Thus, faced with an entropic world, the European Union faces the same dilemmas as Latin America at the international level, so a deeper strategic association constitutes an opportunity to broaden horizons both from Brussels and from theircumrent American capitals. Facts such as the commitment to democracy, multilateralism, political dialogue, fair trade and an international system based on rules are shared issues that can be deepened to acquire greater autonomy.

Conclusions

The existence of multiple ties between the various international actors has brought a new way of how they relate to each other, especially due to the interpenetration of these at a multilevel scale, which has implied that any action in foreign matters can have repercussions that are not only direct, but indirect and at various intensities. In this sense, interdependence can be both a source of virtue and problems, especially in times of great general challenges.

Therefore, autonomy – as an element – is currently found as a relevant concept within both European and Latin American foreign policies. In this sense, the idea of searching for margins of action through association with other actors, or spaces that allow resilience and adaptability, is an effective and suitable tool to confront the dominant paradigm of the contemporary world. On the other hand, the existence of antecedents and prior development on both sides of the Atlantic is important, since it thus becomes a policy of its own, innate and adjustable to the various realities in which it is to be implemented.

Likewise, an external guideline of this type also implies the development of *whole-of-government* policies. In this way, the development of niche diplomacies based on the comparative advantages of a given actor; and the empowerment of foreign institutions as a selector agent and incubator of those prerogatives, would make it possible to create a solid base to pursue the objectives supported by various Latin American and European countries. However, the mere development of these does not imply a certain autonomy, but must be accompanied by associativity with key actors. In this sense, the relations between the European Union and Latin America become fundamental, since, in addition to sharing common values and principles, they face shared challenges and events capable of putting the international order at risk. In times of change and general uncertainties, the search for a tool that is effective and efficient becomes an immediate imperative.

Consequently, autonomy as an external guideline is a construction that is capable of adapting to new events that may occur in the future, and thereby provide a necessary response to a new world that is increasingly diverse, multiple and in the making. In that sense, both the EU and Latin America should establish policies that enable and construct *autonomy* for both parties, such as resuming the EU-CELAC meetings, deepening the economic ties between both regions, rearticulating the Latin American organizations for a more proper relationship with their European counterparts, advancing in several areas such as the energy transition and climate resilience related areas, and building cooperative agendas in the United Nations. In a troubled world, *autonomy* for the EU and Latin America is a shared path, and not only a stand-alone result.

Bibliography

Actis, E., and B. Malacalza, *Las políticas exteriores de América Latina en tiempos de autonomía líquida*, 2021, https://nuso.org/articulo/las-politicas-exteriores-de-america-latina-en-tiempos-de-autonomia-liquida (last ircum: 2 March 2022).

Arteaga, F., *La autonomía estratégica y la defensa europea*, 2017, https://www.realinstitutoelcano.org/analisis/la-autonomia-estrategica-y-la-defensa-europea (last ircum: 9 March 2022).

Arteaga, F., R. García, I. Molina, A. Ortega, M. Otero, C. Powell, and F. Steinberg, *Autonomía estratégica europea e intereses de España*, 2022, https://www.realinstitutoelcano.org/analisis/autonomia-estrategica-europea-e-intereses-de-espana (last ircum: 7 March).

Astroza, P., and J. Sepúlveda, *¿El enfrentamiento de China y Estados Unidos motivará mayor acercamiento entre la Unión Europea y América Latina?* In: P. Astroza y B. Larraín, (eds.), *Relaciones entre la Unión Europea y América Latina: Escenarios futuros en un mundo de cambios*. Tirant Lo Blanch, Santiago de Chile, 2022.

Ayuso, S., *Macron reclama una mayor "soberanía francesa y europea" para cubrir necesidades básicas*, 2020, https://elpais.com/internacional/2020-03-31/macron-reclama-una-mayor-soberania-francesa-y-europea-para-afrontar-crisis-como-la-del-coronavirus.html (last ircum: 8 March 2022).

Barbé, E., *Relaciones Internacionales*. Editorial Tecnos, Madrid, 2020.

Bonialian, M., Relaciones económicas entre China y América Latina. Una historia de la globalización, siglos XVI–XXI. *Historia mexicana*, vol. 70, n°3, 2021.

Briceño, J., and A. Simonoff, La Escuela de la Autonomía, América Latina y la teoría de las relaciones internacionales. *Estudios Internacionales*, vol. 49, n°186, 2017.

Bywaters, C., D. Sepúlveda, and A. Villar, *Introducción: Hacia un nuevo ciclo progresista para la Política Exterior de Chile*. In: C. Bywaters, D. Sepúlveda, and A. Villar (eds.), *Nuevas Voces de Política Exterior*. Fondo de Cultura Económica, Santiago de Chile, 2021.

Clinton, H., *America's Pacific century*, 2011, https://foreignpolicy.com/2011/10/11/americas-pacific-century (last ircum: 2 March 2022).

Cooper, A., Entrepreneurial states versus middle powers: Distinct or intertwined frameworks?. *International Journal: Canada's Journal of Global Policy Analysis*, vol. 73, n°4, 2018, pp. 596–608.

Covarrubias, A., Latin American integration: ircumstantial regionalism. In: M. Shifter and B. Binetti (eds.), *Unfulfilled promises: Latin America today.* Inter-american Dialogue, Washington D.C., 2019, pp. 121–129.

deLisle, J., International law in the Obama administration's pivot to Asia: The China seas disputes, the trans-Pacific partnership, rivalry with the PRC, and status quo legal norms in U.S. foreign policy. *Case Western Reserve Journal of International Law*, vol. 48, n°1, 143–176, 2016.

Direction générale des relations internationales et de la stratégie de France, *Revue stratégique de défense et de sécurité nationale*, 2017, https://www.vie-publique.fr/sites/default/files/rapport/pdf/174000744.pdf (last access: 4 March 2022).

Dueck, C., *The Obama doctrine: American grand strategy today.* Oxford University Press, Nueva York, 2015.

El Mundo, *Cruce de acusaciones en una cumbre de alta tensión entre EE. UU. y China: "¿Es así como quieren negociar?"*, 2021, https://www.elmundo.es/internacional/2021/03/19/60550decfc6c8309028b4682.html (last access: 4 March 2022).

El País, *China y Rusia rechazan una nueva ampliación de la OTAN*, 2022, https://elpais.com/internacional/2022-02-04/china-y-rusia-expresan-su-apoyo-mutuo-en-politica-internacional-y-rechazan-una-nueva-ampliacion-de-la-otan.html (last access: 8 March 2022).

Escudé, C., *Realismo periférico: bases teóricas para una nueva política exterior argentina.* Planeta, Buenos Aires, 1992.

European Commission, *Comunicación de la Comisión al Parlamento Europeo, al Consejo, al Comité Económico y Social Europeo y al Comité de las Regiones: Un nuevo modelo de industria para Europa*, 2020 https://eur-lex.europa.eu/legal-content/ES/TXT/PDF/?uri=CELEX:52020DC0102&from=FR (last access: 6 March 2022).

European Commission, *Communication from the commission to the European parliament, the council, the European Economic and Social Committee and the Committee of the Regions: Trade policy review – An open, sustainable and assertive trade policy*, 2021, https://trade.ec.europa.eu/doclib/docs/2021/february/tradoc_159438.pdf (last access: 9 March 2022).

European Commission, *La Commission dévoile des actions significatives visant à contribuer à la défense européenne, à stimuler l'innovation et à remédier aux dépendances stratégiques*, 2022, https://ec.europa.eu/commission/presscorner/detail/fr/ip_22_924 (last access: 10 March 2022).

European Council, *Papel internacional del Euro*, 2021, https://www.consilium.europa.eu/es/policies/international-role-euro (last access: 6 March 2022).

Fagaburu, D., Afinidades entre la Cooperación Internacional y la Integración Regional en América Latina. *Revista Cultural*, n°2, 2017.

Franke, U., and T. Varma, *L'Europe: En Quête d'Autonomie Stratégique*, 2020, https://ecfr.eu/paris/publication/leurope_en_quete_dautonomie_strategique (last access: 5 March 2022).

Gomes, M., A diplomacia brasileira e as visões sobre a inserção externa do Brasil: institucionalistas pragmáticos x autonomistas. *Mural Internacional*, vol.1, n°1. 2010.

Government of the Netherlands and Government of Spain, *Non-paper on strategic autonomy while preserving an open economy*, 2021, https://www.permanentrepresentations.nl/documents/publications/2021/03/24/non-paper-on-strategic-autonomy (last access: 10 March 2022).

High Representative of the European Union for Foreign Affairs and Security Policy, *Implementation plan on security and defence*, 2016, https://data.consilium.europa.eu/doc/document/ST-14392-2016-INIT/en/pdf (last access: 3 March 2022).

Jaguaribe, H., Autonomía periférica y hegemonía céntrica. *Estudios Internacionales*, vol. 12, n°46, 1979.

Kempin, R., and B. Kunz, France, Germany, and the quest for European strategic autonomy: Franco-German Defence Cooperation in a new era. *Notes du Cerfa – Notes de l'Ifri*, n°141, 2022.

Keohane, R., and J. Nye, *Power and interdependence: World politics in transition.* Harper Collins Publishers, Nueva York, 1989.

Lechini, G., *China en África: discurso seductor, intenciones dudosas*, 2013, https://nuso.org/articulo/china-en-africa-discurso-seductor-intenciones-dudosas (last access: 5 March 2022).

Le Gleut, R., and Conway-Mouret, H. *Rapport d'Information n°626, fait: au nom de la commission des affaires étrangères, de la défense et des forces armées (1) par le groupe de travail sur la défense européenne*, 2019. http://www.senat.fr/rap/r18-626-1/r18-626-11.pdf

Lippert, B., N. von Ondarza, and V. Perthes, *European strategic autonomy: Actors, issues, conflicts of interests*, 2019, https://www.swp-berlin.org/publications/products/research_papers/2019RP04_lpt_orz_prt_web.pdf (last access: 7 March 2022).

Míguez, M., La Autonomía Heterodoxa y la Clasificación de las Políticas Exteriores en la Argentina. *Revista de Relaciones Internacionales, Estrategia y Seguridad*, vol. 12, n°2, 2022.

Molina, M., y M. Benedicto, Autonomía Estratégica en Seguridad y Defensa: Un Anhelo Geopolítico que no se hace realidad en la Unión Europea. *Revista UNISCI*, n°55, 2021.

Nye, J., *La rivalidad cooperativa de las relaciones entre Estados Unidos y China*, 2018, https://www.project-syndicate.org/commentary/china-america-relationship-cooperative-rivalry-by-joseph-s--nye-2018-11/spanish (last access: 8 March 2022).

Pellicer, L. *Bruselas se propone impulsar una gran reforma de la OMC tras su cambio de dirección*, 2022, https://elpais.com/economia/2021-02-19/bruselas-se-propone-impulsar-una-gran-reforma-de-la-omc-tras-su-cambio-de-direccion.html (last access: 2 March 2022).

Puig, J., *Doctrinas internacionales y autonomía latinoamericana*, Universidad Simón Bolívar, Instituto de Altos Estudios de América Latina, Fundación Bicentenario de Simón Bolívar, 1980.

Sanahuja, J. A., "*¿Un mundo unipolar, multipolar o apolar? El poder estructural y las transformaciones de la sociedad internacional contemporánea*". In: VV AA, Cursos de Derecho Internacional *de Vitoria-Gasteiz,* Servicio Editorial de la Universidad del País Vasco, Bilbao, 2008.

Sanahuja, J. A., *Pacto verde y «Doctrina Sinatra» ¿Por qué son importantes para América Latina?,* In: Revista Nueva Sociedad, n°241, 2021. https://nuso.org/articulo/pacto-verde-y-doctrina-sinatra/ (last access: 10 March 2022).

Schulz, J., *¿Hacia un mundo multipolar? La emergencia de los BRICS en el escenario global*, IX Jornadas de Sociología de la Universidad Nacional de La Plata, 2016. http://www.memoria.fahce.unlp.edu.ar/trab_eventos/ev.8857/ev.8857.pd (last access: 2 March 2022).

Sénat, *Déclaration franco-britannique sur la défense européenne*, 1998, https://www.senat.fr/rap/r98-167/r98-1679.html (last access: 10 March 2022).

Smith, M., and H. Xie, The European Union, China and the United States: Complex interdependence and bi-multilateralism in commercial relations. In: G. Wiessala, J. Wilson, and P. Taneja (eds.), *The European Union and China: Interests and dilemmas.* Brill, Amsterdam, 2009.

Tocci, N., *European strategic autonomy: What it is, why we need it, how to achieve it*, 2021, https://www.iai.it/sites/default/files/9788893681780.pdf (last access: 2 March 2022).

Tokatlian, J. G., *La Autonomía en nuestra política exterior*. 2022 Available at: https://grupolacapitana.com.ar/la-autonomia-en-nuestra-politica-exterior/ (last access: 10 August 2022).

Tokatlian, J. G., and R. Russell, De la autonomía antagónica a la autonomía relacional: una mirada teórica desde el Cono Sur. *Perfiles Latinoamericanos*, n°21, 2002.

United States Senate, S.1169 – Strategic Competition Act of 2021.

Vigevani, T., and G. Cepaluni, A política externa de Lula da Silva: a estratégia da autonomia pela diversificação. *Contexto Internacional*, vol. 29, n°2, 2007.

Zieliński, T., Strategic autonomy of the European Union in security and defence. *Lithuanian Annual Strategic Review*, vol. 18, n°1, 2020.

Sandra Zapata

EU-LAC Relations in Times of US-China Competition

Introduction

It is hard to escape the feeling that the map of the world is being redrawn in light of the confrontation between the United States and China. As Beijing positions itself as an economic power, a technological giant, and a military force, it challenges the leadership of the United States. None of the other countries seem to be particularly inclined to take sides between the two powers in a binary logic. For this reason, the European Union (EU) is rethinking its international ties and has gone in search of allies, while Latin America (LAC) is looking to its European partners for a third pole on which to rely.

The analytical framework of power transformation considers that the reconfiguration of power relations conditions the foreign policy orientation of states (Kennedy, 1994; Modelski, 1983). There are increasing voices that suggest that the current changes in the international system will give rise to a new Cold War scenario where states have to choose between antagonist poles (Heine, Fortin, Amorim, 2021; Brands & Gaddis, 2021); some others say that in a highly interconnected world, opportunity windows open up and countries do have space for manoeuvre in complex multi-scalar geographies (Schindler & DiCarlo, 2022). Along with the latter, the position defended here is that in the current scenario, no key international actor can remain on the sidelines and the central question is the role they want to play to avoid falling into a position of strategic subordination.

This chapter argues that if the EU and LAC regions do not want to make uncomfortable decisions by taking sides in geopolitics, a stronger bi-regional relation can constitute a "third pole" for reshaping the re-emerging bipolarity, especially if Europe wants to regain international leadership in the global arena, and Latin America, not to accentuate its already peripheral situation in the current international system. Autonomy strategies lie at the heart of the foreign policies on both sides of the Atlantic.

In the case of the EU, autonomy ideas arise as a response to its loss of weight in the redistribution of global power due to the pressure exerted by China landing on the continent. Some recent wake-up calls for Europe are its dependencies on Washington in military terms, on technological inputs from China, and on energy from Russia. Dependency and autonomy are two sides of the same coin, also in Latin America. In this region, in its constant search for functional alternatives to boost its development, it has openly embraced alternative alliances with extra-hemispheric actors such as China. The extent to which the Asian country has re-primarised the Latin American economies and created new dependencies is still debated (Gallagher, 2016).

The chapter proceeds in three parts. It first proposes an analysis of the current rivalry context between China and the US, where the EU still is a relevant actor. Then, it analyses how in a more interconnected world, old and new dependencies have given rise to a geopolitical Europe and to "autonomy strategies" in the bloc. Finally, the discussion addresses how the EU-LAC bi-regional relation fits into this changing scenario and how this opens up opportunities for renewed bi-regional cooperation.

The international structure in dispute

The international system is facing profound shifts and the US-China rivalry has a prominent role on the international agenda. A starting point to analyse the changes in the international system is to reflect on power, cooperation and conflict in a given historical period. Following Cox's ideas, one way to do this is to ask how such a world order is conceived, who benefits, and how the costs and benefits of a determined set of rules are distributed (Cox, 1981; Strange, 1988; Krasner, 1976).

The world order under current transformation is the one that emerged as a set of norms, rules and institutions consolidated by the United States and its allies in the post-World War II period. In economic terms, it was a historical response to the world set up after the Bretton Woods agreements (1944), which institutionalised the international economic order under neoliberal principles of economic openness and financial deregulation (Krugman, 2009). In the political sphere, the visions of the promoters of the liberal order assumed the rapid diffusion of democracy and human rights around the globe. In a broader sense, the hegemonic powers enforced their will on the rest of the world, crafting institutions that served their interests and assured their primacy (Bernal-Meza, 2004).

Some elements of this world order are in dispute today. Specialists of diverse orientations and disciplines agree that we face the beginning of a new historical era, marked by profound changes in the order created by the *Pax Americana* (Huntington, 1998, Krugman, 2009; Nye, 2005; Ohmae, 2005; Bigsten, 2004; Dicken, 2003; Cox & Sinclair, 2001; Rodrik, 1997). The new geo-economic and geo-strategic dynamics are relocating the centres of gravity of world power from the transatlantic axis to the Asia-Pacific axis. Nowadays, China is not only the centre of the Asian complex, but it has become the second largest economy in the globe. In macroeconomic terms, this area has become the largest zone of world trade; its patterns of accumulation are linked to extractive industries, and it has taken a course oriented towards a market economy but regulated by the State. This sets trends in terms of trade, consumption, resources and capital investments.

The rise of its material power capabilities has emboldened China to increasingly question the Western primacy in global politics, prompting new rivalries with other actors, such as the US. This competition among great powers would give rise to what some authors see as a new Cold War, which again confronts the world into a bipolar relationship (Fortin, Heine, Ominami, 2021). This understanding of international relations has economic arguments, as it says that the world is facing a new commercial war (Kapustina et al., 2020); ideological, as there is a direct challenge to the liberal Western model in terms of democracies vs. autocracies (Kroenig, 2020); and in terms of defense as it suggests that the world is divided into zones of influence (Allison, 2017).

Amidst the focus on great power rivalry, the interdependence between the US and China continues to grow thicker, and as Nye describes, "the world is neither unipolar, nor multipolar, nor chaotic; it is all three of these things at the same time" (Nye, 2011). Therefore, it is not a foreordained conclusion that we are moving towards a new Cold War and here are some of the reasons.

Regarding the economic trends, the emerging nature of the global political economy is increasingly deep and complex, not only as international actors have multiplied, but also as they have become interdependent with each other on a myriad of issues. The actors in the international arena experience different kinds of relationships simultaneously, as they can cooperate on some issues and compete in others at the same time, and they experience the reciprocal effects of interdependence (Keohane & Nye, 1987). Between the US and China, a frenemy-like relationship is taking place in an ever-compartmentalised structure (Casarini, 2022). For instance, China-US have been each other's major trading partner for years; their supply chains are increasingly interdependent, and debt holdings are intertwined (Lee, 2020). At the same time, both countries have conflicts, as portrayed in the technology trade dynamics – which is regarded as the most consequential arena for competition (Kennedy et al., 2018). US targeted major technology companies like Huawei, TikTok, ByteDance, and China put foreign US firms on a blacklist.

On ideological terms, global powers today are not immersed in ideological competitions as they were in the past. Drawing lines in international relations pushing China to the autocratic side and the US to the democratic side is a fallacy, as China has long integrated into the capitalist world economy and become a powerful economic driving force. China's economic model is commonly described as "state capitalist" or "party-state capitalism" (Pearson, Rithmire, Tsai, 2022). Xi Jinping pointed out that "the US has American-style democracy. China has Chinese-style democracy" (Xinhua, 2022). With very few exceptions, the world has embraced capitalism as an economic system.

Moreover, in the area of defense, there are no clear zones of influence, and neither China nor the US are the uncontested leaders of any particular group of countries gathered around one common ideological purpose or strategic rationale – as it was the case with the USSR and the US during the Cold War times. There is not a unified West, and the idea that there are two distinctive Wests has strengthened over the last thirty years (Oğuzlu, 2022). For instance, when considering NATO, the EU does not want to play a secondary role to the American primacy in the region. Another striking difference is the way Brussels and Washington have approached Beijing. The former tends to engage China at the bilateral level, and the latter in the framework of the system of alliances in Asia and the commitment to regional security (Casarini, 2022).

Despite the many factors and trends that point to a more contested and volatile world, the future is not predefined. In a more interconnected world, the voices of non-hegemonic actors, middle powers, small countries and regions around the world do matter. Regions can have a "moderation" impact in times of confrontation, as they constitute new geopolitical foundations for the world economy and the construction of a multipolar world-system (Merino et al., 2022).

The case of the EU comes to mind. It constitutes the third-largest economy in the world and continues to be a major power in the international arena. It has been a political actor and a role leader in many areas including championing norms, human rights values and democracy. In Latin America, the EU is associated with leadership in areas such as environmental protection, promotion of world peace, the fight against poverty and inequality. Whether through its absence or its engagement, the EU is a key actor in shaping the current international order (Grevi, 2019).

In a more conflictive scenario, the EU wants to manage the competition responsibly and strengthening alliances with traditional actors constitutes a key feature not to submit to a bipolar logic. For this aim, the strategy that has gained relevance is strengthening the EU's role as a global geopolitical actor. In the words of the EU High Representative for Foreign and Security Affairs, Josep

Borrell, "the awakening of geopolitical Europe" means facing the current word challenges from its own point of view, act to defend the EU's values and interests, and proceed forward in "its own way" (Borrell, 2020). Geopolitics mark the renewed interest to reconnect with international partners such as LAC and the desire to reinforce the existing cooperation ties.

Wake-up calls to strengthen autonomy: Old and new dependencies

The step-change in the EU's external action is framed within the bigger narrative of the new bipolarity between China and the US. In Europe, autonomy lies at the heart of foreign policy as a means of resilience to ensure that Europeans take charge of themselves (Borrell, 2020). The concept is usually defined in terms of the "freedom of choice" or "margin of manoeuvre" of foreign policy (Escudé, 1992). In the Latin American tradition, a certain level of autonomy means conditions that allow free decisions to be taken by persons and agencies that are part of a national or regional system (Jaguaribe, 1979). It encompasses the ideas of self-determination and sovereignty in areas where hegemonic power's economic, political or cultural interferences are expressed – as the achievement of greater autonomy presupposes a previous zero-sum strategic game (Puig, 1980).

In the last decade, as China landed in Europe and in Latin America, new relations of conflict and cooperation have arisen, and there is not a unified vision or a common strategy to deal with them. What is certain is that China is the only country with both the intent to reshape the international order and, increasingly, the economic, diplomatic, military, and technological power to do it (Röttgen, 2022). Beijing's international assertion has triggered some major wake-up calls in both regions to opt for autonomous strategies.

For the EU, autonomy strategies have evolved hand in hand with economic asymmetrical interdependence and the vulnerabilities Europe faces against Beijing's assertiveness. The scholarly literature analysing the triangular Europe-US-China relations is fast-growing (Michalski & Pan, 2017; Zhou, 2016; Wang & Song, 2016; Shambaugh et al., 2008; Kerr & Liu, 2007). A large body of works has examined the US's complex relationship with China from a European perspective, where autonomy for the EU means regaining political space vis-à-vis the US (Hass, 2021; Allison, 2017; Ikenberry et al., 2015; Steinberg & O'Hanlon, 2014). Other authors have attempted to compare US and EU policies towards China and Europe's strategic autonomy in relation to Beijing (Brown, 2017; Aggarwal & Newland, 2014).

In the same vein, in the case of Latin America, the logic of autonomy has been widely practiced, as great powers continue to exert effective control over peripheral economies (Russell & Tokatlian, 2013). With China's assertion in the continent, autonomy was studied as the counter side of new dependencies and the re-primarization of the economies (Bernal-Meza, 2020); other authors highlight the irruption of the Asian country, acknowledging the historic and socio-economic relevance of the US in the region (Dussel Peters et al., 2013). Others account for China's engagement in economic, diplomatic and military activities in the continent (Gallagher, 2016).

The first wake-up call to opt for autonomy in Europe was the recent nationalist withdrawal of its main ally, the US, especially after the arrival of Donald Trump to power. In terms of security and defense, Europe continues to depend on the US for its security; however, the American attention has increasingly been pulled toward China. For the US administrations, the priority is to curb the rise of China and the efforts are concentrated in the Asia and Indo-Pacific, not anymore in the European continent. For the US, this is the most strategically important geographical area and China is considered "the most ominous threat to US security" (Casarini, 2022).

There is not a unified transatlantic strategy to deal with China's assertiveness. While Washington outlines its policies in a confrontative way, the EU's approach with Beijing is one of cooperation, not confrontation (Casarini, 2022). As a matter of fact, Trump's nationalistic administration and the strategic shift of US security policy, reinforced the idea that Europe's problems are a matter for Europeans. Also, there is not a common strategy among the EU members to counterweight Beijing, but there is an increasing belief that their security should not ultimately depend on America. As long as Washington's priorities are in the Indo Pacific and the country continues to have other global commitments such as those in the Middle East (Bergmann et al., 2022), the EU needs to step up to the challenge of taking its security into its own hands.

Beyond the defense sector, dependencies exist in other areas, such as global supply chains – science, technology, trade, data, investments are becoming sources and instruments of force in international politics (Borrell, 2020). The pandemic of Covid-19 was another wakeup call that brought this to light. During the first waves of 2020, various countries in Europe recorded shortages in the supply of personal protective equipment, medicines or masks. Subsequently, these shortcomings affected other areas, such as the pharmaceuticals needed to develop the vaccine or in semiconductors used in various industries, like the automotive sector. These events caused growing consciousness of the EU's strong external dependencies on Asian countries. In the case of Latin America, during the pandemic Beijing's donations of medical equipment to vulnerable countries strengthened its influence and soft power in the continent. The donations have doubled as dialogue facilitators that extend beyond an extra supply of facemasks, testing kits, medical equipment to discussions for widening export agreements with China (Nunell, 2020).

In terms of economy and trade, there is wider awareness in the EU of the industrial and technological dependencies on China. The European market's importance as a destination for Chinese exports is around double that of the Chinese market for Europeans, and China is the EU's largest source of imports since 2011, accounting for 22% (Cooban, 2022). European investment in China has become more concentrated in five sectors – food processing, autos, pharma/ biotech, chemicals and consumer products manufacturing – which make up nearly 70% of all EU FDI to China (Kratz et al., 2022). As a countermeasure, the EU released an Industrial Strategy in 2021 to cut its dependency on the Asian country in six strategic areas such as raw materials, pharmaceutical ingredients, semiconductors and advanced technologies.

In the case of the triangular relationship between China-US and LAC, Beijing has become a serious competitor to US hegemony in the region. Since the beginning of the 21st century, China's presence has been substantial in practically all socio-economic fields. In the financial sphere, the Asian giant has become an alternative source to the private financial market and the Bretton Woods institutions. The China Development Bank and the Export-Import Bank of China are among the region's main financiers. Between 2005 and 2020, cumulative loans amounted to more than 137 billion, with Venezuela, Brazil, Ecuador and Argentina being the main recipients (The Inter-American Dialogue, 2021). China's investments in the region amounted to 140 billion between 2005 and 2021, of which 64 billion correspond to Brazil and 25 billion to Peru, according to data from the Inter-American Dialogue.

In terms of trade, China has displaced the role of the EU and surpassed that of the US in many cases – it is the first commercial partner of Brazil, Chile, Peru, Uruguay and Argentina. The total trade between China and LAC increased from almost US$18 billion in 2002 to US$318 billion in 2020 (The Inter-American Dialogue, 2021). Despite the fact that the US continues to be the most important historical actor in the region, nowadays Beijing constitutes an additional point of reference and for negotiations. For instance, 21 of the 33 countries in the region have joined China's Belt and Road Initiative (BRI).

The latest wakeup call was Russia's invasion of Ukraine. The EU imports around 40% of natural gas from Russia. After the outbreak of the war, the European Commission has established plans to cut EU dependency on Russian gas by two-thirds in 2022 and end its reliance on Russian supplies of the fuel before 2030 (Cesluk-Grajawski, 2022). In LAC, this event made countries start thinking pragmatically about their extra-hemispheric alliance, but partners like Brazil or Peru rely on Moscow for key economic sectors such as agriculture. The former imports 85% of its fertilisers from Russia and the latter 50% (Cross, 2022). Russia is essential for fertilisers required for the agribusiness sector.

Dependencies are identified on both sides of the Atlantic, but there is no consensus on the best way to address them. Regarding the Chinese assertion, in Europe, countries such as France and Germany – highly dependent on the Asian country – are betting on a more assertive shift in EU policy. Their main concern is the loss of competitiveness of their companies vis-à-vis strategic managers of high-added value. On the other hand, the countries of Southern and Eastern Europe have been more receptive to closer ties with Beijing. Italy is the first G7 country to sign the BRI agreement, joining other EU countries that have already done so, including Hungary, Poland, the Czech Republic, Greece, and Portugal.

In the case of Latin America, political fragmentation has become a constant, and external events affect every country in a different way. China will continue to increase its presence in the region, instigating LAC countries to follow its lead in the international sphere. A clear proof is the alignment towards the "One China" policy. Currently, only eight countries in the region recognise Taiwan. Panama, the Dominican Republic, and El Salvador switched recognition to the People's Republic of China between 2017 and 2018, and Nicaragua did so in December 2021.

EU-LAC bi-regional cooperation to avoid international irrelevance

The narrative that the US is gradually declining and China is emerging, facing resistance, conditions the already complex relations between the EU and LAC because it subordinates both regions to be mere rule-takers rather than rule makers. The central question is to avoid this trap. The EU's core strategy is to mitigate the drift towards a zero-sum world by increasingly becoming a global geopolitical power. Brussels intends to achieve greater strategic autonomy and reduce its dependencies. In this scenario, revisiting and strengthening the bi-regional alliance acquire relevance, as it gives the opportunity to promote an innovative partnership to face these challenges.

The EU and LAC relations should be thought of in light of the power transformations. In the early 21st century, the EU's weight in the world has been shrinking, while China is growing as a global power. In the nineties, Europe represented a quarter of the world's wealth. It is foreseen that in twenty years, Europe will not represent more than 11% of world GNP, far behind China, which will represent double it, below 14% for the US and at par with India (Borrell, 2020). The same period of time finds LAC an ever heterogeneous, fragmented and increasingly irrelevant region – Latin America lost positions in all available indicators of relevance: share of the world population, strategic weight, trade volume, military projection and diplomatic capacity (Schenoni & Malamud, 2021).

In this adverse scenario, EU-LAC alliance is key to avoid irrelevance and strengthen the autonomy of both regions. For the EU, strategic autonomy refers to the capacity of the EU to act autonomously, "without being dependent on other countries in strategically important policy areas" (European Parliament, 2022), which can range from defense policy to the economy, and the capacity to uphold democratic values. It is also the "ability of a state to pursue its national interests and adopt its preferred foreign policy without depending heavily on other foreign states" (Borrell, 2020). In the case of Latin America, the region has a long tradition of reflection and experiences that have been oriented towards the search for greater autonomy as means to pursue economic development, peace, restriction of influence of great powers. The mechanisms to put this into practice have been regionalism, the appeal to law or the support of international organizations (Russell & Tokatlian, 2013).

The new cycle of a geopolitical and more autonomous EU has different dimensions and it opens up opportunities for cooperation and re-articulation of ties with Latin America. Some of the cross-cutting elements that should be revisited are the association agreements, trade, energy, norms and regulations.

Regarding the association agreements, the EU and LAC have developed one of the densest networks of association, trade, political and cooperation agreements, between the EU and 27 of the 33 LAC countries. These tools are not only trade agreements, the networks it has created have a geopolitical character with the potential to open up a shared space for policy dialogue, as well as regulatory convergence for changing production and consumption models (Sanahuja, 2022). The central element is to revise the associations in light of the challenging global context, emphasising the green transition, digital transformation, human development, inclusive economy and democratic governance (European Commission, 2022).

In terms of trade, the EU and LAC can cooperate in setting international standards and moving towards agreements, which are not the "business as usual" FTA. For instance, the Mercosur agreement, if ratified, can also be about setting up models of sustainable trade regulations, disseminating norms and promoting sustainable development up to today's challenges. For Latin America, a good negotiation would offer the chance to look for mechanisms to strengthen the local industries. Considering the penetration of China in the South American markets and the possibility of Beijing signing an FTA with Uruguay, the ratification of the Mercosur agreement becomes strategic. It imprints urgency to develop long-term strategic thinking, as whichever actor moves first into these markets will gain competitive first-mover advantage. The EU and LAC are better off as commercial partners and if they lose the opportunity to strengthen ties, there will be other external actors, who will take that place.

In terms of energy, the EU is setting up the global energy plan – RePowerEU, which aims at accelerating the clean energy transition and increasing Europe's energy independence from unreliable suppliers and volatile fossil fuels. For the EU's relationship with Latin America, there will be an increasing demand for critical raw materials such as lithium and niobium, which are important components for the production of electric and high-tech batteries. The EU imports these materials 78% from Chile and 85% from Brazil, respectively (European Commission, 2020). For Europe, there is the risk of moving its current dependency on fossil fuels to a dependency on critical raw materials and minerals. LAC will face again the challenge of making steps forward adding value to its goods and not becoming a primary product exporter. The current energy transition can give opportunities to industrialise those areas in LAC.

Another key issue for the bilateral relation is policy dialogue and regulatory convergence. The EU has set the goal of diversifying its suppliers in different areas so as not to depend on any country or supplier higher than 33%. This is not only included in the action plan on critical materials, but it also extends to other ten areas such as: sustainable and resilient food and health system; decarbonised and accessible energy; capacity in the management of data; security and defense capabilities and access to space; working with global partners to promote peace, security and prosperity (European Commission, 2021). Therefore, in terms of regulations, strengthening the bi-regional relations could open up the space to create new norms and deploy the so-called "Brussels Effect" – the ability to influence different regulatory areas on a global scale through the diffusion of regulations by means of market mechanisms (Bradford, 2020).

Ultimately, in light of the global changes, the EU-LAC relations should be seen as a common space of dialogue to think of innovative policies, setting standards, regulatory convergence, change in production and consumption models in the interest of sustainable development. The framework of bi-regional cooperation needs to be revisited having a long-term sight of where the world is moving towards.

Conclusion

The international system is facing a *Zeitenwende* or an epochal tectonic shift. This critical juncture is characterised by the crisis of globalization, inequality, the climate emergency, the coronavirus pandemic, and the resurgence of the war of aggression and its global socio-economic consequences. China-US rivalry is a significant factor influencing the insertion processes of countries worldwide. Beijing has been gaining influence and political allies in Europe and it has already challenged the traditional EU-Atlantic cooperation in terms of defense. In LAC, China has become a top trading and investment partner for many countries.

These challenging times have prompted some wake-up calls for Europe to rethink its international role and alliances. The EU-LAC bi-regional relations cannot escape from the dynamics that challenge the rationale of the relationship. The EU has sought to respond to these convulsive times by becoming a geopolitical actor and through the search for "strategic autonomy". A renewed cooperation between the two regions is key in terms of building common spaces for dialogue in areas such as trade, energy, norms and regulations. At a moment of crossroads, stronger cooperation between the EU and LAC can constitute a strategic alternative for the international insertion of both regions in the changing world order, especially if they want to avoid being entrenched between the US and China rivalry.

Bibliography

Allison, G. (2017). *Destined for war: Can America and China escape Thucydides' trap?* Boston: Houghton Mifin Harcourt.

Allison, G. (2020). *The new spheres of influence. Sharing the globe with other great powers foreign affairs*. https://www.foreignaffairs.com/articles/united-states/2020-02-10/new-spheres-influence.

Aggarwal, V. and Newland, S. (2014). *Responding to China's rise: US and EU strategies*. Berlin: Springer.

Bergmann, M., Morcos, P., Wall, C., and Monaghan, S. (2022). *Transforming the European defense*. CSIS Briefs. Available at: https://csis-website-prod.s3.amazonaws.com/s3fs-public/publication/220818_Bergmann_European_Defense.pdf?Nv5aOdqnPtDfUlIt_ATghDCNTD4UmVPk

Bernal-Meza, R. (2004). *Multilateralismo y unilateralismo en la política mundial: América Latina ante el orden mundial*. Argentina: Universidad de Buenos Aires. HAOL, N.5, pp. 83–91.

Bernal-Meza, R. (2020). Introduction: Understanding China–Latin America relations as part of the transition of the world order. In: Bernal-Meza, R. and Xing, L. (Eds.), *China–Latin America relations in the 21st century*. International Political Economy Series. Cham: Palgrave Macmillan. https://doi.org/10.1007/978-3-030-35614-9_1.

Bigsten, A. (2004). Globalisation and the Asia–Pacific revival. *World Economics*, vol. 5, no. 2, 1–31.

Borrell, J. (2020a). *Why European strategic autonomy matters*. The Diplomatic service of the European Union. European Union External Action. https://www.eeas.europa.eu/eeas/why-european-strategic-autonomy-matters_en

Borrell, J. (2020b). *The Sinatra doctrine: Building a United European front*. Institut Montaigne, 09 September.

Bradford, A. (2020). *How the European Union rules the world*. Oxford: Oxford University Press.

Brands, H. and Gaddis, J. L. (2021). The new cold war: America, China, and the echoes of history. *Foreign Affairs*, vol. 100, no. 6, pp. 10– 20.

Brown, S. (2017). *Power, perception and foreign policymaking: US and EU responses to the rise of China*. London: Routledge.

Casarini, N. (2022). *A European strategic "third way?" The European Union between the traditional transatlantic alliance and the pull of the Chinese market*. The Institute of International and Strategic Studies (IISS). Peking University. China International Strategy Review. Available at: https://doi.org/10.1007/s42533-022-00095-1

Cesluk, G. (2022). EU strategic autonomy in the context of Russia's war on Ukraine [What Think Tanks are thinking]. Think Thank European parliament. https://www.europarl.europa.eu/thinktank/en/document/EPRS_BRI(2022)729300

Coffman, D. M. (2010). *The ascent of money: A financial history of the world*. By Niall Ferguson. London: Allen Lane, 2008, pp. 442. ISBN 978-1-846-14106-5.£ 25.00. *The Historical Journal*, vol. 53, no. 1, pp. 239–241.

Cooban, A. (2022). *Huge trade partner and "systemic rival." Europe has a China problem Analysis*. CNN Business. Available at: https://edition.cnn.com/2022/11/30/economy/europe-china-trade-tension/index.html#:~:text=China%20is%20Europe's%20biggest%20source%20of%20imported%20goods,the%20year%20before%20the%20pandemic

Cox, R. (1981). Social forces, states and world orders: Beyond international relations theory. *Millennium*, vol. 10, no. 2, pp. 126–155.

Cox, R., and Sinclair, T. (eds.) (2001). *Approaches to world order*. New York: Cambridge University Press.

Cross, A. (2022). *Latin American perspectives on the war in Ukraine.* Oxford Political Review, 22 November. Online: https://oxfordpoliticalreview.com/2022/11/22/latin-american-perspectives-on-the-war-in-ukraine/

Dicken, P. (2003). *Global shift: Reshaping the global economic map in the 21st century.* London, Thousand Oaks CA, and New Delhi: Sage.

Dussel, E., Hearn, A., and Shaiken, H. (2013). *China and the new triangular relationships in the Americas: China and the future of US-Mexico relations.* Mexico: CLAS/University of Miami, CLAS/University of California-Berkeley, UNAM/CECHIMEX.

Escudé, C. (1992). *Realismo periférico: fundamentos para la nueva política exterior argentina.* Planeta.

EU-LAC partnership. *Fact sheet.* https://www.eeas.europa.eu/sites/default/files/documents/Factsheet%20EU_LAC_en_2022_2510fin.pdf

European Comission. (2020). *Resiliencia de las materias primas fundamentales: trazando el camino hacia un mayor grado de seguridad y sostenibilidad.* COM Brussels, September 3th.

European Comission. (2021a). *2021 strategic foresight report. The EU's capacity and freedom to act.* COM, Bruesels, September 8th.

European Commission. (2021b). *China: Countries and regions.* Available at: https://ec.europa.eu/trade/policy/countries-and-regions/countries/china/.

European Commission. (2022). *The EU-LAC partnership.* The diplomatic service of the European Union. The European Union External Action. October.

European Parliament. (2022). *EU strategic autonomy 2013–2023: From concept to capacity.* Think Thank European parliament. https://www.europarl.europa.eu/thinktank/en/document/EPRS_BRI(2022)733589

Gallagher, K. P. (2016). *The China triangle: Latin America's China boom and the fate of the Washington consensus.* New York: Oxford University Press.

Grevi, G. (2019). *Strategic autonomy for European choices: The key to Europe's shaping power.* Discussion paper. Europe in the World Programme. European Policy Center.

Hass, R. (2021). *Stronger: Adapting America's China strategy in an age of competitive interdependence.* New Haven, CT: Yale University Press.

Heine, J., and Ominami, C. (2021). *El no alineamiento activo y América Latina: Una doctrina para el nuevo siglo.* Editorial Catalonia.

Huntington, S. (1998). *The clash of civilizations and the remaking of world order.* New York: Touchstone.

Ikenberry, J., Zhu, F., and Wang, J. (2015). *America, China, and the struggle for world order.* Basingstoke: Palgrave Macmillan.

Jaguaribe, H. (1979). Autonomía periférica y hegemonía céntrica. *Estudios Internacionales* vol. 12, nº 46, pp. 91–130.

Kapustina, L., Lipková, Ľ., Silin, Y., and Drevalev, A. (2020). US-China trade war: Causes and outcomes. In *SHS Web of conferences* (vol. 73, p. 01012). EDP Sciences.

Kennedy, A., and Darren, J. (2018). The innovation imperative: Technology and US-China rivalry in the twenty-first century. *International Affairs*, vol. 94, no. 3, pp. 553–572.

Keohane, R. O., and Nye, J. S. (1987). Power and interdependence revisited. *International Organization*, vol. 41, no. 4, pp. 725–753.

Kerr, D., and Liu, F. (2007). *The international politics of EU-China relations*. Oxford: Oxford University Press.

Krasner, S. (1976). State power and the international trade structure. *World Politics,* no. 28, pp. 317–347.

Kratz, N., Barkin, N., and Lauren, D. (2022). *The chosen few: A fresh look at European FDI in China.* Agatha. Rhodium Group. https://rhg.com/research/the-chosen-few/

Kroenig, M. (2020). *The return of great power rivalry: Democracy versus autocracy from the ancient world to the US and China.* New York: Oxford University Press.

Krugman, P. (2009). *The return of depression economics and the crisis of 2008.* New York: Norton Company.

Lee, Yen Nee (2020). Five charts show how much the US and Chinese economies depend on each other. *CNBC*. https://www.cnbc.com/2020/09/29/5-charts-show-how-the-us-and-chinese-economies-depend-on-each-other.html

Michalski, A., and Zhongqi, P. (2017). *Unlikely partners? China, the European Union and the forging of a strategic partnership*. Berlin: Springer.

Nunell, L. (2020). *China's facemask diplomacy in Latin America.* Fresh perspective. Available at: https://www.internationalaffairs.org.au/australianoutlook/chinas-facemask-diplomacy-in-latin-america/

Nye, J. (2005). The rise of China's soft power. *Wall Street Journal Asia*, vol. 29, pp. 6–8.

Oğuzlu, T. (n/d). *Are we on the eve of a new cold war?* Antalya Bilim University Department of Political Science and International Relations.

Ohmae, K. (2005). *The next global stage: The challenges and opportunities in our borderless world*. Pennsylvania: Wharton School Publishing.

Pearson, M., Rithmire, M., and Tsai, K. (2021). Party-state capitalism in China. *Current history*, vol. 120, no. 827, pp. 207–213. https://doi.org/10.1525/curh.2021.120.827.207.

Puig, J. C. (1980). *Doctrinas internacionales y autonomía latinoamericana*. Caracas: Instituto de Altos Estudios de América Latina, Universidad Simón Bolívar.

Rapoport, M., y Madrid, E. (2002). Los países del Cono Sur y las grandes potencias. In M. Rapoport and A. Cervo (eds.), *El Cono Sur: Una historia común*. Buenos Aires: Fondo de Cultura Económica.

Rodrik, D. (1997). *Has globalization gone too far?* Washington, DC: Institute for International Economics.

Röttgen, N. (2022). *Nie wieder hilflos! Ein Manifest in Zeiten des Krieges*. Dtv München.

Russell, R., and Tokatlian, J. G. (2003). From antagonistic to relational autonomy: A theoretical reflection from the Southern Cone. *Latin American Politics and Society*, vol. 45, n.º 1, 1–24.

Russell, R., and Tokatlian, J. G. (2013). América Latina y su gran estrategia: entre la aquiescencia y la autonomía/Latin America and its grand strategy: between acquiescence and autonomy. *Revista Cidob d'afers internacionals*, 157–180.

Sanahuja, J. (2022). *La Unión Europea y América Latina en el interregno: autonomía estratégica, pacto verde y recuperación pospandemia*. Eurosocial.

Schenoni, L., and Malamud, A. (2021). *Sobre la creciente irrelevancia de América Latina*. Tema Central NUSO Nº 291. Enero-febrero 2021. NUSO.

Schindler, S., and DiCarlo, J. (2022). *Towards a critical geopolitics of China–US rivalry: Pericentricity, regional conflicts and transnational connections*. Area, June 16th.

Shambaugh, D., Sandschneider, E., and Zhou, H. (2008). *China-Europe relations: Perceptions, policies and prospects*. London: Routledge.

Steinberg, J., and O'Hanlon, M. (2014). *Strategic reassurance and resolve: US-China relations in the twenty-frst century*. Princeton: Princeton University Press.

Strange, S. (1988). *States and markets: An introduction to political economy*. London: Pinter.

The Inter-American Dialogue. (2021). *China-Latin America finance database*. Online https://www.thedialogue.org/MapLists/index.html?initialWidth=691&childId=iframeContainer&parentTitle=China-Latin%20America%20Finance%20Databases%20-%20The%20Dialogue&parentUrl=https%3A%2F%2Fwww.thedialogue.org%2Fmap_list%2F#/Policy/List/amount

Tickner, A. (2003). *Colombia: U.S. subordinate, autonomous actor, or something in between?* In Frank O. Mora y Jeanne A. K. Hey (eds.), *Latin American and Caribbean foreign policy*. Lanham: Rowman & Littlefield Publishers.

Verdes-Montenegro, F. (2022). *La autonomía estratégica de la Unión Europea: ¿en qué lugar queda América Latina?*. Documentos de trabajo 65. Fundación Carolina.

Wang, J., and Weiqing, S. (2016). *China, the European Union, and the international politics of global governance*. Basingstoke: Palgrave.

Xinhua. (2022). *So-called "democracy versus authoritarianism" narrative not defining feature of today's world, says Xi*. China Daily. https://www.chinadaily.com.cn/a/202211/14/WS63724c92a310491754329a3f.html

Zhou, H. (2016). *China-EU relations: Reassessing the China-EU comprehensive strategic partnership*. Berlin: Springer.

Paz Verónica Milet and Belén Cabezas Araya

The Challenges of Linking with Latin America and the Caribbean Under Three Crises

In the last decade, Latin America has undergone a series of far-reaching processes that have conditioned the transitions and even the survival of its main multilateral initiatives at the regional level. This chapter will identify these conditioning factors that range from the global to the regional and national level. These factors today determine the Latin American scenario, affect the state of the region's multilateral spaces, and consequently, Latin America and the Caribbean's conditions and capacity to link with Europe and the European Union. The chapter will answer two questions: What is the actual state of Latin America's multilateral processes? And what are the most appropriate spaces to project the link with Europe?

The challenges of three simultaneous crises

Latin America is facing one of the most challenging stages in its history due to the confluence of a crisis process at three levels: global, regional and national. First, at the global level, the consequences of the tension between the prominent world powers, the broad scope of the 2008 economic crisis, the multidimensional effects of the pandemic, and the conflict in Ukraine all make the international environment very challenging for Latin America and the Caribbean (LAC).

At the international level, the differences between the main world powers have wide-ranging consequences in the region, as they generate self-questioning as to how to position and act at the international level, either through active non-alignment, with equidistance or pursuing strategic autonomy, in a scenario in which questions are also being raised as to the region's relevance. While some authors argue that Latin America possesses the geopolitical resources to position itself in a prominent position at the international level, others argue that the region is becoming increasingly irrelevant (Malamud & Schenoni, 2021). This framework conditions any international decision of Latin American countries and their definitions in foreign policy, security, and defense.

The economic crisis of 2008 and the fall in the price of raw materials had vast repercussions in Latin America, conditioning not only the internal policies of the countries of the region but also the capacity to build common projects and institutions, which in those years began to weaken, generating crises in the integration processes (Ocampo, 2009). Some of the main regional initiatives were affected in their capacity for expansion and interregional projection in areas such as connectivity, infrastructure, energy articulation, overcoming poverty, and knowledge integration (Maira, 2009). Priorities had to be re-established in Latin America based on the average growth of 0.7% that the region has experienced in recent years. This figure is far from the 5% annual growth that the region had before 2008, which was accompanied by the export of commodities and the improvement of international reserves (Maira, 2009).

This scenario of regional fragility worsened during the pandemic due to the restrictive measures implemented to prevent the spread of the virus, which affected the logistics of international trade, increasing the time and cost of foreign trade (ECLAC, 2021). The performance of the regional economy has been recorded as the worst in seven decades. The region's countries are experiencing a very delicate situation due to the slowdown in the pace of growth, rising inflation, increases in energy, fuel, and food prices, the slow and incomplete recovery of labor markets, and the rise in inequality and poverty (ECLAC, 2022).

In general, in the face of these global phenomena, there is evidence of the confluence of two variables: the priority of unilateralism and the competition for access to inputs, especially health inputs. In the struggle for access to these resources, a determining factor was the building of alliances and the level of openness of the countries in the region. The sector that had to focus on acquiring sanitary inputs or vaccines is traditionally the one in charge of negotiating free trade agreements.

This takes us to the second level of crises, the regional level, which is characterised by a lack of vision and a forward-looking approach. This was made evident by the Covid-19 pandemic. It was noted that since 2008 one of the sectors with the lowest level of investment was the health sector. This is an area that has also generated little institutionalism. From a regional perspective, only the role of the two institutions stands out. Between 2008 and 2019, the South American Health Council, an organization affiliated with the Union of South American Nations (UNASUR), contributed to the collective confrontation of the H1N1 influenza pandemic, epidemics such as dengue, and the Ebola virus (Buss & Tobar, 2020). However, when faced with the projection of COVID, its capacity for action was limited by the UNASUR crisis itself and the loss of political and economic capital of this initiative.

The institution that had the most significant capacity to act in this context was the Andean Health Organization – Hipólito Unanue Agreement, which worked along the lines of strengthening health systems, identification, and development of actions aimed at caring for people infected by Covid-19; but in general, the region's actions were reactive and focused on specific areas, rather than approaching them from a global and multidimensional perspective.

In regional crises, beyond the specificities, two wide-ranging processes have manifested themselves through different expressions. First, the questioning of the political and economic model applied during the last decades in Latin America. Discontent had different ways of channeling, either through the so-called social outbursts of 2019 or the transitions towards new expressions of political leadership, within the framework of the questioning of traditional political parties and democracy as a form of government (Latinobarometro, 2021). Second, polarization and fragmentation at the regional level, expressed on the one hand in the inability to generate a cohesive response to some of the major crises affecting the region –such as the Venezuelan crisis – and on the other hand in the lack of consensus to work towards greater institutionality.

The third and final level of crisis is the national level. National crises are the result of specific local processes, but also, to a large extent, of the interaction of global and regional circumstances and their impact on the national level. Thus, the existing discontent in some countries of the region in 2019 has led institutions such as the OECD, EU, ECLAC, and CAF to raise the possibility of a new social contract in Latin America (LEO, 2021). This need has deepened due to the worsening of economic and social crises and the inability of current governments to respond effectively to them.

The reality of regional processes: Progress, setbacks, and stagnation

Before delving deeper into some of the main multilateral processes in the region, it is crucial, in addition to the framework already mentioned, to consider other three factors that have conditioned the development of Latin American regionalisms in the last period. First, the tendency to adopt a light regionalism is expressed in the lack of willingness to move towards greater supranational and the option for minimal dispute settlement systems. Second, the lack of regional leadership to promote the creation of mechanisms for concerted action. Third, the lack of willingness to move towards greater institutionality determines an excessive dependence on the priorities of the countries that hold the pro tempore Secretariat or presidency of a process. The chapter analyses five regional multilateral projects: MERCOSUR, UNASUR, the Pacific Alliance, The Andean Community of Nations and CELAC.

MERCOSUR

Until the 2000s, the Southern Common Market was considered the most successful integration experience in the region (Schvarzer, 2001), since it had not only overcome the rivalry between Argentina and Brazil but also, with a fundamental institutional framework, had made substantial progress in the area of intra-regional trade. However, the integration process was gradually weakened due to structural weaknesses in the member countries and insurmountable divergences at the internal level, which had to be submitted to bodies such as the World Trade Organization.

Among these eroding factors can be identified the Argentine economic and political crisis – which had its maximum expression in 2001 with the "corralito" and the departure from power of President De la Rúa (Bernal-Meza, 2002) – but which with different expressions has continued for more than 20 years, affecting the country's capacity to manage the joint project.

These Argentine difficulties have been accompanied by divergences between the partners, some of a more conjunctural nature, others showing deeper tensions; regarding how to project itself in the international scenario and open up to new incorporations. In this context, two issues have been the most controversial: the agreement with the European Union and the incorporation of Venezuela as a full member. The former was negotiated for more than a decade, and during that period, there was resistance from Argentina to greater openness, while the incorporation of Venezuela, which took about five years, was made when the democratic clause had been applied to Paraguay (Portela, 2021). That is to say; it was officially approved by only three of the founding members and, from the beginning, was the subject of discrepancies, first due to the treatment of opponents to the government of Nicolás Maduro and later due to the Venezuelan regime's decision to call elections for a Constituent Assembly, which was considered to usurp the functions of the National Assembly and affect the democratic system.

Tensions over these two processes were added to the deep differences already developing in MERCOSUR due to the confrontation between two identities (De Sierra, 2010). In the political sphere, between the more conservative and progressive sectors, and in the economic sphere, between those who seek – through openness – to consolidate the bloc as a platform for links with other projects and those who opt for a more protectionist strategy.

These discrepancies have been increasing since 2001 and have worsened during the pandemic. Alberto Fernández, who had just taken office, in response to his partners' request to generate agreements that would link him with other regions (Casa Rosada, 2022), was evident in pointing out that this was not the time to sign contracts but rather to rethink why this initiative was created.

These tensions grew, and in 2021, thirty years after the signing of the Treaty of Asunción, the lack of harmony between some of the prominent leaders became evident, and it was feared that some of the founding countries would leave. Although this did not materialise, differences persist and have become apparent in the late treatment of the pandemic and the debate regarding an agreement with China. At the MERCOSUR Summit in early December 2022, Uruguay announced its unilateral decision to negotiate a deal with the Asian power. The Argentine President insisted on re-establishing MERCOSUR and working towards overcoming asymmetries. Fernandez prioritises interests different from those defended by other member countries such as Brazil and Uruguay by expressing the politicization of the organization and, at the same time, seems to bet again on the internal market and trade restrictions, to promote its economic recovery (Caetano & Pose, 2020).

The absence of dialogue between the leaders of the Southern Common Market is evident, generating confrontations between its members in regards to possible unilateral negotiations with other countries (Bartesaghi, 2022). In turn, this absence of dialogue is present in the uncertainty associated with the possible ratification of the agreement with the EU and the definitive disarmament of the Customs Union (Caetano & Pose, 2020). The danger of a possible breakup of MERCOSUR has been constant in recent years. The tensions between the founding countries go beyond their different political trajectories and are related to the perspective that should guide the actions of this initiative and the priorities to be established in the current regional and international context.

UNASUR

This initiative arose under Brazilian leadership, first by Fernando Henrique Cardoso – in the preceding institution, the Summits of South American Presidents – and later by Luiz Inácio Da Silva, already in the process that led to the creation of the Union of South American Nations (UNASUR). By 2008, this instance symbolised Latin American regionalism; however, eight years later, some authors were already categorical in saying that it constituted a missed opportunity (Ramanzini & Serbin, 2016).

A questioning of the neoliberal model and the necessity to generate more autonomy from international leading powers, especially the US, is at the origin of UNASUR. In this context and within the framework of what is known as post-liberal regionalism, the decision was made to move forward with the development of an initiative that would promote a South American identity, prioritise political integration and provide a space for convergence between the Andean Community of Nations, MERCOSUR and Chile, a country that did not participate fully in any other regional integration agreement.

From the outset, it was clear that UNASUR was an option that emerged from the region; that critical issues for regional development, such as the generation of common infrastructure, energy integration, and the treatment of asymmetries, would be rescued and, in addition, something remarkable in the context of the light regionalism that prevailed in the region, was that it would opt to move towards a common institutional framework, which finally materialised through the creation of a series of specialised Councils.

Despite the international support and legitimacy that this initiative acquired, as a counterpart in the region and as an electoral observer, it began to experience the consequences of internal tensions almost from the moment of its official constitution. It was impossible to overcome the differences in narratives between the countries committed to the Bolivarian proposal and the other countries of this initiative.

Finally, the differences became evident in the inability to appoint the General Secretariat. This led seven founding countries to freeze their participation and withdraw definitively from UNASUR. The suspension of the involvement of Argentina, Brazil, Chile, Colombia, Paraguay, and Peru, supposed the further step of UNASUR's disintegration as a geopolitical bloc (Nolte & Mijares, 2018). Yet, at the end of 2022, a group of former Presidents and former Ministers of Foreign Affairs proposed the reactivation of the Union of South American Nations but considering two substantive modifications: incorporating a commercial emphasis and eliminating the ability to veto the election of the Secretary-General. However, questions immediately arose regarding the possibility of rescuing failed experiences due to deep internal divergences (Nolte, 2022).

Likewise, in the current regional and international context, two questions arise regarding the possibility of relaunching UNASUR. Firstly, the concerns about adding the trade and economic dimension to an initiative that is primarily political, thus affecting its identity, structure, and raison d'être, and secondly, concerns on the generation of excessive expectations considered the current political moment. The election of Luiz Inácio Da Silva has generated expectations regarding a rebirth of this institution within the framework of a new pink tide. However, it is important to consider that the scenario is different from when UNASUR was created. There is not the same political harmony; there is not the same financing capacity, and, in the case of Lula, he has a minority representation in Congress, which significantly conditions his actions.

Pacific Alliance

Since its inception, this initiative has been questioned since it arose amid what was considered a post-liberal stage, promoting instead adherence to neoliberalism and with a primarily commercial character.

In the context of these questions regarding the content of its proposals, the Alliance has designed a roadmap for 2030, which includes objectives for deepening the political, institutional, and commercial spheres. The Strategic Vision of the Pacific Alliance for the year 2030 focuses on external and inter-institutional relations, which is why it is proposed to add ten additional associated States by 2030, articulate with international forums such as the OECD and the G-20, reform its commitment to the World Trade Organization (WTO), strengthen economic cooperation with ASEAN, consolidate a free trade area with Asia-Pacific, obtain observer status in APEC, constitute a cooperative relationship with the EU by deepening bi-regional ties, and promote South-South cooperation (Pastrana & Blomeier, 2018).

These proposed reforms are based on the one hand on a positive self-assessment of the achievements made so far, and on the other on the understanding of the challenges imposed by the scenario of regional fragmentation and the difficulties that some of the leading integration initiatives in the region experience. However, amid this process, several conditioning factors emerged that substantially determined the possible advances in these guidelines. The questioning of the neoliberal model; the unwillingness of the political and economic elites to reshape this development model, generating a strong defense of the neoliberal economic international order, of which the PA is an expression; institutions such as the PA associated with that model have produced great social discontent and disenchantment with domestic, regional and international democratic institutions (Pastrana & Blomeier, 2018).

This discontent resulted in two significant expressions. The first is the decision of the Mexican government, led by President López Obrador, to declare that the neoliberal model would no longer be applied in Mexico (Forbes, 2019), and second, the social outbursts that were generated in two of the member countries, Chile and Colombia, which show disagreement with the neoliberal model adopted in the last 30 years.

During the most challenging stage of Covid-19, a lack of coordination among the member countries of the Alliance was evident in several areas. Chile managed to negotiate agreements to acquire vaccines from different laboratories early on, working to immunise a large part of its population. Mexico benefited from agreements with Chinese and US-based laboratories. The other members of the Pacific Alliance received little aid from fellow PA members, and it proved to be necessary for Colombia and Peru to be part of the COVAX Program to immunise their population. Although the Alliance held virtual meetings to address the crisis generated by the pandemic to coordinate positions and joint actions, this was not enough. Part of the expected collective response on issues of regional health governance and, therefore, access to vaccines did not materialise (Oyarzún, 2021).

In recent times, due to fragmentation at the regional level, the ideological transitions of the member countries, and their internal difficulties, the Pacific Alliance has functioned almost "on autopilot" lacking proactivity. The minimal institutional framework developed in the Alliance characterises it as a minimalist regionalism that essentially seeks to flexibly facilitate trade between economic agents and countries. This makes it possible to increase efficiency but ends up generating weakness in the organization (Pastrana & Castro, 2020). Although the countries have increased their initial commitment, the relative importance of intra-PA trade is at most 10% of the total foreign trade of the members. These figures suggest that productivity should be accelerated by restructuring production and strengthening regional value chains (Marchini, 2019).

The weakening of the Alliance has been deepened by the absence of leadership, lack of political will, and internal polarization (Oyarzún, 2021). Within the institutional transformations, a priority requirement is a change in the pro tempore leadership, conditioned by the political will of the administration in office and does not provide adequate tools to overcome crises. A demonstration of this incapacity is what happened in December 2022 in the face of the political turmoil in Peru, which ended with the departure from power of Pedro Castillo. First, the Mexico Summit was postponed due to the lack of authorization from the Peruvian Congress for the President to leave the country, and only weeks later, the new meeting was delayed in Lima due to the dismissal of President Castillo. In other words, there is a direct dependence on the current situation and an inability to generate longer-term guidelines.

In addition, so far, the Alliance, based on the work developed by the working groups, has mainly addressed issues that do not generate significant tensions; one may wonder what will happen when more sensitive issues will be brought to the fore. Likely, divergences may arise that require greater leadership and a more developed institutional framework that considers not only member countries, but also associates and observers, which may be key players in the PA projection to other regions.

Andean Community of Nations (CAN)

This initiative, the oldest at the regional level and with the highest level of supranationality, should, in principle, have a greater capacity to face regional crises. It has institutional backing and has been working together for over forty years. Yet, it has faced a series of ups and downs that have permanently raised questions about its continuity. This uncertainty worsened after the Venezuelan decision to withdraw from the group, among other factors, due to the decision of Colombia and Peru to negotiate free trade agreements with the United States (Acosta, 2006). This fact generated wide differences within the CAN of an ideological, economic, and commercial nature, including vast differences in terms of the international insertion policies of the member countries (Chiriboga, 2009).

Despite these difficulties, this bloc began renewing its priorities in 2019, the fortieth anniversary of its creation, which made it possible to be in a better position to face crises. Among the areas prioritised were the development of an Andean Digital Agenda (XXIX Comité Andino de Autoridades de Telecomunicaciones, 2022), the approval of the Andean Environmental Charter for the protection of regional biodiversity (XXV Consejo Andino de Ministros de Relaciones Exteriores, 2020), the establishment of an Andean Migratory Statute (XXVI Consejo Andino de Ministros de Relaciones Exteriores, 2021) – to face one of the most significant regional challenges, migration and, finally, the establishment of an Andean Agricultural Agenda (Cuarta Sesión Foro Agropecuario Andino, 2021), focused – in a scenario of increasing food insecurity – on turning the Community into a food pantry for the planet.

This development has led to a reasonable adaptation to changes in the international and regional scenario; however, there is still instability and uncertainty in some member countries of this initiative, which permanently affect the achievement of the agreed goals. In 2022, Bolivia, Ecuador, and Peru experienced different instability scenarios, which cast doubts on the viability of the Andean Community of Nations as a catalyst of regional public policies.

CELAC

From its inception, the Community of Latin American and Caribbean States (CELAC) considered the confluence of two experiences, the Rio Group – which had been characterised by emphasising regional coordination – and the Development Summits, a Brazilian initiative. By rescuing the identity of these two experiences, the proposal was to operate with flexibility and no institutionalization; to work on a wide range of issues so as to have a greater margin of action to face possible turbulences; not to overlap with other regional organizations and to assume the role of spokesperson for Latin America in the dialogue with other global actors. This role was previously played by the Rio Group and is facilitated by the fact that CELAC is the most inclusive initiative at the regional level, which seeks to recover its own identity, explicitly leaving out the United States and Canada.

In this framework, the Community of Latin American and Caribbean States proposed to generate a new development paradigm and to address issues such as drugs, sustainable development, natural disasters, physical integration, gender, migrant protection, and culture from a renewed perspective (Díaz & Bertot, 2017). However, increased regional fragmentation affected the achievement of some of these objectives, and CELAC became a space for expressing the particular interests of the member states and subregional realities rather than the global sentiment of the region. This became noticeable in the dialogue with the European Union – stalled since 2015 due to the inability to generate a shared vision – and in the talks with China. The two white papers developed by China towards the region have remained unanswered, and finally, Beijing has opted to maintain the dialogue with CELAC, although with limited expectations and privileging bilateral approaches.

From the thematic point of view, the topics on the agenda were broadened, and, under Mexico's leadership during the pandemic, efforts were made to create spaces for coordination. However, factors such as excessive rhetoric, the lack of clear leadership, and the withdrawal of Brazil have affected the basis for joint work without clarifying a roadmap to achieve regional unity and intergovernmental cooperation (Malamud & Núñez, 2021).

CELAC entered a reflection phase in 2018, and in 2021 it emanated its conclusions: maintaining pragmatic leadership, prioritising common elements over differences, strengthening dialogue with extra-regional partners, sustaining the commitment to a peace zone, and persisting in the founding objectives. The final aim of the document that contains the conclusions is to end with the stagnation of the Community of Latin-American and Caribbean States, that since the year 2017 has been debating in regards to what type of integration to develop (CELAC, 2021).

Linking Latin America and the Caribbean with the European Union

Latin America is the region with the most extensive institutionalised ties with the EU. However, relations have been, in the words of Caetano (2022), "bogged down". Since 2015, there has been a window of opportunity to relaunch bi-regional relations (Sanahuja, 2022), mainly by updating the association agreements, incorporating new issues and the new geopolitical scenario.

The European Union is again interested in Latin America, among other reasons, due to the rivalry between the United States and China since there is a need to expand the margins of strategic autonomy between the two regions and strengthen multilateral spaces. This encounter with Europe could improve Latin American countries' eventual negotiating capabilities in the face of offers from China and the United States (Verdes-Montenegro & Jeger, 2022).

Another challenge to be faced jointly is the conflict between Russia and Ukraine, with wide repercussions at the energy and food levels. A context in which Latin America, a region rich in resources, is becoming increasingly relevant for EU countries to diversify suppliers and gain access to renewable energies under better conditions and consequently acquire greater autonomy concerning the Russian supply. In this context, the need to ratify modernization agreements with Chile, with which it achieved an Advanced Framework Agreement, and Mexico, who, in the XXVIII Meeting of the Mexico-European Union Joint Parliamentary Committee, declared to work on the modernization of the Mexico-European Union Global Agreement (European Commission, 2022).

The European Union and Latin America could, through the bi-regional partnership, cooperate in diversifying the energy matrix and the productive capacities of both parties, also considering potential regional organizations to be global food pantries, being cautious with a new extractivist cycle in the region that may cause a deterioration in its development and structural vulnerabilities (Verdes-Montenegro & Jeger, 2022).

For Latin America, the European Union acquires a new meaning as an alternative in the China-United States confrontation and as access to resources for an impoverished region. It is estimated that 202 million people were living in poverty in 2020, 22 million more than the previous year, of which 78 million would be living in extreme poverty (ECLAC, 2020).

Amid the pandemic, the EU developed proposals for cooperation with the region. First, in the area of migration, through an extraordinary donor conference to address the situation of Venezuelan migrants, and in December 2021, with a bi-regional conference that sought to revitalise the link with the different regional initiatives. In 2019 the EU and the Pacific Alliance signed a joint declaration where they committed to deepening the partnership between the two regional blocs, strengthening political, economic, and cooperation ties and also emphasising the need to enhance cooperation on environmental matters, science, technology, and innovation, as well as support for small and medium-sized enterprises. In line with the Pacific Alliance 2030 Document, the EU is given a central role in future development.

With the Andean Community, the EU developed talks when there was still no consensus among the Andean countries on a possible free trade agreement (Nieto & De la Cruz Guerrero, 2019). Finally, the final talks took place when Venezuela withdrew from the CAN, and Bolivia did not want to be part of the negotiations, so agreements were only established with Peru, Colombia, and Ecuador. On the occasion of the XXI Meeting of the Presidential Council of the Andean Community in July 2021, the European Union reiterated the commitment to the Andean Community to face shared challenges through a positive agenda and in a framework of political dialogue and bi-regional cooperation through a Joint Commission.

Relations between the EU and CELAC have been stagnant since the last EU-CELAC summit was held in Brussels in 2015, but from the second half of 2020, the linkage was invigorated, and a Bi-regional Roadmap 2022–2023 was agreed upon, which promotes renewing the bi-regional partnership to strengthen peace and sustainable development. This was developed at the III Meeting of Ministers of Foreign Affairs CELAC-EU, highlighting in the agenda issues of inclusive, equitable, and sustainable economic recovery in the post-pandemic context, innovation and the fight against climate change, disaster risk management, and the digital agenda, multilateralism, cooperation in security and governance, in addition to promoting and protecting human rights (Verdes-Montenegro & Jeger, 2022). It is expected that this relationship will take a qualitative leap with the July 2023 bi-regional Summit under the Spanish presidency of the European Union.

The EU-Mercosur Agreement is still awaiting ratification. This pact was announced on the 20th anniversary of the start of negotiations during the G20 meeting in Japan, so it was a message of multilateralism to the world and the defense of free trade as opposed to protectionism (Sanahuja & Bonilla, 2022). With this agreement, the EU obtains significant advantages in industrial and service matters and some agricultural products. MERCOSUR improves its access conditions to the European market for agricultural exports. The agricultural sector is undoubtedly where the greatest tensions have arisen. Some EU countries have expressed their dissatisfaction with the impact this agreement would have on farmers, which could also lead to a questioning of the leadership of European countries in environmental matters (Euractiv, 2021).

However, the questions go beyond agriculture. The viability of the agreement and its entry into force presents a ratification process with many complexities, due to the diverse nature of the agreement for the countries of the Union because it contains matters that fall within the competence of both the EU and the member countries themselves. Therefore, there is a possibility that it could get stuck in one of the national parliaments (Bonilla & Sanahuja, 2022).

Although CELAC should be the priority initiative in the political dialogue with the EU, the low levels of progress in recent years condition this rapprochement. Furthermore, the poor state and instability of LAC regional projects make the preferred EU's region-to-region approach to LAC quite problematic. In fact, everything indicates that the bilateral option, agreements with the region's different countries, will have to be chosen first while the fabric of Latin American integration is being rebuilt. This adds another key element to the discussion on the redefinition of the EU role and presence in Latin America and the Caribbean.

Bibliography

Bartesaghi, I. (2022). Uruguay y el Mercosur. In: G. Caetano & D. Hernández (Eds.), *30 años del Mercosur* (pp. 147–160). s.l.

Bernal-Meza, R. (2002). la crisis argentina: Impacto en las relaciones bilaterales argentino-brasileñas y en el MERCOSUR. *Revista Brasileña de Estudios Latinoamericanos, 1*(1), 1–18. https://doi.org/10.11606/issn.1676-6288.prolam.2002.83042

Bertot, H., & Díaz, E. (2017). The Community of Latin American and Caribbean States (CELAC): An approach from an integration perspective. *Cuadernos de Política Exterior Argentina (Nueva Época)*, (126), 47–66.

Briceño-Ruiz, J., Prado Lallande, J., & Legler, T. (2021). *La Alianza del Pacífico a 10 años: Integración profunda e institucionalización sui generis*, GEMAP PB 01, Konrad Adenauer Foundation-Mexico.

Buss, P., & Tobar, S. (2020). *La COVID-19 y las oportunidades de cooperación internacional en salud*, s.l.: Cadernos de Saúde Pública.

Caetano, G. (2022). Análisis y prospectiva del Acuerdo de Asociación Unión Europea-Mercosur. En: J. A. Sanahuja & A. Bonilla (Eds.), *Unión Europea, América Latina y el Caribe: Cartografía de los Acuerdos de Asociación* (pp. 225–259). s.l.:Fundación Carolina.

Caetano, G., & Pose, N. (2020). La debilidad de los regionalismos latinoamericanos frente a los escenarios actuales. *Fundación Carolina* (41).

Casa Rosada. (2022). *Palabras del presidente de la Nación, Alberto Fernández, en la Cumbre de Jefes de Estado del MERCOSUR y Estados Asociados*, desde Uruguay.

Castro Silva, J,. & Quiliconi, C. (2022). Cooperación Regional Latinoamericana: Desafíos y Oportunidades en Pandemia en Josette Altmann Borbón & Francisco Rojas Aravena (Eds.), *América Latina: ¿Hay voluntad política para construir un futuro diferente? 2022* (pp. 132–148), Flacso Secretaría General. Universidad para la Paz.

CELAC. (2021). *Nota conceptual sobre la conclusión del proceso de reflexión*. XXI Reunión de Cancilleres de la CELAC.

CEPAL. (2020). *Social Panorama of Latin America 2020*.

CEPAL. (2021). *Prospects for international trade in Latin America and the Caribbean*.

CEPAL. (2022). *Repercussions in Latin America and the Caribbean of the war in Ukraine: How to face this new crisis?*

CEPAL, EU, OECD Development Centre, CAF. (2021). *Latin American and Caribbean Economic Outlook (LEO)*.

Chiriboga, M. (2009). *¿ Es la CAN un modelo de integración válido?* Friedrich Ebert Stiftung.

Cuarta Sesión Foro Agropecuario Andino. (2021). *Países de la CAN acuerdan Agenda Agropecuaria Andina para impulsar reactivación del sector*.

De Sierra, G. (2010). *Los rostros del Mercosur. El difícil camino de lo comercial a lo social*.

EURACTIV. (2021). *EU lacks defense capabilities to meet "strategic autonomy goals"*, Euractiv, 5 January.

European Commission. (2022). *Sustainability impact assessment in support of association agreement negotiations between the EU and Mercosur*. Brussels: s.n.

Forbes México. (2019). *López Obrador declara formalmente abolido el modelo neoliberal*. https://www.forbes.com.mx/lopez-obrador-declara-formalmente-abolido-el-modelo-neoliberal/

Fortín, C., Heine, J., & Ominami, C. (2020). El no alineamiento activo: un camino para América Latina. *Revista Nueva Sociedad, Opinión*.

Latinobarómetro. (2021). *Report 2021*. Adiós a Macondo.

Maira, L. (2009)..¿Cómo afectará la crisis la integración regional? *Nueva Sociedad, 224*. Online: https://nuso.org/articulo/como-afectara-la-crisis-la-integracion-regional/

Malamud, A. (2022). *Treinta años de MERCOSUR entre flujos declinantes y reglas deficientes n Gerardo Caetano Diego Hernández Nilson, Coordinadores, Treinta años de MERCOSUR*. Trayectorias, flexibilización e interregionalismo, Departamento de Ciencia Política, Facultad de Ciencias Sociales, Universidad de la República, 2022.

Malamud, A., & Carreiras, H. (2020). *Geopolítica del coronavirus*. Recuperado de https://eleconomista.com.ar/debates/geopolitica-coronavirus-n33940

Malamud, R., & Castellano, C. (2021). *La integración latinoamericana: irrelevancia tras el intento de liderazgo mexicano*. Real Instituto Elcano.

Malamud, A., & Schenoni, L. (2021). Sobre la creciente irrelevancia de América Latina. *Revista Nueva Sociedad 291* (January–February 2021), 66–79.

Marchini, G. (2019). La Alianza del Pacífico a ocho años de su creación. Balance Crítico y perspectivas. *Anuario Latinoamericano Ciencias Políticas y Relaciones Internacionales, 7*.

Niebieskikwiat, N. (2022). *El duro mensaje de Alberto Fernández contra Lacalle Pou por la pelea en el Mercosur: "La solución no es que cada uno haga lo que quiera"*, clarin.com, 6 December 2022.

Nieto, D., & De la Cruz Guerrero, L. (2019). Los primeros 18 meses del Acuerdo Multipartes Ecuador-Unión Europea. *PODIUM, 35*, 43–56.

Nieto, S., & Da Costa, R. (2022). Desarrollo en Transición en América Latina en tiempos de la Covid-19. En: J. A. Sanahuja (Ed.), *Relanzar las relaciones entre América Latina y la Unión Europea* (pp. 125–159). s.l.: Fundación Carolina.

Nolte, D. (2022). Una nueva UNASUR: el regreso de un zombie?. *NODAl*, 2 December 2022.

Nolte, D., & Mijares, V. (2018). Regionalismo posthegemónico en crisis. ¿Por qué la Unasur se desintegra? *Foreign Affairs Latinoamérica, 18*(3), 105–112.

Nolte, D., & Mijares, V. (2022). UNASUR: An eclectic analytical perspective of its disintegration. *Colombia International, III*, 83–109.

Ocampo, J. A. (2009). Impactos de la crisis financiera mundial sobre América Latina. *Revista Cepal*, abril. *97*, 9–32.

Oyarzún, L. (2021). *La Alianza del Pacífico en tiempos convulsos*. GEMAP.

Pastrana, E., & Blomeier, H. (2018). *La Alianza del Pacífico; ¿ atrapada en el péndulo del regionalismo y del interregionalismos?* (Primera ed.). Bogotá D.C.: Konrad Adenauer Stiftung.

Pastrana, E., & Castro, R. (2020). *Auge y estancamiento de la Alianza del Pacífico*. Fundación Carolina.

Portela, M. (2021). 30 años del Mercosur: ¿un sobreviviente o una posibilidad? *Nueva Sociedad*.

Puertas, J. A. (2006). La desintegración andina. *Nueva Sociedad* (204). Online: https://nuso.org/articulo/la-desintegracion-andina/

Sanahuja, J. A. (2022). The European Union and Latin America in the interregnum: Strategic autonomy, green pact and post-pandemic recovery. In: Josette Altmann Borbón & Francisco Rojas Aravena (Eds.), *Latin America: Is there political will to build a different future, 2022* (pp. 95–110), Flacso General Secretariat, University for Peace.

Sanahuja, J. A. & Bonilla, A. (2022). The Association Agreements between the EU and Latin America and the Caribbean: Balance and perspectives for bi-regional relations. In: *European Union, Latin America and the Caribbean: Cartografía de los Acuerdos de Asociación* (pp. 265–296). s.l.: Fundación Carolina.

Sanahuja, J. A., & Rodríguez Díaz, J. D. (2019). *Veinte años de negociaciones Unión Europea-Mercosur: Del interregionalismo a la crisis de la globalización*. Documentos de Trabajo.

Schuarzer, J. (2001). *El Mercosur: un bloque económico con objetivos a precisar*. CLACSO, Consejo Latinoamericano de Ciencias Sociales.

Serbín, A., Martínez, L., Romanzini, H., & Serbín, A. (2016). América Latina y el Caribe frente a la encrucijada actual de la globalización. *Anuario de la Integración Regional de* (13).

Tokatlian, J. (2021). *La diplomacia de equidistancia, una propuesta estratégica*, Clarín 10 February 2021.

Verdes-Montenegro, F., & Jeger, E. (2022). Un nuevo tiempo para los acuerdos de Asociación UE-América Latina y el Caribe. En: J. A. Sanahuja & A. Bonilla (Eds.), *Unión Europea, América Latina y el Caribe: Cartografía de los Acuerdos de Asociación* (pp. 1–9). s.l.: Fundación Carolina.

XXIX Comité Andino de Autoridades de Telecomunicaciones. (2022). *Todo sobre la Agenda Digital Andina*. Comunidad Andina.

XXV Consejo Andino de Ministros de Relaciones Exteriores. (2020). *Carta Ambiental Andina*. Comunidad Andina.

XXVI Consejo Andino de Ministros de Relaciones Exteriores. (2021). *Aprueban Estatuto Migratorio Andino que establece Residencia Temporal y Permanente en países de la CAN*.

Part II A Reinvigorated Agenda for EU-Latin America Relations

Gian Luca Gardini

Proposals for a Functional EU-LAC Agenda, with an Underpinning Political Design

The European Union (EU) and Latin America and the Caribbean (LAC) have a dense, highly articulated and comprehensive agenda. This intense interaction spans across a multitude of sectors and actors. It continues almost unaltered in spite of the absence of a formal EU-LAC political summit at the highest level between 2015 and 2023. Up to a point, this may be good news. It certifies the proactive role of bi-regional civil society as much as the solid institutional texture of the bi-regional relationship. Yet, this may also signal some of the limits of interregional mechanisms. Overcrowded and overly ambitious agendas (especially without proper political leadership) are often perceived by policymakers and scholars alike as major limitations of interregional regimes and summits (Gardini & Malamud, 2018). This, in turn, leads to little real commitment and even less compliance.

The EU-LAC agenda is no exception. Declarations of countless points are hardly a credible commitment and doubtfully a selection of real priorities for cooperation, action or even discussion. This certainly presents significant challenges for follow-up and implementation. As an example, the 2013 final declaration of the EU-Community of Latin American and Caribbean States (CELAC) Summit consisted of 48 points, a significant reduction compared to the record 104 points of the 2004 Guadalajara Declaration concluding the EU-LAC summit. Furthermore, at times the contents and provisions of interregional summit declarations and action plans "can at best be regarded as optimistic assumptions" (Eyinla 2004: 176). Yet, agendas and final declarations are a compromise between a large number of countries. This results in an accumulation of items on the agenda that can be acceptable to all participants. While this may ensure a level of consensus, it makes the achievement of tangible results and their communication to stakeholders quite difficult.

Is there a way to overcome these problems while at the same time pursuing a meaningful and ambitious, but not chimeric, agenda? Are there ways to bypass very sensitive political issues that jeopardise more specific and relatively uncontroversial cooperation? Conversely, is a focus on a circumscribed and mainly technical agenda without discarding broader political issues possible? There seem to be three possibilities, ideally complementary and certainly not mutually exclusive, at least in principle.

The first option is a renewed political commitment to EU-LAC relations with significant investment at the technical level. This would imply that politicians on the two shores of the Atlantic conduct serious reflection, including on the political and financial costs, about a self-contained and widely shared bi-regional agenda for the medium and long term. This agenda should be multi-partisan and reach a consensus among states, parties, opposition and civil society with strong support from the business sector both in Europe and Latin America. A deep and articulated exercise in the "two-level game" between diplomacy and domestic politics would be required too (Putnam, 1988). Accordingly, this venture should also include a major refinancing and staffing of the ministries and other technical bodies entrusted with the monitoring and implementation of this agenda, nationally and regionally. Considering the current structural problems at the global and regional levels both in the EU and LAC, and the hurdles and vested interests that such a process would have to tackle domestically, this option remains quite unlikely.

The second possibility is the recourse to "minilateralism" and "multibilateralism" (Hill & Smith, 2011; Le Gloannec, 2004) and "differentiated integration" and "variable geometry" (Bertoncini, 2017; Herolf, 2012) at the bi-regional level. These make multilateral events, summits and commitments – such as the bi-regional ones – convenient to take forward bilateral (and/or minilateral) affairs and agendas. Differentiated integration and cooperation are, in fact, used within the EU to allow those members who wish to cooperate more deeply to do so, without prejudice to the reluctant members, who are granted opt-out. The latest Joint Communication of the European Commission (2019) on EU-LAC relations provides a combination of traditional instruments and innovative and tailor-made solutions to foster EU-LAC cooperation. This opens the way to going beyond the established summit system of political dialogues. It invites EU and LAC states, as well as the EU institutions, who want closer cooperation, to experiment with new formats. On the one hand, this has the advantage of allowing willing countries to move forward without major opposition. On the other hand, though, this procedure further fragments and divides participants, making it hardly a practicable mechanism for region-to-region relations.

There is a third solution: emphasis on functional cooperation as a non-exclusive starting point that decouples the political and the functional agendas. This type of cooperation focuses on a self-contained agenda centred on specific issues of common interest, low controversy, limited political and economic investment, and potentially big and non-conflictive returns. A functional and technical agenda does not exclude a political one. Yet, a decoupling of political and functional cooperation may ease international deals (Carreiras & Malamud, 2020). Emphasis on technical issues avoids major politically sensitive topics. Success in functional and technical cooperation may provide tangible material and political incentives for political cooperation. It can also generate an incremental effect (spill-over), based on the expansion of cooperation to germane policy areas in a neo-functionalist guise (Haas, 1958).

This chapter focuses on a functional, mainly technical agenda for EU-LAC relations. The first section discusses digitalization. The second addresses energy systems. The third analyses entrepreneurship and small and medium-sized enterprises (SMEs). These sections are partly inspired by a one-day seminar on cooperation between the Pacific Alliance and its observer states that I jointly organised in Berlin in 2018 with the Organization for Economic Cooperation and Development (OECD), the Bundesverband der Deutschen Industrie (BDI), and the European Institute of International Studies (EIIS).[1] The conclusion summarises the main arguments and offers three proposals for the EU-LAC political agenda too.

Digitalization

The digital agenda at the national, regional and international levels is a key to the present and future development of any community, especially those that seek a better and more effective international insertion in regional and global value chains (Ha, 2022; Gopalan et al., 2022). The digital agenda, however, comes with both opportunities and challenges. An EU-LAC agenda for digital cooperation has to consider both aspects: how to maximise opportunities and how to minimise or at least diffuse risks and challenges.

Two preliminary warnings before any discussion on content have to be addressed. First, there is a tendency to assume that digitalization is good and has positive effects on society and the economy. This is only one side of the story. Much less attention has been devoted to the negative effects of digitalization. Only recently a significant scholarly debate on the topic has emerged (Trittin-Ulbricht et al., 2021). This focuses on the potentially dark and unexpected sides of digitalization for workers, consumers, activists and democracy. Accordingly,

---

1 I am indebted and grateful to all the experts, colleagues and professionals who made that event possible. In particular, I would like to thank Mario Torres Jarrín, then director of the EIIS, for all the invaluable support.

the proposals for an EU-LAC digital agenda discussed below are not enthusiastically or uncritically embraced. They are only a part of a broader reflection on a functional and technical agenda and they remain subject to further scrutiny.

Second, one of the key challenges to developing an effective and inclusive EU-LAC digital agenda is the awareness – and the ensuing policies – of the impact that government decisions on digital matters may have on the community at large. Governments and civil society have different but equally important roles in the definition and implementation of a digital agenda. While it is mostly companies and civil society that have a prominent role in the development and use of digital technologies, it is for governments to identify priorities for cooperation, commercial deals and regulatory frameworks. Yet, whose task is it to evaluate moral and democratic risks such as overt or stealth control of citizens? The interaction between citizens and public officials, the so-called "public encounter" raises questions and ethical concerns regarding accountability and reskilling of both citizens and public officials (Lindgren et al., 2019). A first preliminary point to any EU-LAC digital agenda ought to be a serious reflection on ethical issues and an agreement on the limits and risks that such an agenda implies.

That said, the possible topics on a bi-regional digital agenda are, of course, as numerous as they are diverse. Digitalization itself is a universe of issues that increasingly pervades every aspect of daily lives and has implications for connected agendas, such as innovation and sustainability (Broekhuizen & Langley, 2021). In the impossibility of addressing all these issues, this section focuses on five areas, which are relevant to a variety of actors. These proposals invariably make reference to education and digital skills as these are the basis for any digitalization strategy for development, which is not possible without digital competence. Likewise, digitalization has a lot to do with business development, the opportunities to access regional and global value chains, employment and therefore wellbeing.

A first issue is an understanding of what a digital transformation actually is and entails. The digital transformation is not only about technology but mostly about a mindset (Neeley & Leonardi, 2022). People, from students to employees, from the young generations to the elderly must be motivated to acquire and use digital skills. They need to see how data, algorithms, and artificial intelligence are useful in their daily lives, which will be ever more technology-intensive. This concept has to be widely disseminated. This can be done with information and awareness campaigns that bring together experts and stakeholders. Digitalization is neither good nor bad per se, but digitalization is what we make of it. This concept and the appropriate campaigns can be jointly organised, coordinated and disseminated as a bi-regional effort.

A second proposal is to gradually advance in a single bi-regional digital market, or at least in areas of it.[2] This would include sectors such as telecom regulation, cybersecurity, media, copyright, platforms and eCommerce. Regulatory frameworks and their capacity for attraction (or imposition) become more and more important for global competition and competitiveness (Schneider-Petsinger et al., 2019; Mc Geachy, 2019). If the EU and LAC don't want to remain passive takers of technical regulations, this is another key item for a functional bi-regional agenda. This is particularly important for the EU and its capacity for both attraction and projection globally. A joint effort in this matter would be a timely and potentially very fruitful initiative.

The creation of a specific EU-LAC Search Engine Advertising Manager (SEA Manager) for the digital job market is a third idea. This is meant to match the skills on offer in the digital job market and the demand of companies and public institutions. Evidence shows that job search has largely moved online, mainly via general search engines or specialised platforms (Karaoglu, 2022). Research also shows that the credibility and reputation of the digital marketing tools, in particular those owned or managed by the company itself (such as LinkedIn), are seen as very relevant for the job application decision (Rodrigues & Martinez, 2020). An EU-LAC SEA Manager platform would reach a very wide audience in two continents, would facilitate job matches in a key sector and would enjoy the credibility that an EU and CELAC seal can grant.

A fourth proposal concerns the pursuit of a skills-for-tasks approach in digital training and education. Empirical research shows that task-based learning in the social sciences develops new ways of learning by integrating knowledge, practice and critical reflection (Purdam, 2016). This concept can be applied to learning digital skills. For instance, an ambitious but feasible EU-LAC technical project could aim to develop and include a skills-for-tasks approach to the teaching of digital skills and digital transformation(s) in the STEM areas in the curricula at schools and university. An accompanying measure could be the improvement of the digital infrastructure at vocational schools in order to mirror industry and company needs. Students would learn skills immediately applicable to perform tasks and find solutions to real problems.

---

2 The 2015 Communication from the Commission on a digital single market strategy for Europe, the 2016 European Economic and Social Committee position paper on the Digital Single Market and the 2016 CAF report on Building a digital single market strategy for Latin America may serve as initial references, but they are already quite dated.

The fifth proposal addresses inclusiveness and the ability to reach disadvantaged audiences and peripheral communities and remote geographical areas. That is to provide digital skills and training through technology itself. The use of technological devices allows us to reach a wide audience, including those with little time or just rudimentary competences to acquire new digital skills, such as workers in the informal sector and senior citizens. The development and use of appropriate mobile applications allow us to train digital competences in a tailor-made approach and according to one's own time and availability. It would also facilitate participation in and consultation of training and certification systems in other regions, including developing regions. Successful examples already exist, as the experience of the company SAP in Africa demonstrates (SAP News, 2022). This can be a benchmark for a joint EU-LAC project.

Energy systems

The energy crisis that struck Europe and other regions in the aftermath of Russia's invasion of Ukraine is only the tip of the iceberg. The energy systems question is much older and much broader. The need to save energy and produce it more efficiently, at lower costs and in a sustainable way, is as old as the debate on the environment and dates back to at least the early 1970s. The question is also much broader and complex, as it has an impact on the environment, the economy and lifestyles at large. To change the matrix of energy sources, production and distribution is imperative. However, the investments required to change sources and suppliers of energy are huge (Bruegel, 2021). Yet, using investments in renewables and the grid is not the only solution, although it remains the crucial one. There are smaller complementary measures that can significantly help too.

Firstly, algorithms can now save on energy consumption and distribution by optimising transportation timetables and velocity. A project on timetabling efficiency carried out by Friedrich-Alexander University in Germany in partnership with the train operator Deutsche Bahn aimed to decrease peak power consumption to bring down electricity costs. Results estimated possible cost savings of 5%, which would be 5 million Euros per year (Bärmann, Martin, & Schneider, 2017). A similar modelling approach can be used for other modes of transport, such as the underground, and also for gas pipelines and networks (Bärmann et al., 2018). This kind of project does not require expensive equipment or infrastructure but capable, even small, teams of researchers. Relatively modest investments can result in huge savings. The EU-LAC technical agenda could promote and disseminate this kind of research and help to apply it to as many sectors as possible.

Secondly, not all renewables are equally suitable and mutually beneficial to EU-LAC relations. Wind power certainly is. One should assess the market before choosing which kind of renewables to promote in a possible bi-regional technical deal. China has already become a leader in manufacturing for both wind and solar equipment. However, while seven of the top ten solar manufacturers are Chinese, the wind turbine market is far more dispersed and competitive, with the top 10 manufacturers in Europe, the US, China and India (Gross, 2020). Furthermore, the large blades of turbines are often manufactured close to where they are installed. 3-D printing has amplified this situation. Considering the favourable climate conditions for wind power almost anywhere in Latin America and Europe's competitiveness in the sector, cooperation in wind power should feature high on the EU-LAC technical agenda.

Thirdly, a joint EU-LAC effort at monitoring the energy and commodities prices along with a clear and truthful joint EU-LAC communication strategy in this field should be a primary concern on the bi-regional agenda. A careful analysis of price variations at production and final consumption points should be constantly carried out to avoid speculation and malpractices. This would protect consumers on the two shores of the Atlantic and maintain a levelled playing field in the energy sector. The record-high profits of energy and fuel companies in 2022 are partly the result of rising demand, scarcity, increased costs of production and transportation. Yet, there is a significant component of speculation, which the EU and LAC and its regional organizations should address.

Record prices of gas and gasoline for consumers in Europe in 2022 were not directly connected to peak prices of the corresponding commodities. As an example, in October 2022, the average price of a barrel of Brent oil was 93.4 USD, against over 132 USD in June and July 2008 or 125 USD in March 2012. Yet, gas and gasoline prices in Europe reached an all-time peak in that period. In August 2022, the Henry Hub price of liquid gas on the New York exchange market reached 8.81 USD per million Btu, against 12.69 in June 2008 and 13.42 USD in October 2005.[3] In the third trimester of 2022, the extra-profit of the big five energy companies against 2021 was +191% for Exxon, +83% for Chevron, +128% for Shell, +106% for Total and +146% for BP (La Stampa, 2022). This chapter does not advocate state control of prices or companies. Yet, some public mechanism to

3 Figures collected and elaborated by the author using historical series of oil prices and the Henry Hub natural gas prices. Data sourced from the US Energy Information Administration (www.eia.gov), macrotrends.net, statista.com and countryeconomy.com.

guarantee fairness for producers and consumers is needed. Perhaps a bi-regional forum would be the right place, at least to initiate such discussion.

Entrepreneurship and SMEs

The ability to stimulate the talent and the sense of initiative of its own people is fundamental to any society. This includes the ability of a community to provide opportunities to operationalise and reward those talents appropriately. This is a key factor for economic and social development. In the case of Latin America, "SMEs comprise 99.5% of firms in the region (with almost 9 out of 10 classified as micro-enterprises) and generate 60% of formal productive employment" (OECD, 2022). In Europe, "Small and medium-sized enterprises are the backbone of Europe's economy. They represent 99% of all businesses in the EU. They employ around 100 million people, account for more than half of Europe's GDP" (European Commission, 2022). It is, therefore, crucial to provide these actors with the instruments to foster their entrepreneurship and their ability to be present and compete in ever larger markets, be it at the regional or global level.

Entrepreneurship, digitalization and vocational training are strictly interconnected. This is the approach taken in this chapter, especially in its policy proposals. Regional integration processes, but also interregional mechanisms, may be a valuable engine to develop these sectors. It is vital to integrate SMEs into trade agreements, trade strategies towards fast-growing markets, and to take their needs into account when designing production repatriation strategies and effective industrial policies. Regional and interregional development strategies are needed to promote entrepreneurship and a better insertion of SMEs in global value chains. This is even more important in the light of recent studies stressing that we are far from deglobalising, even after the Covid-19 pandemic, the war in Ukraine or the hardening of the US-China competition. In fact, the challenge is to harness the benefits of still growing interconnection "while managing the risks and downsides of dependency – particularly where products are concentrated in their places of origin" (McKinsey, 2022).

There are some traditional and very useful measures to support entrepreneurship, especially SMEs. These include domestic agencies for trade and investment, trade missions to increase the visibility and presence of SMEs at the international level, and the simplification of requirements and red-tape procedures through digital platforms. The potential for further cooperation between the EU and LAC in the area of SMEs and entrepreneurship is still largely untapped and worth a profound and creative reflection. Innovative financing systems for SMEs, stimulating the green transition and creating connected jobs, helping

SMEs navigate crises, the promotion of the tourist sector, and developing entrepreneurial educational programs for young people are all suitable areas for bi-regional collaboration.

The first idea concerns the financing system for SMEs. This is especially important for those SMEs that want to go green or improve their energy efficiency. While financing mechanisms should primarily be embarked on a national and regional strategy, interregional cooperation can serve this purpose too. The German KfW-Bank could be a good basis for reflection on how EU-LAC technical cooperation could help in this respect. KfW was established in 1948 under public law and is owned 80% by the federal government of Germany and 20% by its states. It supports individuals, businesses and public organisations with promotional loans and grants. Public funding represents a minimal part of the KfW resources, which come from over 90% from the capital markets (KfW, 2022). These funds are made available to users via a network of partner banks, closer to the people. Priority areas are climate change and the environment, innovation and education projects. The EU and LAC could put in place a similar bi-regional body and scheme to complement the initiatives already in place or to streamline them.

A second proposal or, more appropriately, a crucial precondition for entrepreneurship connected with the green transition is the political will to take change forward. In this respect, EU-LAC dialogue could prove itself to be fundamental. A study by the Inter-American Development Bank and the International Labour Organization concluded that Latin America could create up to 15 million new jobs by 2030 if countries in the region seriously committed themselves to cutting carbon emissions (Maloney, 2020). In fact, 22.5 million jobs would be created mainly in plant-based agriculture, green transport and renewable energy. Though, in the transitional phase, around 7.5 million jobs could be lost in fossil-fuel extraction and livestock farming, which are among the most politically sensitive sectors in the continent. The net gain would be remarkable but the political cost may be initially high. Bi-regional dialogue and support for both the necessary political will and the required financing instruments can be a key to successful green entrepreneurship.

A third suggestion concerns a further push towards the internationalisation of, and research and development by SMEs. A study by the University of Valencia in Spain shows that in times of crisis companies tend to adopt retrenchment strategies. The same study demonstrates that the most apt strategies for companies to survive crises are an increase in international presence and an enhanced research and development activity (Máñez, Rochina Barrachina & Sanchis Llopis, 2020). Yet businesses experience financial constraints in both fields, which comprise important initial costs before obtaining any returns. Hence the need for public policy "focused on easing access to financial resources, providing the incentives to invest in and to commit to R&D activities over the long term, as well as helping firms to continue with their international integration in global value chains" (Máñez, Rochina Barrachina & Sanchis Llopis, 2020: 68). In this sense, proposals number one, two and three are strictly interconnected and provide for an excellent opportunity for EU-LAC functional cooperation.

A fourth proposal is to improve the soft, language, and technical skills available within SMEs. This would facilitate their insertion into international value chains. "In-company training" is a possibility but informality and lack of resources and time make it a complex issue, especially for SMEs. "Skills and entrepreneurship can empower youth to develop knowledge-intensive economic activities to transition successfully from schools to jobs" (OECD/ECLAC/CAF, 2016: 17). The German Apprenticeship Scheme may constitute an initial basis for discussion. Yet it is not easily transferable to other realities for its high costs, the role of an efficient state, and cultural attitudes and traditions (Jacobi, 2014). EU-LAC functional cooperation could look at ways to make a similar scheme applicable to other countries and regions.

A fifth idea is to invest further in the tourist sector to promote entrepreneurship and SMEs. The improvement of the offer as well as the accommodation capacity is crucial. So is the promotion of the natural, architectural and cultural heritage. Still, tourism has by now become a very complex industry facing several interlinked challenges and it requires an integrated policy (Palma Andrés et al., 2019). It has to take into account the needs and expectations of the visitors and the hosts. Tourism has to deal with transportation, energy, supply chains, ecological setting and impact, culture and lifestyles. EU-LAC technical cooperation could go a long way to stimulate the tourist sector in the two regions. A bi-regional discussion on responsible tourism and a joint integrated policy or at least guideline may benefit economic growth, sustainability and the preservation and promotion of natural and cultural heritage.

Conclusion

This chapter has argued that a decoupling of the political and the functional agenda could help relaunch EU-LAC relations and foster bi-regional cooperation. It has also provided a number of policy proposals in three key areas. In the field of digitalization, awareness of what digitalization is and entails, a single bi-regional digital market, a specific EU-LAC Search Engine Advertising Manager, a skills-for-tasks approach to digital training and education, and inclusiveness through digital training with digital technology were discussed. Regarding energy systems, the huge investments that a change of the energy production and consumption matrix would require can be accompanied by more modest but potentially highly rewarding measures, such as algorithms optimising the use and distribution of energy, the emphasis on wind power, and the monitoring of prices to alert on, and avoid speculation. In the area of entrepreneurship and SMEs, EU-LAC cooperation could provide new financing mechanisms, political and material support for the green transition, incentives to companies to overcome crises, innovative forms of training via apprenticeship, and an elan to sustainable tourism.

A key issue is transversal to all these topics: education. Education is not only about higher education. It has a lot to do with the generation and dissemination of technical skills. Vocational education and training (VET) is essential to promote trade, international insertion, and inclusive development. A major challenge for both the EU and Latin America is to achieve better and more targeted technical training to reduce the skills mismatch that both regions face. Technical training can facilitate inclusion in value chains, the grasp of opportunities offered by digitalization and new technologies, and the reduction of gender and ethnic gaps, along with the strengthening of the SME sector.

Accordingly, VET is crucial in the three areas discussed. First, digitalization: training in digital technologies is essential to benefit from the new opportunities that information and knowledge-based economies and societies offer. The digital gap must be reduced to achieve inclusive and sustainable development. Second, energy systems: technical expertise in this field is fundamental to grasp the opportunities offered by "at-the-edge" innovation, such as green technology and renewable energies. Third, entrepreneurship and SMEs: effective technical training is paramount for SMEs to be able to join regional and global value chains, and more broadly to interact internationally and command technological development and devices. This is not the future but the present.

Three additional policy proposals can be made to improve VET at the bi-regional level:

1. *Enhance teacher quality:* Providing training to the trainers is fundamental to the success of any education system. Precise surveys about the quality of the trainers are a precondition to designing new programs for the training of the trainers in collaboration with students and companies, and to invest in the development of soft skills for trainers.
2. *Improve the quality of teaching materials:* Specialised companies, such as Pearson, focus on advanced training materials including content, tests

and certifications in different areas of knowledge. Specific packages can be designed and produced to meet the needs identified by a bi-regional body.
3. *Invest in the proficiency of English and other languages:* This would foster effective communication and language skills of the targeted recipients.

A cultural change is also needed. To insist on technical education only is not enough and is certainly not the approach supported here. On the contrary, a move from a STEM (science, technology, engineering, mathematics) to a STEAM (where A stands for art and humanities) approach is highly recommended. Technical training produces good professionals, but thorough education produces good citizens. STEM disciplines are important, but the inclusion of the Arts and Humanities in technical curricula is fundamental too, hence the acronym STEAM, which also means power, drive and determination. A citizen who is able to think logically and independently, who knows where he/she comes from, who is aware of realities and challenges, will be more creative and innovative. The Arts and Humanities stimulate these assets.

This brings us to the final point. Is it possible and useful to separate technical from more comprehensive education? Similarly, is it possible to separate entirely the functional from the political agenda? The answer is no in both cases. One thing is to place more emphasis on, or give priority to one or the other at certain times, under given circumstances, and for specific purposes. This is what this chapter has tried to indicate. A completely different matter would be to maintain that a bi-regional technical agenda has no political dimension or underpinning political design. Of course the identification of the three fields discussed here, digitalization, energy systems, and entrepreneurship is in itself a political choice. It is ultimately for politics to determine technical and functional priorities and guidelines.

Accordingly, this conclusion cannot avoid making three proposals also in the sphere of EU-LAC political cooperation.

1. Full support for US President Joe Biden's proposal for a summit of democracies (Biden, 2020). In a phase of strain for democratic institutions at the national and international levels, this would be an opportunity to reaffirm shared values.
2. Elaboration of a joint EU-LAC agreement on China's investments. This would give visibility to the EU and LAC globally, more negotiating power to both vis-à-vis China and facilitate the regulation of needed but potentially problematic foreign investments.
3. A new EU-LAC migration scheme that prioritises Latin Americans who want to work in the EU. This would promote legal and dignified migration,

respond to the needs of the EU labour market and attract people more likely to adapt to the social and cultural fabric of the receiving countries.

These may be bold proposals. If they are too bold for the current political climate, this chapter has also discussed a number of less conflictive functional proposals, which are easier to implement. Their impact would be anyway significant.

Bibliography

Bärmann, A., A. Martin, and O. Schneider (2017). A comparison of performance metrics for balancing the power consumption of trains in a railway network by slight timetable adaptation. *Public Transport*, 9(1), pp. 95–113.

Bärmann, A., M. Merkert, T. Gellermann, and O. Schneider (2018). *Staircase compatibility and its applications in scheduling and piecewise linearization.* Online: https://optimization-online.org/wp-content/uploads/2018/01/6435.pdf (last accessed 1 November 2022).

Bertoncini, Y. (2017). *Differentiated integration and the EU: A variable geometry legitimacy, Istituto Affari Internazionali (IAI) paper*, series "EU60: Re-Founding Europe. The Responsibility to Propose". Online: https://www.iai.it/sites/default/files/eu60_7.pdf (last accessed 12 December 2022).

Biden, J. R. (2020). Why America must lead again. *Foreign Affairs*, 99(2), March–April, pp. 64–76.

Broekhuizen, T. L. J., and D. Langley (2021). *Digitalization, innovation and sustainability*, Editors call for papers, Sustainability, special issue forthcoming. Online: https://www.mdpi.com/journal/sustainability/special_issues/digitalization_innovation_sustainability (last accessed 9 December 2022).

Bruegel. (2021). *How much investment do we need to reach net zero?*. Online: https://www.bruegel.org/blog-post/how-much-investment-do-we-need-reach-net-zero (last accessed 5 January 2023).

Carreiras, H., and A. Malamud (2020). Cooperation, the state, and international organizations. In G. L. Gardini (Ed.), *The world before and after COVID-19. Intellectual reflections on politics, diplomacy and international relations.* Stockholm and Salamanca: European Institute of International Studies Press, pp. 19–22.

European Commission. (2019). *Joint Communication to the European Parliament and the Council – European Union, Latin America and the Caribbean: Joining forces for a common future.* Online: https://eur-lex.europa.eu/legal-content/EN/TXT/PDF/?uri=CELEX:52019JC0006&from=en (last accessed 12 December 2022).

European Commission. (2022). *Entrepreneurship and small and medium-sized enterprises (SMEs)*. Online: https://single-market-economy.ec.europa.eu/smes_en (last accessed 1 November 2022).

Eyinla, B. M. (2004). Beyond Cairo: Emerging pattern of Euro-African relationship. *Africa: Rivista trimestrale di studi e documentazione dell'Istituto italiano per l'Africa e l'Oriente*, 59(2), pp. 159–178.

Gardini, G. L., and A. Malamud (2018). Debunking interregionalism: Concepts, types and critique – with a Pan-Atlantic focus. In Frank Mattheis and Andreas Lindegard (Eds.), *Interregionalism across the Atlantic space*. Cham: Springer, pp. 15–32.

Gopalan, S., K. Reddy, and S. Sasidharan (2022). Does digitalization spur global value chain participation? Firm-level evidence from emerging markets. *Information Economics and Policy*, 59. Online: https://reader.elsevier.com/reader/sd/pii/S0167624522000117?token=8788A3917C894D989F0F2FD7659BA90F864E5EEBFB8873F08919A9F7AADD5A07AAB3116DDD656FD15B17171B53C1B9EA&originRegion=eu-west-1&originCreation=20221212183947 (last accessed 9 December 2022).

Gross, S. (2020). *The global energy trade's new center of gravity*. Brookings Institution 14 September 2020. Online: https://www.brookings.edu/articles/the-global-energy-trades-new-center-of-gravity/ (last accessed 1 November 2022).

Ha, L. T. (2022). *Impacts of digital business on global value chain participation in European countries, AI & Soc* (2022). Online: https://link.springer.com/content/pdf/10.1007/s00146-022-01524-w.pdf?pdf=button%20sticky (last accessed 09 December 2022).

Haas, E. B. (1958). *The uniting of Europe; political, social and economic forces, 1950–1957*. Stanford, CA: Stanford University Press.

Herolf, G. (2012). Variable geometry – where could it lead?. *Studia Diplomatica*, 65(1), pp. 57–68. Online: https://www.jstor.org/stable/26531519 (last accessed 12 December 2022).

Hill, C., and M. Smith (2011). *International relations and the European Union*. Oxford/New York: Oxford University Press.

Jacobi, T. (2014). Why Germany is so much better at training its workers. *The Atlantic*, 16 October 2014. Online: https://www.theatlantic.com/business/archive/2014/10/why-germany-is-so-much-better-at-training-its-workers/381550/ (last accessed 1 November 2022).

Karaoglu, G., E. Hargittai, and M. H. Nguyen (2022). Inequality in online job searching in the age of social media. *Information, Communication & Society*, 25(12), pp. 1826–1844.

KWf. (2022). *Several entries*. Online: https://www.kfw.de/kfw.de-2.html (last accessed 1 November 2022).

Le Gloannec, A. (2004). The unilateralist temptation Germany's foreign policy after the Cold War. *Internationale Politik und Gesellschaft*, 1, pp. 27–39.

Lindgren, C., Ø. Madsen, S. Hofmann, and U. Melin (2019). Close encounters of the digital kind: A research agenda for the digitalization of public services. *Government Information Quarterly*, 36(3), pp. 427–436.

Maloney, A. (2020). Latin America urged to boost green jobs for pandemic recovery. *Thomson Reuters Foundation*, 29 July 2020. Online: https://www.reuters.com/article/latam-nature-climatechange-idUKL5N2EZ6PK (last accessed 1 November 2022).

Máñez, J. A., M. E. Rochina Barrachina, and J. A. Sanchis Llopis (2020). Companies' strategies in downturns. In G. L. Gardini (Ed.), *The world before and after Covid-19*. Stockholm and Salamanca: European Institute of International Studies, pp. 65–69.

McGeachy, H. (2019). *US-China technology competition: Impacting a rules-based order*, Report for the United States Studies Centre at the University of Sydney. Online: https://publicsectornetwork.com/wp-content/uploads/2020/01/US-China-technology-competition-impacting-a-rules-based-order.pdf (last accessed 9 December 2022).

McKinsey. (2022). *Global flows: The ties that bind in an interconnected world*. McKinsey Global Institute discussion paper, 15 November. Online: https://www.mckinsey.com/capabilities/strategy-and-corporate-finance/our-insights/global-flows-the-ties-that-bind-in-an-interconnected-world (last accessed 30 November 2022).

Neeley, T., and P. Leonardi (2022). Developing a digital mindset. How to lead your organization into the age of data, algorithms, and AI. *Harvard Business Review*, May–June. Online: https://hbr.org/2022/05/developing-a-digital-mindset (last accessed 9 December 2022).

OECD/ECLAC/CAF. (2016). *Latin American economic outlook 2017: Youth, skills and entrepreneurship*. Paris: OECD Publishing. Online: https://www.oecd.org/dev/americas/E-Book_LEO2017.pdf (last accessed 1 November 2022).

OECD – Organization for Economic Cooperation and Development. (2022). *Supporting SME development in Latin America and the Caribbean*. Online: https://www.oecd.org/latin-america/regional-programme/productivity/sme-development/ (last accessed 1 November 2022).

Palma Andrés, J., A. L. Ladeiras, D. Culic, and M. Gini (2019). *For a new EU integrated tourism policy: Europe – 27 countries, one destination*. Epicah-Interreg Europe. Online: https://projects2014-2020.interregeurope.eu/filead

min/user_upload/tx_tevprojects/library/file_1556119954.pdf (last accessed 1 November 2022).

Purdam, K. (2016). Task-based learning approaches for supporting the development of social science researchers' critical data skills. *International Journal of Social Research Methodology*, 19(2), pp. 257–267.

Putnam, R. D. (1988). Diploma, cy and domestic politics: The logic of two-level games. *International Organization*, 42(3), pp. 427–460.

Rodrigues, D., and Martinez, L. F. (2020). The influence of digital marketing on recruitment effectiveness: A qualitative study. *European Journal of Management Studies*, 25(1), pp. 23–44.

SAP News. (2022). *Graduates of SAP young professionals program paving way to Africa's digital future*, 23 June. Online: https://news.sap.com/africa/2022/06/graduates-of-sap-young-professionals-program-paving-way-to-africas-digital-future/ (last accessed 9 December 2022).

Schneider-Petsinger, M., J. Wang, Y. Jie, and J. Crabtree (2019). *US–China strategic competition: The quest for global technological leadership*. London: Chatham House, the Royal Institute of International Affairs.

Trittin-Ulbrich, H., A. G. Scherer, I. Munro, and G. Whelan (2021). Exploring the dark and unexpected sides of digitalization: Toward a critical agenda. *Organization*, 28(1), pp. 8–25.

Mario Torres Jarrín

Rethinking EU-CELAC Interregionalism in the Digital World: Techplomacy as a Foreign Policy Instrument for Global Tech Governance

Introduction

A new era in the history of international relations began with the European regional integration process. The regional integration organisations became promoters of development policies, representative agents in foreign policy and new geopolitical actors. Nation-states stopped being the only agents elaborating development policies and designing and implementing foreign policy strategies. With the growth of regional integration projects, the international system was reconfigured, and the decision-making processes for international agendas were modified. A "world of regions" (Katzenstein, 2015) was born, led by an "emerging regional architecture of world politics" (Acharya, 2007). In this new international system, relations must be developed between regions, hence the term "inter-regionalism".

The concept of inter-regionalism developed mainly within the framework created by the two international phenomena of "globalisation" and "regionalism" (Molano, 2007). There are various visions of "inter-regionalism", but we will focus mainly on two. On the one hand, there are those who argue that inter-regionalism is a level within global governance (Söderbaum & Van Langenhove, 2005) below multilateralism and above regional, sub-regional and bilateral relations between states (Hänggi, Roloff & Ruland, 2006). On the other hand, there are those that consider inter-regionalism an independent unit of analysis which could complement or replace multilateralism (Aggarwal & Fogarty, 2004). Inter-regionalism has a transformational effect on international relations, on the structures of regional and international governance, as well as society as a whole (Mattheis & López-Lucia, 2021).

According to Hänggi (2000), there are three types of inter-regionalism: traditional, trans-regionalism and hybrid. The first type describes relations between regions, for example, between the European Union and SICA, the European Union and Mercosur or the European Union and Caricom. Trans-regionalism describes the relations between states in the different regional summits like the

Asia-Pacific Economic Cooperation (APEC) summits or those organised between the European Union and Latin American and Caribbean countries in the 1990s. Hybrid inter-regionalism describes the relations between regional groups and emerging economies like the relations between the EU and Brazil, the EU and Chile or the EU and Mexico.

The creation of the Community of Latin American and Caribbean States (CELAC) in 2010 introduced a new type of relations between the EU and Latin American and Caribbean states. CELAC is designated the official counterparty in relations with third countries and regions. This has led to a series of summits CELAC-EU, CELAC-China, CELAC-African Union, CELAC-Russia, CELAC-Turkey and CELAC-India. CELAC's inter-regionalism encompasses the three types described by Hänggi.

Gardini and Ayuso (2015) discuss how to capture EU-CELAC inter-regionalism. Torres Jarrín (2018) calls EU-CELAC inter-regionalism a "multiplayer inter-regionalism", arguing that, unlike the other inter-regionalism developed by the EU, that with CELAC is based on an inter-regional dialogue with different players from different sectors of society and at different levels of dialogue: governmental, commercial, civil society, academic, etc. Until now, EU-CELAC inter-regionalism has prioritised economic, commercial, investment and international cooperation themes, focusing on issues like the fight against poverty, education, science, technology, innovation, environment and climate change.

The world is experiencing times of great changes. We are living through a phase of transition in the world order. The rise of new global and regional powers, disputes between old and new powers, and the changes in economic-trade axes reflect the transfer of the geopolitical and geoeconomic centre of gravity from the Atlantic to the Pacific. The Asia-Pacific and Indo-Pacific regions have become key. The first of these regions is led by China, the second by India. Each of these countries has its own trading partners and political allies, and its own geopolitical strategy at both the regional and inter-regional level.

In this sense, few regions of the world share common values and principles or, above all, a joint view of the world. Europeans, Latin Americans and Caribbeans share an inter-regional heritage which can serve as a basis for re-thinking how they want to participate in the new world order. They must decide whether to be political protagonists or antagonists.

This chapter seeks to explore two variables which until now have not been considered in the study of inter-regionalism: cyberspace and big tech companies. Both need to be regulated. The chapter first analyses how European, Latin American and Caribbean countries have dealt with issues related to digital transition until now. The following section explains the importance of the big tech companies and their activities in cyberspace. The chapter concludes by arguing that if the strategic alliance between Europeans, Latin Americans and Caribbeans served to promote and secure the first effective agreement on climate change – an agreement that was negotiated between government representatives and those from different sectors of society – then it should also be possible to think about regulating big tech companies and their activities in cyberspace, creating international norms and standards. Techplomacy could become a foreign policy instrument for EU-CELAC inter-regionalism. A bi-regional Techplomacy would allow both regions to play a leading role in the digitalisation process which confronts the world, conceiving a new way of doing international relations and a new way of taking decisions in the sphere of global governance. This would recognise the big tech companies as geopolitical actors in their own right and welcome their participation in designing a global governance for the future: a new global tech governance.

EU-CELAC and digital transition

In October 2022, during the Argentine presidency of CELAC, a meeting was organised in Buenos Aires at the ministerial level of the countries of EU-CELAC with the aim of restoring the system of bi-regional EU-CELAC summits, which had been suspended since 2015 due to the political crisis in Venezuela. The meeting in Buenos Aires agreed to the CELAC-EU bi-regional roadmap for 2022–2023 and to renew the bi-regional partnership to strengthen peace and sustainable development, which contemplated the creation of a "EU-LAC Digital Alliance" (European External Action Service 2022a).

The EU-LAC Digital Alliance sought to create a new framework for cooperation which would allow both regions to confront the challenges of the digital era. The regions hoped to unite forces to promote a bilateral agenda which could be extrapolated at the global level. This new agenda would create and promote the establishment of global rules and standards in digitalisation.

There are four important points in the EU-CELAC bi-regional roadmap for 2022–2023. Firstly, the organisation of the second "High-level event D4D Hub in Action for EU-LAC Digital Cooperation" is envisaged for December 2022 under the Czech presidency of the EU. The meeting will tackle two themes. The first will be the design of a bi-regional EU-CELAC focus to develop an inclusive digitalisation centred on the human being with the support of digital technologies. The second theme is the creation of a "Global Gateway digital investment package for LAC". The second and third points envisage the launch of the "Digital

Alliance" and the "First High-Level Dialogue on Digital Policies" in 2023 during the Swedish Presidency of the EU. Finally, the fourth point is the restoration of EU-CELAC summit meetings, with the next one already scheduled for July 2023 during the Spanish Presidency of the EU.

An important aspect of the D4D (Digital for Development), launched during the Slovenian Presidency in December 2021, is that it is conceived as a "strategic multistakeholder platform" to promote digital cooperation between European countries and their global partners, including regions like Latin America, the Caribbean and Africa (European Commission, 2021). The idea is to exchange experiences of the regulatory framework created by the EU for the digitalisation of the EU economy.

The EU is conscious that the global digitalisation process is changing the lives of its citizens and that governments must create norms and regulate the behaviour and activities of technology companies, especially the so-called disruptive technologies like Artificial Intelligence, Big Data, the Internet of Things, 5G and facial recognition. These disruptive technologies are important because they are innovations which replace processes, whether of the creation, production or commercialisation of specific goods or services.

The EU regulations include: The Digital Service Act, the Digital Markets Act, the European Chips Act, the European Digital Identity, the Artificial Intelligence Act, the European Data Strategy and the European Industrial Strategy (European Commission, 2022). Each of these regional European norms could serve as a point of reference for other regions and serve as a model for implementation at the global level. The inter-regionalism developed by the EU with other regions could be the ideal mechanism for promoting these norms at an international level.

The latest "Development Cooperation Instrument 2014–2020: Multi-annual Indicative Regional Programme for Latin America" included a budget of 925 million euros to cover the following priority areas: security – development nexus – good governance, accountability and social equity; inclusive and sustainable growth for human development; and environmental stability and climate change (European External Action Service, 2014). The roadmap agreed upon in Buenos Aires does not abandon these themes but emphasises the need to re-think the strategic EU-CELAC association and begin to create a new cooperation agenda centred on the challenges of digitalisation.

A digital era generated by the Fourth Industrial Revolution and led by big tech companies presents us with a world in which the physical, digital and biological converge (Schwab, 2015), which will have an impact on governments and global governance as a whole (Schwab, 2016). The EU and CELAC are not immune to the impact of the disruptive technologies created by the big tech companies, which, due to their economic and political power, have become the new geopolitical actors in the current digital world order.

Latin America and the Caribbean as a region face problems like the lack of connectivity, the modernisation of its economies in the digital world, and the regulation and control of cyberspace. Within the framework of the Organisation of American States (OAS), the Latin American and Caribbean countries have established meetings at a continental level to discuss the future in terms of the digital economy, the protection of human rights online, the stability of cyberspace and the fight against cybercrime. In fact, the major achievements of the inter-regionalism developed by the countries of North America, Latin America and the Caribbean within the framework of the OAS include 17 national cybersecurity strategies and more than 20 reports focused on cybersecurity, critical infrastructure, cybersecurity education and workforce development, digital security, online gender violence and data classification (OAS, 2022).

The EU-LAC partnership has long contemplated the inclusion of the promotion of cyberspace stability within its bi-regional cooperation agenda. In fact, both regions share the idea that the internet should be free and open and that a safe cyberspace should be based on rules and rights (Van Raemdonck, 2020). But they have not made progress in the negotiations to develop cooperation at bi-regional or global levels.

The Development Cooperation Instrument 2014–2020: Multi-annual Indicative Regional Programme for Latin America designated two types of cooperation, one at the continental level and the other at the sub-regional (Central America). What is interesting in this programme is that it was the first time that the European Commission used the term "continental cooperation" to refer to Latin America and the Caribbean. The use of the term was not accidental or arbitrary. In the EU's earlier global strategy "A Global Strategy for the European Union's Foreign and Security Policy" (European External Action Service, 2016), the European Commission spoke of the "revival of the Atlantic area" through a new focus on the Atlantic alliance. Until that moment, every time that the term "transatlantic alliance" was used, whether by politicians or academics, it referred to EU-US relations. However, in the 2016 global strategy, it was described as being based on three or even four pillars: the EU, the US-Canada, Latin America and the Caribbean and Africa. This redefinition of the Atlantic axis was responding to a geopolitical consideration: counteracting the growing influence of the economic and political weight of the Pacific axis, whose leadership was defended by the countries from the two Asia-Pacific and Indo-Pacific regions.

Although this new vision of the Atlantic area favoured Latin American and Caribbean countries, it did not materialise for external reasons, principally the election of Donald Trump as US President. Trump attributed no importance to relations with the EU or his continental neighbours. These external factors included the trade war between the US and China, Brexit and subsequent process, the political crisis in the CELAC integration process and the stagnation of EU-CELAC inter-regionalism (the latter two both produced by the political crisis in Venezuela). The disinterest was mutual. Both Europeans and Latin Americans and Caribbeans during the last decade preferred to prioritise their relations with Asia and in particular with China.

The rate of development of the digital ecosystem in Latin American and Caribbean countries is 60% that of Asian countries, 35% of the population in LAC does not use the internet. In terms of corporate competitiveness, 90% of companies in LAC have access to the internet but only 75% use digital banking. Between 40 and 80% of Latin American and Caribbean companies have a webpage but only 8–23% sell through the internet (European Union, 2022). These figures show major areas for cooperation between the EU and CELAC.

Latin American and Caribbean "tech start-up ecosystems" can be found in Sao Paulo, Buenos Aires and Mexico City. It is estimated that there are 1,005 technology companies "Technolatinas" in the region that raised over $1 million. These companies are collectively worth $221 billion, raised $28 billion, include 28 companies worth more than $1 billion, and have over 245,000 employees (Peña, 2021). In Europe, the "tech start-up ecosystem" is found in cities as: Amsterdam, Stockholm, Munich, Paris and London, etc (European Institute of Innovation & Technology, 2022).

According to Westcott (2008), the internet has impacted international relations in three ways. Firstly, it has multiplied and amplified the number of voices and the interest in decision-making in international relations. Secondly, it accelerates the free circulation of information (whether the information is true or not). Finally, it allows traditional diplomatic services to connect more rapidly, both to the citizen and the government, including those of other countries. Both regions face the common challenge of the digital transition, and the EU-LAC digital alliance can be the mechanism for designing a new bi-regional cooperation agenda based on common approaches to the challenges of the digital era.

Big tech companies, cyberspace and techplomacy

The rapid growth of the digital economy makes innovation essential for companies. The pandemic showed that governments, companies and populations throughout the world were not prepared for the digital era. Thus, the challenge of a transformation towards a digital economy is four-fold: national, regional, inter-regional and global.

The ten top companies at a global level by earnings belong to the tech sector, also called Industry 4.0, such as Apple, Alphabet, Microsoft, Amazon, Meta or PayPal. These companies enjoy significant control of cyberspace infrastructure and know how to make the best use of the internet in comparison with governments and citizens.

The European Commission has imposed sanctions and fines on some of these big tech companies for abusing their "dominant use" or "dominant position" in cyberspace. This has led to the European Commission to prosecute Facebook (now called Meta). These companies were also related to companies which used the personal data bases of their respective users to develop disinformation campaigns and in some cases to alter commercial investment decisions and even electoral processes in some countries. In 2017 the European Commission imposed a fine of 110 million euros on Facebook for providing incorrect or misleading information to its clients during its 2014 acquisition of WhatsApp (European Commission, 2017). EU legislation obliges companies to inform users about the change in conditions when there is a merger or takeover between companies (Council of the European Union, 2004). The European Commission determined that Facebook had not done so.

After these incidents which affected the normal functioning of the EU economy, it was realised that the activities of big tech companies not only had commercial repercussions but also impacted on the human and fundamental rights of its citizens and even the democratic systems of EU member states. In 2018 European Commissioner Vestager said that the use of digital technologies is changing democracy, creating new forms of participation in democratic debates, at the same time as also generating new ways of persuading us and manipulating us (Vestager, 2018).

In 2017 the Danish Ministry of Foreign Affairs presented its Foreign Policy Strategy, which presented three new concepts in international relations: Techplomacy, Techembassy and Techambassador. With this strategy Denmark became the first country in the world to raise technology and digitalisation to a cross-cutting priority in its foreign and security policy. At the same time, the strategy mentions Latin America as a region of emerging economies with which Denmark had to work (Ministry of Foreign Affairs of Denmark, 2017).

This Techplomacy presented the thesis that international relations had to be rethought. Starting from the premise that the earnings of big tech companies are greater than the GDP of the majority of economies in the world. Thus, they enjoy a political influence greater than any nation-state and are, in fact, geopolitical actors and agents of change in the international system.

The Danish government thought it necessary to design a specific foreign policy for these big tech companies to understand the latest technological advances and to anticipate them in the creation of international norms which could reduce, mitigate or prevent the negative effects of certain disruptive technologies in society. Thus, they opened a Techembassy with triple headquarters (Silicon Valley, Copenhagen and Beijing) and in 2017 named Caspar Klynge as its first Techambassador. Later in 2020 it named Anne Marie Engtoft Larsen as its Techambassador when Klynge was headhunted by a big tech company, Microsoft, as its European Vice-President for European Government Affairs. This shows the effectiveness of Techplomacy as an instrument for foreign policy to regulate the behaviour of big tech companies and their activities in cyberspace.

Until now companies in general have always created goods and services which governments have then regulated in relation to their design, use and commercialisation. Normally there existed a period of time which lasted some years before these goods and services were regulated. But in recent years, technological advances have been frequent and disruptive for society as a whole which means governments have had to accelerate the creation of specific legislation. But as these technologies are used and commercialised at a global level the norms and standards have to be global too.

Given that big tech companies develop, manage and operate in cyberspace, cyberspace is one of the fields that has to be regulated. The Danish Minister of Foreign Affairs stated: "We have been too innocent for too long about the technological revolution. We have to ensure that democratic governments establish the limits for the technology sector, not the other way round. This is where the Danish initiative for Techplomacy comes into play" (Office of the Techambassador of Denmark, 2021).

EU-CELAC cooperation and values in a broader scenario

The EU-CELAC interregionalism developed during the last decades has created a "bi-regional acquis" mechanism that can serve to rethink the future of their relations. Cyberspace and Big Tech Companies are two international issues that cannot be left out of the EU-CELAC bi-regional agenda. Just as EU-LAC interregionalism contributed to establishing legal norms to achieve global governance on climate change, Europeans, Latin American and Caribbean can create international norms to regulate cyberspace and Big Tech Companies' activities.

The EU-CELAC partnership represents a third of the United Nations General Assembly, World Bank, International Monetary Fund. At the same time, many of their countries are considered economic powers worldwide. Proof of this is that they are members of the OECD or participate in the main international forums linked to global governance, such as the G20. Both regions can exercise an influential power in the decision-making in the main international topics of global governance.

However, before proposing new international norms and standards, Europe, Latin America and the Caribbean must consider two issues related to the broader international context. Firstly, to recover the EU proposal of reviving the Atlantic Area. A relaunch of transatlantic relations is essential, but it may be not enough to do it at a bi-regional level (EU-LAC or EU-United States). Perhaps the bi-continental level (America and Europe) may serve this purpose better. Secondly, to include China in the negotiations on international norms and standards. This is crucial to achieving truly globally accepted regulations of the big tech and the cyberspace.

Still, in a broader international context, also the issue of common values that has long characterised the EU-LAC relation has to be reconsidered. The EU-CELAC roadmap agreed during the 2022 includes a number of key clauses. The importance of clauses 4 and 7 in the communique issued after the meeting is worth noting. In clause 4, taking into account the challenges of the current geopolitical context, the ministers stress the importance of the common values shared by both regions based on the promotion and respect for human rights and fundamental freedoms, democracy and the rule of law. In clause 7, the ministers agreed to strengthen multilateralism and cooperation in international forums through the strategic association of EU-CELAC, considering that this bi-regional partnership is founded on shared values and a vision for the future of democratic, free and equitable societies (Co-Chairs' Communique CELAC-EU 3rd Foreign Ministers Meeting, 2022).

These two clauses in the communique are important because they reaffirm the supposedly shared values that unite the two continents. The European Union seems to be seeking to avoid that LAC countries abandon these principles: a clear reference to the relations that various LAC countries are developing with China and Russia. Thus, shared values are emphasised, such as a vision of the future of democracy, liberty and equitable societies, precisely the values that are not shared with China and Russia. The Democracy Summit Initiative, promoted and led by US President Joe Biden (US Department of State, 2021), should not be forgotten. The Initiative enjoys the support of the Europeans. This initiative is meant, among others, to identify which countries are ready to align themselves with those who defend democracy and which ones are ready to downplay democratic values in exchange for economic or political returns, starting from the premise that an authoritarian country cannot defend democracy.

In this respect, Latin American countries find themselves at a diplomatic crossroads, which they must resolve through a balancing act between their main trading partners, investors and aid donors. In this context, the US, China and the EU play a relevant role as each of them thinks of themselves as promoters or defenders of their own models of democracy and free and equitable societies. The US model can be defined as a democracy with a liberal economic model. The European model is a democracy based on a social market economy. In contrast, China is a socialist state with an economy directed by a single political party, the Chinese Communist Party, headed by a secretary general who acts as a supreme leader. The absence of other political parties and the lack of elections are just some of the arguments for why China is not a democracy. However, in recent years China's foreign policy has sought to present Beijing as a promoter of a new model of democracy. The Chinese Communist Party has long maintained that that "there is no democracy without socialism and there is no socialism without democracy" (US Joint Publications Research Service, 1961). In 2021, the PRC's State Council Information Office published a document titled "China: Democracy that Works" that argues that "democracy is a common value of humanity and an ideal that has always been cherished by the Communist Party of China and the Chinese people" (The State Council Information Office of the PRC, 2021). The new superpower competition involves values and their definition, as much as more traditional political and economic elements.

Latin America finds itself in between Washington and Beijing, with other competitors also playing a significant role in the continent. The geoeconomic chessboard has already been affected by the trade war between the US and China. This started during the Trump presidency and has continued under the new Biden administration. Russia's second invasion of Ukrainian territory in February 2022 has changed the balance of the world order. The position of Latin American and Caribbean remains unclear. The votes in favour of the March 2022 UNGA resolution condemning the Russian invasion of Ukraine can serve as a test. There were 141 votes in favour, 5 against and 35 abstentions (United Nations, 2022). Bolivia, Cuba, El Salvador and Venezuela were absent for the vote. That is to say that a number of important countries in the LAC region did not agree with condemning Russia for its military actions in Ukraine. To this, we must add Brazil's abstention on the 30 September 2022 UNSC resolution which declared that Russia's annexation of Ukrainian territory violated the UN Charter. Furthermore, the ambiguous statements by the presidents of the three largest economies in the region – Mexico, Brazil and Argentina – made constant calls for peace, diplomacy and dialogue but did not position themselves against Russia and avoided criticism of President Putin's actions.

Europeans, Latin Americans and Caribbeans form part of a common history, the history of the West (Torres Jarrín, 2017), and among the contributions of the West to the world are democracy, the rule of law and human rights. All are questioned today. In this sense, EU-CELAC inter-regionalism has a double strategic relevance. On the one hand is the broad question of values, such as the defence of democracy. On the other is the topical need to create norms which regulate the behaviour of big tech companies and their external activities in cyberspace. These are main challenges for the years to come.

Conclusions

The international system is witnessing a change in world order where there is a dispute between old, new, and emerging powers. The European, Latin American and Caribbean countries find themselves with a lack of strategic autonomy and limited geopolitical weight as global actors. These are variables that have to be acknowledged and carefully considered by countries and regional organisations in Europe and Latin America and the Caribbean. Perhaps the awareness of this weakness may generate a common strength. Geopolitics is changing, not only in geographical terms but also thematically. If at the beginning of the 20th century geopolitical theories focused on the conquest of the "Heartland" region of Central Asia (Mackinder, 1904), at the beginning of the 21st century the cyberspace is the "new non-physical region" to be conquered (Torres Jarrín, 2021).

Today techplomacy can serve as a foreign policy instrument to establish a formal relation with Big Tech Companies, regulate their activities and reduce the impact of disruptive technologies on societies. If the collective leadership of the member states of EU-CELAC made the difference in the approval of the Paris Accords and the adoption of Agenda 2030, it could do the same in the adoption of an international agreement to regulate cyberspace. In this sense, the EU-CELAC inter-regionalism can use Techplomacy to pursue a new global governance: a Global Tech Governance.

The pandemic provoked by Covid-19 showed the vulnerability of global health systems as well as the vulnerability of humanity to disease. But it also showed the lack of preparation of countries (both governments and societies) for the digital age. It showed how the inequality divide, caused by the lack of opportunities, often by a lack of education, combines with the digital divide caused by the lack of training in everything related to digital skills. The war launched in

Ukraine by Russia showed the weakness in international security the world faces. Wars today are also fought out in cyberspace, through cyberattacks, in what is known as hybrid war.

On 21 March 2022, the European Council approved a document entitled "Strategic Compass" which contemplates an action plan to reinforce EU security and defence policy up to 2030 (European External Action Service 2022b). It is expected that the EU will become a stronger and more capable provider of security. This includes developing cybersecurity instruments and developing associations, including with Latin America and the Caribbean.

In August 2022, the European Union opened an embassy in Silicon Valley, as Denmark had done in 2017, and created the position of EU Special Envoy to the Tech Sector, making the EU the first organ of regional integration to designate a representative to big tech companies. In the same way, at the multilateral level, the UN Secretary General has also decided to name a UN Special Envoy to the Tech Sector. At the national level, Australia, France, Germany, Switzerland and Estonia have begun to design strategies for cyberspace and the tech sector. Latin America seems to lag behind. EU-LAC cooperation in techplomacy and cyberspace may well help reduce this gap.

Bibliography

Acharya, A. (2007). The emerging regional architecture of world politics. *World Politics, 59*(4), 629–652. Retrieved 9 December 2022 from: https://doi.org/10.1353/wp.2008.0000

Aggarwal, V., and Fogarty, E. (2005). The limits of Interregionalism: The EU and North America. In F. Sörderbaum and L. Van Langenhove (Eds.), *The EU as a global actor and the role of interregionalism. European Integration, 27*(3), 327–346.

Council of the European Union. (2022). *CELAC-EU 3rd foreign ministers meeting – co-chairs' Communiqué*, Buenos Aires, 27 October 2022. Retrieved 9 December 2022 from: https://www.consilium.europa.eu/es/press/press-releases/2022/10/27/celac-eu-3rd-foreign-ministers-meeting-co-chairs-communique-buenos-aires-argentina-27-october-2022/

Council of the European Union. (2004). *Council regulation (EC) N 139/2004 of 20 January 2004 on the control of concentrations between undertaking (the EC merger regulation)*. Retrieved 9 December 2022 from: https://eur-lex.europa.eu/legal-content/EN/ALL/?uri=CELEX:32004R0139

European Commission. (2017). *Mergers: Commission fines Facebook €110 million for providing information about WhatsApp takeover*. Retrieved 9

December 2022 from: https://ec.europa.eu/commission/presscorner/detail/pl/IP_17_1369

European Commission. (2021). *EU launches the digital for development hub for Latin America and the Caribbean*. Retrieved 9 December 2022 from: https://ec.europa.eu/commission/presscorner/detail/en/IP_21_6835

European Commission. (2022). *A Europe fit for the digital age: Empowering people with a new generation of technologies*. Retrieved 9 December 2022 from: https://commission.europa.eu/strategy-and-policy/priorities-2019-2024/europe-fit-digital-age_en

European External Action Service. (2014). *Development Cooperation Instrument (DCI) 2014–2020. Multiannual indicative regional programme for Latin America*. Brussels: European External Action Service, European Commission-Directorate General for Development and Cooperation-Europeaid.

European External Action Service. (2016). *Shared vision, common action: A stronger Europe. A global strategy for the European Union's foreign and security policy*. Retrieved 9 December 2022 from: https://www.eeas.europa.eu/sites/default/files/eugs_review_web_0.pdf

European External Action Service. (2022a). *CELAC-EU. Bi-regional roadmap 2022–2023. Renewing the bi-regional partnership to strengthen peace and sustainable development*. Retrieved 9 December 2022 from: https://www.eeas.europa.eu/eeas/celac-ue-bi-regional-roadmap-2022-2023_en

European External Action Service. (2022b). *A strategic compass for security and defence*. Retrieved 9 December 2022 from: https://www.eeas.europa.eu/eeas/strategic-compass-security-and-defence-1_en

European Institute of Innovation & Technology. (2022). *EIT digital. For a strong, digital Europe*. Retrieved 9 December 2022 from: https://eit.europa.eu/our-communities/eit-digital

European Union. (2022). *EU-Latin America and the Caribbean digital alliance*. Retrieved 9 December 2022 from: https://europa.eu/capacity4dev/file/123432/download?token=wC2Jd7Ek

Gardini, G. L., and Ayuso, A. (2015). *EU-Latin America and Caribbean interregional relations: Complexity and change*. Retrieved 2 June 2017 from: https://www.cidob.org/en/publications/publication_series/project_papers/atlantic_future_papers/scientific_paper/eu_latin_america_and_caribbean_inter_regional_relations_complexity_and_change

Hänggi, H. (2000). Interregionalism: Empirical and theoretical perspectives. Paper prepared for the Workshop "Dollars, Democracy and Trade. External Influence on Economic Integration in the Americas". Los Angeles, May 18.

Hänggi, H., Roloff, R., and Ruland, J. (2006). Interregionalism. A new phenomenon in international relations. In H. Hänggi, R. Roloff, and J. Ruland (Eds.), *Interregionalism and international relations* (pp. 31–62). Abindgdon-New York: Routledge.

Katzenstein, P. (2015). *A world of regions: Asia and Europe in the American imperium*. Ithaca and London: Cornell University Press.

Mackinder, H. J. (1904). *The geographical pivot of history*. Cosimo Classics, 2020.

Mattheis, F., and López-Lucía, E. (2021). *The unintended consequences of interregionalism. Effects on regional actors, societies and structures*. Abingdon: Routledge.

Ministry of Foreign Affairs of Denmark. (2017). *Government's foreign and security policy strategy 2017–18*. Retrieved 9 December 2022 from: file:///C:/Users/Mario%20Torres/Downloads/Publikation_Udenrigsministeriet_UK_01%20(002).pdf

Molano, G. (2007). *El interregionalismo y sus límites. Estudios Internacionales* 158. Santiago de Chile: Instituto de Estudios Internacionales, Universidad de Chile.

OAS. (2022). *Cybersecurity program*. Retrieved 9 December 2022 from: https://www.oas.org/en/sms/cicte/prog-cybersecurity.asp

Peña, I. (2021). *Tecnolaltina. The LAC startup ecosystem comes of age 2021*. Inter-American Development Bank. Retrieved 9 December 2022 from: https://publications.iadb.org/en/tecnolatinas-2021-lac-startup-ecosystem-comes-age

Schwab, K. (2015). *The fourth industrial revolution. What it means and how to respond*. Foreign Affairs, December 2015. New York: Council on Foreign Relations.

Schwab, K. (2016). *The fourth industrial revolution*. Geneva: World Economic Forum.

Söderbaum, F., and Van Langenhove L. (2005). The EU as a global actor and the role of interregionalism. *European Integration, 27*(3), 249–262.

The State Council Information Office of the People's Republic China. (2021). *China: Democracy that works*. Retrieved 9 December 2022 from: https://news.cgtn.com/news/whitepaper/China+Democracy+That+Works.pdf

Torres Jarrín, M. (2017). *El acervo integracionista en Europa y América: Una historia común*. Salamanca: Ediciones Universidad de Salamanca.

Torres Jarrín, M. (2018). EU-CELAC: A multiplayer interregionalism. Redefining the atlantic area. In G. L. Gardini, S. Koschut, and A. Falke (Eds.), *Interregionalism and the Americas*. Lanham, MD: Lexington Book.

Torres Jarrín, M. (2021). Indo-Pacific region: A political concept or a geopolitical reality? In J. Argumosa, A. Garofali, and M. Torres Jarrín (Eds.), *The future of the Asia-Pacific in the new world order. Emerging markets & emerging powers.* Valencia: Tirant Lo Blanch.

United Nations. (2022a). *Rusia veta la resolución que habría condenado la anexión de territorios ucranianos.* Retrieved 9 December 2022 from: https://news.un.org/es/story/2022/09/1515842

United Nations. (2022b). *La mayoría del Consejo de Seguridad rechaza la "resolución humanitaria" sobre Ucrania presentada por Rusia.* Retrieved 9 December 2022 from: https://news.un.org/es/story/2022/03/1506112

US Department of State. (2021). *Summit for democracy 2021.* Retrieved 9 December 2022 from: https://www.consilium.europa.eu/es/press/press-releases/2022/10/27/celac-eu-3rd-foreign-ministers-meeting-co-chairs-communique-buenos-aires-argentina-27-october-2022/

Van Raemdonck, N. (2020). Cyber diplomacy in Latin America. *Digital Dialogue.* 24 June. Retrieved 9 December 2022 from: https://eucyberdirect.eu/research/cyber-diplomacy-in-latin-america

Vestager, M. (2018). *"Time is over" for digital world to escape the rules.*

Retrieved 9 December 2022 from: https://www.drinks-insight-network.com/digital-disruption/margrethe-vestager-digital-world-rules/

Westcott, N. (2008). *Digital diplomacy: The impact of the internet on international relations, Research report (16).* Oxford: Oxford Internet Institute.

Jeanne W. Simon

Decentralising Cooperation Through Regional Policy Dialogues: Exportation of the European Smart Specialization Strategy to High- and Middle-Income Latin American Countries

Introduction

For more than a decade, the European Union (EU) has developed a more pragmatic relationship with Latin America and the Caribbean, creating a complex network of interrelations. Since 2010, seeking to advance towards a more horizontal partnership of international cooperation, the Directorate-General for Regional and Urban Policy (DG REGIO) of the European Commission (EC) has promoted the European smart specialization strategy as a mutual learning process in six Latin American countries: Argentina, Brazil, Chile, Mexico, Colombia and Peru.[1] Within this context, the first milestone is the so called RED Initiative established between the EC and the Chilean government in 2010 to provide technical support to sub-national governments to design and establish regional innovation strategies (European Commission, 2011). This decentralisation of EU cooperation builds on and/or is formalised through bilateral "regional policy dialogue" (RPD) in which each country defines its collaboration priorities in science, technology and innovation for sustainable development, seeking to improve sub-national innovation policy and governance.

In parallel, the DG REGIO has also promoted the "smart specialization strategy" (S3) in numerous regions in the EU as part of the cohesion policy and S3 has also become a main component of cooperation in the framework of the European Neighbourhood Policy. Originally an economic development strategy, S3 has evolved into a place-based intersectoral policy that helps regions[2] identify

1 https://s3platform.jrc.ec.europa.eu/international-cooperation

2 The paper uses the terms "region" and "regional" preferentially to denote sub-national territories. However, in some cases, these terms are used to describe cooperation between the European Union and Latin America and the Caribbean, for example, "regional organizations" or "interregional cooperation".

territorial resources in research and innovation and prioritise actions to build critical mass in economic sectors in which there is a comparative advantage (Uyarra, 2019). From the EU perspective, the diffusion of S3 beyond its borders allows other countries to benefit from this innovative approach and methodology that is adaptable to distinct territorial contexts and can contribute to strengthening regional innovation systems throughout the world (Gómez Prieto, Demblans and Palazuelos Martínez, 2019).

This decentralised cooperation that is centred around S3 emphasises dialogue and policy learning between sub-national territories, facilitating internationalisation of private enterprises and sub-national territories. It promotes a bottom-up methodology based on the entrepreneurial discovery process that involves stakeholders in the definition of strategic priorities at the sub-national level. Further, due to the EC's rapid appropriation of S3 as a European policy instrument, the limited orientation for its implementation at first allowed for different interpretations and flexibility in its adaptation to existing institutional planning contexts (Kroll, 2015).

Considering the growing interest in S3 in Latin America and the Caribbean (LAC), the present chapter uses the ideational perspective of policy translation to analyse how the bottom-up nature of the European S3 strengthened EU-LAC cooperation through RPDs in six high and middle-income countries in Latin America. The decentralised nature of the technical collaboration and capacity permitted greater flexibility and empowered cities and regions to play a greater role in EU-LAC cooperation.

This chapter is structured as follows. The next section presents the concept of "policy translation" used to analyse the exportation of European S3 through the RPDs established between the EU and six Latin American countries. The third section situates the growing importance of the DG REGIO within the framework of EU-LAC cooperation. The fourth section analyses the growing importance of S3 in bilateral and EU-LAC relations, and the chapter concludes with reflections on the RPDs as a mechanism of decentralised cooperation between the EU and LAC.

Translating a policy idea into different national contexts

In the study of the effects of international cooperation, there is a growing body of literature that analyses the diffusion of policy ideas between countries (Stone et al., 2020; Osorio, 2018). The literature on policy diffusion and transfer analyses the process and the role that actors play in exporting a policy idea (Hassenteufel & Zeigermann, 2021). Within the policy transfer literature, the concept of policy translation emphasises the selective adoption of global/transnational policy ideas by actors in the target contexts (Stone, 2012; Beeson & Stone, 2013) and highlights the role actors play in debating and creating meaning, drawing on both technical and political discourses. In this way, policy translation emphasises discursive elements and visibilises different interpretations, voices, meanings and practices (Lendvai & Stubbs, 2007).

Drawing on Latour (1986), this chapter conceptualises policy translation as a communicative process between different social worlds. Successful translation requires mutual points of understanding ("words in common") and then a reinterpretation that can be understood in and adapted to the receiving context. In this sense, the exportation of a policy idea involves its adaptation to a different cultural and institutional context, where transnational and domestic policy entrepreneurs interpret and adapt the policy idea (for example, S3). In this way, translation involves a dynamic back-and-forth circulation of ideas (Hassenteufel & Zeigermann, 2021), although not necessarily a mutual learning process. From this perspective, differences in policy application between contexts are not problematic.

To promote the policy idea, development cooperation projects, trainings and conferences provide opportunities for transnational actors to share language and concepts with domestic actors (Lendvai & Stubbs, 2007). Transnational policy entrepreneurs provide generic storylines and normative guidelines to achieve policy goals at national and sub-national levels, while domestic actors can collaborate, transform, or block its introduction. In this way, domestic intermediaries also play an important role as translators that construct policy meaning and relevance within the domestic context (Song et al., 2019). Further, even when international organizations and industrialised countries are the principal promoters of policy ideas, Stone et al., (2020) highlight that there is a growing circulation from and within the Global South.[3]

International organisations, such as the European Union (EU), the World Bank, the Organization of Economic Cooperation and Development (OECD), and the United Nations (UN) agencies, are conceptualised as "forceful agents of policy transfer", although policy ideas often fail to penetrate domestic policy-making due to domestic political, institutional, and cultural factors (Stone et al., 2020). Since international organizations do not have formal power, their influence depends on their ideas and expertise, reflecting Latour's insight on the power of convincing translations (Latour, 1986). For example, Jacob et al.

3 See for example, Osorio (2018).

(2008), in their study of the incorporation of international objectives of sustainable development, show that the incorporation of this perspective in the official speeches does not always imply the creation of instruments that can achieve the desired results. For Hassenteufel and Zeigermann (2021), policy translation analysis contemplates three dimensions: discourse, actors and institutional contexts. In short, the principal agents can be transnational or domestic actors who act as translators, negotiating meanings and understandings as they adapt proposed policies into the institutional context. The present study focuses on how the adaptation of S3 by several Latin American countries strengthened decentralised EU-LAC cooperation.

Exporting EC regional policy to Latin America

Even when the relationship is based on historical ties, shared values and important economic and social exchanges, EU cooperation with Latin America and the Caribbean (LAC) continues to evolve and can be characterised as a network of overlapping dialogues, negotiations and cooperation initiatives (Garcia, 2016). Indeed, this network of EU-LAC cooperation probably emerged as a strategy to address the significant asymmetries in socioeconomic development between these two regions and in the institutional capacities of the EU with its numerous Latin American counterparts. The EU's adoption of a more pragmatic and practical inter-regional cooperation with Latin America became clearly evident in 2014 (Selleslaghs, 2019; Macaluza, 2021).

In short, EU efforts to strengthen relations with regional organizations in Latin America are often parallel to their efforts to develop mutually beneficial bilateral trade agreements, which also encompass collaboration on political and social issues (García, 2016; Selleslaghs, 2019). Moreover, since several Latin American countries can no longer receive official development assistance (ODA) due to their status as upper-middle-income countries, the EU developed a new approach with these countries based on horizontal and triangular cooperation (ECLAC, 2018; Selleslaghs, 2019). The introduction of S3 through bilateral relations with a limited number of countries connects the economic objectives of innovation and competitiveness with the social objectives of sustainability and equity. Its coherence with the Sustainable Development Goals has surely contributed to its generally positive reception.

In this new period, two regional organizations that include the 33 Latin American and Caribbean states have played key roles in facilitating EU cooperation: the Community of Latin America and Caribbean States (CELAC[4]) and the Economic Commission for Latin America and the Caribbean (ECLAC). Even though CELAC has limited financial and human resources, the EU-CELAC relationship provides a large-scale interregional platform for cooperation, facilitating the transfer of policy ideas from the EU and between member countries. In turn, ECLAC, which is an organization of the United Nations, contributes with technical support and the management of cooperation projects in different LAC countries, especially with respect to the Sustainable Development Goals (SDGs).

Between 2007 and 2015, the EU (through DG REGIO) established formal agreements for regional policy dialogues (RPD) with Brazil, Chile, Argentina, Peru, Mexico, Colombia and the Central American intergovernmental organization SICA. As a bilateral dialogue, the RPD seeks to create mutually beneficial relations between sub-national territories, establishing partnerships and providing access to EU policy platforms. The inclusion of RPD in bilateral agreements strengthened over time and became part of the priorities of bi-regional collaboration established in the EU-CELAC Action Plan in 2015 (EU-CELAC, 2015). For the EU, these RPDs are a mechanism to transfer European policy ideas and practices to non-EU partners interested in emulating the EU regional development model. In this way, RPD institutionalises decentralised cooperation, complementing trade agreements that open national markets to facilitate trade and investment. There are few studies on RPDs, although Dabrowski et al. (2018) provide an interesting analysis of the RPDs established with Brazil and China.

Within the EU, regional development policy is a central component of the cohesion policy that seeks to reduce disparities between sub-national territories, targeting investment to create dynamic knowledge-based economies. Since many regional governments were not acting (or investing these funds) strategically, the European Commission (EC) drew on the concept of "smart specialisation" that had recently been developed by the Knowledge for Growth advisory committee to orient regional authorities (Kroll, 2019; Foray et al., 2009). Later, in 2012, the EC established the regional innovation and smart specialisation strategy (RIS3) as a precondition to receive the European Regional Development Funds (ERDF) for research and innovation initiatives, focusing on recently incorporated countries (EU-13). In this way, the application of S3 in the EU builds on their earlier regional innovation strategy (RIS) and seeks to strengthen the

4 Since 2012, CELAC has been recognised as the Latin American counterpart of the EU for bi-regional relations.

connections between actors of the regional innovation system and promote the internationalisation of sub-national territories.

The focus of RIS3 has evolved over time, but it essentially consists of the prioritisation of a few competitive economic activities, scientific fields and technological domains that have potential market opportunities for the territory in a global context. A central element of the RIS3 methodology is the entrepreneurial discovery process (EDP), which is data-driven and based on collaboration among the actors of the regional innovation system. Indeed, the EDP should be based on "a structured, inclusive dialogue with local actors" that creates territorial identity and empowers local agents representing the public sector, business organisations, research and academic institutions and civil society (Demblans et al., 2020: 12). In this way, it seeks to connect investment in science and technology to economic activities. To achieve place-based economic transformation, RIS3 should be bottom-up and integrate different types of explicit and tacit knowledge in the shared vision, analysis of endogenous economic potential, define strategic priorities and policy instruments to maximise innovation and economic progress (Iacobucci, 2012). Finally, the RIS3 strategy should include a public-private governance structure and have an effective monitoring and evaluation system. The following figure summarises the principal components of S3.

Figure 12.1: Principal components of a Smart Specialisation Strategy
Source: Author elaboration.

The DG REGIO has developed numerous materials to better orient policy-makers, providing methodological support and advice through the Smart Specialisation Platform[5] that can be used by both EU and non-EU authorities for collaboration and mutual learning (Gomez Prieto et al., 2019). In this way, S3 also connects to EC cooperation on research and innovation as contemplated in

5 https://s3platform.jrc.ec.europa.eu/

the Strategic Plan 2020–2024 of the Directorate-General for Research and Innovation (DG Research and Innovation, 2020).

There is a growing number of studies on the implementation of smart specialisation in the EU. For example, Kroll (2015) analyses the RIS3 in EU-13 countries, observing limited internationalisation of their economies. Capello et al. (2020) draw on studies of S3 to develop quantitative tools that can map the technological and innovation dimensions, providing a more effective knowledge base for the collaborative design process. The Joint Research Centre of the European Commission systematised the experiences of S3 in Latin America, declaring that S3 is "inspirational" for Latin America even when the report recognises differences with the European RIS3 (Gomez et al., 2019).

Bilateral and Bi-regional EU-LAC cooperation in smart specialisation

This section describes the introduction and appropriation of S3 as a policy idea whose transfer is facilitated through decentralised EU cooperation. Its introduction in Latin America first builds on the bilateral relations that the EU had already developed with several countries since 1990 in the four priority sectors of economic development and trade; human resources (science cooperation) and mutual understanding; social cohesion; and the environment.[6] Further, ECLAC's promotion of the social cohesion concept in Latin America surely contributed to a growing interest in RIS, especially in Chile.

Its initial introduction in Latin America, through the RPDs established by DG REGIO, built upon and connected with prior EU-LAC cooperation programs in science, technology and innovation (STI), which originally focused on private enterprises and academic exchange. In this way, the transfer of the S3 approach complements traditional cooperation programmes with small and medium enterprises (SMEs), such as the AL-INVEST programme offered from 1994 to 2018. AL-INVEST provided financing to improve the productivity and competitiveness of micro, small, and medium-sized enterprises and fostered economic relations within the LAC and with the EU through the sharing of experience and knowledge in the area of innovation. It also facilitated relationships between LAC and European companies through an internationalisation strategy.

The following table provides a timeline of the bilateral and bi-regional relations that are relevant for S3, identifying three stages. The first stage is exploratory

6 Further information can be found in Sanchez (2018).

and involves a diversity of strategies and programs. In the second stage, there is a clear strategy to establish RPDs based on S3. The third stage is a consolidation of this methodology through partnership programs.

Table 12.1: Principal events in bilateral and bi-regional relations in regional development and innovation

2007	Strategic partnership and RPD Bilateral Relations	
1994 2018	Cooperation framework in innovation and competitiveness with **Chile**	
2009	Strategic partnership with **Mexico**	
2010	**RPD Chile** RED Project	EU-CELAC Joint Initiative for Research and Innovation (JIRI)
2011		URBELAC through DG REGIO – IADB cooperation (2011–2017)
2012		CELAC becomes the official counterpart of the EU
2013	**RPD Peru**	
2014	**RPD Mexico**	
2015	**RPD Colombia**	**RPD SICA (Central America)** Innopro
2016	**RPD Argentina**	

2016	International Urban Cooperation (IUC) Programme (2016–2019)
2017	International Urban and Regional Cooperation programme (2017–2022)
2017	INNOVACT: RIS3 and cross-border integration (2017–2020)
2018	EU-CELAC INNOV-AL I & II (2018–2020)

Sources: Author elaboration based on official information of DG REGIO and https://www.innoval2.eu/innovation-policies/the-project/eu-al-cooperation_204_1_ap.html.

The first stage begins with the establishment of strategic partnerships with Brazil in 2007 and Mexico in 2009. This bilateral relation facilitated the development of RPDs as a form of decentralised cooperation. Indeed, in 2007, the EU established their strategic partnership with Brazil and signed the RPD defining bilateral collaboration priorities at the sub-national level. The principal objectives of this RPD are to reduce regional inequalities and encourage the exploitation of endogenous potential. Still, Brazil's motivation was "not to take off-the-shelf solutions, but rather to gain insights, examples and ideas that could be adapted to the Brazilian context" (Dabrowski et al., 2018: 1175). The principal instruments have been study visits, conferences, training events and studies. Although important advances were made in S3 implementation, the change of government at the national level weakened the relations with the EU, affecting its continuity. Despite this setback, there are other agreements that continue to promote S3 in specific states, such as Pernambuco.[7]

In 2008, the Chilean government and the EC established a cooperation framework in innovation and competitiveness, signing an RPD in 2010. Within this

7 See https://ec.europa.eu/regional_policy/es/policy/cooperation/international/latin-america/

framework, the EC provided support for the RED project, which is considered a milestone in the introduction of S3 in Latin America (Barroeta et al., 2017). With EC support, the Undersecretary of Regional Development (SUBDERE), in collaboration with the Chilean Council of Science and Technology (CONICYT), worked with the 11 regional governments and stakeholders (universities and industry) in the elaboration of an RIS3 that would orient public spending for a 10-year period. This program resulted in policy learning, even when only a few regions established RISs (Maggi & Maza, 2017).

Based on this experience, in 2014, the Chilean Corporation for Reconstruction and Industrial Development (CORFO) led the design of the Strategic Programs of Smart Specialisation with the goal to improve the competitiveness of strategic sectors (Gomez Prieto & Dos Santos, 2017). The design process was multi-level, integrating public and private actors at the national and regional levels to develop knowledge-based companies; its analysis focused on identifying coordination and production failures. Hernández y Lebert (2019) conclude that the EU's cooperation with Chile has contributed to more effective public policies by addressing inequality and social participation, although changes in funding priorities between governments have affected greater continuity. A more flexible and horizontal relationship is observed in these first RPDs, while later RPDs present a more standard approach with a stronger sub-national focus that is strengthened and structured through their connection to city-to-city cooperation programs.

In this first stage, a series of bi-regional collaborations complemented the existing RPDs. In 2010, the EU and CELAC established the Joint Initiative for Research and Innovation (JIRI) and a two-year Action Plan that emphasises "science, research, innovation and technology" to consolidate bi-regional cooperation through policy learning. This same year, DG REGIO and the Inter-American Development Bank (IADB) created the URBELAC network to support national, regional and local governments in Latin America for the 2011–2017 period. Drawing on European policy, this program understood urban development as an integrated process, addressing social development, productivity, and environmental protection in urban areas. Although the network did not explicitly include S3, its financing of partnerships between cities facing similar challenges contributed to relationship building through the exchange of knowledge, experiences, good practices, and lessons learned (Demblans et al., 2020). In 2012, CELAC is recognised as the official counterpart of the EU in Latin America.

In the second phase from 2013 to 2016, DG REGIO established five more RPDs. The RPD established in 2013 with the Ministry of External Relations of the Republic of Peru included S3 and introduced border integration. This program financed capacity building, exchange of information and good practices for an integrated approach to sub-national development. As part of this RPD, DG REGIO highlights that the focus on regional innovation enabled decentralised cooperation between Europe and Latin American sub-national authorities, contributing to collaboration and exchanges between private actors. In short, "regional innovation is good business". Granda et al. (2015) and Esparza y Ipanaqué (2021) analyse the development of S3 in different sub-national territories in Peru, highlighting the challenges facing an effective adaptation to the institutional and political context. Despite the differences with European sub-national regions, both authors highlight that the S3 methodology, and especially the EPD, favoured a more inclusive process. However, the business sector's limited interest in innovation remains an important challenge (Barroeta et al., 2017).

In 2014, DG REGIO signed the RPD with Mexico, cooperating with the Secretary for Agricultural, Territorial and Urban Development (SEDATU) to develop regional and urban policies. Among the areas of cooperation are the reduction of internal economic and social disparities, multi-level governance and decentralization issues, including transborder regional cooperation. The focus is on the exchange of information and capacity building, resulting in the application of the S3 methodology in several sub-national territories. Studies, like Solleiro-Rebolledo et al. (2020), describe the process and identify the principal challenges.

In 2015, the EU and Colombia established an RPD. Among the priorities are the promotion of economic, social and territorial cohesion, innovation and technological development; cross-border, transnational and interregional cooperation; development policies in post-conflict situations; the setting up and implementation of regional and cross-border development and integration policies, including the strengthening of administrative capacity, in particular at regional and local levels; issues relating to decentralisation and multi-level governance; issues relating to sustainable economic development and corporate social responsibility at the territorial level.

Subsequently, DG REGIO established an RPD with the multilateral organization Central American Integration System (SICA) in 2015 and with Argentina in 2016. Even when these letters of intent maintain a standard format that emphasises the exchange of knowledge and experiences in the areas of urban and regional policy, there is weak incorporation of S3. The RPD with SICA addresses regional integration in Central America; the RPD with Argentina did not apply the S3 methodology to define its innovation strategies that remain highly national in their focus (Barrota et al., 2017).

Complementary to these experiences of bi-lateral cooperation, the EU-CELAC bi-regional cooperation agreements began to strengthen the sub-national cooperation component beginning in 2015 with an EU-LATAM cooperation project that identified and created a database for potential long-term partnerships where the EU experience could be both used and recycled (Innopro, 2015). Then, in 2016, a new stage begins with the establishment of several programmes that specifically transfer S3 to several countries with RPDs: International Urban and Regional Cooperation, INNOVACT and INNOV-AL. These programmes build on the already mentioned URBELAC network that was active between 2011 and 2017.

In 2016, the establishment of the International Urban Cooperation (IUC) Programme facilitated 20 city-to-city partnerships between the EU and LAC, with a focus on local and regional development, contributing to the globalization of the Covenant of Mayors. Further, this programme "stimulated the development of mutual business opportunities and the strengthening of regional strategies" (Demblans et al., 2020). In the second phase that began in 2017, the International Urban and Regional Cooperation (IURC) expanded its coverage, organising around thematic networks and strengthening its coherence with the SDGs.

In 2017, the INNOVACT programme was established to share European cross-border experiences with similar Latin American counterparts. Working within an S3 framework, this programme provided technical assistance and training for cross-border cooperation, innovation systems, clusters and competitiveness in seven cross-border areas in Latin America, where Peru participates with four cross-border areas.[8] This program builds on an earlier triangular cooperation program between Chile and Peru with European financing and technical assistance.

The subsequent INNOV-AL programme developed in two phases from 2018 to 2020[9]. In the first stage, this programme collaborated with national authorities to facilitate cooperation between specialised agencies and regional authorities. The objective was to develop further cooperation between national and regional authorities and specialised agencies in Argentina, Brazil, Chile, Colombia, Peru and México (only Phase II). The programme specifically focused on the decentralised definition and implementation of RIS3, facilitating knowledge exchange through region-to-region partnerships, where the EU partners are defined according to the innovation needs of the participating regions in Latin America.

8 See the web page: http://www.innovactplatform.eu/index.php/
9 See the web page: https://www.innoval2.eu/descripcion/

A subsequent evaluation of this process concludes that "the path of European competitiveness and innovation policy towards a model with a multi-sectoral and systematic approach for the economy (national and regional) forms a point of reference and a starting point for Latin American countries in the process of articulating decentralised innovation policies" (EU-CELAC, 2021).

Indeed, since 2019, there is growing recognition that S3 is beneficial for both European and Latin American countries: "Not only would this generate economic transformation and contribute to building robust regional innovation ecosystems, possibly integrating the sustainability dimension, but it could also foster learning and new cooperation and business, thereby facilitating integration in global value chains" (Demblans et al., 2020: 4). Further, this *Science for Policy Report* declares: "Smart Specialisation has acted as a genuine inspirational driver of regional innovation and specialisation in several countries and regions of Latin America. Indeed, it [Latin America] is considered to be a privileged laboratory for the export of Smart Specialisation outside EU borders", arguing that S3 can build on the mutual knowledge and earlier partnerships to improve the effectiveness of EU collaboration (Demblans et al., 2020). The positive evaluation appears to be based on Latin American interest in S3, and the EU believes that its application outside of the EU will have a multiplier effect "by fostering learning and opening up avenues for inter-regional and international synergies, complementarities and collaboration" (Gomez Prieto et al., 2019: 4).

Indeed, S3 has become a key concept orienting EU-LAC cooperation in regional innovation and increasingly in science and technology, working to make these territories "global, inherently local and definitely sustainable" (Demblans et al., 2020: 7). In this stage, the strategy of city-to-city / region-to-region cooperation has become the principal component of bilateral cooperation expressed in RPDs. An increasing number of sub-national partnerships throughout Latin America will be a likely outcome of these EU-LAC bi-regional cooperation programmes, such as INNOVACT and INNOV-AL.

Adaptation of the European smart specialisation strategy in Latin America

Despite many shared values, the differences between European and Latin American institutional contexts remain, and consequently, there are important differences between the implementation of S3 in the EU and the six Latin American countries. Indeed, the multi-level governance structure in EU countries resulted in a top-down translation process of S3 policy ideas. Based on the goals set at the supranational level, national and regional governments set specific objectives that are coherent with the European S3 framework: policymakers design policy instruments coherent with the territorial context; monitor and assess their advances, reporting their advances to the EU; and revise their objectives when necessary (Marianelli et al., 2019). Further, due to its rapid implementation, the framework was relatively flexible and the regions could consider territorial specificities in the definition of priority sectors. Further, the inclusion of stakeholders and their knowledge in monitoring was fundamental for collective learning and S3 effectiveness (Marianelli et al., 2019).

In contrast, the cooperation priorities for sub-national development were negotiated at the national level in the six Latin American countries with RPDS. Consequently, they present differences with the European S3 model (Barroeta et al., 2017). First, despite certain advances in bottom-up formulation, the national level continues to be central in the definition of innovation strategies. In the case of Chile, the national level promoted the development of RIS3 throughout the country. In contrast, in Peru, Brazil, Mexico and Colombia, the application of the S3 methodology was targeted to a limited number of sub-national territories; and was not followed in Argentina (Barroeta et al., 2017).

Further, the application of the S3 methodology at the sub-national level also varied between countries. The coordination of the entrepreneurial discovery process was led by a university in Peru, by a municipal government in Colombia and by the regional government in Chile. While the involvement of non-governmental actors in the EU favoured the identification of emerging sectors such creative and cultural industries, social innovation and the blue economy, among many others, the objective of LAC innovation strategies is not to support new initiatives but rather to add value to traditional sectors, such as food and tourism (Demblans et al., 2020). Even when an important number of stakeholders participated in the process, public-private coordination and monitoring of the advances are weak in the six Latin American countries, limiting the generation of collective knowledge.

In this way, DG REGIO did not promote S3 emulation, but rather focused on the "consolidation of customised approaches through a shared understanding of the S3 methodology, where both contribute to a learning process between different territorial contexts" (Demblans et al., 2020: 11). Among the principal indicators for success are: the growing importance of territorial dimension in competitiveness strategies, greater relevance of innovation policies as complementary to science and higher education policies, greater availability of data for the initial characterization, the establishment of social dialogues and monitoring mechanisms.

Still, important barriers remain within Latin American countries that have limited an effective learning and translation process. In contrast with most European sub-national territories, public institutions at the sub-national level are weaker and less efficient in Latin America; there is limited financing and they have limited experience in innovation policy (Barroeta et al., 2017). A further complication is when new political authorities are not interested in decentralised development strategies that involve public-private decision-making. Despite these challenges, S3 remains an attractive policy idea and there is a strong interest in European technical support as well as learning from the experiences of similar territories in the EU (Demblans et al., 2020). Consequently, sub-national territories in Latin America principally learn from their European counterparts and adapt S3 to their priorities and institutional contexts. Indeed, there is no evidence of horizontal collaboration between the EU and these six countries. For the period studied, knowledge transfer on S3 is principally from the EU to Latin America. However, in the future, the city-to-city partnerships around an economic sector could facilitate the integration of both partners into a global value chain, favouring a more equal relationship. Further studies should analyse these effects.

Decentralised cooperation through Regional Policy Dialogues

The present chapter analyses decentralised EU cooperation with six high and middle-income Latin American countries established in bilateral RPDs. This decentralised cooperation emerged incrementally as both a strategic and pragmatic response within the multiple levels of EU-LAC cooperation. The EU first developed strategic partnerships with Brazil and Mexico, and then RPDs with Brazil and Chile. In particular, Chile's interest in and adaptation of EU innovation policy paved the way for RPDs with Peru, Mexico, Colombia, Argentina and SICA. Within the same period, the EU-CELAC also prioritised research and innovation in sub-national territories in their Actions Plans, further facilitating S3 strategies.

Even when the RPDs provide a framework for decentralised cooperation between sub-national territories, DG REGIO supervision and financing did not establish specific mechanisms for mutual knowledge exchange. Further, since 2017, decentralised cooperation is more structured to transfer S3 more effectively through the EU-CELAC INNOV-AL programme, while the IURC programme facilitates partnering. The combination of these programs has favoured multiplier effects in scientific and business collaboration in innovative sectors.

However, there is no mutual knowledge exchange on S3 as a policy idea because European experts teach their LA counterparts. Still, the next stage contemplates triangular cooperation in which LA experts will teach their counterparts in LAC, effectively translating the European version of S3.

In conclusion, the RPD provided a new bilateral cooperation mechanism that sought to establish a more horizontal relationship at the sub-national level with high- and middle-income countries in LAC. Even when it maintained a one-way knowledge transfer from the EU to LAC, its flexible approach resulted in cooperation in mutually beneficial areas. It also laid the ground for triangular cooperation through the agreement with the Central American intergovernmental system (SICA) and bi-regional agreement with CELAC.

Bibliography

Barroeta, B., Gómez Prieto, J., Paton, J., & Palazuelos M. (2017). *Innovation and regional specialisation in Latin America*. Luxembourg: Joint Research Centre, European Commission.

Beeson, M., & Stone, D. (2013). The European Union model's influence in Asia after the global financial crisis. *European Journal of East Asian Studies, 12*(2), 167–190. https://doi.org/10.1163/15700615-13120202.

Capello, R., Kleibrink, A., & Matusiak, M. (2020). *Quantitative methods for place-based innovation policy*. Cheltenham: Edward Elgar Publishing.

Dabrowski, M., Polverari, L., & Musialkowska, I. (2018). EU–China and EU–Brazil policy transfer in regional policy. *Regional Studies, 52*(9), 1169–1180. https://doi.org/10.1080/00343404.2018.1431389.

Demblans, A., Cagnin, C., & Gómez Prieto, J. (2020). *Smart specialisation, an innovation bridge between the EU and Latin America – evidence and lessons learned from the International Urban Cooperation Programme, Science for Policy Report*, EUR 30232 EN. Luxembourg: Publications Office of the European Union. https://doi.org/10.2760/39443, JRC120873.

DG Research and Innovation. (2020). *Strategic plan 2020–2024*. https://ec.europa.eu/info/sites/default/files/rtd_sp_2020_2024_en.pdf

ECLAC, Economic Commission for Latin America and the Caribbean. (2018). *The European Union and Latin America and the Caribbean: Convergent and sustainable strategies in the current global environment* (LC/TS.2018/56/Rev.1). Santiago: ECLAC.

Esparza Masana, R., & Ipanaqué, W. (2021). Regionalizing innovation strategies in Peru based on smart specialization: implications and challenges. Regional *Studies, 55*(7), 1194–1208. https://doi.org/10.1080/00343404.2020.1869202.

EU-CELAC. (2015). *Action plan 2015*. https://www.consilium.europa.eu/media/23757/eu-celac-action-plan.pdf.

EU-CELAC. (2021). *EU-CELAC INNOV-AL Platform II – final report*. https://www.innoval2.eu/politicas-de-innovacion/documentos-del-proyecto/documentos-finales_301_1_ap.html

Foray, D., David, P. A., & Hall, B. (2009). "Smart specialisation: the concept", *Knowledge Economists Policy Brief No. 9*, European Commission. https://ec.europa.eu/invest-in-research/pdf/download_en/kfg_policy_brief_no9.pdf?11111

Garcia, M. (2016). *EU trade relations with Latin America: Results and challenges in implementing the EU-Colombia/Peru Trade Agreement*. Study for the European Parliament. http://www.sice.oas.org/tpd/and_eu/Studies/EXPO_STU_EU_COL_PER_2016_e.pdf

Gomez Prieto, J., & Dos Santos, P. (2017). *Smart specialisation in EU and Chile, challenges and opportunities. Towards a transcontinental policy learning dialogue methodology*. JRC106872. Luxembourg: Publications Office of the European Union.

Gomez Prieto, J., Demblans, A., & Palazuelos Martínez, M. (2019). *Smart specialisation in the world, an EU policy approach helping to discover innovation globally*. Luxembourg: European Union. https://doi.org/10.2760/962643, JRC117005.

Granda Alva, G., Ropert, M., Planas, L., Boero, M., & de Bustos, E. (2015). *Estudio sobre sistemas regionales de innovación en el Perú: lecciones de política*. Universidad del Pacífico.

Hassenteufel, P., & Zeigermann, U. (2021). Translation and translators in policy transfer processes. In *Handbook of policy transfer, diffusion and circulation*. Cheltenham: Edward Elgar Publishing.

Hernández, B., & Lebret, P. (2019). Dos décadas de cooperación europea en Chile: una asociación para el desarrollo. *Estudios Internacionales, 51*(192), 35–56. https://doi.org/10.5354/0719-3769.2019.52812.

Iacobucci, D. (2012). Developing and implementing a smart specialisation strategy at regional level: Some open questions. *c.Met Working Paper* 15/2012.

Innopro. (2015). *Final project report. EU-Latin America Cooperation on regional innovation strategies in the framework of regional policy*. Phttps://ec.europa.eu/regional_policy/sources/cooperate/international/pdf/final_report_ris_latam_en.pdf

Kroll, H. (2015). Efforts to implement smart specialization in practice – leading unlike horses to the water. *European Planning Studies, 23*(10), 2079–2098. https://doi.org/10.1080/09654313.2014.1003036.

Kroll, H. (2019). Eye to eye with the *innovation paradox: Why smart specialization is no simple solution to policy design. European Planning Studies*, 27(5), 932–951. https://doi.org/10.1080/09654313.2019.1577363.

Lendvai, N., & Stubbs, P. (2007). Policies as translation: Situating transnational social policies. In S. Hodgson & Z. Irving (Eds.), *Policy reconsidered: Meanings, politics and practices* (pp. 173–190). Bristol: The Policy Press.

Maggi, C., & Maza, J. (2017). Evolución y Desafíos de Gestión Pública en el fomento a la Innovación Tecnológica en Chile. En *Transformaciones en La Política y Desafíos para Gobernar En El Siglo XXI*. Concepción: Sello Editorial Universidad de Concepción.

Marinelli, E., Guzzo, F., & Gianelle, C. (2019). Building smart specialisation strategies monitoring systems: Evidence from the EU. *L'industria 1*, 27–44. https://doi.org/10.1430/94058.

Osorio, C. (2018). *Aprendiendo o emulando? Cómo se difunden las políticas sociales en América Latina*. Santiago: Lom Ediciones.

Sanchez, B. (2018). New horizons shaping science, technology and innovation diplomacy: The case of Latin America and the Caribbean and the European Union, *EL-CISD Working Paper 20*. https://www.el-csid.eu/working-papers

Selleslaghs, J. (2019). The EU and Latin America. In R. A. Wessel & J. Odermatt (Eds.), *Research handbook on the EU's engagement with international organisations.* Cheltenham: Edward Elgar Publishing.

Solleiro-Rebolledo, J. L., García-Martínez, M. B., Castañón-Ibarra, R., & Martinez-Salvador, L. (2020). Smart specialization for building up a regional innovation agenda: The case of San Luis Potosí, Mexico. *Journal of Evolutionary Studies in Business, 5*(1), 81–115.

Stone, D. (2012). Transfer and translation of policy. *Policy Studies, 33*(6), 483–499.

Stone, D., Porto de Oliveira, O., & Pal, L. (2020). Transnational policy transfer: The circulation of ideas, power and development models. *Policy and Society, 39*(1), 1–18, https://doi.org/10.1080/14494035.2019.1619325

Uyarra, E. (2019). Smart specialization as a place-based policy. Lessons learnt? In *Regional insights: A selection of articles providing a fresh take on Regional Studies*. https://doi.org/10.1080/13673882.2018.00001022.

Mauricio J. Rondanelli-Reyes

Action for Climate and Life in Terrestrial Ecosystems: Sustainable Development Goals in the European Union and Latin America and the Caribbean – A Synoptic Vision

Introduction

There is no doubt that the global change that affects our planet is manifested without respite (Cabrera Silva, 2019). Natural ecosystems are collapsing and human society is being affected. The causes of this global change include the increase in the human population, alterations in biochemical cycles, changes in land use, alterations in biodiversity and climate change. Certainly what initially began in the mid-19th century with the intention of providing a greater well-being of life to humanity and is now referred to as "The Industrial Revolution", brought with it a high environmental cost that we are all paying today – rich and poor; more and less guilty; humanity and nature. Perhaps, as is often said in the face of the great and serious problems that afflict us, it is no longer important how it began but what we do and how we do to it to mitigate these problems.

This chapter deals with two of the causes that are responsible for this global change: Climate change and loss of biodiversity. Both topics are crucial in the 2015 United Nations Sustainable Development Goals (SDGs): 13, Climate Action and 15, Life of Terrestrial Ecosystems (United Nations Development Program [UNDP], 2015). We will discuss them with a relational approach so that we can visualise how they are interlinked. Furthermore, we will analyse the issue of climate and biodiversity in the current context of interregional cooperation between the European Union and Latin America and the Caribbean.

Climate change and biodiversity

Climate change is a variation in the climate of planet Earth directly or indirectly attributable to anthropogenic action, which causes the increased use of fossil fuels and other industrial processes and results in the alteration of the composition of the atmosphere, with a greater presence of carbon dioxide and other greenhouse gases (GHGs), which translates into an increase in the planet's average temperatures and leads to an alteration of the global climate with the presence of greater and recurrent extreme events, including mega floods and mega droughts (Ministry of Environment, n.d.).

The greenhouse effect is a phenomenon that enables life on planet Earth. Solar radiation reaches our planet and is absorbed, in part, by the Earth's land and water surfaces; another part is returned to the atmosphere which, due to its diverse gaseous composition, prevents the total outflow of this rebound energy and projects it back onto the planet's surface, allowing sustained temperatures that favour the development of life. The planet's greenhouse effect is thus a normal phenomenon that has been destabilised by the rapid and explosive industrial development since the mid-18th century. This has caused the excessive increase of GHGs in the atmosphere and has created a barrier that prevents the solar radiation that enters from also leaving towards space, and this closed bubble allows the temperature of the planet to rise, affecting life and the biogeochemical processes present in it. The main GHGs present in our atmosphere and which have been increasing their concentration along with industrial progress are nitrous oxide (N_2O), carbon dioxide (CO_2) and methane (CH_4); they represent less than 1% of the atmosphere; however, this small percentage is sufficient to strengthen the greenhouse effect of the planet, increasing its temperature (Mendoza de Armas & Jiménez Narváez, 2017).

However, it must be said that these changes in climate are not new. The Earth has experienced changes in weather patterns throughout its development over almost 4.5 billion years of history. We have gone from torrid periods of extreme heat to glacial periods, mediated by interglacial epochs; the natural climatic cycle this time differs from the historical one in that the change is forced and accelerated, as GHGs do not increase due to natural causes but mediated by human action which is recurrent, relentless and does not adjust to the natural reaction times of the planet (Government of La Rioja, n.d.).

Climate action

The targets of SDG 13 are to (a) strengthen resilience and adaptive capacity to climate-related risks and natural disasters in all countries, (b) incorporate climate change measures into national policies, strategies and plans, (c) enhance education, awareness and human and institutional capacity for climate change mitigation, adaptation, mitigation and early warning, (d) meet the commitment of developed countries that are parties to the United Nations Framework Convention on Climate Change to achieve by 2020 the goal of jointly mobilising US$ 100 billion per year to address the needs of developing countries to develop concrete mitigation actions and operationalise the Green Climate Fund, and furthermore, to promote mechanisms to enhance capacity for effective climate change planning and management in the least developed countries (UN, n.d.-b).

These goals have not made the progress that was expected with respect to the commitments and goodwill expressed by the 193 signatory states of the 2015 Paris Agreement (UN, n.d.-a) at the 21st United Nations Climate Change Conference (COP21). Shortly after that meeting, the Covid-19 pandemic broke out, we were forced to stop and shut ourselves away, at least for a while. Unfortunately, despite the marked global economic slowdown caused by the pandemic, the climate crisis has inexorably continued without major changes. It is, therefore, imperative to pursue more vigorously the goal of reducing GHG emissions and strengthening resilience to climate change. Economies must move towards carbon neutrality and adapt to the effects of climate change, which states committed to the Paris Agreement do voluntarily through their Nationally Determined Contributions (NDCs) where each state prepares, communicates and maintains the NDCs it expects to achieve. As of May 2021, 192 Parties had submitted their first NDCs to the UNFCCC Secretariat (UN, 2021).

Terrestrial ecosystem life

The targets of SDG 15 (UN, n.d.-c) are as follows:

(a) By 2020, ensure the conservation, restoration and sustainable use of terrestrial and inland freshwater ecosystems and the services they provide, particularly forests, wetlands, mountains and drylands, in accordance with international agreements.
(b) By 2020, promote sustainable management of all types of forests and halt deforestation.
(c) By 2030, combat desertification, rehabilitate degraded land and soils, including land affected by desertification, drought and floods, and strive for a world where land degradation is neutral.
(d) By 2030, ensure the conservation of mountain ecosystems, including their biodiversity, to enhance their capacity to provide essential benefits for sustainable development.
(e) Take urgent and meaningful action to reduce the degradation of natural habitats, halt the loss of biodiversity, protect threatened species and prevent their extinction by 2020.
(f) Promote the fair and equitable sharing of the benefits arising from the utilisation of genetic resources and promote appropriate access to these resources, as internationally agreed.

(g) Take urgent action to stop poaching and trafficking of protected species of flora and fauna and address illegal demand and supply of wildlife products.
(h) By 2020, take action to prevent the introduction of invasive alien species and significantly reduce their impacts on terrestrial and aquatic ecosystems and control or eradicate priority species.
(i) By 2020, integrate ecosystem and biodiversity values into national and local planning, development processes, poverty reduction strategies and accounting.

All of the 2020 targets for monitoring the state of the art have been affected by the Covid-19 pandemic. Working together to halt the environmental deterioration of the planet remains a top priority. However, the isolation experienced by much of humanity as a result of the coronavirus has not stopped the clearing of forests and the deterioration of terrestrial ecosystems. Soil degradation affects one fifth of the Earth's surface, wildlife trafficking threatens human health, increasing the risk of zoonotic diseases, which are those transmitted from animals to humans (Covid-19 is one example); today, we are still witnessing, from time to time and recurrently since 2019, the appearance of new viral outbreaks of global importance (BBC News World, 2022). The more we alter the natural biodiversity of ecosystems, the more we are affecting ourselves, putting our own survival at risk.

As the UN's Sustainable Development Goals Report 2021 points out, human activities are causing the most rapid decline in biodiversity in human history. Beyond the pandemic (or independent of it), none of the targets set for 2020 were met. Twenty-eight percent of the species assessed (more than 37,400 species) by the International Union for Conservation of Nature (IUCN) for its red list are in danger of extinction. Among these, 41% of amphibians, 34% of conifers, 33% of coral reefs, 26% of mammals and 14% of birds; the main causes are agricultural and urban development, uncontrolled hunting and fishing, logging and invasive alien species (UN, 2021). The protection of key biodiversity areas (KBAs) is vital for the conservation of terrestrial, freshwater and mountain ecosystems. As of 2020, no more than 45% of CBAs were within protected areas (UN, 2021).

Forests are home to most of the world's biodiversity. They are vital ecosystems for regulating the water cycle, evapotranspiration processes, soil nutrient cycles and atmospheric cycles; they regulate climate change and are part of all biotic and abiotic interactions of terrestrial ecosystems. By 2021, global sustainable forest management indicators for Europe and Latin America and the Caribbean show a concordance in terms of levels of positive change in relation to the stock of forest biomass on the ground, the proportion of forest area in protected and legally established areas, the proportion of forest area under long-term protection plans and certified forest area. Only in terms of the annual rate of forest area change index does Latin America and the Caribbean show little or no change between 2000–2010 and 2010–2020, in contrast to Europe, which shows positive changes for both periods (UN, 2021).

Situation in the European Union and Latin America and the Caribbean

If we do not tackle climate change and do not protect biodiversity and ecosystems, the effects will be dramatic as climate and biodiversity are intrinsically related. Working with nature (ecosystem approaches to climate change adaptation and mitigation) to solve problems caused by climate change brings many important benefits (Directorate General for the Environment of the European Commission [DG ENV], 2010). The ecosystem approach is cost-effective, not complex to implement and easily accessible to the world's population, which favours the implementation of sustainable development strategies and helps to improve precarious or subsistence economies. For example, restored coastal ecosystems (wetlands, shorelines, reefs) offer natural protection from storms and can also serve as nursery grounds for marine species. Currently, the perception of biodiversity loss is less compelling than that of climate change (DG ENV, 2010). While climate change occupies a major place on the public agenda, biodiversity conservation appears as a minor problem, generally associated only with the protection of endangered flora and fauna. The close relationship between climate change and the loss of biodiversity is lost or simply unknown.

The 2030 Agenda and its seventeen Sustainable Development Goals, together with the Paris Agreement on Climate Change, form part of the roadmap for joint international cooperation on sustainable development. Let us see, then, where we are on this roadmap with respect to sustainable development goals 13 and 15, in relation to the European Union and Latin America and the Caribbean.

The European Union (EU) is currently facing a less than promising outlook. The European Commission's 2022 report on the state of progress in achieving the sustainable development goals indicates that the region will have to make a major effort if it is to achieve the proposed goals by 2030 (UN News, 2022). The aforementioned report points out the goals and targets on which greater and urgent attention is required. With regard to climate and environment issues, the EU must urgently reverse trends around deforestation, biodiversity and climate change policies. The main challenges include further reductions in the emission of greenhouse gas, waste generation and treatment, sustainable use of natural resources and the conservation of ecosystems. The report also highlights that at least 40% of the targets cannot be measured due to a lack of data from several EU regions and this causes a serious problem for progress in achieving the Agenda's targets.

The United Nations Economic Commission for Europe (UNECE) in its 2022 report states that, at present, the EU will achieve only 26 objectives of the 2030 Agenda, 64 objectives require accelerated progress to be achieved and for 15 objectives the current trend will need to be reversed if they are to be met by 2030. More specifically, in relation to SDG 13, Climate Action, the objective on resilience and adaptive capacity will need to accelerate its progress to reach its target, the objective on climate change policy will need to reverse its current trend to reach its target; other three objectives (climate change awareness; UNFCCC Change agreements and climate change planning and management) cannot be assessed due to insufficient data. For SDG 15, Life of Terrestrial Ecosystems, several objectives (terrestrial and freshwater ecosystems, conservation of mountain ecosystems, utilisation of genetic resources, invasive alien species, and resources for biodiversity and ecosystems) will need to accelerate progress to achieve their targets by 2030. Objectives related to sustainable forest management and biodiversity loss will need to reverse their current trend. For other objectives (desertification and land degradation, trafficking of protected species, local and national biodiversity planning, resources for forest management, and trafficking of protected species), there is no assessment due to insufficient data.

In relation to climate and environmental issues, the problem in the EU with regard to the commitments made in the Paris Agreement and embodied as targets in the 2030 Agenda continues to focus on the increase of GHGs in the atmosphere by developing states. The region also needs to act quickly to reverse trends in sustainable forest management and biodiversity loss. For critical areas such as waste generation and treatment, sustainable use of natural resources and ecosystem conservation, the EU must accelerate progress.

In Latin America and the Caribbean (LAC), the situation is not very different. In 2018, at the Second Meeting of the Forum of Latin American and Caribbean Countries on Sustainable Development (Economic Commission for Latin America and the Caribbean [CEPAL], 2018) held in Santiago de Chile, the ministers and High Representatives of the region, among their thirty agreed conclusions and recommendations, indicated their recognition of the synergies between the Paris Agreement, the Sendai Framework (disaster risk reduction), the New Urban Agenda, the Samoa Pathway, the Vienna Programme of Action (for landlocked developing countries) and the 2030 Agenda for Sustainable Development, visualised through the seventeen Sustainable Development Goals. They stressed the importance of multilateral cooperation at regional and global level. They also noted the need to accelerate the pace of implementation and awareness of the SDGs at all levels. Specifically, they recognised the need to promote progressive structural change towards sustainable development and the protection of ecosystems and biodiversity by reducing deforestation, combating desertification and land degradation and promoting strategies for the sustainable use of natural resources and ecosystem services in the region. They also highlighted the importance of increasing climate finance in addition to that officially received for development. These conclusions and recommendations arise in a scenario prior to the subsequent and successive manifestations of social revolt that have been affecting several countries in the region and, of course, prior to the declaration of a state of pandemic and its consequences at the global level. This has undoubtedly had a negative impact on the planning and implementation of actions in favour of the proposed sustainable development goals. Having said this, let us look at how the LAC regional scenario looks today and what the current urgencies are.

According to the 2020 report of the Centre for Sustainable Development for Latin America (CODS in its Spanish acronym) at the University of Los Andes, Bogotá, the region shows trends towards stagnation in meeting most of the SDGs. The CODS compares under the same criteria, called SDG index, the 232 indicators established to assess progress in meeting the SDG targets in LAC countries. There is a high probability that LAC will not achieve the targets by 2030. The study, which covered 24 of the 33 countries in the LAC region,[1] indicates a modest progress in the targets set, with a significant lag mainly in the Caribbean countries. These results are associated, in most cases, with the degree of poverty in the countries of the region. The best results are achieved in relation to SDG 13 (Climate Action), SDG 11 (Sustainable Cities and Communities), SDG 6 (Clean Water and Sanitation), and SDG 1 (End Poverty). Regarding SDG 1, the tasks remain challenging for the region, which has 62 million people living in extreme poverty. The three SDGs with the worst average performance in LAC are SDG 9 (industry, innovation and infrastructure), SDG 10 (reducing inequalities), SDG 15 (living terrestrial ecosystems), and SDG 16 (peace, justice and strong institutions) (Morales-Estay, 2021).

In relation to SDGs 13 and 15, in the LAC region there is clearly a marked dichotomy between SDG 13, with the best percentage of achievements per

1 Argentina, Belize, Bolivia, Brazil, Chile, Colombia, Costa Rica, Ecuador, El Salvador, Guatemala, Guyana, Haiti, Honduras, Jamaica, Mexico, Nicaragua, Panama, Paraguay, Peru, Dominican Republic, Suriname, Trinidad and Tobago, Uruguay and Venezuela.

proposed target, versus SDG 15, which achieves in the region just over 50% of the targets proposed. SDG 13 highlights the low levels of carbon dioxide emissions into the atmosphere due to the generation of increasingly cleaner energy in the economies of the region. The SDG index for Climate Action, calculated in 2019, experienced a nominal variation of −0.02 and in a percentage variation equal to 0%, when considering that in the period 2015–2019 the average value of the index varied from 88.84 to an average value of 88.82 (Cods, 2020); this is the best result of the SDG index in the LAC region. The main reason for this achievement, which signals the region's opportunity to make further progress on this climate change challenge, is that countries have defined their Nationally Determined Contributions (NDCs) and have the necessary institutional frameworks in place to implement this commitment.

Yet, these NDCs are still insufficient to keep the temperature increase below 2°C, making it necessary to redouble efforts to make the aid pledged by the more developed countries effective. A few lessons can be learned in the process: (a) to have an adequate framework of disaster indicators; (b) to move towards renewable energies in a short period of time; (c) to implement laws on climate change, with citizen participation; and (d) to consolidate national decarbonisation plans with a view to 2050 (CEPAL, 2019). SDG 15 reaches an SDG index of 57.5, one of the lowest indexes in relation to all the SDGs. The main reason for this is the indiscriminate advance of deforestation of forests and jungles, concentrated in the Amazon region and the Caribbean territories, to satisfy the demand for agricultural land and the timber industry. The affected ecosystems contain unique biodiversity on the planet, and the loss of biodiversity is irretrievable. Among the opportunities that the region has to improve significantly the percentages of achievements of this SDG is the use of biotechnology to improve agriculture, in addition to promoting new forms of organisation of value chains associated with biodiversity and the creation of circular economies. Furthermore, forest management with sustainability criteria is feasible and represents a productive and conservation alternative. For highly degraded areas, restoration through the establishment of natural or second-generation plantations can contribute positively to zero deforestation (2030 Agenda in Latin America and the Caribbean [ALC 2030], s.f.). This is a sensitive SDG for both LAC and EU regions but there are different causes for this common problem. In LAC, the "technologization" of agricultural processes, the development of more sustainable and socially just food systems, the development of sustainable natural energies, the sustainable generation of goods and services, and learning that environmental problems can be solved from nature itself are part of the actions that are called upon to contribute significantly to the life of terrestrial ecosystems. The problem in the EU is that the pressure on biodiversity due to land occupation continues, which has intensified since 2010. This loss of habitat has had an influence in the long term, for example, to reduce the number of birds and pollinators in the territory of the Union, which is serious. In addition, the lack of accurate and reliable official statistics on resources and ecosystems from EU developing countries prevents the development of adequate technical analyses to facilitate fact-based policy making (Eurostat, 2021).

SDG 13 and SDG 15 in EU-LAC bi-regional cooperation

The problem of climate change and loss of biodiversity is global. The 2030 Agenda for Sustainable Development and its stated SDGs require global action on a daily basis. So far, we have outlined the situations in the EU and LAC. We will now attempt to take a synoptic look at the cooperation that has been established between the two regions on the subject.

Since 1999, Latin America and the Caribbean and the European Union have maintained a strategic bi-regional relationship in political and economic matters. Over the years, this joint work has been strengthened by facing other issues that the global contingency brought to the fore. One of these is the strong commitment to the 2030 Agenda for Sustainable Development and the Paris Agreement on climate change. The Community of Latin American and Caribbean States (CELAC), made up of thirty-three countries, has been positioning itself as an increasingly influential international actor in the debate on climate and biodiversity issues. Considering that the two regions are asymmetrical in terms of their political, economic and social developments, it is not difficult to understand that they are also asymmetrical in terms of the environment and environment-related policies. Yet a common interest in fighting against climate change and biodiversity loss lay the ground to further strengthen the bi-regional relationship and cooperation.

In July 2018, the joint declaration of the second Meeting of EU and CELAC Foreign Ministers reiterated the commitment to bi-regional cooperation to face the global challenges of the 2030 Agenda for Sustainable Development. The declaration accepted the principle of shared but differentiated responsibilities, depending on the needs, capacities and resources of each state. For CELAC and the EU, the environment and energy are priorities. The two regions have established common responsibilities in the areas of resources, technology transfer and multilateral initiatives such as the Green Climate Fund (Green Climate Fund, s.f.). According to Ayuso (2019), the international framework for joint and collaborative work between the EU and LAC, under the Paris Agreement and the

2030 Agenda, consists of SDG 7 (affordable and sustainable energy), SDG 11 (sustainable cities and communities), SDG 12 (responsible production and consumption), SDG 13 (climate action), SDG 14 (underwater life) and SDG 15 (life of terrestrial ecosystems). There is a consensus among the parties that for a successful implementation of the environmental agenda, citizens must be fully involved. Various organisations (governmental and non-governmental), both in the EU and in LAC, aim at observing and monitoring the environmental situation. They contribute with educational programmes on the subject which are disseminated to the school system and the general public, instructing, for example, to promote the use of alternative, natural and clean energies and to raise awareness of the rational and responsible use of natural resources. The support given in both regions to citizens' movements that defend and work for the care of the environment is vital.

Among the issues that the EU has recently proposed to deepen cooperation with its LAC partners is the transition towards a green economy. The document issued by the parties states that both regions must move towards more sustainable production and consumption (European Commission [EC], 2019). EU research, technology and expertise could help LAC in areas related to the region's tremendous potential, such as hydroelectric, wind, solar, ocean and geothermal energy, thereby creating jobs and business opportunities. Regarding the specific situation of the Caribbean region, the EU should support the development of clean energy, renewable energy and energy efficiency. In addition, the EU has experience in harnessing resources from private financing for sustainable development, which is ultimately vital for this bi-regional cooperation.

In relation to the climate issue, the EU's climate change resilience programme aims to manage climate risks and promote ecosystem-based approaches to move towards a low-carbon economy. It proposes that cooperation be based on the approach of the EUROCLIMA+ programme, with funding from the European Investment Bank (EIB), for projects associated with Climate Action (SDG 13) (Euroclima+, n.d.). In terms of environment and diversity, the LAC region accounts for just under half of the total biodiversity on the planet and possesses 7 of the world's 25 biodiversity hotspots (Mittermeier, 2000). Hence, the environmental challenge is not minor. It is essential to consider the issues associated with biodiversity loss, unsustainable extraction, management of natural resources, degradation of land, forests and coastal environments, in addition to the scarcity of fresh water, which is part of SDG 15. The EU proposes to continue the implementation of the short-term plan on ecosystem restoration (1992 Convention on Biological Diversity), the Strategic Plan for Biodiversity 2011–2020

(Convention on Biological Diversity [CBD], 2010) and the post-2020 Biodiversity Framework (CBD, 2019).

In March 2021, the European Commission and the United Nations Environment Programme (UNEP) announced the common priorities for EU-LAC environmental cooperation for the next five years (United Nations Regional Information Centre, 2021). The main areas will be: biodiversity; climate change; pollution and waste management and circular economy. In this framework, for the area of biodiversity related to SDG 15, a number of actions stand out: an integrated management of landscapes and seascapes, with special emphasis on land use planning and ecosystem restoration; the inclusion of biodiversity in all policies through the implementation of nature-based solutions; public and private finance for green purposes; environmental justice and sustainable tourism development; and improved knowledge management and scientific information to inform ad hoc policy making, with particular reference to monitoring and verification of biodiversity information. In the area of climate action (SDG 13), the following undertakings are relevant: strengthening public and private financing for climate change mitigation and adaptation to enable the disclosure of climate finance within regulatory frameworks; implementation of nature-based solutions, crucial to achieve climate goals while conserving biodiversity; and a transition to zero carbon emissions in energy, transport and construction (Sustainability for All, n.d.-a). On the latter, LAC will need to develop more ambitious policies, increase investments for this purpose and incorporate carbon-neutral technologies such as green hydrogen technology (Sustainability for All, n.d.-b).

A major turning point in the cooperation between the EU and LAC from March 2020 onwards was the Covid-19 pandemic. The scientific world had been announcing for years the increasing likelihood that zoonotic diseases could become global threats. These would obviously have adverse effects on the planning and execution of the 2030 Agenda for Sustainable Development and the Paris Agreement commitments. The coronavirus, in addition to its toll of lives (by June 2022 there were nearly 6.3 million people dead (Orús, 2022)), highlighted the structural differences between the EU and LAC regions. The 2021 United Nations Sustainable Development Report presents the progress and setbacks of 165 countries in matters related to the implementation of the Sustainable Development Goals (SDGs) committed to for the period 2020–2030 (UN, 2021). The significant progress made in many regions prior to the pandemic has been limited by Covid-19. Targets have turned out to be unachievable by 2030 in many cases. This was of course completely unpredictable in 2015 when the SDGs were established in the wake of the Paris Agreement.

In LAC, greater efforts will be needed to break the vicious circle associating economic growth with negative environmental consequences, mainly in relation to SDGs 13 and 15. Yet, this can be turned into a virtuous circle, combining economic growth and environmental protection, and the EU cooperation can play a major role. The EU should contribute to prioritise and accelerate targets related to climate action and the life of terrestrial ecosystems in LAC. The EU should also focus on GHG emissions from the least developed countries, both in the EU and in LAC. It will therefore be necessary to reinforce bi-regional co-operation between the EU and LAC by strengthening multilateral collaboration mechanisms that enhance and accelerate the fulfilment of the SDGs. This will be key to a more solid global governance embracing the 2030 Agenda, which still remains the best possible roadmap at the disposal of humanity and the planet (Pajín, 2021).

Final considerations

Climate Change is not the umbrella under which other changes observed on the planet are covered, such as the loss of biodiversity, among others. It is just one more change that together with other environmental situations currently out of balance on our planet constitutes what is known as Global Change. This widely spread misperception gave rise to an almost paradoxical difference in public and political attention. SDG 13 (Climate Action) is the SDG that, until the onset of the pandemic, had the highest percentage of compliance of the 17 SDGs. One of the reasons is that the restrictions and regulations associated, for example, with the control of GHG emissions, are ultimately the laws of the countries and must be complied with. On the other hand, the issue of ecosystems and biodiversity loss, comprised in SDG 15 (life of ecosystems), seems to have less relevance in the collective consciousness, as if it were a secondary objective and, of course, often associated with a direct consequence of climate change, probably due to a lack of information and inadequate education on the subject. It is one of the SDGs that has experienced the lowest percentage of achievements in relation to its established targets and, therefore, should be one of the priority goals between now and 2030.

The whirlwind speed of events in both the EU and LAC, in the political, economic and social spheres, goes hand in hand with consequences in the environmental sphere. These are turbulent times not only in terms of climate. The historical instability of a large part of the LAC region with respect to building solid political institutions, establishing social justice, equity and environmental protection is a constant that truly threatens the best intentions of its nations to advance towards the fulfilment of the SDGs. With a territory that is rich and abundant in natural resources, that possesses a unique ecosystem on the planet, that is home to a biodiversity of great genetic richness, LAC is a valuable and strategic partner for multilateral cooperation on Global Change. The EU has understood this and has made its own experience in environmental issues available for this cooperation, collaborating with high-impact technologies and its expertise in obtaining funding for projects associated with environmental sustainability. Importantly, these projects include the design and dissemination of governmental and non-governmental initiatives developed with the citizens themselves. Environmental education empowers citizens, encourages participation and ultimately strengthens local, regional and global governance in environmental issues.

Still, the structural differences between the EU and LAC as well as the emergence of other strategic partners on the scene, have somehow meant that progress in bi-regional cooperation in environmental matters has not progressed as much as it would have been desirable. Yet, joint work has been maintained, an example of which is the persistence and commitment to the 2030 Agenda for Sustainable Development; both regions have expressed their willingness and commitment to advancing towards the fulfilment of the Agenda's goals, especially now, in the so-called post-pandemic times. Covid-19 has been a relevant factor in all matters. Accordingly, it will have a drastic and negative influence on the environmental issue. It may not matter much how dramatic the effects of the pandemic are today as the current record may be largely outperformed by the even more dramatic results of the well documented Global Change affecting our planet. The concentrations of GHGs in the atmosphere continue to rise, and the loss of biodiversity is accelerating and insufficiently quantifiable. The post-pandemic reconfiguration of EU-LAC bi-regional cooperation on the environment is uncertain. Efforts and good intentions are in place and the 2030 Agenda remains on track. Yet this may not be enough to avert global disaster.

Bibliography

2030 Agenda in Latin America and the Caribbean. (n.d.). *SDG 15: Sustainably manage forests, fight desertification, halt and reverse land degradation, and halt biodiversity loss.* https://agenda2030lac.org/es/ods/15-vida-de-ecosistemas-terrestres

Ayuso, A. (2019). The EU and LAC: United by the commitment to sustainable development. *Why should the European Union be relevant to Latin America and the Caribbean? And why should Latin America and the Caribbean be relevant to the European Union?* (EULAC Bulletin 07/2019), 10–12. https://eulacfoundation.org/sites/default/files/documents/ESP_IMP_d.pdf

BBC News World. (23 July 2022). *Smallpox of the monkey: The WHO declares the maximum alert by the increase of cases in the world.* Accessed 25 July 2022 at https://www.bbc.com/mundo/noticias-62277365.

Cabrera-Silva, S. (2019). Global change: A look from biology. *Revista Chilena de Enfermedades Respiratorias*, *35*(1), 9–14. http://dx.doi.org/10.4067/S0717-73482019000100009.

Centre for the Sustainable Development Goals for Latin America. (2020). *SDG index 2019 for Latin America and the Caribbean.* Cods. Bogotá, Colombia. https://cods.uniandes.edu.co/indice-ods/

Convention on Biological Diversity. (2010). *Biological diversity strategic plan 2011–2020.* https://www.cbd.int/undb/media/factsheets/undb-factsheet-sp-es.pdf

Convention on Biological Diversity. (25 January 2019). *Post-2020 global biodiversity framework: Discussion paper. CBD/POST2020/PREP/1/1/.* https://www.cbd.int/api/v2013/documents/1B916F4E-F266-2A3F-7BEF-CEE7AA879500/attachments/208086/chile.pdf

Directorate General for the Environment of the European Commission. (2010). *The role of nature in climate change.* Communications Office of the European Commission for the Environment. https://op.europa.eu/es/publication-detail/-/publication/c366ac10-33e8-4204-94e3-a2e9ba8f25e9/language-es/format-PDF/source-279693334

Economic Commission for Latin America and the Caribbean. (April, 2018). *Conclusions and recommendations agreed at the second meeting of the forum of the countries of Latin America and the Caribbean on sustainable development.* https://repositorio.cepal.org/bitstream/handle/11362/44965/2fororegional_conclusiones_recomendaciones.pdf?sequence=1&isAllowed=y

Economic Commission for Latin America and the Caribbean. (2019). *Third meeting of the forum of the countries of Latin America and the Caribbean on sustainable development. Quadrennial progress report on regional progress and challenges of the 2030 agenda for sustainable development in Latin America and the Caribbean.* https://www.cepal.org/es/publicaciones/44551-informe-avance-cuatrienal-progreso-desafios-regionales-la-agenda-2030-desarrollo

Euroclima+. (n.d.). *Monitoring climate finance in Latin America and the Caribbean.* https://www.euroclima.org/2/seguimiento-y-monitoreo-a-los-flujos-de-financiamiento-climatico-en-america-latina-y-el-caribe

European Commission. (16 April 2019). *Joint communication to the European Parliament and the Council. The European Union, Latin America and the*

Caribbean: Joining forces for a common future. EUR-Lex. https://eur-lex.europa.eu/legal-content/ES/TXT/?uri=CELEX:52019JC0006

Eurostat. (2021). *Sustainable development in the European Union*. Luxembourg: Publications Office of the European Union. https://ec.europa.eu/eurostat/documents/3217494/12878705/KS-03-21-096-EN-N.pdf/8f9812e6-1aaa-7823-928f-03d8dd74df4f?t=1623741433852

Government of La Rioja. (n.d.). *Greenhouse effect and climate change*. Larioja.org. https://www.larioja.org/medio-ambiente/es/calidad-aire-cambio-climatico/cambio-climatico/efecto-invernadero/efecto-invernadero-cambio-climatico

Green Climate Fund. (n.d.). *About GCF. GCF is the largest global fund dedicated to help fight climate change*. https://www.greenclimate.fund/about#:~:text=The%20Green%20Climate%20Fund%20(GCF,emissions%2C%20climate%2Dresilient%20pathways.

Mendoza de Armas, C., & Jiménez Narváez, G. (2017). Relationship between the greenhouse effect and climate change from the perspective of the agrarian sector. *Revista Facultad Nacional de Agronomía Medellín*, *70*(2), 8120–8122.

Ministry of Environment. (n.d.). *What is climate change?* https://cambioclimatico.mma.gob.cl/que-es-el-cambio-climatico/

Mittermeier, R. (2000). Conservation international and biodiversity conservation. *Nature, 405*, 254. https://doi.org/10.1038/35012266.

Morales-Estay, P. (19 March 2021). *The progress of the SDGs in Latin America and the Caribbean*. Library of the National Congress of Chile (BCN), No. SUP: 130168. https://obtienearchivo.bcn.cl/obtienearchivo?id=repositorio/10221/31965/1/El_avance_de_los_ODS_en_Ame__rica_Latina_y_el_Caribe.pdf

Orús, A. (23 June 2022). Number of people who died as a result of the coronavirus worldwide as of June 12, 2022, by continent. *Statista*. https://es.statista.com/estadisticas/1107719/covid19-numero-de-muertes-a-nivel-mundial-por-region/

Pajín, L. (2021). Europe and Latin America and the Caribbean face the challenge of a just, inclusive, and sustainable recovery. *Pensamiento Iberoamericano*, ISSN 0212-0208 (11), 31–41.

Sustainability for All. (n.d.-a). *Mitigation of the effects and adaptation to climate change*. Sustainability.com. https://www.sostenibilidad.com/cambio-climatico/mitigacion-adaptacion-cambio-climatico/?_adin=02021864894

Sustainability for All. (n.d.-b). *What is green hydrogen?* Sustainability.com. https://www.sostenibilidad.com/desarrollo-sostenible/que-es-el-hidrogeno-verde/?gclid=EAIaIQobChMI56Kj_Ouh-QIVDjSRCh3ZxQuzEAAYASAAEgLPXPD_BwE&_adin=02021864894

UN News. Global look human stories. (24 March 2022). *The European region on track to achieve only 26 of the 169 goals for sustainable development in 2030.* Organization of the United Nations. https://news.un.org/es/story/2022/03/1506142

United Nations. (n.d.-a). *Climate action. Paris agreement.* https://www.un.org/es/climatechange/paris-agreement

United Nations. (n.d.-b). *SDG 13: Take urgent action to combat climate change and its effects.* https://www.un.org/sustainabledevelopment/es/climate-change-2/

United Nations. (n.d.-c). *SDG 15: Sustainably manage forests, fight desertification, halt and reverse land degradation, halt biodiversity loss.* https://www.un.org/sustainabledevelopment/es/biodiversity/

United Nations. (2021). *Report on the sustainable development goals 2021.* https://unstats.un.org/sdgs/report/2021/The-Sustainable-Development-Goals-Report-2021_Spanish.pdf

United Nations Development Program. (2015). The SDGs in action. https://www.undp.org/es/sustainable-development-goals

United Nations Economic Commission for Europe. (2022). *Progress in the UNECE region.* https://w3.unece.org/sdg2022/progress-assessment.html

United Nations Regional Information Centre. (31 March 2021). *The EU and UNEP announce common priorities for environmental cooperation in Latin America and the Caribbean.* United Nations. https://unric.org/es/la-ue-y-pnuma-anuncian-prioridades-comunes-para-la-cooperacion-ambiental-en-america-latina-y-el-caribe/

Alwine Woischnik

The Ecological and Social Transition: An Approach from the Context of the European Union

Introduction: The origin of the concept "ecological and social transition"

The ecological and social transition may be considered a relatively new paradigm, but in fact, it is the result of criticism of the productivist and consumerist model that emerged in the 1970s in several industrialised countries. This is confirmed by the fact that it is a model "that in economic and social terms presents enormous imbalances, which is ethically unjust and unsustainable on a planetary scale" and that Western societies developed "a misunderstood progress" that means "a wrong equation between economic growth, technological progress and human welfare" (Woischnik, 2019a: 1).

It is since the beginning of the 2000s and as a result of increasing environmental degradation (loss of biodiversity, pollution of various kinds), increasing natural disasters and greater concern about climate change, especially by scientists, that a proper debate on the issue has started. A number of initiatives and publications, both at the national and international levels, have highlighted the social dimension associated with the environmental question. Accordingly, social aspects in conjunction with environmental and climatic aspects have come to the fore. Several examples can be made.

One is the "Commission on the Measurement of Economic Development and Social Progress", created in 2008 by the then French President Nicolas Sarkozy, whose most prominent members are Joseph Stiglitz and Amartya Sen (both Nobel Prize winners) and the economist and sociologist Jean-Paul Fitoussi. The published document, entitled Report by the Commission on the Measurement of Economic Performance and Social Progress, stresses that the measurement of GDP does not reflect – among other things – environmental degradation and its negative social impacts on the health and quality of life of citizens (Stiglitz, Sen, Fitoussi, 2009). Ten years later, Joseph Stiglitz added: "What we measure affects what we do, and if we measure the wrong thing, we will do the wrong thing" (Stiglitz, 2018).

Another example is the United Nations Environment Programme's (UNEP) "Green Economy" projects and documents from 2008 and the Organisation for Economic Co-operation and Development's (OECD) "Green Growth" initiatives from 2009. With regard to the OECD, the promotion of green growth was initially considered the way out of the 2008 financial crisis. Yet, shortly afterwards, the OECD highlighted the importance of the social dimension too in the context of green growth (Woischnik, 2015). This and many other precedents led to the concept of the "ecological and social transition". As far as the conceptual framework is concerned, there is no single definition, i.e. different documents as well as the respective debate handle different terms: "social and ecological transition", "eco-social transition", "just ecological transition" or "just and inclusive transition". All these concepts have a common denominator, which is the need and the demand for a profound change in our economic and social model.

The origin of the term "Just Transition" provides an illustration of the link between the ecological and the social dimension of any green transition. The expression "Just Transition" is attributed to the US trade union leader Tony Mazzocchi and was later taken up by the International Labour Organisation (ILO) in the context of the loss of workers' jobs due to environmental policies and the necessary financial support in the transitional phase. The ILO states that "just transition is not just another transition", but is a key issue in the process of "environmentally sustainable economies and societies for all" (ILO, 2018: 5). The link between the ecological and the social was established in both empirical and theoretical terms.

The chapter first discusses the European experience with the environmental and social transition focusing on the European Green Deal. Then it analyses problems of implementation in the European case, stressing factors such as waste disposal, energy transition issues including nuclear technology, supply and security, economic costs and the necessary resources, and the Spanish experience with implementation. Finally, analysis moves to the necessary cultural change for a successful green and social transition. The concluding remarks discuss how the European experiences can help Latin America and foster EU-LAC bi-regional cooperation.

The European perspective: The European Green Deal

With regard to Europe, the planning of an ecological and social transition was the response to the financial and economic crisis of 2008. In Germany, both the prestigious Wuppertal Institute for Climate, Environment and Energy and members of the political party The Greens (Die Grünen) proposed the need for a

New Social Contract. This should enshrine the link between the environment and social sustainability. The Greens, who published an extensive analysis on the subject (Bündnis 90/Die Grünen, 2011), argued that the ecological and social transition and the Green New Deal express the same vision, similar criteria and demands with the aim of initiating a change in the economic and social model.

In this context, reflections on a Green New Deal provided an interesting analogy to the New Deal, the interventionist policy through a set of economic measures adopted by US President Franklin D. Roosevelt with the aim of alleviating the effects of the Great Depression of the 1930s.

> The Green New Deal proposes a cycle of green innovation characterised by direct state investment in green infrastructure, as well as the creation of a favourable framework for the growth of an environmental market for products and services. The social component of the Green New Deal is reflected in the generation of green jobs through increased spending in education and training, as the new jobs require much higher qualifications than traditional industrial production (Woischnik, 2019a: 3).

The Green New Deal was advocated in Europe and beyond. US Democratic congresswoman Alexandria Ocasio-Cortez and US senator Bernie Sanders (Sanders, 2021), or the former UK Labour party leader Jeremy Corbyn (Hancox, 2019) supported it, demanding a profound transformation of the economy that is capable of tackling climate change and that manages to reduce economic and social inequalities. In the context of the 2019 elections to the European Parliament, Yanis Varoufakis (2019), the former Greek finance minister, presented the European Spring document, an ambitious draft of radical political, economic, social and ecological proposals.

The European Union has taken on a leading role in the ecological and social transition. In December 2019, Ursula von der Leyen, President of the European Commission, presented the European Green Deal. Its objective is to make Europe the first continent in the world to achieve climate neutrality by 2050, as the European Commission (2022) emphatically states on its webpage presenting its strategy and policy priorities. The necessary social and ecological as well as digital transitions can be considered the essence of the European Green Deal, which includes the energy transition and thus the decarbonisation of economies.

The European Green Pact is set against the backdrop of the devastating effects of the Covid-19 pandemic and, as a consequence, the economic recovery. In terms of financing the Green Pact, a package of 1.8 trillion euros was approved in 2020, of which just over 1 trillion euros corresponds to the new multiannual financial framework 2021–2027, while 750 billion euros are qualified as the exceptional temporary recovery instrument Next Generation EU (European

Commission, 2020). The confluence of economic, social and ecological aspects of the Green Deal is clearly manifested in the Just Transition Fund too, which aims to compensate European regions that have to cope with considerable socio-economic impacts in their transition to climate neutrality. According to José Antonio Sanahuja, director of the Carolina Foundation, the European Green Pact includes "the need to reorient the financial system and speculative capital towards the ecological transition" and "gives a central role to massive public investment" (Sanahuja, 2021).

A wide range of directives, strategies and laws support the implementation of the European Green Pact. Among the most important are the European Climate Act (2021), the Fit for 55 legislative proposals, the Biodiversity Strategy 2030, the new Energy Efficiency of Buildings Directive and the (proposed) Diligence Directive on global supply chains, which requires companies to respect human rights and the environment. – The European Climate Act and the Fit for 55 packages have as their main goal the reduction of net greenhouse gas emissions by at least 55% by 2030 compared to 1990. Recent decisions include the provisional agreement on a CO_2 tax on imports of products such as iron, steel, cement, aluminium, fertilisers, electricity and hydrogen. This tariff, which would be applied gradually from October 2023, is part of the fight against climate change, but also aims to protect European industry.

A key role in the fight against climate change is played by the (first and second) Circular Economy Action Plan, an alternative to the linear economic model. In the words of Luis M. Jiménez Herrero, a Spanish expert and author of several books on the subject:

> "The so-called Circular Economy has evolved from an initial vision focused on providing a solution to the problem of waste, to now emerge as an alternative backbone of a more sustainable economic model with broad implications for the transformation of lifestyles. The idea-force is to maintain products, components and materials at their highest level of usefulness and value, under the principle of not unnecessarily destroying resources" (Jiménez Herrero, 2019: 28).

In this context, the book *Cradle to Cradle* (*Cradle to Cradle* instead of *Cradle to Grave*) is a milestone. The authors, the German chemist-ecologist Michael Braungart and the US landscape architect William McDonough, are forerunners and promoters of the circular economy. The book argues that the reduction of resource consumption is more pressing than ever, precisely because of the increasing scarcity of raw materials. Once again, the link between the environmental and the social and their mutual impact is highlighted.

However, it is worth noting that the issue was addressed by scientists more than 30 years ago. For example, Ernst-Ulrich von Weizsäcker, author of several books on the consequences of climate change, was, together with Friedrich Schmidt-Bleek, the founder of the Wuppertal Institute for Climate, Environment and Energy in Germany. Both are notable for having elaborated early on the reduction of resource consumption by industrialised countries. Schmidt-Bleek proposed in the 1990s that the reduction should be achieved by a "Factor 10" (Factor X, in Roman) and in 2008 he created the Faktor 10 Institute. Von Weizsäcker later postulated that a "Factor 4" could double wealth and halve resource consumption (von Weizsäcker, Lovins & Lovins, 1997).

The European perspective: The question of implementation

One of the challenges of the Green Deal is its implementation by the 27 EU member states, as it is an extremely ambitious and far-reaching strategy. On the one hand, experience shows that some countries have great difficulties in transposing EU directives and laws into national legislation. On the other hand, despite the fact that the European Commission has a demanding Circular Economy Action Plan and some countries have advanced national legislation, some industrialised countries still export their plastic waste or e-waste to developing countries, which have neither the technical nor the financial capacity to deal adequately with this type of waste. There is no doubt that strict legislation and control by the European Union and national governments are needed to prevent such practices.

Furthermore this is an economic and ecological contradiction on the part of the industrialised countries. On the one hand, disposal of special waste in developing countries does not guarantee its proper recycling due to lack of technology and resources thus posing an ecological problem. On the other hand, the increasing scarcity of raw materials makes it unprofitable and inefficient not to recycle it in the appropriate way. Moreover, it is socially and ethically unacceptable vis-à-vis developing countries. In most cases, it is women and children who scavenge the mountains of rubbish for items which they then sell for a meagre income.

As for the energy transition – a key pillar of the social and ecological transition, one issue of conflict is the so-called green taxonomy. While the European Commission considers nuclear energy as a "bridging technology" (Brückentechnologie) related to climate change mitigation and adaptation, several countries – including Spain, Portugal, Luxembourg, Germany and Austria – are opposed to recognising nuclear energy as a transitional energy. Cristina Narbona, currently first vice-president of the Spanish Senate and formerly an advisor to the Spanish Nuclear Safety Council, recently pointed out that "although it does not emit carbon dioxide while the plants are operating, it does so throughout its very long life cycle. And it has high production costs and dangers such as the Fukushima catastrophe" (Narbona, 2022). It was precisely in the wake of the 2011 Fukushima nuclear disaster that Chancellor Angela Merkel of the Christian Democratic Union party decided to withdraw Germany from nuclear energy.

In this context, it should also be mentioned that radioactive waste, deposited in permanent storage or in so-called "nuclear graveyards", retains radiation for hundreds of years, which is irresponsible towards future generations and therefore contradicts the 1987 Brundtland Report's definition of sustainable development, which refers to "meeting the needs of the present without compromising the needs of future generations" (United Nations, 1987: n.p.). The intersection between the issue of energy supply and energy security may be a crucial debate in the energy transition. Russia's war in Ukraine powerfully shows this. Virtually all EU countries are affected and even countries on other continents are feeling the impact on their economies.

The situation in Germany exemplifies the dilemma. The problem in Germany is not only a lack of energy supply, but that politics and public debate have taken an unexpected turn from energy transition to concern about the energy crisis and thus energy security. This concern has stopped a part of the public from paying as much attention to the climate emergency. The fear of being left without heating in winter, high energy prices and the government's substantial aid to Ukraine in terms of money and weapons are affecting social cohesion. Despite the government's important economic measures for businesses, families, pensioners, and the vulnerable segments more broadly, the link between environmental transition and social dynamics remains a sticky point on the agenda, especially for the implementation of green policy.

The implementation of green policies is first and foremost subject to the economic resources available. Josep Borrell, the European Union's High Representative for Foreign Affairs and Security Policy and Vice-President of the European Commission, stresses that "the ecological and energy transition cannot be made at zero cost; it will have a cost, and it must be shared out fairly. Those who worry about the end of the month cannot be asked to worry about the end of the world" (Borrell, 2019). Indeed, green policies do not affect all people in the same way, i.e. the economic and social impact may differ: "the CO_2 price in the transport and building sectors would affect more than 1% of the net income of low-income households, while for high-income households, it would mean on average 0.4% of their net income" (Woischnik, 2019b).

The protests of the so-called "yellow waistcoats" movement in France also serve as an example. The increase in petrol prices as a consequence of President Macron's climate policy had more economic impacts on people living in sub-urban, peripheral and rural areas and less on those living in the cities. The reason is that people in the outskirts and the countryside drive several kilometres every day between their home and their workplace of business. This may not be easily affordable for low-income families. Therefore, "public policies must consider ecological measures and their social impacts from the outset and in parallel. If not approached and acted upon in this way, public policies, even if they have the best intentions and commitment from an environmental and climate point of view, will be doomed to failure" (Woischnik, 2022: 22).

In this respect, Jofre Carnicer, a researcher at the University of Barcelona and one of the authors of the latest report of the Intergovernmental Panel on Climate Change (IPCC), believes that the ecological transition cannot take place if the social transition is not also taken into account. He points out "that the challenge for the coming decades is 'very complex'... and calls for engaging society through 'deep and calm' dialogues, with data, to gain a broadly informed perspective" (Carnicer, 2022). The report also advocates strong institutions that guarantee social protection systems that facilitate the ecological transition without leaving anyone behind.

Spain is one of the most advanced countries in the European Union in terms of social and ecological transition. The country has a Ministry for Ecological Transition and the Demographic Challenge (MITECO) and a Just Transition Strategy. The strategy points out the opportunities with regard to employment generation, but at the same time emphasises that the ecological transition has to consider the social effects of its implementation. It is therefore useful to look at the Spanish experience to see how Madrid has dealt in particular with implementation.

Specifically, the Government of Spain (2020) highlights in its Just Transition Strategy:

> We are facing an opportunity to improve productive and transport systems, as well as the characterisation of services, to make them much more efficient in the use of resources and offer the solutions that a decarbonised world needs. In addition, the transition to a greener economic model will generate significant employment opportunities.

At the same time, the government notes that while these opportunities are particularly important for Spain, "for the transition to a greener economic model to be socially beneficial, in a country with high unemployment rates, this transition must be the engine of new quality jobs" (Government of Spain, 2020).

A key aspect of the Spanish transition strategy is that it is being implemented in very concrete terms. This implies, among other things, a shift from polluting energies to a greater promotion of renewable energies. The Just Transition Strategy itself stresses that restructuring can lead to negative impacts on certain economic activities, giving as an example the areas of extractive activity in mining areas. Just Transition Agreements have been set up to provide financial support to regions with difficulties in coping with the energy and ecological transition. For the period from 2019 to 2021, the budget reached 130 million euros. These agreements provide for "an action plan aimed at generating comprehensive territorial development projects that guarantee employment in the medium and long term, and dynamise the transition towards a new productive scenario" (Government of Spain, 2019).

As noted above, in order to achieve a more sustainable and fairer Europe and to be able to implement the ambitious Green Pact, significant economic resources are required. In this respect, environmental taxation is key in terms of investments to reduce greenhouse gas emissions, reduce pollution of any kind and curb the loss of biodiversity. In the opinion of Cristina Narbona, "we need taxation that is not only fair, but sufficient" (Narbona, 2022). While this may seem an obvious consideration, its practical implementation, as well as its acceptance, faces significant challenges. This is precisely where one of the great difficulties lies.

In fact, recent trends show a decline in environmental taxes, according to a report by the European Environment Agency (EEA). Specifically: "In the EU, revenues from environmental taxes were €330 billion in 2019. The share of environmental taxes in total tax revenues decreased from 6.6% in 2002 to 5.9% in 2019. The trend varies across Europe, but critically, the share decreased in pioneer countries implementing environmental taxes, such as Denmark, Norway and Sweden" (RETEMA, 2022). This is not a good signal. It not only stresses the political impact and sensitivity of the nexus between the environmental and the social but also indicates that there are areas and lobbies of resistance.

This is partly but significantly connected with the relationship between the ecological transition and employment. There are fears in several European countries that a transition towards sustainability will lead to job losses in some economic sectors, often among the most politically sensitive or those more prone to social mobilization. However, the green transition – same as digitalization – implies opportunities for the generation of new jobs too in areas such as renewable energy, energy efficiency, sustainable construction, green agriculture, sustainable tourism, sustainable transport, sustainable architecture, smart cities, circular economy, etc.

A cultural change for an environmental turn

The ecological and social transition towards a sustainable economy not only requires programmes, plans and financial support from governments, but also a new business culture, focused on the ecological reconversion of productive sectors through processes and products that reduce negative effects on health and the environment. This in turn increases the efficient use of natural resources (through the circular economy) and contributes to the decarbonisation of industry. At the same time, green policies must create decent jobs – not just green jobs, but sustainable jobs – and promote the well-being of society as a whole, with an emphasis on social equity.

All this implies the promotion of Research, Development and Innovation (R&D&I), both in production and marketing. The development of new methods to increase the added value of products, a greater orientation towards quality requirements on the part of consumers, greater speed in satisfying customer demand, all constitute the basis for a cultural paradigm shift. This new situation calls for a reorganisation within companies and, at the same time, greater openness and collaboration with universities. In this context, the reconversion of human capital takes on a significant and growing importance, a reality that is closely linked to education and training.

Let us not forget the role of the consumer in this path towards a new economic model. This implies sustainable consumption, i.e. the responsibility of citizens as consumers. There are many options available to consumers to contribute directly and significantly to the ecological transition. Individual behaviour is as important as collective action and regulation. Less use of one's own car, use of bicycles, purchase of less polluting cars, energy saving, reduction of food waste, active participation in reducing and separating waste and avoiding the use of plastics are all small but significant virtuous choice that every and any citizen can do. This requires a cultural shift and a change in habits and lifestyle.

This connects us to the principle of sufficiency, which in the words of Cristina Narbona:

> is a principle that will be increasingly taken into account, due to the growing depletion of many raw materials (including some necessary for decarbonisation). It goes beyond the principle of efficiency and, in my opinion, should be understood as a basic element to reduce waste and inequalities, particularly in the richest countries (Narbona, 2021).

An interesting aspect related to the sufficiency principle is the Degrowth or Post-Growth social movement, which is active internationally and present above all in countries such as Germany and Austria. The different currents – which have their nuances – go beyond the Green Growth concept, which according to this movement focuses above all on technical innovations, efficiency, the circular economy, etc. The Degrowth movement goes beyond technical solutions to tackle the depletion of resources and advocates a more radical approach that constitutes a sort of "second wave of growth criticism" (D'Alisa, Demaria & Kallis, 2016). The Degrowth scientific-analytical basis takes up the radical thinkers of the so-called first wave of the critique of growth, such as Nicholas Georgescu-Roegen (1971) or André Gorz (1975, 1977).

At the same time, the movement goes beyond this first wave with more radical aspects. For instance, while the "steady-state" concept of the ecological economist Herman Daly is key for many critics of economic growth, it does not suffice for some of the theorists of the Degrowth movement (D'Alisa, Demaria & Kallis, 2016). More radical steps were undertaken at the Degrowth Congresses between 2014 and 2022. Topics such as the right to housing and organic farming expanded the concept (TAZ, 2020). New instances such as open borders, queer people and rules of sexuality and gender perhaps overstretched the original purpose. It may not be easy to understand or accept the new aims of the movement, especially the battle to overcoming capitalism altogether.

Perhaps the best approach to take stock of the Degrowth concept and a way to reconcile the first and second wave of criticism of growth was taken by Cristina Narbona (2021). She differs from Degrowth in that "degrowth should occur in all polluting activities or those whose competitiveness depends on unacceptable conditions for workers. On the other hand, sectors that are essential to guarantee progress should grow, particularly in the poorest countries (health, education, basic infrastructures, etc.)". The link environment-social remains central.

With regard to the subsistence and sufficiency economy in the context of the post-growth debate, Niko Paech, a prominent German economist, was very critical of consumers and their role with regard to the consequences of the greed economy. He argued that:

> Criticism of the system is often an elegant alibi for downplaying the responsibility of the individual. A systemic view would have to properly include the demand side, i.e. the cultural footprint of consumer behaviour. Consumers have never been as politically powerful as they are today, never have they had so much disposable income – and yet they are seen as passive victims of economic conditions. The dogma of growth cannot be described solely as capitalist logic, but is part of a transcendental principle of upward mobility. Competition, profit maximisation and capital accumulation can only ruin a planet if they find insatiable buyers (Folkers & Paech, 2020: 24).

In this respect, it should be recalled that among the voluntary commitments made at the international level was the United Nations 10-Year Framework of

Programmes on Sustainable Consumption and Production Patterns (10YFP), adopted at the 2012 UN Rio+20 conference by the heads of state. The final document, entitled "The Future We Want" provides a framework made up of six specific programmes (UNEP, 2012):

- Consumer Information
- Sustainable Public Procurement
- Sustainable Lifestyles and Education
- Sustainable Tourism (including Ecotourism)
- Sustainable Construction
- Sustainable Food Systems

The 2030 Agenda for Sustainable Development, with its 17 goals and 169 targets, deepens the 10YFP programmes. It is worth recalling that Agenda 2030 was adopted in September 2015 by 193 UN Member States. On the consumption side, Goal 12 "Ensure sustainable consumption and production patterns" is a compelling call for consumers to responsible behaviour. On the production side, Target 12.c calls for "restructuring tax systems and phasing out harmful subsidies", such as "inefficient fossil fuel subsidies" and "wasteful consumption by removing market distortions". Agenda 2030 is an important transformative agenda, which gives quite precise guidelines for a social and ecological transition, even though it does not express it in these terms.

Ultimately, what is utterly needed for a successful ecological and social transition is a cultural change. As the years go by, we have analysed environmental and climate problems in depth, we have undoubtedly made some progress, we have invented new technologies. Yet, we still find it difficult to understand that our planet has limits, and that nature reacts when those limits are crossed by human beings and their behaviour. A cultural change must primarily address and disseminate this understanding.

Conclusion

It is not an easy task to compare the situation described above, centred on the social and ecological transition in the European Union, with similar processes in other continents. Ecological awareness is much more evident and concrete when certain levels of well-being have already been achieved. Nevertheless, the preamble of the 2030 Agenda for Sustainable Development states "we pledge that no one will be left behind". This connects with Goal 17: "Strengthen the means of implementation and revitalise the Global Partnership for Sustainable Development". This clearly implies greater solidarity between countries in a relatively good economic situation and countries in need of technical and financial assistance.

What has been said about the European Union (EU) above links us to Latin America and the Caribbean (LAC), where different governments are making considerable efforts to decarbonise their economies (promotion of renewable energies and energy efficiency, closure of thermoelectric plants, etc.) due to their international commitments, on the one hand, and their great vulnerability to the negative effects of climate change, on the other. It is worth noting that the Covid-19 pandemic has deepened the already existing inequalities in Latin America, with devastating impacts on health, the economy, education and other social aspects, such as, for example, the alarming increase in the so-called "energy poverty".

These and other circumstances led in 2020 to an alliance between academics, social and environmental activists from several Latin American countries to create the Social, Ecological, Economic and Intercultural Pact for Latin America (Pacto Ecosocial del Sur, N/D). This initiative cannot be compared to the European Green Pact, which is a large-scale strategy, involving the 27 EU member states, and has at its disposal large economic resources that the LAC countries lack in order to initiate their own ecological and social transition. In the case of the Latin American Ecosocial Pact of the South, it is more of a manifesto calling for a "radical socio-ecological transition" in four areas: redistributive justice, gender justice, ethnic justice and environmental justice.

International cooperation undoubtedly has a key role to play in renewing and strengthening bi-regional relations between the EU and LAC. In the preface to the book *Relaunching EU-Latin America Relations: Strategic Autonomy, Advanced Cooperation and Digital, Green and Social Recovery*, Josep Borrell, EU High Representative for Foreign Affairs and Security Policy, wrote that "democratic values form part of the common acquis between Latin America and Europe, at a time when these values are being challenged on a global scale", therefore, "it is necessary to deepen our political dialogue, and it is crucial to guard against those who try to make us see the world with old logics of bipolarity" (Borrell, 2022).

Political dialogue is of paramount importance, but so is the willingness of European countries to learn from each other. It is also essential for the EU to take a holistic approach to Latin America's economic and social difficulties. All this is within the framework of greater solidarity between the countries in good economic conditions and the countries that need technical and financial assistance. This would be expressed – in my opinion – no more and no less through a Social, Ecological and Global Transition.

Bibliography

Borrell, J. (2021). *Contestación al cuestionario de la FIIAPP relativo al informe "La incipiente articulación entre las transiciones social, ecológica y digital en la Unión Europea y en América Latina y el Caribe"*, abril 2022, Madrid, España.

Borrell, J. (2022). *Prefacio en libro "Relanzar las relaciones entre América Latina y la Unión Europea. Autonomía estratégica, cooperación avanzada y recuperación digital, verde y social"*. Fundación Carolina, 18 de mayo, Madrid. Online: https://www.fundacioncarolina.es/la-fundacion-carolina-lanza-el-libro-relanzar-las-relaciones-entre-america-latina-y-la-union-europea-autonomia-estrategica-cooperacion-avanzada-y-recuperacion-digital-verde-y-social/ (last accessed 10 January 2023).

Braungart, M., & McDonough, W. (2002). *Cradle to cradle: Remaking the way we make things*. London: Vintage.

Bündnis 90/Die Grünen. (2011). *Die sozial-ökologische Transformation der Wirtschaft: Der Grüne New Deal*, Kiel, Germany.

Carnicer, J. (2022). *La mitigación del cambio climático implica transformaciones estructurales en la mayoría de los sistemas de nuestra sociedad*, interview by Marc Font, *Público*, 17 April 2022. Online: https://www.publico.es/entrevistas/entrevista-jofre-carnicer-jofre-carnicer-mitigacion-cambio-climatico-implica-transformaciones-estructurales-mayoría-sistemas-nuestra-sociedad.html/amp (last accessed 10 January 2023).

D´Alisa, G., Demaria, F., & Kallis, G. (Eds.). (2016). *Degrowth. Handbuch für eine neue Ära*. Munich: Paech, N.: Vorwort zur deutschen Ausgabe.

European Commission. (2020). *Recovery plan for Europe*. Online: https://commission.europa.eu/strategy-and-policy/recovery-plan-europe_en

European Commission. (2022). *A European green deal*. Online: https://commission.europa.eu/strategy-and-policy/priorities-2019-2024/european-green-deal_en (last accessed 10 January 2023).

Folkers, M., & Paech, N. (2020). *All you need is less. Eine Kultur des Genug aus ökonomischer und buddhistischer Sicht*, pág. 24. München: Alemania.

Georgescu-Roegen, N. (1971). *The entropy law and the economic process*. Cambridge, MA: Harvard University Press.

Gorz, A. (1975). *Écologie et politique*. Paris : Galilée.

Gorz, A. (1977). *Écologie et liberté*. Paris: Galilée.

Government of Spain. (2019). *La Estrategia de Transición Justa será el marco de actuación para optimizar las oportunidades de la transición ecológica*, 22 de febrero, Madrid, España.

Government of Spain. (2020). *Estrategia de Transición Justa. Marco estratégico de energía y clima*, noviembre, Madrid, España.

Hancox, D. (2019). At last, the Labour party is bein led from the bottom up. *The Guardian*, 16 May 2019. Online: https://www.theguardian.com/commentisfree/2019/may/16/labour-party-jeremy-corbyn-green-new-deal (last accessed 10 January 2023).

Jiménez Herrero, L. M., en Jiménez Herrero, L. M., & Pérez Lagüela, E. (Eds.). (2019). *Economía Circular-Espiral. Transición hacia un metabolismo económico cerrado*, pág. 28, Madrid, España.

Narbona, C. (2021). *Contestación al cuestionario de la FIIAPP relativo al informe "La incipiente articulación entre las transiciones social, ecológica y digital en la Unión Europea y en América Latina y el Caribe*, abril 2022, Madrid, España.

Narbona, C. (2022a). *Energía nuclear: ni verde ni barata ni segura*, El País, 8 January 2022. Online: https://elpais.com/opinion/2022-01-08/energia-nuclear-ni-verde-ni-barata-ni-segura.html (last accessed 10 January 2023).

Narbona, C. (2022b). *Comentarista en el acto de presentación del informe "La incipiente articulación entre las transiciones social, ecológica y digital en la Unión Europea y en América Latina y el Caribe"*. Organizado por la Fundación Internacional y para Iberoamérica de Administración y Políticas Públicas (FIIAPP), 15 de septiembre, Madrid, España. Online: https://www.youtube.com/watch?v=nlGqccPRw6E (last accessed 10 January 2023).

OIT. (2018). *Transición justa hacia economías y sociedades ambientalmente sostenibles para todos*. Reseña de políticas OIT-ACTRAV, Ginebra, Suiza.

RETEMA. (2022). *"Los impuestos ambientales en Europa están en declive a pesar de su potencial" con referencia al informe de la Agencia Europea de Medio Ambiente (AEMA): "El papel de la fiscalidad ambiental en el apoyo a las transiciones hacia la sostenibilidad"*, 8 de febrero, Madrid, España.

Sanahuja, J. A. (2021). *Transiciones en el desarrollo: el Pacto Verde Europeo y América Latina*, publicado por la OCDE en el marco de la serie *Development matters*, 22 de marzo. Online: https://oecd-development-matters.org/2021/03/22/transitions-in-development-the-european-green-deal-and-latin-america/ (last accessed 10 January 2023).

Sanders, B. (2021). NEWS: Sanders and Ocasio-Cortez rollout green new deal for public housing act, sen. *Sanders Senate webpage* 19 April 2021. Online: https://www.sanders.senate.gov/press-releases/news-sanders-and-ocasio-cortez-rollout-green-new-deal-for-public-housing-act/ (last accessed 10 January 2023).

Schmidt-Bleek. (2008). Factor 10: The future of stuff. *Sustainability: Science, Practice, & Policy*, 4(1), 1–4.

Stiglitz, J. E. (2018). *Más allá del PIB*, El País, 30 December 2018. Online: https://elpais.com/economia/2018/12/27/actualidad/1545929295_139969.html (last accessed 10 January 2023).

Stiglitz-Sen-Fitoussi-Commission-report.pdf. (2009). *Report by the Commission on the Measurement of Economic Performance and Social Progress*. Online: https://ec.europa.eu>eurostat (last accessed 10 January 2023).

TAZ. (2020). *Eine Zukunft für alle*. Degrowth-Kongress in Leipzig, 26.08, Berlín, Germany.

UNEP. (2012). *10YFP – 10 Year Framework of Programmes on sustainable consumption and production patterns*. UN Environment Programme. New York. Online: https://www.unep.org/explore-topics/resource-efficiency/what-we-do/one-planet-network/10yfp-10-year-framework-programmes (last accessed 10 January 2023).

United Nations. (1987). *Our common future*. Report of the World Commission on Environment and Development transmitted to the General Assembly as an Annex to document A/42/427 – Development and International Cooperation: Environment. New York: United Nations.

Varoufakis, Y. (2019). A European spring is possible. *The Nation*, 14 March 2019. Online: https://www.yanisvaroufakis.eu/2019/03/14/a-european-spring-is-possible-the-nation/ (last accessed 10 January 2023).

von Weizsäcker, E. (1998). *Factor four: Doubling wealth, halving resource use – a report to the club of Rome*. London: Routledge.

von Weizsäcker, E.-U., Lovins, A., & Lovins, H. (1997). *Faktor Vier. Doppelter Wohlstand – halbierter Naturverbrauch*. Der neue Bericht an den Club of Rome, München.

Woischnik, A. (2015). *Crecimiento verde en el contexto de la realidad chilena*, Tribuna ASYPS, n° 3, 3 September 2015. Online: tribunaasyps03crecimientoverdechilealwinewoischnik.pdf (last accessed 10 January 2023).

Woischnik, A. (2019a). *Green New Deal y Transición Eco-Social: ¿respuestas a la Crisis Climática?, nuevatribuna.es*, 4 December 2019. Online: https://www.nuevatribuna.es/articulo/sostenibilidad/green-new-deal-transicion-eco-social-respuestas-crisis-climatica/20191204113458168791.html (last accessed 10 January 2023).

Woischnik, A. (2019b). *La descarbonización de la economía. Hacia una transición justa*, Mesa redonda, El Periódico, 31 October 2019.

Woischnik, A. (2022). *La incipiente articulación entre las transiciones social, ecológica y digital en la Unión Europea y en América Latina y el Caribe*. Informe elaborado por encargo de la Fundación Internacional y para Iberoamérica de Administración y Políticas Públicas (FIIAPP), April 2022. Online: https://www.youtube.com/watch?v=nlGqccPRw6E (last accessed 10 January 2023).

Millán Requena Casanova

Towards Forward-Looking Migration Governance: The Global Compact on Migration from a Bi-regional Perspective

The global migration governance regimes

The 2030 Agenda and the UN Global Compact on Migration

In the absence of a binding and coherent international migration regime, the global governance of migration relies on normative narratives produced by UN agencies and other intergovernmental processes. Among the normative narratives of the UN agencies that address migration cooperation, we can highlight the 2030 Agenda for Sustainable Development (2030 Agenda) and the United Nations *Global Compact for Safe, Orderly and Regular Migration* (hereinafter, GCM) . Such normative narratives impact migrants, asylum seekers and refugees because they support certain policy frameworks and common rules among United Nations member States. The *Global Compact for Migration* and the *Global Compact on Refugees* (UN, General Assembly, A/73/12 (Part II), 2018), have been developed in response to these realities and challenges. In addition to committing States to reduce negative and structural drivers of migration, such as conflict, violence, and climate change, the GCM stresses the need to support "legal migration pathways", which are especially needed by people living in countries affected by conflict and underdevelopment, and who are often the ones compelled to undertake irregular and unsafe journeys.

When the 2030 Agenda was adopted in 2015, the positive contribution of migrants to sustainable development was also recognised. Target 10.7 of the Sustainable Development Goals specifies this objective, which seeks to achieve *safe, orderly, regular* and responsible migration. What does *safe*, *orderly* and *regular* migration mean? There is no definition of this term within the 2030 Agenda. In the Declaration adopted at the *2013 High-level Dialogue on International Migration and Development*, Member States recognised "the need for international cooperation to address, in a holistic and comprehensive manner, the challenges of irregular migration to ensure safe, orderly and regular migration, with full respect for human rights" (UN, General Assembly, 2013: p. 2, par. 5), and Member States further advocated for the inclusion of migration in the negotiation of the post-2015 development agenda.

The IOM defined these categories to help in the negotiations leading to the GCM. According to the IOM, we can define *orderly migration* as: "the movement of a person from his or her usual place of residence to a new place of residence, in keeping with the laws and regulations governing exit of the country of origin and travel, transit and entry into the host country". IOM defines *regular migration* as "migration that occurs through recognised, authorised channels". A migrant can be in an *unsafe situation* while or after having migrated through regular channels; conversely, a migrant can be in a situation that is both safe and irregular. A migrant's situation can change from safety to unsafety throughout the various phases of their migratory process, and thus the definition should encompass all stages of the process, including at the country of origin, transit, country of first asylum and country of destination.

Climate migration and capacity-building mechanism: The United Nations Network on Migration

The *United Nations Network on Migration* coordinates system-wide support for States in the implementation of, follow-up to and review of the GCM at the national, regional and global levels. It offers a platform for stakeholders to engage in dialogue and the development of tools and guidance in support of the implementation of the Compact.

The GCM calls for the establishment of a *capacity-building mechanism* (CBM) in the UN, building upon existing initiatives, that supports efforts of Member States in its implementation (UN, General Assembly, 2018: pp. 3–4, par. 43). The *Migration Network Hub* combining both the *Global Knowledge Platform* and the Connection Hub, was launched in March 2021 and is a vital element of the GCM to ensure that relevant knowledge, experience, and expertise can be drawn upon in developing tailor-made solutions in response to the requests of Member States.

The *Network* established the migration multi-partner trust fund in 2019, the first UN inter-agency pooled funding instrument in the field of migration. Aligned with the 2030 Agenda, the programmatic scope of the trust fund embraces the 360-degree approach of the GCM, clustering *all 23 objectives* under five thematic areas. The steering committee of the fund includes countries of origin, destination and transit, donors, stakeholders and network entities.

In May 2022, under the auspices of the UNGA, took place in New York the *International Migration Review Forum* (IMRF). In the framework of the GCM, Member States decided that the *International Migration Review Forum* should serve as the primary intergovernmental global platform to discuss and share progress on the implementation of all aspects of the Global Compact, including as it relates to the 2030 Agenda, and with the participation of all relevant stakeholders.

The *IMRF* shall take place every four years beginning in 2022. Each edition of the Review Forum will result in an intergovernmentally agreed "Progress Declaration". The first Review Forum concluded with the adoption of a "Progress Declaration" on 7 June 2022. In fact, the "Progress Declaration of the International Migration Review Forum", incorporates an "Annex" that contains a series of actions recommended by States to accelerate the implementation of the *Global Compact* and to strengthen international cooperation on international migration. In relation to the consequences of climate change on migration, the States signatories recognised: "The adverse effects of climate change, environmental degradation and natural disasters are among the drivers of migration, which are influenced by economic, social, political and demographic contexts (UN, General Assembly, 2022: p. 5, par. 27).

For this purpose, among the measures to accelerate the *Global Compact*, the States committed to: "strengthen our efforts to enhance and diversify the availability of pathways for safe, orderly and regular migration, including in response to demographic and labour market realities, and for migrants in vulnerable situations, as well as those affected by disasters, climate change and environmental degradation [...]" (UN, General Assembly, 2022: p. 10, par. 59).

Regional mechanisms on migration cooperation in Latin America: The informal dialogues on migration

South America region

Migration in the context of climate impacts: non-binding regional mechanisms on the protection of people displaced across borders

Addressing *irregular migration* is a key component of achieving the Global Compact's overall goal of safe, orderly, and regular migration. Among its shared responsibilities, for example, the GCM aims "to facilitate safe, orderly and regular migration while reducing the incidence and negative effects of irregular migration through international cooperation" (IOM, 2018: p. 15). Several Global Compact commitments have a direct bearing on irregular migration, such as "ensuring that desperation and deteriorating environments do not compel them to seek a livelihood elsewhere through irregular migration" (objective 2).

At the 26th session of the *Conference of the Parties to the United Nations Framework Convention on Climate Change*, and as part of the Glasgow Climate

Pact, State parties urged greater efforts on mitigation and adaptation and action and support to avert, minimise and address loss and damage, including displacement. In terms of cross-border migration, one obvious response is to develop more visa options available to those who cannot remain in, or return to, areas of origin due to slow-onset impacts of climate change, as set out in GCM (objective 5). Such visas could, for instance, be granted on humanitarian grounds to those fleeing extreme environmental degradation, on the model of humanitarian visas offered by Brazil to Haitian migrants after the 2010 earthquake.

Member countries of the *South American Conference on Migration* developed and adopted *non-binding guidelines* to protect persons displaced across borders due to disasters. The guidelines build on existing practices that promote the use of regular and exceptional immigration law on humanitarian grounds. Even if non-binding, the guidelines represent an innovative policymaking example of how South American countries can cooperate at the regional level to minimise environmental drivers of migration and manage the admission and stay of affected people.

Supporting legal pathways for regular migration: Temporary protection for Venezuelan migrants

In the *South America region*, since 2018 to the present, 5.9 million Venezuelan migrants have left their country. The millions of people who have fled Venezuela in recent years must be received, welcomed and protected by neighbouring countries. Some of these migrants lacked regular status and access to social protection. In April 2018, the UN Secretary-General asked UNHCR and IOM to coordinate and lead the operational response to the situation of Venezuelan migrants and refugees. In September of the same year, the two agencies established the "Regional Inter-agency Coordination Platform" with the aim of "implementing a regional approach by which to guarantee an operational, consistent and coordinated response (UNHCR & IOM, 2019: p. 12). Subsequently, UNHCR and IOM drew up a *Regional Refugee and Migrant Response Plan for Refugees and Migrants from Venezuela* to complement and strengthen the national and regional responses of the Governments, including through their national plans and the proposed *Quito Plan of Action*, in line with the principles set out in the *New York Declaration for Refugees and Migrants*, the *Global Compact on Refugees* and its comprehensive response framework, and the *Global Compact for Safe, Orderly and Regular Migration* (Amnesty International, 2019: p. 16).

Colombia, Peru and Ecuador are the three South American countries that have received a greater number of Venezuelan migrants. Colombia has been the country that has had the best response, especially due to the creation in 2021 of the "Temporary Protection Permit", a complementary mechanism to the international refugee protection regime *valid for 10 years* that authorises Venezuelan migrants to remain in the country under conditions of special migratory regularity and carry out any activity or legal occupation. To access this, it is indistinct if the entry to the country has been regular or irregular. Also noteworthy are the different Special Permanence Permits, access to medical care, recognition of the nationality of boys and girls born in Colombian territory, the Administrative Registry of Venezuelan Migrants (RAMV) to register the needs, census and regularization of the Venezuelan population residing in the country.

In 2017, Peru created a "Temporary Residence Permit" ("PTP" in Spanish) for Venezuelans in Peru, enabling them to access work and some basic services. The PTP is only valid for a year, however, leaving those who manage to obtain it in a temporary and precarious situation. The authorities imposed a time limit on PTP requests, limiting it to those who arrived in Peru before 31 October 2018 and with applications accepted only up to 31 December 2018.

In the case of Ecuador, there are three immigration statuses: visitors temporary, temporary residents and permanent residents. The problem lies in the fact that the category granted to those who request international protection while their case is being processed is that of a temporary visitor who does not allow them to carry out work activities, which is insensitive to the needs of Venezuelan migrants fleeing the country, and it even increases their vulnerability by having to resort to irregular jobs that risk their integrity (Gan Galavís, 2022: p. 56).

On the other hand, the *Global Compact on Refugees*, based on the Convention relating to the Status of Refugees adopted in 1951, was generated with the main objective of developing a multilateral cooperation model, a tool that can be implemented in practice based on the *Comprehensive Response Framework for Refugees* that would include burden and responsibility sharing mechanisms (UNICEF, 2019). Regarding this framework, the IOM points out that there are still difficulties related to the distribution of responsibility, such as insufficient funds to support host countries, as well as the lack of spaces for the resettlement of refugees. Likewise, by 2019, USD 125 per Venezuelan migrant and USD 1,500 per Syrian migrant had been allocated in the world, making it one of the migration crises with the least funds allocated to address the problem of displaced persons (Bahar & Dooley, 2019).

During the pandemic, migrants faced hate speech, racial slurs, stigma and violence, as well as discriminatory policies and programmes that impaired their well-being. In 2019, Colombia adopted legislation to outlaw the use of xenophobic narratives about Venezuelan migrants and refugee communities (UN,

Secretary-General, 2021: p. 14). The IACHR also has information regarding serious xenophobic and discriminatory practices against Venezuelans in countries of transit and destination, including insults, abuses by authorities and individuals, extortion, and rhetoric that stigmatises and criminalises Venezuelans by blaming them for increases in rates of violence and taking jobs away from nationals (OAS, Inter-American Commission on Human Rights, 2018: p. 2).

Providing migrants at different skill levels and in different situations of vulnerability with opportunities for entry and stay reduces the need to move, live or work in unsafe or irregular conditions. In 2020, Chile approved an immigration law (Law No. 21,325 of 20 April 2021) to strengthen children's rights in the context of migration, which includes a special visa for children and permits children to enter the territory without travel documentation and prohibits immigration sanctions against them (objective 13). Argentina strengthened consular support through its one-stop virtual mechanism and collaborated with diaspora communities to provide food and housing (UN, Secretary-General, 2021: p. 9, par. 32).

The commitment to providing proof of legal identity received relatively limited attention during regional reviews, despite its foundational role in fulfilling many other commitments (provide legal identity for all, including birth registration). With regular pathways out of reach, migrants who lack proof of legal identity may resort to irregular channels, frustrating the Compact's vision. Well-functioning civil registration systems, including with the capacity to register births and issue documents abroad through consular networks, are crucial for safe, orderly and regular migration. In countries such as Colombia and Ecuador, efforts to provide proof of legal identity for migrants have received considerable support (UN, Secretary-General, 2021: p. 16).

Mesoamerica region

In the *Mesoamerica region* – made up of the countries of Central America and Mexico – the majority of migrants, both intra-regionally and extra-regionally, are mobilised for labour purposes. In this region there are various platforms for dialogue and regional coordination where the governance of labour migration is addressed.

Among the platforms mentioned is the *Regional Conference on Migration* (RCM), a space made up of all the countries of *Mesoamerica*, Belize, Canada, the United States and the Dominican Republic. These countries had the opportunity to analyse the gaps and challenges present in migratory matters for strategic coordination in measures for its attention before the *International Migration Review Forum*. The *Regional Conference on Migration* addressed the regional position before the Review Forum, and issued an *extraordinary Declaration* before the First Review Forum (IMRF) urging the adoption of a "shared responsibility approach" to migration in order to "strengthen international cooperation, optimise the benefits of migration and contribute to improving the lives of migrants, their families and the communities of the countries of origin, transit, destination and return" (Conferencia Regional sobre Migración, 2022).

Therefore, from this regional platform, this first forum is an unprecedented opportunity to review how the commitments made on the issue of migration materialise from an approach based on "shared responsibility". Likewise, the *RCM* has identified regional priorities that constitute the main elements of the *Regional Action Plan for Safe, Orderly and Regular Migration*, grouped around key themes, as well as two transversal priorities (Annex). In particular, within "thematic Pillar 2", the following objectives are identified as priorities: (i) "Increase regular migration pathways" (objective 5); (ii) "Increase the certainty and predictability of immigration procedures" (objective 12); (iii) "Strengthen the transnational response to the smuggling of migrants" (objective 9) (Conferencia Regional sobre Migración, 2022).

The flexibility of immigration procedures to ensure that the largest number of migrant workers have regular immigration status was identified as a good practice. For instance, some important elements are providing the necessary information and protective equipment to avoid contagion and protect health. This will present new challenges to States, including ensuring that the migrant population can participate in health and social protection schemes, according to the GCM (objective 15 offer protection to all migrants, so that they can "access basic services" in safety conditions), and establishing clear regulations regarding the hiring of foreigners remotely (Chaves & Aragón, 2021: pp. 77–82).

The EU pact on migration and asylum: Between a regional migration governance and migration pragmatism

With the adoption of the 2020 *New Pact on Migration and Asylum*, the European Commission (EC) proposed a "fresh start", with a comprehensive package to ensure a strong and balanced migration and asylum system equal to the challenges of the future. It builds on a major stepping-up of work on migration in recent years. However, this European Pact is not really *a pact between EU member States* – as the 2008 *European Pact on Immigration and Asylum,* adopted by the Council – but rather an *action plan* of the EC in the short and medium term to adopt rules of EU secondary law on border controls, migration and asylum aimed at overcoming the deficiencies of the current framework (Morgades, 2022: p. 28).

"Instrumentalisation" of irregular migration by State actors

A highly worrying phenomenon observed recently is the increasing role of State actors in artificially creating and facilitating irregular migration, using migratory flows as a tool for political purposes. A worrying development has been the "instrumentalisation of migration" for political ends at different EU external borders. Since June 2021, a new and serious development intended to destabilise the EU and its Member States, has been observed with Belarus retaliating to EU sanctions by organised State-sponsored smuggling of migrants into the EU by plane from several third countries (mainly from Iraq, as well as from the Republic of the Congo, Cameroon, Syria and others), usually with a valid visa or visa-free. Belarus announced the suspension of the EU Readmission agreement ratified in 2020 and refused to take back those irregular migrants who transited through Belarus. Migrant smugglers have taken advantage of the situation, notably of the actions of the Belarusian authorities, offering illicit services and online guidance to migrants on how to illegally reach Belarus and irregularly cross the EU external border to Lithuania, Latvia or Poland. Irregular arrivals in Lithuania in 2021 have been more than fifty times higher than arrivals in 2020, and Poland and Latvia have also seen vastly increased irregular border crossings from Belarus.

The *renewed EU action plan against migrant smuggling* (2021–2025) (European Commission, COM(2021)591 final, 2021: p. 2) sets out the key pillars and concrete actions needed to counter and prevent smuggling, and to ensure that the fundamental rights of migrants are fully protected. The renewed EU action plan contributes to the implementation of the New Pact, by aiming to prevent the loss of life, reduce unsafe and irregular migration and facilitate orderly migration management and the establishment of a sustainable EU migration and asylum policy.

The forced displacement crisis in 2022: Temporary protection for displaced Ukrainians

Since 24 February 2022, the war between the Russian Federation and Ukraine has led to one of the largest refugee emergencies since World War II. In November 2022, the Office of the United Nations High Commissioner for Refugees (UNHCR) placed the number of refugees and asylum seekers at more than 7.8

million, a number that exceeds the total arrivals in Europe of immigrants and refugees from other regions in the last seven years (UNHCR, 2022).

On 4 March 2022, the EU Council activated the *Temporary Protection Directive*, which aims to relieve pressure on national asylum systems and allow displaced people to enjoy harmonised rights across the Union . These rights include residence, access to the labour market and housing, medical assistance and access to education for children. UNHCR estimates that there are more than 4.6 million Ukrainians who have registered for temporary protection in Europe. Most of the population that has had to leave the country has fled to the Russian Federation and Poland, but a significant number have taken refuge in Germany, the Czech Republic, Italy, Turkey and other European countries (UNHCR, 2022).

This Decision is intended to introduce temporary protection for Ukrainian nationals residing in Ukraine who have been displaced on or after 24 February 2022 as a result of the military invasion by Russian armed forces. In accordance with Article 2 of the Decision, the persons to whom the temporary protection applies to are:

(a) Ukrainian nationals residing in Ukraine before 24 February 2022;
(b) stateless persons, and nationals of third countries other than Ukraine, who benefited from international protection or equivalent national protection in Ukraine before 24 February 2022; and,
(c) family members of the persons referred to in points (a) and (b)

Introducing temporary protection is also expected to benefit the Member States, as the rights accompanying temporary protection limit the need for displaced persons to immediately seek international protection and thus the risk of overwhelming their asylum systems. Furthermore, Ukrainian nationals, as visa-free travellers, have the right to move freely within the EU after being admitted into the territory for a 90-day period. On this basis, they are able *to choose the Member State* in which they want to enjoy the rights attached to temporary protection and to join their family and friends across the significant diaspora networks that currently exist across the EU. Since that directive provides that EU States may adopt or retain more favourable conditions, Spain for instance, has applied more favourable conditions for temporarily displaced Ukrainians, also including those who were in an irregular situation in Spanish territory before 24 February 2022 (Royal Decree 220/2022, on 29 March 2022).

Nevertheless, the *New Pact on Migration and Asylum* proposed to repeal the Temporary Protection Directive, because it was an instrument that was difficult to apply to major migration crises in the past (for instance, the Syrian migration crisis). In situations of forced displacement crises that are of such a magnitude that they risk overwhelming Member States' asylum and migration systems, the practical difficulties faced by EU Member States would be recognised through some limited margin to temporarily derogate from the normal procedures and timelines, "[…] and in view of the fact that the new legislation would lay down rules for granting immediate protection status in crisis situations, the Temporary Protection Directive would be repealed" (Pact on Migration and Asylum, 2020: p. 11). For this reason, a new legislative instrument would provide for the *temporary* and *extraordinary* measures necessary in the face of the crisis (European Commission, COM, (2020)613, 2020).

In addition, the European Commission has adopted a proposal for Cohesion's Action for Refugees in Europe (CARE) allowing Member States and regions to provide emergency support to people fleeing from Russia's invasion of Ukraine. These needs include access to services such as temporary accommodation, food and water supplies or medical care (Cohesion's Action for Refugees in Europe (CARE), 2022).

Reinforcing "legal pathways" for regular migration: Some steps

Supporting legal pathways to Europe is another key pillar of work with the EU Pact and its external partners ("6.6 Developing legal pathways to Europe"). In line with the "Commission Recommendation on legal pathways to protection in the EU" (European Commission, C(2020)6467, 2020), the European Commission has started outreach to promote, in addition to resettlement, complementary pathways linked to study and work. The EU policies need to foster a "level playing field" between national labor markets as migration destinations. In the *area of legal migration*, a number of pilot projects exploring options for targeted labor migration in the interests of Member States and partners are underway, chiefly in North Africa. For example, a pilot project "Addressing Labour Shortages through Innovative Labour Migration Models" is boosting cooperation between Belgium and Morocco in the management of regular migration, offering a safe and lawful option to young professionals willing to gain qualified working experience in the ICT sector. The *talent partnerships* will draw on this experience.

The legislative proposals framed by the EU Pact represent an overarching approach covering all aspects of migration and asylum policy. An important step forward on *legal migration* was achieved with the political agreement reached on the new *Blue Card Directive* in October 2021 (Directive (EU) 2021/1883, 2021). In accordance with Article 1 of the Council Directive 2009/50/EC (Council Directive, 2009), the purpose of this instrument is to determine:

(a) the conditions of entry and residence for more than three months in the territory of the Member States of third-country nationals for the purpose of highly qualified employment as EU Blue Card holders, and of their family members;
(b) the conditions for entry and residence of third-country nationals and of their family members under point (a) in Member States other than the first Member State.

The new scheme proposed in 2021 will introduce efficient rules to attract highly skilled workers to the EU, including more flexible admission conditions, enhanced rights and the possibility to move and work more easily between EU States.

Also, the EU Pact provides guarantees that each Member State will deal with the *asylum* applications it is responsible for, and that a structured, predictable mechanism for solidarity will ensure that no Member State bears a disproportionate burden. To achieve a truly common migration and asylum policy requires political will and vision, and the engagement and commitment of all (European Commission, COM(2021)590 final, 2021). The new *EU Asylum Agency*, approved in December 2021 (EU, Regulation 2021/2303, 2021), that replaces and succeeds the European Asylum Support Office (EASO), "shall contribute to ensuring the efficient and uniform application of Union law on asylum in the Member States in a manner that fully respects fundamental rights" (art. 1.2 of the Regulation (EU) 2021/2303). The EU Asylum Agency will be able to work on capacity building and operational support to third countries, and support EU and Member State resettlement schemes, building on the existing cooperation with UN agencies such as the UNHCR and the IOM.

The EC has also presented further proposals to complete the comprehensive reform set out in the EU Pact, some of them in line with the GCM (objective 5). On 27 April 2022, the EC presented a Communication setting out an approach towards a new and sustainable EU legal migration policy, *Attracting the skills and talent that the EU* needs to address labor shortages and reply to the demographic change in Europe (European Commission, COM(2022) 657 final, 2022). On the same day, the EC also presented proposals to modernise the *Long-term Residents Directive* and the *Single Permit Directive*. To provide a more effective framework for "legal pathways" to the EU, the Commission is proposing to revise the Single Permit Directive (European Commission, COM(2022), 655 final, 2022) and the Long-Term Residents Directive (European Commission, COM(2022), 650 final, 2022). Specifically, with the aim of facing the demographic and migratory challenges in Europe, the EC proposes:

(a) A streamlined procedure for the *single permit* for combined work and residence will make the process quicker and easier for applicants and employers.
(b) The revision of the *Long-term Residents Directive* will make it easier to acquire the EU long-term residence status by simplifying the admission conditions.

The main objectives of these proposals are the following: (a) reduce costs and the administrative burden for employers; (b) prevent labor exploitation; and (c) support further integration and mobility within the EU of nationals of non-EU countries that are already residing and working in the EU.

Conclusions

Global and regional migration governance regimes are emerging, especially with *soft law* instruments such as the 2018 *Global Compact on Migration* and the *New Pact on Migration and Asylum*, proposed by the Commission in 2020. The GCM is indeed an unprecedented success of *multilateralism* and represents, together with the 2030 Agenda, the beginning of the global governance of migration. The GCM has created a migration "cooperation framework" that is key to strengthen the contribution of migrants and migration to the SDGs and the 2030 Agenda.

At the EU level, although the EU and its Member States missed the opportunity to demonstrate a *pragmatic multilateralism* through a common position regarding the GCM, in recent years, there have been relevant developments regarding some proposals contained in the *New Pact on Migration and Asylum*. For instance, the progress made on the Blue Card Directive and the new EU Asylum Agency shows that it is possible to move forward and find compromises on reforms in the area of legal migration and protection of asylum seekers. Likewise, although the EU Pact proposed its repeal, the Council has unanimously agreed to apply the Temporary Protection Directive to Ukrainian nationals after the Russian invasion of February 2022.

At the LAC level, some countries have been forerunners to a global trend towards the regional governance of migration. The *regional consultative mechanisms* have become, especially in the regions of South America and Mesoamerica, specialised forums to define a LAC migration approach. A coordinated regional approach should incorporate four key components:

1. Providing humanitarian assistance to the most vulnerable migrants (including children, pregnant women or refugees).
2. Investing in host communities that make it possible to strengthen basic services to cover all displaced persons.

3. Strengthening the national asylum system and offering regularization alternatives, for example, for work or family reunification.
4. Cracking down on migrant smugglers.

There are some positive developments: Colombia has offered "Temporary Protected Status" to Venezuelan migrants; and most of the countries in the region recognise that they must cooperate to find the opportunities offered by migration within the framework of the GCM, in order to make human mobility a safer and more dignified process for migrants.

Lastly, EU-LAC relations should incorporate in the near future a common bi-regional agenda on human mobility whose main strategy must implement the principles and objectives of the Global Compact. Specifically, countries in both regions should increase the availability and flexibility of regular migration pathways, humanitarian or work visas, reduce vulnerabilities in the migration process, and manage borders in an integrated and safe manner. A good opportunity to relaunch EU-LAC relations could take place in 2023, under the Spanish Presidency of the EU and in coincidence with the EU-CELAC Summit – the first after eight years, in which one of the priorities of the bi-regional agenda must be the coordination of concrete measures within the framework of the GCM.

Bibliography

(2020). *Agreement between the European Union and the Republic of Belarus on the readmission of persons residing without authorization.*

(2020). *Communication from the Commission to the European Parliament, the Council, the European Economic and Social Committee and the Committee of the Regions on a New Pact on Migration and Asylum [Pact on Migration and Asyulm], (COM(2020) 609 final).* Brussels.

(2022). *Nota de Orientación sobre el Foro de Examen de la Migración Internacional destinada a las redes nacionales y regionales y los equipos de las Naciones Unidas en los países.* Obtenido de file:///D:/EU-LAC-project/Book/imrf_guidance_for_country_and_regional_networks_final-_es[1172].pdf.

Amnesty International, Welcome Venezuela, People fleeing massive human rights violations in Venezuela. (2019).

Bahar, D., & Dooley, M. (2019). *Venezuela refugee crisis to become the largest and most underfunded in modern history.* Recuperado el 17 de November de 2022, de Brookings: https://www.brookings.edu/blog/up-front/2019/12/09/venezuela-refugee-crisis-to-become-the-largest-and-most-underfunded-in-modern-history/

BOE. (2022). *Real Decreto 220/2022, de 29 de marzo, por el que se aprueba el Reglamento por el que se regula el sistema de acogida en materia de prot, por el que se aprueba el Reglamento por el que se regula el sistema de acogida en materia de protección internacional.* BOE.

Chaves, M., & Aragón, E. (2021). *Mecanismos sobre Migración Laboral en Mesoamérica. Organización Internacional para las Migraciones.* San José, Costa Rica: OIM.

Cohesion's Action for Refugees in Europe (CARE). (2022). *CARE.* Recuperado el 30 de 04 de 2022, de https://ec.europa.eu/regional_policy/sources/docgener/factsheet/care_supporting_refugees_en.pdf

Conferencia Regional sobre Migración, Declaración Extraordinaria ante el Foro de Examen de la Migración Internacional, 2022, Anexo. (2022). Ciudad de México.

Council of the European Union. (2008). *European pact on immigration and asylum.* Brussels.

EU. (2021a). *Directive (EU) 2021/1883 of the European Parliament and of the Council of 20 October 2021 on the conditions of entry and residence of third-country nationals for the purpose of highly qualified employment, and repealing Council Directive 2009/50/EC.* Brussels.

EU. (2021b). *Regulation (EU) 2021/2303 of the European Parliament and of the Council of 15 December 2021 on the European Union Agency for Asylum and repealing Regulation (EU) No 439/2010.* Brussels.

EU Council. (2009). Directive 2009/50/EC, of 25 May 2009, on the conditions of entry and residence of third-country nationals for the purposes of highly qualified employment. (s.f.). Brussels.

EU Council. (2022). *Council implementing Decision (EU) 2022/382, of 4 March 2022, establishing the existence of a mass influx of displaced persons from Ukraine within the meaning of Article 5 of Directive 2001/55/EC, and having the effect of introducing temporary protection.* Brussels.

European Commission. (2020a). *Commission recommendation on legal pathways to protection in the EU: Promoting resettlement, humanitarian admission and other complementary pathways, C(2020)6467.* Brussels. Recuperado el 31 de 03 de 2022.

European Commission. (2020b). *Proposal for a regulation addressing situations of crisis and force majeure in the field of migration and asylum, COM(2020) 613, 23 September 2020.* Brussels.

European Commission. (2021a). *Communication from the Commission to the European Parliament, the Council, the European Economic and Social Committee and the Committee of the Regions, on the Report on Migration and Asylum, COM(2021) 590 final, Brussels, 29 September 2021.* Brussels.

European Commision. (2021b). *Communication from the Commission to the European Parliament, the Council, the European Economic and Social Committee and the Committee of the Regions, A renewed EU action plan against migrant smuggling (2021–2025), COM (2021) 591 final, Brussels, 29.9.20.* European Commision, Brussels.

European Commission. (2022a). *Communication from the Commission to the European Parliament, the Council, the European Economic and Social Committee and the Committee of the Regions, Attracting skills and talent to the EU, COM(2022) 657 final, Brussels, 27 April 2022.* Brussels.

European Commission. (2022b). *Proposal for a Directive of the European Parliament and of the Council, concerning the status of third-country nationals who are long-term residents (recast), COM(2022) 650 final, Brussels, 27 April 2022.* Brussels.

European Commission. (2022). *Proposal for a Directive of the European Parliament and of the Council, on a single application procedure for a single permit for third-country nationals to reside and work in the territory of a Member State and on a common set of rights for third-country.* Brussels.

European Council. (2001). *Council Directive 2001/55/EC of 20 July 2001 on minimum standards for giving temporary protection in the event of a mass influx of displaced persons and on measures promoting a balance of efforts between Member States, 8 July 2001.* Europen Council.

Gan Galavís, N. (2022). *Abordaje de la crisis migratoria venezolana bajo una perspectiva de seguridad humana: Acciones centradas en las personas para orientar respuestas más allá de la restricción,* en Capriles, V. (Coord.), *Refugiados y migrantes venezola.* Caracas.

Inter-American Commission on Human Rights, IACHR, Resolution 2/18, Forced Migration of Venezuelans, 2018. Available at: https://www.oas.org/en/iachr/decisions/pdf/Resolution-2-18-en.pdf. (2018).

International Organization of Migration [IOM]. (2017). *Facilitation of safe, regular and orderly migration. Global compact, thematic paper.* Geneva. Recuperado el 31 de 03 de 2022, de www.iom.int/sites/default/files/our_work/ODG/GCM/IOM-Thematic-Paper-Facilitation-of-Safe-Orderly-and-Regu lar-Migration.pdf.

IOM. (2011). *Glossary on migration,* 2nd ed. Geneva. Recuperado el 31 de 03 de 2022, de www.iom.int/key-migration-terms.

IOM. (2018). *Migration and the 2030 agenda, a guide for practitioners.* Geneva.

Migration Network Hub. (18 de 03 de 2021). Recuperado el 31 de 03 de 2022, de https://migrationnetwork.un.org/hub.

Morgades, S. (2022). El Pacto Mundial sobre los Refugiados y el nuevo Pacto de la Unión Europea sobre Migración y Asilo: Derecho Informal y Jurisprudencia Europea en materia de acceso a la protección. *Revista Españala de Derecho Internacional*, 28.

Slovenian Presidency Statement on the situation at the external borders with Belarus. (2021). *Declaration of 30 July 2021 by the high representative on behalf of the European Union on the instrumentalisation of migrants and refugees by the regime of Belarus.* Recuperado el 31 de 03 de 2022, de https://www.consilium.europa.eu/en/press/press-releases/2021/07/30/belarus-declaration-of-the-high-representative-on-behalf-of-the-eu-on-the-instrumentalisation-of-migrants-and-refugees-by-the-regime/.

UN, General Assembly. (2013). *Declaration of the high-level dialogue on international migration, draft resolution submitted by the President of the General Assembly, A/68/L.5.* United Nations, Globalization and interdependence: International migration, New York. Recuperado el 31 de 03 de 2022, de file:///F:/EU-LAC-project/Book/Declaration%20of%20the%20High-level%20Dialogue%20on%20International%20Migration.pdf

UN, General Assembly. (2015). *Transforming our word: The 2030 agenda for sustainable development.* Obtenido de http://www.sela.org/media/2262361/agenda-2030-y-los-objetivos-de-desarrollo-sostenible.pdf.

UN, General Assembly. (2018). *Global compact for safe, orderly and regular migration [GCM].* Recuperado el 31 de 3 de 2022, de http://undocs.org/es/A/CONF.23/231/3.

UN, General Assembly, A/73/12 (Part II). (2018). Global compact on refugees.

UN, General Assembly. (2022). Progress declaration of the international migration review forum, resolution adopted by the General Assembly on 7 June 2022, A/RES/76/266, 14 June 2022.

UN, Secretary-General. (2021). *Global compact for safe, orderly and regular migration, A/76/642, 27 December 2021.* New York. Recuperado el 31 de 03 de 2022, de file:///F:/EU-LAC-project/Book/Report%20of%20the%20Secretary-General_2021.pdf.

UNHCR, Operational Data Portal, 2022, Situation Ukraine Refugee (unhcr.org). (s.f.).

UNICEF. (2019). *Regional refugee and migrant response plan, for refugees and migrants from Venezuela.* Obtenido de https://reporting.unhcr.org/sites/default/files/2019%20RMRP%20Venezuela%20%28December%202018%29.pdf.

United Nations Network on Migration. (31 de 03 de 2022). Obtenido de https://migrationnetwork.un.org/.

United States-Mexico-Canada Agreement (USMCA). (July de 2020). Recuperado el 31 de 03 de 2022, de https://www.trade.gov/usmca.

Beatriz Larraín Martinez

Europe in Chile: Its Influence on the New Constitutional Design

This chapter examines the role and influence that Europe played in the recently concluded constitutional process in Chile. To achieve this, it provides a brief background of historical information. Subsequently it explores different forms in which Europe influenced the constitutional process: (a) academic publications and expert opinions; (b) EU political cooperation through seminars, visits, and documents; (c) proposals presented to the Constitutional Convention. The study does not focus on whether these proposals or ideas made it into the final draft of the Constitution, as that would require a different, more extensive study. Instead, the emphasis is on Europe's role and participation in the constitutional reform process in Chile.

Background

In October 2019, Chile experienced an "estallido social", or "social outburst", a massive wave of social protests that occurred throughout the country (Contardo, 2020; De la Fuente, 2020; Jiménez-Yañez, 2021; Rivera-Aguilera et.al, 2021). People filled the streets to protest against the political and economic model that Chile had maintained during the last 30 years because it had caused grave inequalities and had only favoured the economic and political ruling class. The marching and protesting all over Chile paralysed the country for several weeks, causing unrest and fear among the citizenry and the government. Police forces were sent into the streets, resulting in violations to human rights, further fueling the rage of protesters (Guala, 2020).

Almost a month into the protests, political forces in Congress pushed for a solution and passed a law to create a new Constitution, which would replace the Constitution in force (Constitution of 1980). They claimed that at the root of the inequality lay the economic and political model installed by the Constitution of 1980, Pinochet's illegitimate Constitution. Despite the fact that Pinochet´s government had actually held a plebiscite for the citizens to vote the Constitution in 1980, it was a fraudulent plebiscite. The official information stated that the new Constitution had been approved by 67.04% of the voters, information which few people believed. Thus, the Constitution was considered "illegitimate". Some have even called this plebiscite the biggest fraud in Chilean history (Fuentes, 2013).

Changing the Constitution seemed to be the way to permanently resolve the political and social unrest and to avoid the fall of President Sebastián Piñera's government (Peña, 2020). On 11 November 2019, major political forces in Congress agreed that a new Constitution would be promulgated, and a plebiscite was envisioned as the way for Chileans to decide if they wanted a new Constitution and the mechanism by which the new Constitution would be drafted. In 2020, amid the pandemic, Chileans went to the polls and elected an organ called the "Constitutional Convention" which would be in charge of writing the new Constitution. They also elected the members of this organ, the "Conventionals". In July 2021, the Constitutional Convention began to draft the new Constitution.

Latin American Constitutions in general, and Chilean Constitutions in particular, are not new to European influence (Jimenez, 2021; Campos, 2022). It is worth noting that the Chilean legal system is built and modelled on the European system, which the Spaniards brought to Latin America in the 1500s (Sánchez, 2001; Dougnac, 1998). During the 1800s, Latin America was influenced by the Codification movement which swept across Europe and made its way to the region's legal system (Tomas y Valiente, 2001). As Gargarella (2015) points out, Latin American Constitutions are not a "mess" of different texts, but rather a coherent set which has moved along uniform avenues guided by our common early history (Narváez, 2016; Valdés, 2016).

Furthermore, the global North's influence on legal and political issues in Latin America has not been restricted to European countries. US influence on Latin American legal structures had grown during the 1980s, the 1990s and early 2000s (Esquirol, 2011), either through direct economic assistance or through indirect actions such as congressional or scholarly exchange programs to promote legal and constitutional change in the region. However, American influence over Latin America seems to be diminishing somewhat, as China and Russia seek to increase their influence (Roy, 2022; MacCammon, 2022). In this context, it is interesting to note that Europe remains a major legal-political actor in Latin America, as this chapter will show (Borrell, 2020).

The Chilean Convention had many peculiarities, such as an equal number of men and women as Conventionals and reserved seats for indigenous representatives. This made for a very interesting process which not only Europeans observed, but people from many other countries as well.[1]

1 Many foreign and national film makers are preparing documentary films of the process.

On 4 September 2022, a plebiscite was held and the draft Constitution was rejected by the majority of Chileans (62%). However, the process has not ended. Political actors in Chile have devised another constitutional reform mechanism that should lead to the approval of the new Constitution by the end of 2023. The new process will surely take into account many of the ideas that were incorporated into the draft that is the subject of this chapter.

European role in and impact on the Convention

This section is divided into three parts: (a) academic publications and expert opinions; (b) EU political cooperation through seminars, visits, statements, etc.; (c) proposals presented at the Constitutional Convention.

Academic publications and expert opinions

This section examines some of the academic publications that have been produced as support and input to be used by Conventionals in drafting the new Constitution. Likewise, expert opinions given to the press and at the Convention itself, by both foreign and national experts in Constitutional law, government and democracy, will be examined. It is worth noting that these are not the only academic publications or expert opinions, but rather a sample.

A first example is the book "Fundamental Concepts for the Constitutional Debate", published by the Pontifical Catholic University of Chile (Soto & Hube, 2021). When reading through the pages, one finds that most of the articles begin by tracing the origins of the Constitutional institutions as European. For example, Fermandois, when writing about "Constitutional Supremacy", devotes many paragraphs to describing its European origins and workings (Fermandois, 2021). Peña does the same in writing about "Judicial Revision of the Constitutionality of Laws" (Peña, 2021), as does Concha when he writes about "Sovereignty" (Concha, 2021). Soto, writing about the Governmental Regime, states that despite the fact that Chile has always had a Presidential system (typical of the American continent), it would be better off having a semi-presidential system as some European countries do (Soto, 2021).

Likewise, many other articles point to different constitutional organs which have been a part of the Chilean institutional framework for quite a while and

https://www.emol.com/noticias/Nacional/2022/01/01/1042730/equipos-internacionales-alistan-documentales.html.

under different constitutions, such as those contained in the Constitution of 1980, *all implying* that it would be wise and convenient to keep such constitutional settings. Frontaura (2021), for example, states that the Constitution of 1980 had already successfully incorporated the classic concepts of post-second World War constitutionalism. He especially points out the Constitutional actions destined to protect fundamental rights, as well as the Constitutional Court, as special examples of what needs to remain in the new Constitution.

Another interesting publication in which European ideas are used and defended was edited by the Chilean Senate (Senado de Chile, 2021) called "Constitutional Reflections: Contributions for the new Constitution", which compiles a series of talks and conferences given by national experts in Constitutional matters.

As the previous text, this one is also filled with references to European experiences, all deemed positive. For example, Ponce de León (2021), writing about gender equality, cites the case of France, whose Constitution explicitly contemplates the guarantee of equal access, not only to public but also to private positions and employment. García (2021), writing about the Constitutional Court defends the existence of a Constitutional Court, arguing that it has been an important organ in Europe, especially in the preservation of democracy and Constitutional supremacy, relying on European constitutional doctrine and experience. Zuñiga (2021) argues that the new Constitution should contemplate a Regional form of state, a typically European form, despite the fact that Chile has been a unitary state since its independence.

The Chilean Public Study Center (CEP), a well-known think tank, published a book called *Propuestas Constitucionales: La academia y el cambio constitucional en Chile* (Sierra, 2019). This one also contains many references to successful European ideas that should be included in the new Constitution, according to many of the authors. For example, Gajardo (2019), in writing about Constitutional rights, cites the German, Spanish, Portuguese and Italian Constitutions as effective texts that defend citizens' rights. Gomez (2019), writing about the political system and contemplating the possibility of adopting a parliamentary system in Chile, suggests the new Constitution should adopt a model such as the English, Spanish or German model.

Besides the books examined, experts and professors poured out their expertise not only through formal academic publications but also through the press. Journalists actively sought out both Chilean and European experts for interviews and opinions. Many of these interviews reflect the influence and defense of European Constitutional ideas. For example, regarding the success of the European

Central Banks, two Chilean experts argue through the press in favour and against different types of European models for the new Chilean Constitution.[2]

Roberto Viciano, a Spanish expert in Constitutional processes, professor of the University of Valencia assisted a special event hosted by the Chilean Constitutional Court.[3] He expressly advocated for changes in the administration of the Chilean judicial system, so that a separate organ should be created to administer the Judiciary, taking this power away from the Chilean Supreme Court. This system exists, says Professor Viciano, in countries like Spain, Italy and France, where it has worked very well.[4]

The Conventionals themselves also sought out the press to express their opinions on these matters. For example, Conventional Cozzi said in an interview that renaming the Judiciary, as the Convention proposed, was a mistake. In effect, changing the name to "Justice Systems" was wrong, and the new Constitution should keep the name "Judicial Power" as Germany, Spain and other countries name their Judiciary.[5]

Many more interviews were published. For example, regarding the Chilean Constitutional Court, a group of professors and experts[6] defended the Constitutional Court model and gave background information regarding how the idea of a Constitutional Court was born in Europe and how they currently work in different European countries. The main conclusion was the need to have Constitutional Courts to protect democracy.

The EU and political cooperation with the Constitutional Convention

Another important situation to analyse is the direct collaboration of the EU and its public organs with Chile and the Constitutional Convention.

---

2 https://www.ciperchile.cl/2021/01/25/el-futuro-del-banco-central-en-la-convencion-constitucional/ In Contrast, see https://www.ciperchile.cl/2021/01/25/el-futuro-del-banco-central-en-la-convencion-constitucional/, who argues that European central banks handled the 2008 economic crisis poorly.

3 See https://www.latercera.com/politica/noticia/academica-y-transversal-la-apuesta-del-tc-para-incidir-en-la-convencion-y-defender-una-justicia-constitucional-especializada/BYMJSK2XOVFDJL2YHXFSJ37PY4/

4 https://app.vlex.com/#vid/poder-judicial-debe-controlado-881617546

5 See the interview https://www.latercera.com/la-tercera-pm/noticia/constituyente-ruggero-cozzi-y-cambios-al-poder-judicial-daza-y-gutierrez-tienen-propuestas-irresponsables-que-favorecen-a-los-poderosos/FAEEQG4B2VF6BIJMPCSJFKXHG4/

6 https://www.pauta.cl/factchecking/constitucheck/reformas-tribunal-constitucional-nueva-constitucion-watchdog-pauta

A particular initiative, the "Chile-EU Forum" organised all kinds of activities, seminars and webinars in order to "support" and lend cooperation to Chile in the Constitutional process. The Delegation of the EU in Chile hosted a series of webinars in coordination with other European institutions such as FIAPP,[7] a Spanish foundation, the EUROsociAL Program, AGCID,[8] a Chilean public organism which coordinates foreign cooperation, among others. The EU Delegation in Chile even set up a special part of its web page with information referring to the Chilean Constitutional process.[9]

One of the webinars held was called "Dialogues: Chile-European Union".[10] They were organised to serve as a basis for sharing ideas regarding the Constitutional process and basic content such as social cohesion, access to a welfare system and guarantees of individual rights, among others. FIAPP's web page[11] states that the Chilean process is one of the most innovative of modern times with the incorporation of representatives of indigenous peoples and gender parity, among other features.

In inaugurating the webinars, Josep Borrell said that the EU and Chile are partners, and they share fundamental values such as democracy, respect for the rule of law, and respect for human rights. All political social and economic groups have asked to have access to European constitutional experiences, he stated, and therefore these webinars will provide a space for dialogue.[12]

The seminars were later compiled in book form, "Ciclo de Dialogos Chile-Unión Europea".[13] The introduction of the book expresses that Chile and Europe

---

7 Fundación Internacional y para Iberoamérica de Administración y Políticas Públicas, a Spanish foundation which cooperates with South American governments in the implementation and funding of public policies, https://www.fiiapp.org/noticias/la-union-europea-acompana-chile-proceso-constituyente/. Accessed February 2022.

8 https://www.agci.cl/. Regarding information on the webinars see https://www.agci.cl/sala-de-prensa/2127-chile-y-la-union-europea-reflexionan-sobre-los-modelos-de-bienestar-social-y-la-constitucionalizacion-de-los-derechos-sociales

9 https://www.eeas.europa.eu/delegations/chile/ue-chile-proceso-constituyente_en

10 Access to the webinars online at https://eurosocial.eu/seminarios-web/dialogos-chile-union-europea-lanzamiento-de-la-serie-de-webinarios/

11 https://www.fiiapp.org/noticias/la-union-europea-acompana-chile-proceso-consti tuyente/.

12 https://www.fiiapp.org/noticias/la-union-europea-acompana-chile-proceso-constituye nte/. Accessed April 2022.

13 Available online at https://eurosocial.eu/wp-content/uploads/2021/09/CICLO-DE-DIALOGOS-CHILE-UE-todo_compressed.pdf

share common core values such as democracy, freedom, and the rule of law. Chile has been, therefore, one of the EU´s main Latin American partners. It goes on to say that every nation must find its own way, but they must all maintain certain common characteristics such as having a social democratic state, based on strong democratic institutions, a respect for minorities, and a market economy with relevant state participation as the guardian of social justice. "We hope that the experiences of the member states and of the EU´s institutions (…) may be a valuable element to the Chilean public debate", it concludes.

Another series of talks or webinars "Counterpoints Chile-European Union for the Constitutional Process", was organised by the EU and Chilean universities.[14] Again, they were conferences where experts talked about comparative European experiences and the lessons Chile can learn. In one of such seminars, an Italian expert stated that the Chilean constitutional process will be a good opportunity to "try out" new instruments that allow citizens to participate directly in politics as a way of dealing with low levels of trust in governments and politicians.[15]

In November of 2020, another conference, "New Constitution and New Public Policy", was held. It was hosted and organised by Casa America de España[16] (a Spanish public entity) and CED[17] (a Chilean NGO). It was inaugurated by Roberto Ampuero, the Chilean Ambassador to Spain and the Spanish Ambassador to Chile, Enrique Ojeda Vila.[18]

The Convention itself has invited many European experts to talk about Constitutional issues. One of these experts was Boaventura de Sousa Santos, director

---

14 See for example of one of these conferences regarding the Constitutional right to housing https://www.elmostrador.cl/dia/2021/08/18/debate-constituyente-expertas-analizaron-dos-ejemplos-de-derecho-a-la-vivienda-en-paises-de-la-union-europea/dignified. Many of these talks may be seen on YouTube at: https://www.youtube.com/watch?v=C7U37c7vcHA

15 See https://www.elmostrador.cl/nueva-constitucion/2021/06/16/expertos-europeos-ante-el-proceso-constituyente-el-caso-chileno-puede-ser-una-oportunidad-para-experimentar-nuevos-instrumentos-de-participacion-directa/

16 Casa de América is a Spanish public consortium formed by the Ministry of Foreign Affairs, the Community of Madrid, and Madrid City Hall, which seeks to strengthen ties between Spain and the American Continent, especially Latin America and the Caribbean. https://www.casamerica.es/

17 CED is a Chilean NGO. Its objective is to propose public actions with the objective of promoting a development process with political, economical and environmental sustainability. https://www.ced.cl/cedcl/nosotros/#quienes.

18 The conference may be seen online at http://www.ced.cl/cedcl/2020/11/13/mesa-redonda-nueva-constitucion-politica-publica/

of the Center for Social Studies of the University of Coimbra in Portugal.[19] He spoke of installing legal pluralism in the new Chilean Constitution, as his thesis is that the Global South has an imposed patriarchal culture, and the states follow a colonialist model which has undermined ancestral cultures that had their own way of solving conflicts. This is wrong, he concludes, and the state should contemplate the possibility of having different legal systems (De Sousa, 2014).

In September of 2021, a delegation of Members of the European Parliament arrived in Chile, in order to get to know firsthand the Chilean constitutional process which "has surprised many Europeans", as they stated upon arrival, and to offer their help in facilitating the process and serving as a link between Chilean and European MPs in topics of mutual interest, such as gender equality, decentralization, social security, etc. The press stated that the group of European MPs would meet with indigenous organizations, and human rights organizations among others. They were received by president Sebastian Piñera, the Chilean secretary of foreign affairs, and by several members of the Chilean congress.[20] The group of MPs said to the press they were even more impressed with the Chilean constitutional process, after meeting with the President and Vice President of the Convention.[21]

The Head of the European delegation, Inmaculada Rodríguez-Piñeiro, said they were very pleased with the fact that a woman was president of the convention and especially a Mapuche (the Chilean native population) woman, as well as the fact that there was an equal number of men and women in the Constitutional Convention.

However, not everyone was happy with the delegation's visit. A group of Convention members signed a declaration stating that Europeans were trying to interfere with the constitutional process and put pressure on the government, as one of the objectives of the delegation was to talk to Chilean authorities regarding the modernization of the Association Agreement between the EU and Chile. The president of the delegation said she was surprised by these statements as they were in no way trying to interfere and merely wanted to observe and

19 See https://www.pauta.cl/nacional/boaventura-de-sousa-santos-pluralismo-juridico-convencion-constitucional?utm_mc=e209d516f7794b74aa804ebaef4d546b

20 See https://www.elmostrador.cl/dia/2021/09/21/grupo-de-eurodiputados-se-reunira-con-la-mesa-de-la-convencion-constitucional-quieren-conocer-avances-en-el-trabajo-y-realizar-intercambios-estrategicos/

21 https://www.biobiochile.cl/especial/una-constitucion-para-chile/noticias/2021/09/22/diputados-de-la-union-europea-elogiaron-proceso-constituyente-chileno-es-un-ejemplo-para-el-mundo.shtml

accompany the Chilean constitutional process. Hoppe, one of the Conventionals who signed the declaration, said it was not prudent for the government to host a delegation from a continent whose companies have exploited Chilean national resources, damaging the land's inhabitants, especially in the middle of a Constitutional reform process.

A month later, 36 members of the European Parliament asked that the EU not update the Association Agreement between Chile and the EU, as negotiators were getting ready to seal the agreement in November, in the middle of the presidential campaign, and while the Convention was still at work. The Convention, they argued, will change the Constitution on crucial topics such as natural resources, energy, protection of investments, agriculture, etc. Therefore, negotiations should stop for now until Chile's new Constitution comes to light, as there may be relevant changes that put the EU's interests at risk, they argued.[22] Despite these negative opinions, negotiations moved forward and the political conclusion between the parties was announced on 9 December 2022, with the publication of the Trade and Investment pillar of the EU-Chile Advanced Framework Agreement.[23]

Spain has been particularly involved in the process. In May of 2021, the Spanish government declared that it wished to support the work of the Convention by sharing its own constitutional experience, given the values that Chile and Spain share, as brother countries.[24]

In January 2022, Elisa Loncón, president of the Constitutional Convention, received from the Basque Government of Spain the René Cassin Prize for her commitment to Human Rights in Chile. In receiving the prize, she not only thanked the Basque government but also the "Instituto de Derechos Humanos, Democracia, Cultura de Paz y no Violencia (DEMOSPAZ)" of the Autonomous University of Madrid, as well as other organizations such as WILPF-España,[25] for the important role they have played in the Chilean constitutional process.

22 https://radio.uchile.cl/2021/10/13/36-eurodiputados-piden-a-la-union-europea-que-no-se-actualice-tlc-con-chile-mientras-no-termine-el-proceso-constituyente/

23 https://policy.trade.ec.europa.eu/eu-trade-relationships-country-and-region/countries-and-regions/chile/eu-chile-agreement/text-agreement_en

24 https://www.europapress.es/nacional/noticia-espana-ofrece-compartir-experiencia-proceso-constitucional-abre-chile-20210517113514.html

25 https://www.elmostrador.cl/dia/2022/01/20/discurso-de-elisa-loncon-al-recibir-premio-en-espana-con-el-proceso-de-la-convencion-constitucional-hoy-chile-vive-una-nueva-historia/

In April 2021, Iñigo Errejón, a well-known Spanish politician, co-founder of "Podemos", and a referent for Gabriel Boric's[26] political sector, sent a message to the Convention. He said that the new Constitution cannot be a "leftist" Constitution. It must be a Constitution for everyone, even for the "enemies" of the process. If not, it will only last as long as the Leftist government lasts. Agreements must be reached which suit all political sectors.[27]

The involvement of Spain is not particularly striking, as there are many reasons for Chile and Spain to have close political ties. Naturally, as ex-Spanish colonies, all Latin American countries have at least a mixed indigenous and Spanish culture. Further, most people in Chile do not speak a foreign language. Naturally, proposals presented in Spanish would be the most readily understandable. The idea that Chilean politics mimics and is heavily influenced by Spanish politics, is part of political and popular culture, and it has been so for many decades.[28] Therefore, Spanish influence in this process appears as an almost natural occurrence.

Maybe the most important contribution of a European institution is that of the Venice Commission. Originally created by the state members of the Council of Europe in order to help the countries of Eastern Europe in creating Constitutions after the fall of the Berlin wall, nowadays the Commission is a consultant organ. It has more than 60 members (Chile is a member) and helps countries who are modifying their Constitutions, making recommendations and answering questions the countries set forward.

In January of 2022, a group of Chilean Congressmen and women posed several questions for the Commission to answer. In the first place, questions regarding how the 2/3 majority should be interpreted. In second place, a series of questions regarding the general process such as how can a neutral and stable standard be reached by the commission in order to avoid the risk of a simply contingent and unstable Constitution. They further asked for the Commission's opinion regarding the possibility of eliminating the Senate and leaving only one

26 The current president of Chile.

27 See https://www.latercera.com/la-tercera-domingo/noticia/la-advertencia-de-errejon-al-fa-por-el-proceso-constituyente-no-puede-ser-la-constitucion-de-las-izquierdas/FZWJEAK23VC4VAKDIQGXQ6BGD4/

28 See among other opinions in the press made by politicians and social actors regarding this link between Spanish and Chilean politics: https://www.pauta.cl/internacional/elecciones-madrid-diaz-ayuso-lecciones-chile; https://radio.uchile.cl/2018/06/04/chile-y-espana/; https://www.latercera.com/politica/noticia/la-mirada-los-partidos-chilenos-puesta-espana/633342/.

chamber of Congress, this being a particularly controversial topic given the fact that our country has always had a bicameral Congress. Further, they asked whether it would be correct to eliminate the Constitutional Court, and what the Commission thought about the Court's a priori control of legislation, whether it is proper of democratic regimes or not.

The Commission responded in a document dated March 22 of 2022, stating that "The Commission aims to provide a concrete contribution to the successful work of the Constitutional Convention of Chile, by providing information on international standards and on comparative experience of other modern democracies with a view to helping the Constitutional Convention make its choices in the most informed manner." It answered the questions taking into account diverse constitutional experiences from around the globe, and especially from Europe.

The Commission´s answer was widely publicised in the media. It was both defended and attacked, in the political and academic world, as well as by the Conventionals themselves.

Proposals presented to the Constitutional Convention

In July of 2021, the Convention began its work. Thematic commissions were set up in order to treat the central constitutional topics.[29]

Of all of these commissions, we chose to examine three of them: Number 1: "Political System, Government, Legislature and Elections", Number 3: "Form of State, Order, Autonomy, Decentralization, Fairness, Territorial Justice, Local Governments and Fiscal Organization", and Number 6: "Justice System, Autonomous Control Organisms and Constitutional Reform" in order to determine the way in which European institutions and ideas have become a part of these Commissions' proposals. We chose these topics, as we believe they represented the basic forms that Chile would acquire if the draft was approved in the plebiscite.

Commission 1: "Political System, Government, Legislature and Elections"

---

29 These commissions are: (1) Political System, Government, Legislature and Elections; (2) Constitutional Principles, Democracy, Nationality and Citizenship; (3) Form of State, Order, Autonomy, Decentralization, Fairness, Territorial Justice, Local Governments and Fiscal Organization; (4) Fundamental Rights; (5) Environment, Nature's Rights, Common Natural Goods, and Economic Models; (6) Justice System, Autonomous Control Organisms and Constitutional Reform; (7) Knowledge Based Systems, Cultures, Science, Technology and Historical Patrimony; (8) Popular Participation; (9) Indigenous Peoples' Rights and (10) Common Links.

We examined the main proposals this Commission worked on and found that many were influenced by European ideas.[30]

- Establishing limits to public authorities' salaries: The proposal states that Chilean authorities, especially members of Congress, receive more than twenty times the average Chilean salary and it is therefore necessary to establish a limit to this income. The proposal says it was explicitly influenced by the Swedish system, in which members of Congress receive "normal" salaries, much closer to an average Swedish worker's salary. The document also states it was inspired by the French, Greek, Portuguese, Austrian, and UK system which set limits to Congressmen's salaries.[31]
- Establishing legal duties of the state and rights of the presidency with regards to the Armed and Internal Order Forces: This proposal seeks to give the Armed Forces constitutional stature and by doing so introduces an article with regards to terrorism, inspired by the Spanish and German Constitution that refer explicitly to terrorism, noting that not all Constitutions do.[32]
- Use of the Mixed Member Proportional System: The new Legislative Organ proposed would be elected under the Mixed Member system, which was born in Germany and has spread successfully throughout Europe. This has been one of the most controversial proposals, as it eliminates the Senate from the political system.[33]
- Regarding a pluri-national Congress: Proposes the creation of a Legislative Commission based on the UK and Wales model. It is a technical organ, which would not only aid the creation of laws, but would assist in the general functioning of the legal system in order to propose necessary changes.[34]

Commission 3: "Form of State, Order, Autonomy, Decentralization, Fairness, Territorial Justice, Local Governments and Fiscal Organization"

- Regional State: Many proposals saw this as the ideal form of state for Chile, a system created in Europe. One proposal cites the definition of the region given by the Council of Europe in 1978 directly, as well as extensive European

30 The proposals hereinafter referred to may all be found on the Constitutional Convention's website: www.chileconvencion.cl under the corresponding commission.
31 Proposal 167-1c.
32 Proposal 174-1c.
33 Proposal 213-1c.
34 Proposal 234-1.

literature on the regional state.[35] Another document cites the Portuguese Constitution as an ideal example of the regional system.[36] A third document cites the first decentralization law of France (1983), which was later incorporated into the French Constitution (2003), by virtue of which the regions cease to be controlled by the central state.[37] Another proposal cites the French and Italian constitution in order to justify and explain the independence that the autonomous regions have vis a vis the central state.[38]

- In effect, the Regional form of state was approved by the Convention and made it to the final draft of the Constitution. Not everyone agrees, however, that this is right for Chile. Many believe this system has worked well in Europe but that for many reasons (cultural, economic, etc.) will not work in Chile.[39]
- New fiscal principles to be incorporated into the Constitution: This proposal cites the case of Croatia, Portugal and Spain, who have incorporated these principles into the Constitution.[40]
- Concerning local governments: Spain and Germany establish municipalities as local governments with broad powers in their Constitutions.[41] The French Constitution of 1958 is also cited as establishing legal principles that ensure an effective decentralization process giving ample powers to local governments.[42]
- "Special zones": These are geographical areas qualified as special zones, such as Easter Island, and Antarctica, among others. The proposal cites the case of the Spanish cities Ceuta and Melilla which have a special statute and the case of French overseas territories in America and Oceania. The reason for this qualification would be the need for these territories to have certain autonomy while maintaining their link to the central government.[43]
- The creation of a special system of fundamental rights for Chileans overseas and the establishment of the "overseas region": The proposal refers to French Constitution which has contemplated this for years. The Vatican, which has

35 Proposal 91-3.
36 Proposal 99-3.
37 Proposal 157-3.
38 Proposal 197-3-c.
39 See Zarco Luksic's opinion https://www.latercera.com/reconstitucion/noticia/columna-de-zarko-luksic-la-copia-ilusoria-del-estado-regional/T4DDHLNR3ND5JKV6OX5O5JEHQM/
40 Proposal 200-3.
41 Proposal 329-3.
42 Proposal 384-3.
43 Proposal 341-3.

very little territory and whose main authorities do not reside in the Vatican State, also has a system for Vatican nationals to participate legally in its administration.

Commission number 6: "Justice System, Autonomous Control Organisms and Constitutional Reform"

- The citizen's defenders or Ombudsman: The ombudsman is proposed by many Conventionals. One of these proposals states that its historical roots lye in the Swedish institution. It also cites the Spanish and French Constitution, both of which have a citizen's defense council.[44] Another proposes the creation of a similar institution, citing the case of Germany, UK, France, Italy, Portugal, Spain, Ireland, Netherlands, also pointing out that the Swedish have had this institution for many years, and was born as a way to limit monarchic power.[45]
- The Judicial Council: Other proposals seek to establish a Judicial Council, which would be in charge of naming judges to the bench, imposing sanctions in case of judicial misconduct, and the general administration of the judiciary. The proposals point out the fact that most European countries already have such a council, with more than positive results.[46] Another proposal cites the case of France which has had a Judicial Council since 1883, and the exemplary case of the Italian Judicial Council which has shielded judges from external influence during dictatorships and the World War II.[47]
- A complete overhaul of the current judicial system: This proposal points to the current judicial systems that the Italian, Portuguese and Spanish Constitutions contemplate as models both in form and in substance.[48]
- Rules for the Chilean Central Bank: one proposal states that in Europe the existence of the Central Bank is contained in the EU Treaties, regardless of what the national Constitutions contemplate[49] and that mostly all new European constitutions contemplate a Central Bank for their countries.[50]
- The Constitutional Court: In talking about the importance of having a separate entity which controls the constitutionality of the law, and rejecting the claims of those who say that the Constitutional Court should be eliminated

---

44 Proposal 25-6.
45 Proposal 77-6.
46 Proposals 88-6, 98-6, 198-6, 466-6, among others.
47 Proposal 95-6.
48 Proposal 90-6.
49 Proposal 172-6-c.
50 Proposal 349-6.

from the Chilean Constitution, various proposals state that almost all European and even Latin American countries have a Constitutional Court.[51]

- Referendum as the way to approve a Constitutional reform: The proposals all cite the case of the Irish, French, and Swiss Constitutions, which contemplate mandatory referendums in case of Constitutional reform.[52]
- Neighbourhood justice: This proposal cites the case of Spain which has alternate resolution systems to solve small claims, adding that mediation has been highly recommended by the Committee of Ministers of the Council of Europe in different instruments, since 1998. Furthermore, most European countries have laws that regulate mediation.[53]
- Special feminist courts: To judge cases of violence against women, among other issues. The proposal cites the UK and Spain has having especially effective courts that pursue these cases.[54]

Conclusions

There are many European ideas and much European influence on the Constitutional framework that the Convention worked on. This is not strange, as Latin America began its independent republican life by "importing" ideas from Europe.

There seems to be a great deal of concern on behalf of Europeans about Chile following their main "core values" or travel the same roads that Europeans have travelled. It is interesting to note that it is not just Europeans who are looking to "impose" a certain political avenue, but Chileans themselves believe that European constitutionalism is the best model for the country. Spain seems to be the country that has most significantly intervened and influenced the process due to cultural, language and historical commonalities that bind Spain and Chile in many ways. This concern may be fueled not only by politics but also by commercial interests, especially given what occurred with the EU-Chile Association Agreement.

In thinking about the central idea of the book regarding the reconfiguration of the presence of Europe in Latin America, it seems fair to say that at least in the Chilean Constitutional realm, Europe has maintained and strengthened

51 Proposals 184-6-c, and 325-6.

52 Proposals 198-6-c, 223-6, 425-6 and 467-6.

53 Proposal 233-6.

54 Proposal 324-6.

the fundamental presence it has always had. All the direct and indirect ways in which European ideas have tried to influence the Constitutional draft are remarkable. Similarly, it shows the way in which the Chilean legal community continues to view Europe as an important (if not *the* most important) model for political and legal action. This is very important to consider, especially when many have stated that the influence of the US over Latin America has dwindled. As China and Russia are looking to expand their influence in Latin America, Europe continues to be a constitutional guiding light with which we still seek to illuminate our path.

Bibliography

Borrell, Josep. "Latin America-Europe: The 'other' transatlantic relationship". *European External Action webpage*. Available at: https://www.eeas.europa.eu/eeas/latin-america-europe-%E2%80%98other%E2%80%99-transatlantic-relationship_en

Campos Harriet, Fernando. *Historia Constitucional de Chile*. Santiago: Editorial Jurídica, Edición 2022.

CEP (editores). *Propuestas Constitucionales: La Academia y el Cambio Constitucional en Chile*. Santiago: Centro de Estudios Públicos, 2019.

Concha, Jorge. "Soberanía". In Soto, Sebastian and Hube, Constanza (coordinators). *Conceptos Fundamentales para el Debate Constitucional*. Santiago: Pontificia Universidad Católica de Chile, 2021, p. 38.

Contardo, Oscar. *Antes de que fuera octubre*. Santiago: Editorial Planeta, 2020.

De La Fuente, Gloria. *El pueblo en movimiento: del malestar al estallido*. Santiago: Catalonia, 2020.

De Sousa Santos, Boaventura. *Epistemologies of the South justice against epistemicide*. Abingdon: Routledge, 2014.

Dougnac, Antonio. *Manual de Historia del Derecho Indiano*. México: McGraw-Hill, 1998.

Esquirol, Jorge. "The turn to legal interpretation in Latin America." *American University International Law Review* 26, n° 4, 2011, p. 1031.

EUROsociAL+ (editors). "Ciclo de Diálogos Chile-UE: Compartiendo Experiencias sobre Procesos y Contenidos Constitucionales", 2021, disponible online https://eurosocial.eu/wp-content/uploads/2021/09/CICLO-DE-DIALOGOS-CHILE-UE-todo_compressed.pdf

Fermandois, Arturo. "Supremacía Constitucional". In Soto, Sebastian and Hube, Con stanza (coordinators), *Conceptos Fundamentales para el Debate Constitucional*. Santiago: Pontificia Universidad Católica de Chile, 2021, p. 23.

Frontaura, Carlos. "La Constitución de 1980". In Soto, Sebastian and Hube, Constanza (coordinators), *Conceptos Fundamentales para el Debate Constitucional.* Santiago: Pontificia Universidad Católica de Chile, 2021, p. 80.

Fuentes, Claudio. *El Fraude.* Santiago: Editorial Hueders, 2013.

Gajardo, Jaime. "Otras Propuestas sobre Derechos Constitucionales". In *Propuestas Constitucionales: La Academia y el Cambio Constitucional en Chile.* Santiago: Centro de Estudios Públicos, 2019, p. 51.

García Barzelatto, Ana. "Rol del Tribunal Constitucional y Nueva Constitución". En Senado de Chile (editor), *Reflexiones Constitucionales: Aportes para la Nueva Constitución.* Santiago: Ediciones Senado de la República, Biblioteca del Congreso Nacional, 2021, p. 125.

Gargarella, Roberto. "La «Sala de Máquinas» de las Constituciones Latinoamericanas: Entre lo Viejo y lo Nuevo." *Nueva Sociedad,* n° 257, July–August 2015.

Gómez, Gastón. "Propuesta Inicial sobre Régimen Político". In *Propuestas Constitucionales: La Academia y el Cambio Constitucional en Chile.* Santiago: Centro de Estudios Públicos, 2019, p. 126.

Guala, Johanna. "Estallido Social y Violaciones a los Derechos Humanos en Chile". *Espacio Regional,* vol. 1, n° 17, Osorno, January–June 2020, p. 95.

Jimenez Loosli, Fernando and Jimenez Larraín, Fernando. *Historia Constitucional de Chile.* Ediciones UCSC, 2021.

Jiménez-Yañez, César. "#Chiledespertó: causas del estallido social en Chile". *Revista Mexicana de Sociología,* vol. 82, no.4, octubre-diciembre (2020), available online at https://doi.org/10.22201/iis.01882503p.2020.4.59213.

MacCammon, Ron. "American influence in Latin America is rapidly declining". Available online at https://www.washingtontimes.com/news/2022/jul/18/american-influence-in-latin-america-is-rapidly-dec/

Martuccelli, Danilo. *El Estallido Social en Clave Latinoamericana.* Santiago: Lom Ediciones, 2021.

Narvaez, José. *Pensar una historia del derecho latinoamericano matizada.* Universidad Autónoma de Mexico, Instituto de Investigaciones Jurídicas. 2016. Available online http://ru.juridicas.unam.mx:80/xmlui/handle/123456789/36683

Peña, Carlos. *Pensar el malestar. La crisis de octubre y la cuestión constitucional.* Santiago: Editorial Taurus, 2020.

Peña, Marisol. "Revisión Constitucional de las Leyes". In Soto, Sebastian and Hube, Constanza (coordinators), *Conceptos Fundamentales para el Debate Constitucional.* Santiago: Pontificia Universidad Católica de Chile, 2021, p. 25.

Ponce de León, Viviana. "Incorporando una perspectiva de género al Proceso Constituyente y a la Nueva Constitución: un análisis desde la participación política de las mujeres". En Senado de Chile (editor), *Reflexiones Constitucionales: Aportes para la Nueva Constitución.* Santiago: Ediciones Senado de la República, Biblioteca del Congreso Nacional, 2021, p. 24.

Rivera-Aguilera, Guillermo, Imas, Miguel and Jimenez-Diaz, Luis. "Jóvenes, Multitud y Estallido Social en Chile". *Revista Latinoamericana de Ciencias Sociales, Niñez y Juventud,* vol. 19, no. 2, p. 230.

Roy, Diana. "China's Growing Influence in Latin America". *Council on Foreign Relations.* 2022. Available online at https://www.cfr.org/backgrounder/china-influence-latin-america-argentina-brazil-venezuela-security-energy-bri.

Sanchez Arcilla, José. *Historia del Derecho Español.* Barcelona: Calamo, 2001.

Senado de Chile (editor). *Reflexiones Constitucionales: Aportes para la Nueva Constitución.* Santiago: Ediciones Senado de la República, Biblioteca del Congreso Nacional, 2021.

Sierra, Lucas (editor). *Propuestas Constitucionales: La academia y el cambio constitucional en Chile.* Santiago: Centro de Estudios Públicos, 2019.

Soto, Jorge. "elació de Gobierno". In Soto, Sebastian and Hube, Constanza (coordinators), *Conceptos Fundamentales para el Debate Constitucional.* Santiago: Pontificia Universidad Católica de Chile, 2021, p. 54.

Soto, Sebastian and Hube, Constanza (coordinators). *Conceptos Fundamentales para el Debate Constitucional.* Santiago: Pontificia Universidad Católica de Chile, 2021.

Tomás y Valiente, Francisco. *Manuel de Historia del Derecho Español.* Madrid: Editorial Tecnos, 4 edición, 2001.

Valdés, José M. Portillo. *Historia Mínima Del Constitucionalismo En América Latina.* Colegio de Mexico, 2016. http://www.jstor.org/stable/j.ctt1jd943t.

Zuñiga Urbina, Francisco. "Acerca del Estado Regional y la Nueva Constitución". En Senado de Chile (editor), *Reflexiones Constitucionales: Aportes para la Nueva Constitución.* Santiago: Ediciones Senado de la República, Biblioteca del Congreso Nacional, 2021, p. 177.

Juan Carlos Aguirre

Region-to-Region Approach: The EU and the Pacific Alliance

Introduction

The Pacific Alliance (PA) is an economic and development initiative. It was officially created in June 2012 with the signing of the "Pacific Alliance Framework Agreement" by the Presidents of Chile, Colombia, Mexico and Peru. Fundamentally, the PA is a business-oriented integration project (Kuwayama, 2019). The constitution of the PA Business Council is evidence of this. In addition, the PA has proposed to generate "deep integration". However, its critics (Prieto & Betancourt, 2014; Pastrana & Castro, 2020; Sanahuja, 2019) point out that it only intends to generate an "expanded" free trade area, as it would simply be the harmonisation of the Free Trade Agreements already signed by the four signatory countries. However, the PA member states argue that it is possible to achieve progress in Latin American regionalism by promoting the free movement of goods, services, capital and people. They define as one of their main target markets the Asia-Pacific rim, which, according to the PA members themselves, is one of the key regions of the global economy (Pacific Alliance, 2022).

The European Union (EU) defines its objectives in a more complex way, obviously considering that the EU's institutionality has been evolving since the last century. Thus, in a broad sense, the principle underpinning the EU is to promote peace and security and to respect fundamental rights and freedoms and spread European interests and values in the world (including ensuring a strong trade policy in line with multilateralism and the rules-based international order) (European Union, 2022). Considering these different but compatible worldviews, values and founding principles, one may wonder what space for convergence and cooperation exists between the two blocs, even though the PA looks with special attention to the Asia-Pacific.

This chapter is organised as follows. Firstly, a comparative analysis of the PA and the EU is conducted. Secondly, a conceptual framework will be developed to analyse the possibilities for future linkages between the PA and the EU on the basis of the co-constitution of regional institutions and collective identity. In this way, the structural variables of Latin American regionalism will be analysed to subsequently define the agential variables that could lead to a strengthening of the links between the PA and its European observer partners through the use of emerging flexibility mechanisms. Thirdly, the chapter will discuss specific emerging flexibility mechanisms that could strengthen and reshape PA-EU relations. Finally, the concluding remarks address the most relevant possibilities for collaboration for the future of the interregional partnership between the PA and the EU.

The PA and the EU: A comparative theoretical and institutional analysis

The PA and the EU have co-constituted similarities with respect to structural variables within the international system. The collective identities of both blocs are in many ways similar if one considers the co-constitution variables that specialists in Latin American regionalism identify as central to the success of a regional organisation. From the structural point of view, we can find: (a) a common vision regarding the relationship with the hegemon(s) (Gardini, 2010): mainly about the United States' hegemony but China too; (b) similarity in development models (Gardini, 2010): open markets economies); (c) similarities in institutional models (Malamud & Castro, 2007); (d) convergence around regional leadership (Gardini, 2010; Nolte, 2006): Mexico in the case of the PA and Germany in the case of the EU.

Meanwhile, from the agential perspective similarities are more nuanced. We have the importance of the role of presidentialism in the foreign policy decision-making process (Bernal-Meza, 2013; Malamud, 2008) (especially in the case of the PA) and the interaction of regional agents at the regional decision-making level (Aguirre, 2021) as Ministers, Vice-Ministers, diplomats and political advisors. However, the PA has been criticised for its institutional weakness or lack of institutional setting altogether (Prieto & Betancourt, 2014), which would prevent it from expanding to further stages of integration or regionness (Hettne & Söderbaum, 2000). This is certainly not the case of the EU. Then, if one considers the above-mentioned similarities: How to take advantage of this identity similarity to reconfigure Latin America-European Union relations? I argue that a purposeful rapprochement to the EU (thirty-one European states are observer members of the PA) can help strengthen the collective identity and, therefore, the institutional design of the PA, taking advantage of its main feature, its institutional flexibility and the similarities in terms of the collective identity of the two blocs.

Institutionalism and institutionalisation matter in regionalism and in interregionalism too. While the literature on regional institution building is closely linked to the generation of an institutional collective identity and vice versa (Checkel, 2016), it is a fact that the institutional design of the PA has not managed to build a solid collective identity (strong institutionality based on a dense bureaucratic structure), despite its more than 10 years of existence. And it is in this peculiar, hybrid and flexible sense that the EU can support the strengthening of the organisation. This can be done in two ways. On the one hand, generating an "Otherness" (Wendt, 1994) can lead to the re-signification of the PA's collective identity, taking the institutional evolution of the EU as a mirror. On the other hand, through technical-institutional advice to create solid but flexible minimum bureaucratic (intergovernmental) structures that allow the PA to project itself as a global actor and have the "Actorness" capacity, which means behaving actively and deliberately in relation to other actors in the international system (Sjöstedt, 1977). At the same time, only after the institutional strengthening of the PA, can the EU also support the PA directly with concrete cooperation policies and agreements, where cross-regional mechanisms would greatly help.

One of the main characteristics of the PA is what its Constitutive Treaty and its member states have called "institutional flexibility".[1] This is an essential feature of the organisation, in contrast to the institutional rigidity of other projects in the region. It is precisely the institutional flexibility of the PA that allows it to incorporate, more easily than other organisations in the region, diverse actors into the institution's decision-making processes. These actors, such as the business sector, give continuity to the organisation through mechanisms of emergent flexibility (Búzás & Graham, 2020: 2) or ad hoc flexibility like cross-regional initiatives (Garzón & Nolte, 2017; Prieto & Betancourt, 2014). Thus, the emergent flexibility is defined as "a property of international agreements that is not intentionally crafted by rule-makers when a rule is formally established, but rather is subsequently discovered, activated, and accessed by creative rule-users to change agreements in ways unintended by design" (Búzás & Graham, 2020: 2).

These flexibilities confer agency upon the PA members. This characteristic may well allow the PA to play a role in the reconfiguration of relations between Latin America and the EU. In this sense, I argue that the PA and the EU should

1 Specifically, the Framework Agreement of the Pacific Alliance, signed in 2012, defines its institutional design based on the creation of a Council of Ministers, the highest deliberative body, which meets once a year. It also has a High-Level Group, a rotating Pro Tempore Presidency and ad hoc working groups. In addition, the Agreement is open to the incorporation of new members (subject to approval by the Council of Ministers) and establishes the figure of the Associated States and the Observer States.

cooperate to provide the PA with a minimum of institutionalisation before they start elaborating any more specific cooperation agenda through emerging flexibility mechanisms. The first of these mechanisms came in 2013 when the EU became the special guest at the Pacific Alliance Summit in Cali, Colombia. The second *momentum* in the inter-regional relationship took place in 2018 in Brussels, where a roadmap on the most relevant issues for the parties was agreed upon with the EU High Representative Federica Mogherini and the Pacific Alliance Foreign Ministers. The third event took place in 2019 when the two blocs signed a Joint Declaration, a document that discusses similar issues to those being negotiated by the PA with ASEAN.

The co-constitution of agent-structure and collective identity building

The specialised literature on Latin American regionalism explains the low performance of regional projects according to five variables: (1) the relation with the hegemon(s) of the international system; (2) similarities between development models; (3) consensus on regional leadership; (4) the role of presidentialism[2] in the processes of creation and disappearance of regional projects; (5) the socialisation of regional agents. In that sense, the external relations of regional organisations will also be defined according to the convergence, or lack of it, with external partners with regard to co-constituted structural (points 1, 2 and 3) and agential variables (points 4 and 5). Thus, following Wendt (1987, 1992a, 1992b), both agency and structure are co-constituted and generate collective identities and institutionality.

In this regard, co-constitution between agents and structures exists when

> An institution is a relatively stable structure or set of identities and interests. These structures are usually codified in formal rules and regulations, but these only have value by virtue of the socialisation of actors and their sharing of collective knowledge. Institutions are fundamentally cognitive entities that do not exist independently of actors' ideas about how the world works (Wendt, 1992b: 9).

2 The role of presidentialism in regionalism of Latin America has been studied in depth, and there is considerable academic consensus on its relevance (see also Mattli, 1999; Malamud, 2005; Bernal-Meza, 2002; Colacrai & Lorenzini, 2005; Tickner, 2007; Russell & Tokatlian, 2009; Dellanegra, 2012). However, it is necessary to broaden its explanatory capacity by incorporating actors that surround the decision-making process in Latin American foreign policy, despite the prevailing presidentialism.

Therefore, both agency and structure are created, maintained and, above all, modified, as collective identities change interests.

From the interregional point of view, when similarities exist between two blocs, collective identity could play a key role in the relationship, especially through the "Otherness" concept. To generate convergence of initiatives (with regional and extra-regional partners) the structural variables must be moderately aligned among their members, i.e. the parties must coincide in their relations with the hegemon(s), in their institutional and development models, and their vision of regional leadership. Concerning the agential variables in Latin America, the parties must promote the socialisation of the Presidents, as these are the agents who drive the creation and implementation of regional norms. At the same time, Latin American countries should ensure the interaction of other regional agents, such as ministers, diplomats, state officials and, especially, civil society. It is the regional agents who can reinforce the collective identity of an organisation through inter-group socialisation and decision-making at the regional level.

Only a few studies on regional institutions and collective identity in Latin America exist (Prieto, 2015, 2020; Oelsner, 2013). Yet, it is possible to develop an analytical framework of regional collective identity based on the structural and agential variables identified. That is to say: The convergence between the countries involved at the regional level of the structural variables (relations with the hegemons, development model, and acceptance or rejection of regional leadership) provides a first layer of collective identity. Next, agential factors emphasising socialisation through emergent flexibility mechanisms allow adding new partners internationally and to relate normatively to them, thus adding to or reinforcing the existing regional collective identity. Regional institutions can be more or less rigid (with institutional inertia and a solid bureaucratic framework) or more or less flexible (with little bureaucracy). In any case, both species contain mechanisms of emerging flexibility in their design. Emerging flexibility mechanisms allow associating new members to the regional organisation. To strengthen these relations between blocs, agential effort and socialisation are required.

Emergent flexibility in action: Cross-regional mechanisms between the Pacific Alliance and the European Union

Applying the analytical model proposed above, the relations between the PA and the EU have enormous potential for convergence. Firstly, from the point of view of the relationship with the hegemon, both blocs have good and close relations with the United States. The PA countries have FTAs with the United States, while the EU is close to Washington across the board, in cultural, political, commercial and also military terms. However, it is important to point out that the two blocs have substantial differences concerning their relationship with China. For PA members, it is a key partner and the main trading partner, while for the EU, it is a "strategic competitor" (Tovar, 2021).

Secondly, from the point of view of development models, many of the countries that make up the EU are seen by the PA countries as "like-minded countries", fundamentally because they have free market economies. At the same time, from an institutional point of view, there is closeness between the blocs, especially regarding the support of liberal democracy, the rule of law, the protection of human rights and the autonomy of institutions such as the Central Bank. It is also worth mentioning, given the evolution of regionalism in the sub-region, that the four members of the PA coincide in terms of their development model (neoliberal) and, to a certain extent, in terms of institutional models. In fact, it is this economic model that mainly made the creation of the PA possible and generated a degree of common identity among its members, despite internal political changes.

At the same time, the strategy of "cross-regionalism" is an element of the emergent flexibility mechanism used by PA to maintain relations with the EU. The cross-regional mechanism refers to "the new practice or strategy of negotiating multiple parallel bilateral trade agreements with partners belonging to different regions" (Garzón & Nolte, 2017). It also affects the balance of power within Latin America because the creation of the PA, with the inclusion of Mexico, called into question Brazil's leadership role in the sub-region, since Mexico was included in the PA because the other member countries needed a paymaster to counterbalance the power of Brazil and, eventually, Venezuela, which had already created ALBA. Neither Chile, Colombia nor Peru have the material and ideational capacities to match the sub-regional paymasters. This strategy has a meeting point with the partnerships that the EU has established in Latin America. Faced with the fragmentation of regional integration initiatives in Latin America, the EU has adjusted its external approach over time and has opted to strengthen its relations with individual countries. Specifically, this mechanism has been underpinned by strategic agreements signed with Brazil, Mexico and Chile, as well as trade agreements with Colombia and Peru.

Now, from the point of view of the agential variables, presidentialism has been a relevant factor in the development of the PA. The organisation is the clearest example of presidentialism playing a relevant role, at least in its creation of the organisation. This is usual across Latin America's regional integration projects (Mattli, 1999). The particular interest that former Peruvian President Alan García had in this regard during his second term in office is well known. This idea arose, firstly, for the creation of the political coordination forum called the Pacific Arc (García Belaúnde, 2015; Guerra-Barón, 2019), which resulted in what we know today as the PA. The role played in those years by the former President of Chile, Sebastián Piñera, was also key, as he saw an opportunity to strengthen his foreign policy (Nolte & Wehner, 2013; Guerra-Barón, 2019), once again under the auspices of the Free Trade Agreements and a supposed boost to regional value chains.

The role of other so-called "regional actors" has been important in addition to the presidential priorities and impulses for the creation of new regional or sub-regional organisations. It is now important to focus attention on the role of the agents who effectively socialise in regional institutions since it is not exclusively presidents who are involved in the institutional development of projects, Rather, it is foreign ministers, diplomats, advisors, businessmen and other types of representatives who generate the *habitus* of an organisation, even when this organisation does not have formal institutionality, as in the case of the PA.

On this last point, the relationship between the PA and the EU has been mediated by an important presence of regional agents from both sides, who have generated a series of attempts to strengthen the relationship between the two blocs. On the PA side, foreign ministers from member countries, as well as diplomats, officials and businessmen, have been key actors in trying to generate a stronger partnership. On the European side, the action of EU diplomats and businessmen has been complemented by that of a broad spectrum of non-traditional actors. More specifically, universities, businesses and civil society organisations have taken part in the various actions that have been carried out between the parties. In this sense, the first cross-regional rapprochement took place at the VII Presidential Summit of the PA in Cali (2013). Former Spanish Prime Minister Mariano Rajoy took part in the meeting on behalf of the EU. At the same time, two new European observer states, France and Portugal, were accepted. On the occasion, Rajoy pointed out:

> It is simply a step towards progress and an adaptation to the new, more open and more global world" (...) "this is what leads to employment and people's well-being" (...) "We wanted to come here for 24 hours to give my backing and support to this association and to say that Spain wants to collaborate and help build this Alliance (ABC, 2013).

Rajoy's attendance was followed by a Seminar organised in Hamburg (Germany) by the EU-LAC Foundation and a Business Roundtable organised by the Lateinamerikaverein von Hamburg, an opportunity where the former German Foreign

Minister, Guido Westerwelle, celebrated the Pacific Alliance's commitment to free trade (Zarandi, 2014). Both events mark not only the convergence of interests between the parties but also the first emerging flexibility mechanism used by the PA in its relations with external actors. In this regard, it should be noted that the PA was not conceived to establish relations with the EU. Thus, this first rapprochement shows the parties' interest in pursuing strategic alliances beyond their own core objectives. It is understandable that under the logic of "Actorness" the EU wants to move closer to new regional blocs that share its founding principles. But for the PA this relationship is explained more by its interest in generating international support, with its "like-minded" partners, in order to add strategic support to its project.

Another cross-regional initiative as an emerging flexibility mechanism took place in Brussels in 2018. At the meeting, the High Representative for Foreign Affairs and Security Policy/Vice-President of the European Commission, Federica Mogherini (a key actor in the reshaping of PA-EU relations), organised a meeting with representatives of the four Pacific Alliance countries. On the occasion, the participants confirmed the willingness of the EU and the PA to strengthen relations based on common values of democracy, protection of human rights and the rule of law, and a shared vision of open trade and investment and sustainable development. The parties also agreed on the importance of promoting multilateralism and a rules-based global order, as well as open, transparent and inclusive free trade agreements, in line with the World Trade Organisation, to enhance competitiveness and foster sustainable socio-economic development and social inclusion (Pacific Alliance, 2019). On the occasion, the European High Representative, in addition to emphasising European standards that can serve to strengthen the relationship with the PA (European Union, 2022), also wanted to be more pragmatic and offered the establishment of a roadmap in specific areas of dialogue, cooperation and mutually beneficial activities in the form of the exchange of experiences and information to draw relevant lessons from each other's integration processes.

As a result of the two previous cross-regional initiatives, in 2019, the two blocs signed a Joint Declaration in which they agreed to deepen their partnership. This is a further sign of the use of flexibility mechanisms in the relationship between the two blocs. In that context, High Representative Federica Mogherini pointed out:

> The European Union is committed to strengthening its political, economic and cooperation ties with the Pacific Alliance. The Alliance is a driver of regional integration in Latin America, with whom we have a strong friendship and share fundamental values, a

strong belief in multilateralism and a mutual commitment to promote the 2030 Agenda and the Sustainable Development Goals (Pacific Alliance, 2019).

Basically, the declaration points to the classic themes in the collaboration between the parties, already defined in the roadmap agreed upon in 2018. The difference here lies in the operational approach meant to identify actions to address the priorities mutually identified by the Pacific Alliance and the EU. The modalities of the specific actions will be agreed upon by Pacific Alliance and EU experts, who will report regularly to the Pacific Alliance national coordinators and EU representatives (European Union, 2022). By now, these priorities have been clearly defined: entrepreneurship and gender, strategies for digital markets, education and university exchange, and a green economy. In this sense, the PA is moving away from the classic conception of interregional trade and is beginning to incorporate more strategic areas in its development, using mechanisms of emerging flexibility (cross-regionalism). For its part, the EU has the opportunity to strengthen specific areas of cooperation with Latin America through the PA, adding non-traditional actors to the process, such as universities, women's entrepreneurship groups, and ecologically aware entrepreneurs, among others, paving the way towards a genuine strategic bi-regional alliance (Ghymers, 2016). However, the problem at this point is the long-term sustainability of cooperation initiatives between the two blocs because the PA lacks both legal personality and a significant institutional structure.

It is true that the member states of the PA "have always emphasised that they do not want to create cumbersome institutions and do not intend to have a community or supranational institutions. However, it is also true that the Alliance's agenda and its foreign projection seem to be saying the opposite, as it is necessary to have permanent institutions to count internationally, as the PA aims to. A permanent and relatively stable team representing the Alliance will facilitate the external representation and positioning that the Alliance aspires to (Torres, 2016: 32). The PA Pro Tempore Secretariat leaves the PA's agenda of priorities to the discretion of the government of the day. Furthermore, it leaves the PA unable to sit at the negotiating table with other blocs (Torres, 2016: 32).

In fact, the Pacific Alliance's lack of legal personality prevents it from deepening and consolidating its initiatives with the EU and other blocs since it cannot sign agreements on behalf of its members and cannot commit them either. While the Pacific Alliance as a bloc cannot sign an agreement with the EU, it can use the emerging flexibility mechanisms, such as cross-regionalism, as it has done so far. This, in turn, reinforces its own collective identity and perhaps, with time, its will to institutionalise. This would imply, to an extent, the use of the EU as an institutional mirror to reinforce its intergovernmental institutionalism, for example by creating a permanent executive secretariat or a Council of Ministers and/or a General Secretariat. This is where the EU can play an important role based on its institutional experience, thereby giving the Pacific Alliance the capacity to act. After this process, the chances that the two blocs could sit down to negotiate a common agenda for cooperation would greatly increase.

The necessity for further institutionalisation of the PA can be demonstrated by the case of the development of digital markets in the PA-EU relationship. The PA more or less follows the European doctrine in this regard (General Data Protection Regulation rules). However, here the main attribute of the PA, flexibility, has also shown its weakness in addressing relevant societal issues. Following Corredor (2020), none of the normative or legal reactions to the technological giants has been prepared or even debated to establish a doctrine or standard. At present, there is no common understanding of the scope of cross-border data flows or the appropriateness of data localisation as part of concerted strategies to protect the privacy of PA countries' citizens. All of these seemingly disconnected issues are relevant to the creation of digital ecosystems, and coherence is best achieved through institutionalisation and legally binding commitments by PA members. In this sense, then, EU collaboration can be crucial, if only if the EU could persuade the PA to generate, for example, a minimum of institutionalisation to drive a common cybersecurity policy.

Conclusions

Thinking about the role that the PA and the EU can play in the reconfiguration of relations between Latin America and Europe implies analysing two completely different cases. Evidently, the PA prioritises its relations with Asia-Pacific countries, which are quite distant from the interests pursued by the EU, at least geographically.

However, when certain analytical criteria are applied to the PA-EU relationship, it can be understood that these are two regional projects with similarities about their collective identity. Due to the above-mentioned, my argument focused on three main issues. The first relates to the search for similarities between the collective identities of both the PA and the EU, to argue that it is on the basis of those commonalities that a rapprochement between the parties should begin.

Firstly, following Wendt (1987, 1992a, 1992b, 1994), I suggested that a reassertion of Otherness (PA vis-à-vis the EU) can help the PA to strengthen its institutionality in order to have a better capacity for Actorness in the future. Secondly, I pointed out that the PA's own flexibility allows it to use emerging flexibility mechanisms, such as cross-regionalism, without institutional constraints, to seek out and include new strategic partners that allow it to position itself internationally. Thirdly, I pointed out that although cross-regionalism as a mechanism of emerging flexibility has allowed the PA to approach the EU on three occasions until the signing of the Joint Declaration in 2019, today it is not enough. This is because cross-regionalism generates the conditions for a rapprochement between the parties, but does not allow for the deepening of PA-EU relations in the long term.

The main conclusion of this chapter is that if the PA intends to be a strategic partner in relations with the EU, the EU must first persuade the PA to bring about changes in its current institutionality, moving towards the establishment of a permanent General-Secretariat or some intergovernmental body that allows it to have more capacity for Actorness in the international system. This does not imply losing institutional flexibility, because flexibility is the result of the agency in terms of the capacity of actors socialised in specific institutional frameworks. Thus, the challenge is to persuade actors on both sides. Especially if we consider that since Josep Borrell took office as High Representative of the Union for Foreign Affairs and Security Policy and Vice-President of the European Commission, the Pacific Alliance has lost prominence within the EU agenda. In this sense, it seems that the EU looks favourably at the PA's initiatives. But at the same time, it recognises the complexity of advancing the deepening of relations between the parties, insofar as the PA does not acquire greater degrees of institutionalisation. Moreover, the current stalemate and even internal clashes that the PA is experiencing further complicate relations with the EU, especially the deepening of such relations. In any case, the EU is the best ally the PA can have to improve its institutional framework or to move towards some kind of common policy in a specific area, considering the EU's own experience and history, but maintaining its characteristic hallmark, flexibility. In this way, it will be possible to establish a structured cooperation relationship with the EU, which will allow the deepening of bi-regional ties. This specific and pragmatic cooperation agenda would have to foster the PA's global positioning in the future and, at the same time, reinforce the EU's normative power in the international system.

Bibliography

ABC (2013). "Rajoy, en Cali: "La Alianza del Pacífico es un paso hacia el progreso»". *Newspaper ABC* (own translation). https://www.abc.es/espana/20130523/abci-rajoy-cumbre-pacifico-201305231632.html (accessed at 10 April 2022).

Aguirre, J. C. (2021). "El regionalismo latinoamericano: una propuesta de análisis desde los agentes". En G. Álvarez, C. Ovando, M. Deciancio & G. Molano (Eds.), *Teoría y Práctica de las Relaciones Internacionales en América Latina*, INTE-Chile, FLACSO Argentina, IEPRI Colombia.

Bernal-Meza, R. (2002). Política exterior argentina: de Menem a De La Rúa¿ Hay una nueva política? *Sao Paulo em perspectiva, 16*, 74–93.

Bernal-Meza, R. (2013). *Modelos o esquemas de integración y cooperación en curso en América Latina (UNASUR, Alianza del Pacífico, ALBA, CELAC): una mirada panorámica*. Ibero-Online. Ibero-Amerikanisches Institut, Berlín. Available at: <http://www.iai.spk-berlin.de/publikationen/ibero-online.html> (accessed 10 March 2022).

Briceño Ruiz, J. (2013). Ejes y modelos en la etapa actual de la integración económica regional en América Latina. *Estudios internacionales (Santiago), 45*(175), 9–39. https://dx.doi.org/10.5354/0719-3769.2013.27352.

Búzás, Z. & Graham, E. (2020). Emergent flexibility in institutional development: How international ruleselaciónhangee. *International Studies Quarterly, 64*(4), December 2020, 821–833. https://doi.org/10.1093/isq/sqaa049.

Checkel, J. T. (2016). Regional identities and communities [Identidadeselacións y Comunidades]. In T. Börzel & T. Risse (Eds.), *The Oxford handbook of comparative regionalism*. Oxford: Oxford University Press.

Colacrai, M., & Lorenzini, M. E. (2005). La política exterior de Chile: ¿excepcionalidad o continuidad? Una lectura combinada de "fuerzas profundas" y tendencias. *CONfineselaciónn. internaci. ciencia política* [online], *1*(2), 45–63. ISSN 1870-3569.

Corredor, G. (2020). The Pacific Alliance towards a strategy on digital economy? *Anuario Colombiano de Derecho Internacional (acdi) 13*, 165–186. https://doi.org/10.12804/revistas.urosario.edu.co/acdi/a.8343.

European Union. (2002). Website: https://european-union.europa.eu/index_es

European Union. (2022). Joint declaration between the European Union and the Pacific Alliance. https://www.eeas.europa.eu/eeas/joint-declaration-partnership-between-states-parties-framework-ag (accessed at 12 April 2022).

Foster, K. (2020). The future of the Pacific Alliance. *Harvard International Review*. Available at: https://hir.harvard.edu/the-future-of-the-pacific-alliance/ (accessed at 5 March 2020).

García Belaunde, J. (2015). Política exterior y diplomacia peruana: pasado, presente y future. In F. Novak & J. García (Eds.), *La Política Exterior Peruana en el Siglo XXI: Agenda y Propuestas* (pp. 39–50). IDEA-Konrad Adenauer Stiftung.

Gardini, G. L. (2010). Proyectos de integración regional sudamericana: Hacia una teoría de convergencia regional. *Relaciones Internacionales, 15*, 11–31.

Garzón, J., & Nolte, D. (2017). The new minilateralism in regional economic governance. Cross-regionalism and the Pacific Alliance. In P. Riggirozzi & C. Wylde (Eds.), *Handbook of South American governance* (1st ed., pp. 160–178). Routledge. https://doi.org/10.4324/9781315661162.

Garzón, J., & Prieto, G. (2017). Estrategias de inserción económica internacional de Colombia y Brasil: regionalismo cruzado y estrategia de tamaño. En D. Flemes, E. P. Buelvas, & M. Carpes (Eds.), *Estado y perspectivas de las relaciones colombo-brasileñas* (1st ed., pp. 119–146). Pontificia Universidad Javeriana.

Ghymers, C. (2016). The Pacific Alliance a potential catalyst for strengthening the CELAC and paving the way towards a genuine strategic alliance with the EU. In M. Torres & J. Violante (Eds.), *Emerging marketsthee Pacific Alliance perspectives and opportunities for Latin America. Stockholm and Salamanca: European Instituto of International Studies* (pp. 203–242).

Guerra-Barón, A. (2019). The foreign policies convergence as a factor of the establishment of the Pacific Alliance. *Studia Politica: Romanian Political Science Review, 19*(2), 187–213. https://nbn-resolving.org/urn:nbn:de:0168-ssoar-63165-8

Hettne, B., & Söderbaum, F. (2000). Theorising the rise of regionness, 2000. *New Political Economy, 5*(3) (December 2000), 457–473. Available at: SSRN: https://ssrn.com/abstract=2398942 https://doi.org/10.2307/j.ctv86dgnp

Kuwayama, M. (2019). *Pacific Alliance: A Latin American version of "Open Regionalism" in practice*, Discussion Paper Series DP2019-02, Research Institute for Economics & Business Administration, Kobe University.

Malamud, A. (2005). Presidential diplomacy and the institutional underpinnings of Mercosur. An empirical examination. *Latin American Research Review, 40*(1), 138–164.

Malamud, A. (2008). Jefes de Gobierno y procesos de integración regional: Las experiencias de Europa y América Latina. En P. de Lombaerde, S. Kochi, y J. Briceño Ruiz (Eds.), *Del regionalismo latinoamericano a la integración interregional* (pp. 137–162). Madrid: Fundación Carolina/Siglo XXI.

Malamud, A., y Castro, P. (2007). ¿Son los bloques regionales los que conducen a los Estados nacionales a la gobernanza global? Una visión escéptica desde América Latina. *Iberoamericana. Nordic Journal of Latin American and Caribbean Studies, 37*(1), 111–130.

Mattli, W. (1999). *The logic of regional integration: Europe and beyond*. Cambridge: Cambridge University Press.

Nolte, D. (2006). *Potencias regionales en la política internacional: Conceptos y enfoques de análisis*. GIGA Research Programme, No. 30, Hamburg.

Nolte, D., & Wehner, L. (2013). *The Pacific Alliance casts its cloud over Latin America* (GIGA Focus International Edition, 8). Hamburg: GIGA German Institute of Global and Area Studies – Leibniz-Institut für Globale und Regionale Studien. https://nbn-resolving.org/urn:nbn:de:0168-ssoar-360988

Novak, F., & Namihas, S. (2018). La Alianza del Pacífico: Situación, perspectivas y propuestas para su consolidación (2da. ed.). *Pontificia Universidad Católica del Perú Instituto de Estudios Internacionales (IDEI) and Konrad Adenauer Stiftung (KAS)* (160 pp.). Perú: Lima.

Oelsner, A. (2013). The institutional identity of regional organizations, or Mercosur's identity crisis. *International Studies Quarterly, 57*(1), 115–127.

Pacific Alliance. (2019). *The European Union and Pacific Alliance commit to deepening their partnership.*https://alianzapacifico.net/the-european-union-and-pacific-alliance-commit-to-deepening-their-partnership/ (accessed at 12 April 2022).

Pacific Alliance. (2022). Website: https://alianzapacifico.net/

Pastrana, E., & Castro, R. (2020). Auge y Estancamiento de la Alianza del Pacífico. *Análisis Carolina*, 7/2020, 1–20. https://doi.org/10.33960/AC_7.2020.

Prieto, G. C. (2015). Collective identity in the Andean community: An institutional account. *Papel Político, 20*(2), 585–604.

Prieto, G. C. (2020). Identity in Latin American regionalism: The Andean community. In Harry E. Vanden & Gary Prevost (Eds.), *Oxford encyclopedia of Latin American politics*. Oxford: Oxford University Press.

Prieto, G. C., & Betancourt, D. (2014). Entre la soberanía, el liberalismo y la innovación: un marco conceptual para el análisis de la Alianza del Pacífico. In E. Pastrana & H. Gehring (Eds.), *Alianza del Pacífico: mitos y realidades* (pp. 76–113). Cali: Editorial Universidad Santiago de Cali.

Russell, R., & Tokatlian, J. (2009). *Modelos de política exterior y opciones estratégicas: El caso de América Latina frente a Estados Unidos*. Revista CIDOB d'Afers Internacionals, No. 85/86, Los retos de América Latina en un mundo en cambio (Mayo, 2009), pp. 211–249 (39 pp.). https://www.jstor.org/stable/40586393

Sanahuja, J. A. (2019). La crisis de la integración y el regionalismo en América Latina: giro liberal-conservador y contestación normativa. En M. MESA (coord.), *Ascenso del nacionalismo y del autoritarismo en el sistema internacional – Anuario CEIPAZ 2018–2019* (pp. 107–126). Madrid: CEIPAZ.

Sjöstedt, G. (1977). The exercise of international civil power: A framework for analysis. *Cooperation and Conflict*. https://doi.org/10.1177/00108367770 1200102.

Tickner, A. (2007). Intervención por invitación. Claves de la política exterior colombiana y de sus debilidades principales. *Colombia Internacional* (65),

90–111. January–June 2007. http://colombiainternacional.uniandes.edu.co/view.php/93/view.php.

Torres, M. (2016). The new model of regional integration for emerging countries in Latin America: The Pacific Alliance. In M. Torres & J. Violante (Eds.), *Emerging markets the Pacific Alliance perspectives and opportunities for Latin America*. Stockholm and Salamanca: European Institute of International Studies (pp. 19–44).

Tovar, J. (2021). *Biden y el futuro de la relación EE.UU-UE*. Real Instituto Elcano. Available at: https://www.realinstitutoelcano.org/analisis/biden-y-el-futuro-de-la-relacion-eeuu-ue/ (accessed at 30 March 2022).

Wendt, A. (1987). The Agent–structure problem in international relations theory. *International Organization, 41*(3), 335–370.

Wendt, A. (1992a). Anarchy is what states make of it: The social construction of power politics. *International Organizations, 46*(2), 391–425.

Wendt, A. (1992b). Levels of analysis vs agents and structures. *Review of International Studies, 18*(2), 181–185.

Wendt, A. (1994). Collective identity formation and the international state. *American Political Science Review, 88*(2), 384–396.

Wight, C. (2020). *Agents, structures and international relations politics as ontology* (pp. 1–361). Cambridge: Cambridge University Press.

Zarandi, M. (2014). Perspectivas del Interrgionalismo entre la Alianza del Pacífico y la Unión Europea. En E. Pastrana y H. Gehring (Eds.), *Alianza del Pacífico, mitos y realidades* (pp. 431–476). Editorial Universidad Santiago de Cali-Konrad Adenauer Stiftung.

Gian Luca Gardini

Context, Foreign Policies, Tools and Ideas: Concluding Remarks on a Continuous Reconfiguration of the EU-LAC Relation

The seventeen chapters of this book have explored recent developments in the bi-regional relation between the European Union (EU) and Latin America and the Caribbean (LAC). The book addressed EU-LAC relations taking into due consideration both the EU and the Latin American perspective and interest. This is certified by the well-balanced academic background of the contributors as well as by the topic and perspective of their contributions. At the same time, the overall standing point of the book leans towards a European view. This does not express any particular preference of the team or any specific view of global affairs. This perspective simply reflects the aim of the Jean Monnet project "The redefinition of the EU presence in Latin America and the Caribbean" (EUin-LAC), which generated this book. As the title suggests, the whole intellectual exercise was designed to rethink the presence and positioning of the EU in Latin America and the Caribbean. While considering both sides, the EU remained the centre of our reflections.

The aim of our analysis was three-fold: (a) to dissect the context within which EU-LAC relations are taking place; (b) to assess the foreign policies of some key state actors, which have the potential to steer EU-LAC relations; and (c) to identify and discuss topical issues relevant to the EU-LAC agenda.

This set of aims was reflected in the book structure. In part I, purposefully entitled "foreign policies and contextual factors moulding EU-LAC relations", we tried to balance systemic and agential factors that shape the bi-regional relation. We dealt with the foreign policies of individual state actors, such as Spain, Portugal, Germany, Italy, UK and Brazil as potential drivers of EU-LAC relations. At the same time, we also considered systemic factors affecting the context of EU-LAC relations, such as the impact of the US-China competition, the quest for autonomy pursued by both the EU and Latin America, and the objective difficulties that the EU faces to link with Latin America and the Caribbean due to the concomitant crises that struck the continent. This approach also provides a healthy balance in the debate between structure and agency, to which I will return below.

In part II, entitled "a reinvigorated agenda for EU-Latin America relations", we critically addressed some topics already present on the EU-LAC agenda and suggested some new ones or at least some new ways to look at them. We blended theoretical and empirical considerations on the bi-regional agenda. On the one hand, we discussed more conceptual issues such as the idea of decoupling the political and functional agendas, to introduce techplomacy and the role of big tech, to link strongly the ecological and the social transition and to examine underexplored forms of soft power such as European engagement with key debates within Latin America, for example, the constitutional reform in Chile. On a more practical level, we also discussed key issues on the technical agenda such as digitalization, energy systems, entrepreneurship, the smart specialization strategy, actions for climate and biodiversity, migration in its multiple dimensions, and the challenges of a region-to-region approach.

Two shifts in empirical observation and theoretical thinking

As early as the 18th century, the philosopher Giambattista Vico theorised the courses and recourses of history, arguing that history unfolds in cycles that tend to repeat themselves (Vico, 2015). The idea of finding patterns and regularities is certainly not new to any social science and to International Relations in particular. It suffices to think of George Modelski's cycles of systemic change where he argued that power transition repeats itself broadly with the same modalities across history (Modelski, 1981). Not surprisingly, there seem to be cycles of empirical and theoretical focuses also in the study, and therefore one would guess in the practice, of European Union-Latin America and the Caribbean relations. On the one hand, the tension between agency and structure, and on the other, that between values and interests, have often characterised the policy and the academic debate on EU-LAC relations.

In this respect, we have observed two significant shifts in the last few years. First, there has been a move from predominantly agent-focused studies to more context-oriented analyses. Second, there has been a pragmatic shift from a shared value-based relationship to one founded on common interests. In principle, we welcome both shifts as more apt to capture the realities of politics and international relations. At the same time, we tried to keep a balanced approach acknowledging that the two dyads always inform international politics, with a varying degree of intensity and combination in different historical, political, economic and social moments. Hence, this is one of the primary reasons for the continuous redefinition of the EU's presence in Latin America and the Caribbean.

More specifically, on the debate between agency and structure, the book has sought to rebalance discussion by stressing the role of structure as a limiting factor of the agent's preferences and actions. This – we hope – was evident in part I, where the focus was on both the individual foreign policy of key state actors and the contextual factors constraining their choices and behaviour. Part II has pursued a blend of structural and agential considerations when dissecting key issues on the bi-regional agenda. This largely reflects the approach of the English School of international relations, for which international outcomes, organisation and organisations, including therefore interregional regimes, are largely the result of the agent's preferences within the limits posed by structure and context (Linklater, 2001).

The debate between agency and structure has a long tradition in International Relations. For at least the last fifty years it has been present in the theoretical and methodological discussion in various disciplines in the human and social sciences, such as sociology, geography and philosophy (Lukes, 1968; O'Neill, 1973; Gregory, 1981; Wallerstein, 1974). Political science and especially International Relations have also followed this pattern (Rosenau, 1986; Waltz, 1979; Wendt, 1987). If the debate dates back to the 1960s and the problem of the level of analysis (Singer, 1961), in the 1970s and 1980s, neorealism prevailed in the diatribe within International Relations, prioritising systemic factors and arguing that it is essentially the context that defines the modalities and contents of interactions at the international level (Waltz, 1979; Gilpin, 1981). In the mid-1980s, the discussion became more balanced and since the 1990s, with the constructivist wave in International Relations (Wendt, 1987, 1992; Checkel, 2003; Finnemore & Sikkink, 1998), the role of agency has been quite prominent. More recently, the emphasis on agency has blossomed to include different theoretical approaches such as post-structuralism, reflexivist theories, actor-network theories, and new concepts and new areas of research have been developed (Braun, Schindler & Wille, 2019; Schindler, 2014). Events such as the Covid-19 pandemic, the war in Ukraine and the need for an ecological transition have shown that structure and context do matter a lot.

In more geographically and thematically circumscribed terms, the EU-LAC bi-regional relationship has been analysed from various perspectives over the last thirty years, and until very recently there was a noticeable tendency to focus on agency, preferences and opportunities (Borrell, 2020; Haider & Clemente Batalla, 2020; Gardini & Ayuso, 2015; Krakowski, 2008). This approach tends to concentrate on actors and their behaviour, often stressing shortcomings in political will. Yet this tends to downplay the analysis of structural and systemic factors, which constrain the actors' choices, and which were left almost as a secondary aspect with limited impact on the bi-regional relationship. In the last couple of years, emphasis on contextual factors has vehemently returned to the fore (Gardini, 2021a; Nolte, 2023; Maihold, Muscio Blanco & Zilla, 2023). This book fully acknowledges the value of agency, but at the same time, it seeks to focus on the systemic framework of the EU-LAC relationship in order to understand its current state and explain its limits and opportunities. Despite the unfavourable international context, and precisely with this in mind, the EU-LAC relationship is solid, and the seemingly inauspicious context itself also provides opportunities to deepen the EU-LAC relationship. The July 2023 EU-CELAC summit, after 8 years of absence, was perhaps the most relevant manifestation of how context prompts actors to alter their policies. This provides a second reason for a continuous redefinition of EU-LAC relations.

The second tension, between values and interests, is intertwined with the debate on agency and structure. The book has sought to establish a bridge between the two debates. Furthermore, our approach attempted to go beyond the debate on whether agents shape social structures or vice versa. It tried to escape the logic that analyses the European Union and its members on the one hand, and Latin America, its regional organisations and states on the other, as agents detached from the international context in which they operate. Until very recently, with the coming to the international fore of context-changing factors such as Covid-19 or the war in Ukraine, it seemed as if the values and interests that supposedly bind the EU and LAC together do not have to take into account the structural and systemic constraints. The EU-LAC relationship does not take place in a vacuum and cannot be understood only in a bi-regional context. It takes place in a historical, political and social context in which other actors and circumstances also play a leading role. This in turn shapes both values and interests, the way in which they are defined and defended.

The academic literature has often focused on the values that supposedly bind the EU and LAC together but it has also stressed the importance of common interests to maintain a solid relation (Sanahuja, 2013; Gardini & Ayuso, 2015; Gardini, 2021b). Policy-makers and civil society too have often emphasised shared values (Maas, 2019, Borrell, 2020, Euractiv, 2022; Jung, 2021), to the point that this has sometimes occurred to the detriment of the importance of interests. This was very likely due more to reasons of political opportunity and etiquette rather than lack of reflection or analysis. Not surprisingly, also EU and EU-LAC official documents have broadly followed this path (European Commission, 2022; EU-CELAC, 2015). Yet, a discourse analysis of the final declarations that emanated from the eight EU-LAC summits celebrated between 1999 and 2015 reveals that the word values was mentioned 22 times and the word interests 33.

References to shared and common values were only 9 though, while references to common and mutual interests were 20.[1] This is – I believe – a fair reflection of the actual weight of interests and values in international relations and also EU-LAC relations.

Indeed, the EU-LAC partnership is not only based on supposedly shared values, which are at least wobbling at the moment of writing, but also on common interests. The war in Ukraine and the diatribe between certain Latin American governments and the United States about the invitation of Venezuela, Cuba and Nicaragua to the 2022 Summit of the Americas show that the continent is, at best, divided on the meaning and defence of values such as democracy, human rights, the rule of law and non-interference, all of which are very cheered in Europe. In spite of these questions of principle, the EU and Latin America and the Caribbean share several interests at the international level. These are the primary base on which to construct a meaningful political relation and a fruitful cooperation. Interests are partly shaped by values and world views but also the other way around. As the most recent literature shows (Nolte, 2023; Maihold, Muscio Blanco & Zilla, 2023) interests rather than values may be the engine for a renewed EU-LAC relationship. This should be true for both the political and the functional agendas. Yet, if it were not so, there is always the possibility of decoupling them as I argued in Chapter 10 in this book.

Overall, actors and structures change. Values and interests do so too. Therefore also policies need a continuous redefinition to adapting to shifting circumstances, preferences and goals. The EU-LAC relationship is no exception. This dimension is a central legacy of this book.

Four lessons drawn from the encounter of individual foreign policies and their context

After discussing the importance of context and the centrality of interests in international relations, it is now time to resume the key findings and lessons to be learnt from the analysis of the foreign policy of specific actors. Four aspects stand out: the varying degrees of interest in Latin America that EU member states display across time; the tension between change and continuity and the wariness of big slogans and announcements; the importance of interlocutors and

---

1 Discourse analysis conducted by the author in preparation for the presentation “When Geopolitics meets values” (“Cuando la geopolitica se une a los valores”) delivered for the EU-LAC Foundation, 25 November 2020.

the understanding of their views and priorities; and once again that politics and policies are very much context-dependent.

Perhaps the big lesson for the European Union institutions is that relations with Latin America and the Caribbean cannot invariably count on the unwavering support of member states, even those more closely involved in Latin America. This is manifest in two respects. The first, EU member states have their own national agendas and strategies towards Latin America, including bilateral strategies and alternative multilateral strategies. Compatibility and mutual reinforcing of national and EU strategies have not to be taken for granted but carefully assessed, pursued and built. Second, interest in and support for initiatives about Latin America, be at the national or the community level, may vary in member states across time, depending on the government in office and its priorities, the national political and social climate, and the national and international circumstances. Support for closer relations with Latin America may be constant in discourse but is quite swinging in practice.

The chapters by Caballero on Spain, Fonseca on Portugal, Beneduzi on Italy and León Gonzalez on Germany have clearly shown this. Spain has consistently placed Latin America among its foreign policy priorities. Still, different administrations have taken quite different approaches and assumed different degrees of commitment, often privileging in practice other regions of the world. The Ibero-American system also deserves scrutiny in that it is an alternative region-to-region approach to the EU's. The "yo-yo" policy (Fonseca in Chapter 2) that Portugal has maintained towards Latin America further reinforces the argument that even European countries with consolidated political and economic links with Latin America face ups and downs in their commitment to the continent. Italy has shown more or less interest towards Latin America largely depending on the economic national agenda and the economic international climate, in spite of the ever present issue of the Italian diaspora in Latin America. Germany has made considerable political efforts and overtures towards Latin America but prioritising its own economic and societal mood and interest as the energy partnership in Brazil, Mexico and Chile show.

A second lesson has to do with the wariness of announced major policy changes that result in little practical effects and the problematic balance between change and continuity in international relations. As Maria Garcia discussed, the "Global Britain" campaign and London's foreign policy offensive in Latin America after Brexit have in fact changed very little in terms of policy and results as compared to the UK pre-Brexit times. Overall, the whole Brexit issue has not affected the EU presence in Latin America and the latter's relevance for the EU in any significant way (Astroza, 2019; Gardini, 2019). On a similar note, in 2019 Germany trumpeted a new approach to Latin America making the continent a priority of its foreign policy and a "neighbour of values" (Maas, 2019). As Germany took over the EU presidency in the second semester of 2020, Latin America almost disappeared from the agenda (German Presidency, 2020). Something quite similar happened when Portugal took over the EU presidency in the first semester of 2021 and a clear priority was given to Africa (Portuguese Presidency, 2021). The combination of change and continuity of the foreign policy approach of single EU member states towards Latin America also impacts the EU role and policy in the continent and the support for it. Expectations of the EU Spanish presidency in the second half of 2023 would better take this into account.

A third key lesson has to do with the interlocutors that the EU finds in Latin America and the Caribbean. As Elena Lazarou and Diego Ponce discussed in their chapter, Brazil had long been viewed in Brussels as a privileged and strategic partner and as a possible engine for stronger EU-Latin America relations. Economic difficulties and the Bolsonaro administration, but not only this one, have shown that the positions, support and command of the counterparts in Latin America have not to be taken for granted. In a similar vein, Juan Carlos Aguirre argued how the Pacific Alliance, in spite of a promising recent past and a problematic present, can be a suitable partner for the EU's region-to-region approach. Still, nuances in collective identity and institutional issues may hamper an effective relationship. On a similar note, Paz Verónica Milet and Belén Cabezas Araya have argued in their chapter how the concomitant crises that have recently struck Latin America along with the paralysis of Latin American regional organisations make it difficult for Brussels to find reliable counterparts in the continent, especially when it comes to the EU's cheered region-to-region approach.

Fourthly, any social and political relationship is ultimately context-dependent, arguably even more than it is actor-dependent. Paulina Astroza Suárez and Javier Sepúlveda Estrada discussed how the quest for autonomy is being pursued in both Europe and Latin America, although with different instruments and political traditions. The results of this newly autonomous posture are not yet clear but they certainly pose both challenges and opportunities to the EU-LAC relation. At the same time, the growing US-China competition at the global level may restrict room for manoeuvring for other actors. Still, as Sandra Zapata argues in her chapter, this too provides Europe and Latin America and the Caribbean with both challenges and opportunities. This is perhaps where, in our view, theory and practice meet at this historical juncture: the EU-LAC relationship depends on the actors' predisposition and preferences but within the structural limits posed by the context and its interpretations.

A humble decalogue for EU-LAC relations and the bi-regional agenda

After analysing foreign policies and context, the contributors have also tackled a number of issues that are present on the EU-LAC agenda or that may be worth considering for it. New perspectives or perhaps just different ways of looking at things have resulted in a humble set of policy indications that are here summarised in the form of a decalogue to reinvigorate the EU-LAC agenda and bi-regional relations more broadly.

1. *Decoupling the political and functional agenda.* Ideally, political and functional agendas should go hand in hand. However, as Gardini observed in his chapter, when this is not possible, a decoupling of the political and the technical agenda with a focus on the latter may ease relations and bring advance in relative uncontroversial issues. This provides at least for effective technical cooperation and lays the ground for future broader political entente.
2. *Introduce techplomacy as a major component of the EU engagement in Latin America.* Torres suggested in his chapter that a new technological era characterised by continuous technological advance and the global role of the big tech companies requires new diplomatic instruments and a new governance. Techplomacy could well be one of these tools, in an area where both the EU and LAC risk marginalisation.
3. *Further deepen differentiated approaches per geographical area and development level.* Brazil is not Latin America and the latter does not follow the former easily (Gardini, 2016). The idea of strategic partnerships ought to be revised. A selection of privileged or more significant partners is almost a natural phenomenon. Yet, this should facilitate dialogue and inclusion and not hamper them. At least in this respect, shared values on a stable basis should be a prerequisite. On a related note, special tools to foster cooperation with high- and medium-income Latin American countries should be encouraged, following the example of the exportation of the Smart Specialisation Strategy analysed by Jeanne W. Simon in her chapter.
4. *Activate all forms of soft and normative power.* The EU soft and normative power is still very relevant in Latin America, also in underexplored forms. As the chapter by Beatriz Larraín Martinez has shown, European participation in debates, also internal, cheered by Latin Americans can be an instrument to show interest, care and eventually to exercise influence. By a similar token, the chapter by Beneduzi argues that the communities of European origins in Latin America can be a tool for economic, political and societal partnership.

There are many national cultural centres in Latin America, from the British Council to the Alliance Française, from the Instituto Cervantes to the Goethe Institute. Why not to think of a genuinely European Cultural Institute to promote European and EU values and actions around the world, also to counter organically the action of the Confucius Institute?

5. *Promote and finance the ecological and the social transition at the same time.* Alwine Woischnik showed in her chapter how the two processes are interlinked and how the former also brings negative consequences for the latter. Woischnik mentioned the Spanish Just Transition Agreements that help regions with difficulties in the energy and ecological transition. These agreements provide comprehensive territorial development projects that guarantee employment in the medium and long term. This could be an example for the EU cooperation strategy towards Latin America.
6. *Promote awareness and meaning campaigns to reach a wide common understanding on key issues even before public policies are put in place.* This would facilitate the implementation and success of public policies. Such joint EU-LAC campaigns can include information and communication strategies to explain the real meaning and consequences of digitalization, as Gardini explains in his chapter. Joint efforts to stimulate awareness of the targets of the sustainable development goals and virtuous behaviours to achieve them as Rondanelli urges in his chapter, or widespread awareness of rights and regulations for migrants as discussed by Millán Requena.
7. *Improve consistency between discourse and practice on both sides.* On the one hand, the EU and its member states' repeated announcements of a new elan towards Latin America have often remained paper tigers. Also the EU aid effort during the pandemic was perceived as insufficient in Latin America. On the Latin American side, recent positions on democracy, human rights, the rule of law and non-interference cast serious doubts on the commitment of these countries to such values. Not to take a position has consequences as much as taking one. Brazil's president Ignacio Lula da Silva stated that "If one doesn't want to, two can't fight" with reference to Russia's war in Ukraine (Politico, 2023). This is exactly the type of inconsistency and incomprehensible provocation to European eyes that make confidence building and political entente such a problematic exercise at the bi-regional level.
8. Strictly connected is the question of *better marketing and communication by the EU.* The EU does a lot of good but its image does not benefit proportionally from it. On the contrary, the EU image in Latin America is often less positive than it should (Latinobarometro, 2018). Improvements have occurred in 2022 but the EU is not perceived as a strong partner (NUSU, 2022; Hirst,

Schiffer & Blanke, 2022). This certainly remains an area that deserves attention. China is gaining positions also as a result of an intense information and media campaign and Russia actively manipulates and distorts opinions in Latin America and worldwide on the war in Ukraine (Brandt & Wirtschafter, 2022). The EU shall explore ways to counter this and lead its own effective branding and information strategy. On a related note, the EU normative approach should not be mistaken for a charitable approach. The EU has its own agenda and legitimately defends European interests. This point too should be clearly communicated. Too often Latin Americans have expectations of the EU closer to a charitable institution rather than a proper geopolitical and economic actor. This may cause undue incomprehension.

9. *Keep focusing on the topical issues on the international agenda and renew efforts on those topics that are of concern to Latin America.* Focus on common interests shall include major issues on the international agenda that are also perceived as major problems in Latin America such as climate change and the environment (Rondanelli in this book) and migration (Requena in this book). At the same time, a more effective cooperation should also target those problems that represent a specific concern for Latin Americans, such as extreme poverty and the consequences of the pandemic (NUSU, 2022). To list these issues on the bi-regional agenda is not enough. Appropriate resources shall be raised and effective policies designed, implemented and communicated.
10. *Value what we already have.* It is important to put the EU-LAC relation in perspective and context. Even at pre-Covid and pre-Brexit level, the 33 countries of Latin America and the Caribbean accounted for less than 6% of the EU's global trade (Chiacchio, 2017). LAC will not be a top priority for the EU and ought not to be. The pandemic, the rise of China and other players in Latin America, the crisis of Western multilateralism, globalisation in transition, the redefinition of the US international projection, and Latin America's growing international irrelevance (Schenoni and Malamud, 2021) are all unpropitious factors for the EU-LAC bi-regional relation. Still, this relationship remains solid, cordial and significant to both parties. Both consistently express the desire to strengthen their bond further. These are important results. All this makes the EU-LAC relationship today valuable and worth appreciating. This must be the positive starting point of any analysis.

In times of alleged European decline (Webber, 2016), this book argues that the EU is still a very important actor in Latin America and the Caribbean and that there is considerable unexplored potential. Yet, in order to untap this potential, the first indispensable step is to acknowledge the existing difficult global scenario as well as the differences in values and interests and to work hard on the commonalities that also exist. Both political will and the ability to see opportunities also in an objectively unpropitious context are necessary. After all, EU-LAC relations are what their stakeholders make of them.

Bibliography

Astroza, P. (2019). "Brexit ¿Qué impacto para America Latina?". Análisis 22/2019, Fundación Carolina, Madrid. Online: https://dialnet.unirioja.es/servlet/articulo?codigo=7110487 (last accessed 13 January 2023).

Borrell, J. (2020). "Latin America-Europe: The 'other' transatlantic relationship", Blog post: 19 October 2020. Online: https://www.eeas.europa.eu/eeas/latin-america-europe-%E2%80%98other%E2%80%99-transatlantic-relationship_en (last accessed 13 January 2023).

Brandt, J. and V. Wirtschafter (2022). "Working the Western Hemisphere. How Russia spreads propaganda about Ukraine in Latin America and the impact of platform responses", Brookings Institution, Washington DC, December. Online: https://www.brookings.edu/research/working-the-western-hemisphere/ (last accessed 10 February 2023).

Braun, B., S. Schindler and T. Wille (2019). "Rethinking agency in International Relations: Performativity, performances and actor-networks". *Journal of International Relations and Development*, 22, pp. 787–807.

Checkel, J. (2003). "'Going Native' in Europe?: Theorizing social interaction in European Institutions". *Comparative Political Studies*, 36:1–2, pp. 209–231.

Chiacchio, F. (2017). "The European Union with the Community of Latin America and the Caribbean: Where do we stand?", Bruegel blog post. Online: https://www.bruegel.org/blog-post/european-union-community-latin-america-and-caribbean-where-do-we-stand#:~:text=Member%20countries%20of%20the%20Community,still%20representing%20a%20relatively%20small (last accessed 10 February 2023).

Euractiv. (2022). "EU-Latin America relations: Shared values and missed opportunities", Event report June-July. Online: https://en.euractiv.eu/wp-content/uploads/sites/2/special-report/EU-Latin-America-relations-shared-values-and-missed-opportunities.pdf (last accessed 13 January 2023).

European Commission. (2022)."Latin America and the Caribbean". European Union external action, strategic communications, 20.01.2022. Online: https://www.eeas.europa.eu/eeas/latin-america-and-caribbean_en (last accessed 13 January 2022).

EU-CELAC. (2015). "Political declaration: A partnership for the next generation". EU-CELAC Summit, Brussels. Online: https://www.consilium.europa.eu/media/23749/eu-celac-political-declaration.pdf (last accessed 13 January 2023).

Finnemore, M. and K. Sikkink (1998). "International norm dynamics and political change". *International Organization*, 52:4, pp. 887–917.

Gardini, G. L. (2019). "Brexit: seis consideraciones para la integración latinoamericana". *Pensamiento Propio*, 24:49–50, November 2019, pp. 395–405.

Gardini, G. L. (2021a). "El contexto sistémico de las relaciones Unión Europea-América Latina y el Caribe: Convertir los desafíos en oportunidades", in P. Astroza and B. Larraín (Eds.), *Relaciones entre la Unión Europea y América Latina: Escenarios futuros en un mundo de cambios* (pp. 13–28). Valencia: Tyrant lo Blanch.

Gardini, G. L. (2021b). "The European Union in Latin America: A 'neighbour'of values", in G. L. Gardini (Ed.), *External powers in Latin America* (pp. 29–43). Abingdon: Routledge.

Gardini, G. L. and A. Ayuso (2015). "EU-Latin America and Caribbean Interregional relations: Complexity and change". Atlantic Future project, Scientific Paper No. 24. Online: https://www.cidob.org/en/publications/publication_series/project_papers/atlantic_future_papers/scientific_paper/eu_latin_america_and_caribbean_inter_regional_relations_complexity_and_change (last accessed 13 January 2023).

Gardini, G. L. and M. H. Tavares de Almeida (Eds.). (2016). *Foreign policies responses to the rise of Brazil*. New York: Palgrave MacMillan.

German Presidency. (2020). "Together for Europe's recovery. Programme for Germany's Presidency of the Council of the European Union". Online: https://www.eu2020.de/blob/2360248/e0312c50f910931819ab67f630d15b2f/06-30-pdf-programm-en-data.pdf (last accessed 13 January 2023).

Gilpin, R. (1981). *War and change in world politics*. Cambridge: Cambridge University Press.

Gregory, D. (1981). "Human agency and human geography". *Transactions of the Institute of British Geographers*, 6:1, pp. 1–18.

Haider, W. and I. Clemente Batalla (2020). *Revisiting bi-regional relations: The EU-Latin American dialogue and diversification of cooperatio*n. Hamburg: EU-LAC Foundation.

Hirst, M., R. Schiffer and S. Blanke (2022). "Europe's lost opportunities in Latin America?", Euraktive/Friedrich Ebert Stiftung, 27 June 2022. Online: https://www.euractiv.com/section/politics/opinion/europes-lost-opportunities-in-latin-america/ (last accessed 10 February 2023).

Jung, T. (2021). "A new cycle in Euro-Latin American cooperation: Shared values and interests", Documentos de Trabajo 47EN/2021. Madrid: Fundación Carolina.

Krakowski, M. (2008). "The relations between the European Union and Latin America and the Caribbean. Current state and perspectives". *Intereconomics*, 43:2, pp. 112–120. Online: https://www.intereconomics.eu/contents/year/2008/number/2/article/the-relations-between-the-european-union-and-latin-america-and-the-caribbean-current-state-and-persp.html (last accessed 13 January 2023).

Latinobarometro. (2018), Analisis Online, several entries. Online: https://www.latinobarometro.org/latOnline.jsp (last accessed 10 February 2013).

Linklater, A. (2001). "Rationalism", in S. Burchill, R. Devetak, A. Linklater, M. Patterson, C. Reus-Smit and J. True (Eds.), *Theories of international relations* (pp. 103–128). Basingstoke and New York: Palgrave.

Lukes, S. (1968). "Methodological individualism reconsidered". *British Journal of Sociology*, 19, pp. 119–129.

Maas, H. (2019). "Opening speech by Foreign Minister Heiko Maas at the Latin America-Caribbean conference", German Ministry of Foreign Affairs, 28 May 2019. Online: https://www.auswaertiges-amt.de/en/newsroom/news/maas-latin-america-caribbean-conference/2222232 (last accessed 13 January 2023).

Maihold, G., T. Muscio Blanco and C. Zilla (2023). "From common values to complementary interests", Stiftung Wissenschaft und Politik (SWP), SWP Comment No. 1, January.

Modelski, G. (1981). "Long cycles, Kondratieffs, and alternating innovation", in C. Kegley and P. McGowan (Eds.), *The political economy of foreign policy behaviour* (pp. 63–83). Beverly Hills: Sage.

Nolte, D. (2023). "The European Union and Latin America: Renewing the partnership after drifting apart", GIGA Focus, N. 2, January.

NUSU (Nueva Sociedad). (2022). "The image of Europe", database. Online: https://data.nuso.org/en/the-image-of-europe/ (last accessed 10 February 2023).

O'Neill, J. (coord.). (1973). *Modes of individualism and collectivism*. New York: St. Martins.

Politico. (2023). "Brazil's Lula snubs Olaf Scholz with Ukraine war remarks", 31 January 2023. Online: https://www.politico.eu/article/ukraine-war-luiz-ina cio-lula-da-silva-mercosur-olaf-scholz/ (last accessed 10 February 2023).

Portuguese Presidency. (2021). "Programme for the Portuguese Presidency of the Council of the European Union", 1 January to 30 June 2021. Online: https://

www.2021portugal.eu/media/rohpisqf/portuguese-presidency-en.pdf (last accessed 13 January 2023).

Rosenau, J. (1986). "Before cooperation: Hegemons, regimes, and habit-driven actors in world politics". *International Organization*, 40, pp. 849–894.

Sanahuja, J. A. (2013). "Towards a new framework of relations between the European Union and Latin America and the Caribbean". Hamburg: EU-LAC Foundation. Online: https://eprints.ucm.es/id/eprint/44784/1/EU_LAC_Broschuere_RZ.pdf (last accessed 13 January 2023).

Schenoni, L. and A. Malamud (2021). "Sobre la creciente irrelevancia de América Latina", *Nueva Sociedad*, No. 291, January-February. Online: https://nuso.org/articulo/sobre-la-creciente-irrelevancia-de-america-latina/ (last accessed 10 February 2023).

Schindler, S. (2014). "Man versus state: Contested agency in the United Nations". *Millennium*, 43:1, pp. 3–23.

Singer, D. (1961). "The level-of-analysis problem in international relations". *World Politics*, 14:1, pp. 77–92.

Vico, G. (2015). *The new science of Giambattista Vico*. Ithaca NY: Cornell University Press.

Wallerstein, I. (1974). "The rise and future demise of the world capitalist system: Concepts for comparative analysis". *Comparative Studies in Society and History*, No. 16, pp. 387–415.

Waltz, K. (1979). *Theory of international politics*. Reading, MA: Addison-Wesley.

Webber, D. (2016). "Declining power Europe: The evolution of the European Union's world power in the early 21st century". *European Review of International Studies*, 3:1, pp. 31–52.

Wendt, A. (1987). "The agent-structure problem in international relations theory". *International Organization*, 41:3, pp. 335–370.

Wendt, A. (1992). "Anarchy is what states make of it: The social construction of power politics". *International Organization*, 46:2, pp. 391–425.

www.ingramcontent.com/pod-product-compliance
Ingram Content Group UK Ltd.
Pitfield, Milton Keynes, MK11 3LW, UK
UKHW041825100926
8556IPUK00002B/27